# GREEK AND LATIN
*in Scientific Terminology*

# OSCAR E. NYBAKKEN

# GREEK AND LATIN

## IN SCIENTIFIC TERMINOLOGY

*The Iowa State University Press, Ames*

Oscar E. Nybakken is professor emeritus and was formerly chairman of the Department of Classics at the University of Iowa, and besides holding the doctor of philosophy degree from the State University of Iowa, he has studied at Harvard and the American Academy in Rome.

He has been a trustee of the Vergilian Society of America, a member on the Managing Committee of the American School of Classical Studies in Athens, Greece, and president of the Classical Association of the Middle West and South. He is a member of the American Philological Association, the Archaeological Institute of America, the Classical Association of the Middle West and South, and the Virgil Society of Great Britain.

Professor Nybakken has published numerous articles in the professional classical journals of his field. For ten years he was assistant editor of *The Classical Journal*. Besides authoring this book, he is the translator of selections from Horace's Satires and Epistles in *Latin Literature in Translation* (1952).

⊗ Printed on acid-free paper in the United States of America

Authorization to photocopy items for internal or personal use, or the internal or personal use of specific clients, is granted by Iowa State University Press, provided that the base fee of $.10 per copy is paid directly to the Copyright Clearance Center, 27 Congress Street, Salem, MA 01970. For those organizations that have been granted a photocopy license by CCC, a separate system of payments has been arranged. The fee code for users of the Transactional Reporting Service is 0-8138-0721-2/59 $.10.

First edition, 1959 (*through nine printings*)
First paperback edition, 1985
*Second printing, 1986*
*Third printing, 1987*
*Fourth printing, 1990*
*Fifth printing, 1993*
*Sixth printing, 1994*
*Seventh printing, 1995*

Library of Congress Card Number:   59-5992
International Standard Book Number:   0-8138-0721-2

# PREFACE

... Nobis parienda sunt imponendaque nova rebus novis nomina.
Quod quidem nemo mediocriter doctus mirabitur, cogitans in omni
arte cuius usus vulgaris communisque non sit multam novitatem
nominum esse cum constituantur earum rerum vocabula quae in
quaque arte versentur. (Cicero, *De Finibus* III, 3)

"We are obliged to create a vocabulary and to find names to attach
to new discoveries. This will not cause surprise to any moderately
well-informed person, when he reflects that in every branch of
knowledge lying outside the most elementary ones there must be a
large measure of "newness" about its vocabulary. This "newness"
grows out of the necessity for each area of knowledge to express the
particular concepts with which it deals."

When Marcus Tullius Cicero, the Roman statesman, orator, and
man of letters, in the year 45 B. C. wrote the Latin words quoted
above, he revealed that the problem of finding suitable names for
things and ideas was already recognized in his day. But even as
he reflected on the problem and wrote those words so many centuries
ago, Cicero could have had only a faint idea of how many names
(*nomina*) would be required for identifying the enormous number of
"new things" (*res novae*) yet to be discovered. Pride and faith in his
own country and in its language encouraged Cicero to believe that
the Latin tongue would long be the chief vehicle of communication
and the main source of names for new phenomena and concepts.
Cicero was justified in that belief, as subsequent history has proved.
And yet it is doubtful that even the intellectual Cicero could have
predicted the great significance of the role, both direct and indirect,
which his native Latin and the antecedent Greek were to have in the
formation of languages and words to be used by mankind for the
communication of knowledge.

This book, in its broader aspect, deals with the subject of communication in science. In its narrower aspect, and most particularly,
however, the book deals with the role of the Greek and Latin languages

in the construction of the technical terms, names, and specific epithets used in the medical and biological sciences. Some consideration is given to a few of the more common linguistic and practical factors that relate to the structure, meaning, and pronunciation of scientific terms. The scope and arrangement of its contents are such that the book may be used for supplementary work in courses in language or in science, or it may be used as a textbook for a special course in the derivation of technical terms of science and medicine.

I wish to express my sincere gratitude to The State University of Iowa for granting me, through its Research Professorships Program, a semester's leave from teaching duties in order to complete this work; to the Graduate College of The State University of Iowa and to the Iowa State University Press through whose special efforts the publication of this material has been made possible; and to Norma D. Young, Associate Professor of Physical Education at The State University of Iowa, who read the manuscript and offered many valuable suggestions.

Iowa City, Iowa
August, 1958

Oscar E. Nybakken

# CONTENTS

|                                                                          | *Pages*   |
|--------------------------------------------------------------------------|-----------|
| SOME SUGGESTED INSTRUCTIONAL PROCEDURES                                   | ix-xi     |
| CHAPTER I. Introduction and Definitions                                  | 1-8       |
| 1. Introduction                                                          | 1-2       |
| 2. Definitions of Some Frequently Used Terms                             | 3-8       |
| CHAPTER II. Language: General and Scientific                             | 9-23      |
| 1. General and Scientific Language                                       | 9-12      |
| 2. The Vernacular in Scientific Language                                 | 12-15     |
| 3. Some Characteristics of Scientific Nomenclature                       | 15-23     |
| CHAPTER III. The Latin and Greek Languages                               | 24-61     |
| 1. Latin and Greek in Scientific Nomenclature                            | 24-29     |
| 2. The Latin and Greek Languages. Transliteration                        | 29-61     |
| a. The Latin Language                                                    | 30-44     |
| b. The Greek Language                                                     | 44-61     |
| CHAPTER IV. Word Lists                                                    | 62-230    |
| 1. Introduction to the Word Lists                                        | 62-66     |
| 2. Latin Prefixes                                                        | 66-74     |
| 3. Latin Suffixes                                                        | 75-83     |
| 4. Latin Numerals                                                        | 83-84     |
| 5. General Latin Vocabulary                                              | 85-131    |
| 6. Greek Prefixes                                                        | 132-139   |
| 7. Greek Suffixes                                                        | 139-145   |
| 8. Greek Numerals                                                        | 145-146   |
| 9. General Greek Vocabulary                                              | 146-223   |
| 10. Word-Elements Frequently Confused                                    | 224-230   |
| CHAPTER V. Practical and Linguistic Factors                              | 231-307   |
| 1. Compound Words: Gender, Stems and Bases, Combining Vowels             | 231-242   |
| 2. Pronunciation                                                         | 243-249   |

3. Synonymy                                    249-263
4. Shortening, Malformations, Misnomers        264-274
5. Hybrid Words                                274-280
6. Eponyms                                     280-286
7. Codes and Rules of Scientific Nomenclature  287-307

BIBLIOGRAPHY                                   308-313
    Dictionaries                              308-309
    Books                                     309-311
    Bulletins and Tracts                      311
    Codes and Rules of Scientific Nomenclature 311-312
    Periodicals                               312-313
INDEX                                          315-321

# SOME SUGGESTED INSTRUCTIONAL PROCEDURES

For those who may wish to use this book as a basic text for a special course in the nomenclature of science and medicine, the following suggestions may be of some value:

1. Major attention should be given to the lists of Latin and Greek words and the scientific terms derived from them. Only by learning the meanings of more and more word-elements and by constant practice in the recognition of those word-elements as they appear in varying combinations in compound terms can the student acquire the ability to compute the meanings of technical words by observing their structure. The student's efforts in this direction should be systematic and persistent throughout the course.

A good starting point for a systematic study of the word lists is the list of Latin prefixes. Latin prefixes not only are the most frequently appearing Latin elements in compound scientific terms, but many of them are likely to be familiar to the student already. After a period of special attention to the prefixes, the student should proceed systematically through the rest of the word lists, learning all or most of the words which are marked with asterisks. The same procedure should then be followed in studying the Greek word lists. If desired, the Greek word lists may be studied before the Latin lists.

2. The number of words to be assigned at one time must be adjusted to the achievement level of the students and to the length of the course. For this reason, the more important words in the General Vocabulary lists have been identified by asterisks. In most situations, better results will be obtained if words from the General Vocabulary lists are assigned in several selective "rounds" rather than in an unaltered sequence as they appear in the lists. This means that only the most extensively used words of those marked with asterisks are selected for study the first time through the list, and that the rest of the words so marked are left for the second "round." When the students have learned all the words marked with asterisks, a third "round," or even a fourth, may include as many of the other words in the list

as time and class ability warrant. Such procedure will insure the giving of maximum attention to the most valuable words, will obviate any feeling of tedium that the learner may develop at facing an "unending" list of words, and will enable the instructor better to gauge the number of words that a class can effectively learn in the time available. No omissions should be permitted in the lists of prefixes and suffixes.

3. When studying the derivatives under a Latin or a Greek entry-word, the student should concentrate his first attention on those derivatives with which he is already familiar; after that, he should take special note of those terms which incorporate word-elements that have been studied or which will be included in the first (and second) "round"; and finally, he should study the remaining derivatives under the entry-word. Such progression through the lists will enable the student to encounter as early as possible those constructive units which he already knows or which he can most quickly and easily learn. Those more easily learned units will then become valuable keys in the analysis of other words. In the beginning stages when he has yet learned only a few basic words, the student may need considerable assistance from the instructor in analyzing the derivative words, but the amount of such assistance should gradually decrease as he acquires a larger vocabulary and as his analytic ability increases with practice. The student cannot normally be expected to analyze and define all the derivatives under the entry-words selected, especially in cases where the derivatives are very numerous and range over several scientific areas. Apportionment of the derivatives, especially of the less familiar ones, among several students will often be advisable.

4. Sufficient derivatives are given in the word lists to allow the instructor to draw on them for periodic examination material. Items on written examinations may be such as require: (a) the dissecting of compound words into their component parts and stating the basic meaning of each component, (b) matching scrambled terms and definitions and (c) selecting the correct definition of a particular scientific word from among several suggested definitions of it.

5. The student should keep a notebook in which he records the exact definitions of a few derivatives under each entry-word. The

notebook may also be used for gathering historical and linguistic information about some of the source words and their derivatives.

6. Webster's Unabridged Dictionary and a recent comprehensive medical dictionary should be made easily available for use by the students. Other valuable books for reference are The Oxford English Dictionary, specialized scientific dictionaries, International Codes of Nomenclature, elementary Greek and Latin texts, and a standard text on the history of medicine. These, and other reference sources, are listed in the Bibliography of this text.

7. Concurrent with work on the word lists should be assignments and discussions on the linguistic and practical factors treated in Chapters I, II, III, and V. Occasionally the origin, history, form, and meaning of single words (e.g., eponyms from classical myth, legend, or history) or a group of related words can provide the basis for valuable oral or written reports.

CHAPTER I

# Introduction and Definitions

## Introduction

Not all the difficulties encountered in the study of a science are inherent in the subject matter; many are due to the terminology used. In some areas of science the student may spend a year or more in becoming acquainted with the terminology. In medicine the student must become familiar with the terminology of several branches of science, such as anatomy, bacteriology, chemistry, microscopy, botany, psychiatry, and psychology. In zoology several hundreds of thousands of separate animals have been identified and named, and every year some two thousand new generic and ten thousand new specific names of insects are added. Between five hundred thousand and a million species of plants have been named and described. When to this host of names are added those of diseases, drugs, and minerals, the number of names and technical words currently required in scientific speech runs into the millions.[1] A vocabulary already so extensive and still growing rapidly constitutes a problem of considerable magnitude in some scientific areas and a burden of no mean proportions for the present-day student of science.

The purpose of this book is to furnish information and material which will aid in reducing the vocabulary burden for the student of biology and medicine. Its twofold objective is (1) to increase the student's facility in determining the meaning of scientific words by analyzing their structure, and (2) to encourage the student to establish sound nomenclatural criteria for himself and his profession.

The nature and the scope of the book's contents have been largely

---

1. *Jour. Amer. Med. Assn.* CXII, 1939, 1843. Edmund Andrews, *A History of Scientific English*, pp. 6 and 312. L. H. Bailey, "Problems in Taxonomy," *Amer. Jour. Botany* XXXVI, 1949, 22.

determined by the fact that the ancient Greek and Latin languages underlie both the structure and the meaning of most of the technical names and terms used in biology and medicine. Moreover, all scientific names of plants, bacteria, and animals have been latinized and are therefore, in effect, Latin words whose structure, inflection, and syntax are governed by the rules of classical Latin. For these reasons, only Greek and Latin words and scientific names and terms derived from them have been included in the word lists and, with few exceptions, the words used for illustrative purposes throughout the book are words of Greek or Latin origin. Of the numerous principles of word formation and inflection in the Greek and Latin languages, however, only those have been outlined in this text which have had the most direct and extensive application to the construction and the form of modern biological names and terms.

In order to attain its primary objective, and in order to meet the student's most immediate and practical need, this book seeks above all else to provide in ample quantity the kind of material necessary for learning those Greek and Latin roots, stems, and affixes which recur most often in the technical terms of medicine and biology. These essential working materials are furnished in several word lists which contain the Greek and Latin source words and samples of modern scientific names and terms derived from them. In seeking to achieve its secondary objective, the book contains discussions on certain aspects of biological nomenclature which relate directly or indirectly to the origin and the structure of technical terms. Some of the affiliated topics discussed are synonymy, hybrid terms, international codes of nomenclature, eponyms, and pronunciation.

If students at an early stage in their studies acquire an awareness of past and present usages in scientific nomenclature and an appreciation of what are desirable and what are undesirable practices in the formation of scientific terms, it can reasonably be hoped that in time there will be general agreement among scientists about what constitutes sound onomatological practices. The happy result will be that word coinages will rarely result in haphazard terms to add weight to an already heavy burden, but will instead be distinguished memorials to scientists who believed that the name applied to a disease, treatment, drug, plant, or animal should be a help rather than a hindrance to clear and effective communication of ideas.

## Definitions of Some Frequently Used Terms

Throughout the discussions in this book certain terms are used repeatedly. In order that these terms may be fully understood whenever they appear, the following definitions and illustrations of them are given:

## 1. ROOT

A ROOT is that primitive and fundamental verbal element which expresses the basic meaning or suggestion that is common to all the words of a related group; it is the core from which several differentiated words (e.g., nouns, verbs, adjectives, and adverbs) spring up by the addition of formative elements such as prefixes, infixes, and suffixes. For example:

**Gen-** (Gk. *gignesthai*; Lat. *gignere*): beget, come into being, be born, become.

| | | | |
|---|---|---|---|
| auto*gen*y | *gen*ealogy | *gen*us | oxy*gen* |
| exo*gen*ous | *gen*eration | indi*gen*ous | pro*gen*itor |
| *gen*e | *gen*esis | in*gen*ious | |

**Sta-** (Gk. *histanai*; Lat. *stare*): stand, set.

| | | | |
|---|---|---|---|
| amyo*sta*sia | *sta*ble | *sta*men | *sta*ture |
| hypo*sta*sis | *stag*nant | *sta*tic | *sta*tus |
| in*sta*bility | | | |

**Spec-** (Lat. *spectare* or *-specere*): see, look at, spy.

| | | | |
|---|---|---|---|
| intro*spec*tion | *spec*ialist | *spec*ific | *spec*trum |
| per*spec*tive | *spec*ies | *spec*imen | *spec*ulum |

## 2. STEM

The STEM is that part of a word to which inflectional endings are attached. Because of morphological and phonetic changes (e.g., elision, assimilation) that take place when inflectional endings are added, the stem of a Greek or Latin word is not always apparent in the form of the word that is first presented by a dictionary or textbook.

| WORD AND MEANING | STEM | WORD AND MEANING | STEM |
|---|---|---|---|
| *alga*, seaweed | *alga-* | *soma*, body | *somat-* |
| *fungus*, fungus | *fungo-* | *helmins*, worm | *helminth-* |

| | | | |
|---|---|---|---|
| *radix*, root | *radic-* | *genos*, birth, race | *genes-* |
| *lithos*, stone | *litho-* | *gero*, bear, carry | *gere-* |
| | | | *gest-* |

Some stems are SEPARABLE; that is, they may be used alone or in combination with other stems, prefixes, or suffixes. For example:

*askos* (stem, *asko-*), bag, sack:  *asc*us; *asc*ocarp
*ergon* (stem, *ergo-*), work:  *erg*; asyn*erg*ia

Some stems are INSEPARABLE; that is, they always appear in combination with other stems and are never used alone, even though they may have independent meanings. For example:

*algos* (stem, *alg(es)-*), pain:  *alg*esthesia, cardi*alg*ia; but not "algus" alone

*-jectum* (stem, *jecto-*), throw:  in*ject*ion, tra*ject*ion; but not "jection" alone

## 3. BASE

The terms BASE and STEM are often used synonymously. Linguistically, however, only STEM has validity. But BASE is a convenient designation for that part of an inflected word which remains unchanged so that, even though it has no scientific linguistic value, BASE does have a practical value in simplifying explanations of word construction. In the examples below, it will be noted that the BASE and the STEM of a word may be alike but that more often they differ in that the STEM ends in a vowel and the BASE ends in a consonant.

| GREEK OR LATIN WORD | STEM | BASE | DERIVATIVES USING BASE |
|---|---|---|---|
| *mensa, mensae*, table | *mensa-* | *mens-* | *mens*al, comm*ens*al, comm*ens*alism |
| *lac, lactis*, milk | *lact-* | *lact-* | *lact*ary, *lact*iferous, ab*lact*ation |
| *kyklos, kyklou*, circle | *kyklo-* | *kykl-* | *cyclo*stomate, heterocyc*l*ic |
| *sarx, sarkos*, flesh | *sark-* | *sark-* | ento*sarc*, *sarc*ohydrocele |
| *scribere, scriptum*, write | *scribe-* *scripto-* | *scrib-* *script-* | pre*scribe*, nonde*script*, super*scrip*tion |
| *facere, factum*, make, do | *face-* *facto-* | *facie-* *fact-* | calori*facie*nt, *fact*or |

## 4. PREFIX

A PREFIX is an element attached to the beginning of a root, stem, or base. Its function is to elaborate, qualify, or intensify the meaning of a word. It consists of one or more syllables and is generally derived from a preposition or an adverb. For example:

| PREFIX | IN COMPOUND WORD |
|---|---|
| *trans*, across | transocular (*oculus*, eye) |
| *per*, through | permeate (*meare*, to go) |
| *hyper*, over | hypertrophy (*trophe*, nourishment) |
| *ento*, within | entophyte (*phyton*, plant) |

The term PREFIX should not be applied to noun, verb, or adjective stems which are used as the first component of compound words; in "laterocervical" (*latus, lateris*, side), for example, *latero-* is not a PREFIX even though it is "prefixed" to another word.

## 5. SUFFIX

A SUFFIX is an element of one or more syllables attached to the end of a root, stem, or base. In addition to contributing its own particular meaning to a word, a suffix may also indicate part of speech, gender, case, number, person, tense, mood, or voice.

| STEM OR BASE | SUFFIX | WORD |
|---|---|---|
| *flex-* (bend) | *-or* (that which) | flexor |
| *sanat-* (heal) | *-orium* (place where) | sanatorium |
| *steno-* (narrow) | *-sis* (condition of) | stenosis |
| *enter-* (intestine) | *-itis* (inflammation) | enteritis |

## 6. COMBINING VOWEL AND COMBINING FORM

A COMBINING VOWEL is used between two constructive units of a compound word in order to join them euphoniously. The vowels most commonly used are *o* and *i*, although the other vowels also occur. For example:

*hydr-* (water) plus *phob-* (fear) = hydrophobia.
*anthrop-* (man) plus *metr-* (measure) = anthropometry.
*arch-* (chief, main) plus *blast-* (germ cell) = archiblast.

*sudor-* (sweat) plus *fic* (make) = sudorific.
*cervic-* (neck) plus *faci-* (face) = cervicofacial.
*flav-* (yellow) plus *bacteri-* (bacteria) = Flavobacterium.

A COMBINING VOWEL is ordinarily not used when the second constructive member of a compound word begins with a vowel or a diphthong. For example:

*mes-* (middle)    plus *enter-* (intestine) = mesenteron.
                   plus *odont-* (tooth) = mesodont.
*noct-* (night)    plus *ambulat-* (stroll) = noctambulation.

In some words, however, a COMBINING VOWEL has been used even if the second member begins with a vowel. For example:

*gastr-* (stomach)    plus *enter-* (intestine) = gastroenteritis.
*dextr-* (right)      plus *ocul-* (eye) = dextraocular.

A COMBINING FORM is a base plus the combining vowel. In the examples used above, the combining forms are: *hydro-*, *anthropo-*, *archi-*, *sudori-*, *cervico-*, *flavo-*, *meso-*, *gastro-*, and *dextra-*.

## 7. VOWEL GRADATION (ABLAUT)

VOWEL GRADATION, or ABLAUT, are terms applied to changes in the root vowel of closely related words. Such changes can be observed in groups of English words like sit, sat, seat, set; tell, told, tale; sing, sang, sung, song; ride, rode, ridden; spring, sprang, sprung. The same sort of change occurred also in closely related Greek and Latin words and is reflected in their English derivatives. For example:

*annus* (year); *perennis* (perennial): annual, perennial.
*facere* (to do); *deficere* (to fail to do): factual, deficient.
*pherein* (to carry); *phoros* (a carrying): periphery, phosphorus.

## 8. ELISION

ELISION is the omission or the suppression of a vowel when one word element ending in a vowel is prefixed to another element beginning with a vowel. The first element usually loses its final vowel. For example:

magno- (large) plus animus (mind) = magnanimous.
epi- (upon) plus arteria (artery) = eparterial.

## 9. TRANSLITERATION

TRANSLITERATION is the transposition of a word from one language into another. For example:

| GREEK | LATIN | ENGLISH |
|-------|-------|---------|
| ἀμοίβη | amoeba | ameba |
| κόκκος | coccus | coccus |

## 10. LOAN WORDS

LOAN WORDS are foreign words which have been adopted into English (or another language) without any change in spelling. Some familiar examples are apex, antenna, fistula, cancer, serum, genesis, basis, onyx, cosmos, zone, calyx.

## 11. DERIVATIVES AND COINED WORDS (NEOLOGISMS)

DERIVATIVES are words obtained from other languages by slightly modifying the spelling of the original word, or by combining several foreign word elements into new words. COINED WORDS, or NEOLOGISMS, are words which did not exist in the parent languages from which their elements were drawn. Most derivatives in modern scientific terminology are NEOLOGISMS. For example:

| FOREIGN WORDS OR WORD-ELEMENTS | DERIVATIVES |
|-------------------------------|-------------|
| ocularis (pertaining to the eye) | ocular |
| habitus (condition of body) | habit |
| konos (cone) | cone |
| strept- (twisted); cocc- (berry) | streptococcus |
| koin- (common); trop- (turn) | koinotropic (or coenotropic) |
| olig- (few); erythr- (red); cyt- (cell); h(a)em- (blood); -ia (state or condition) | oligoerythrocythemia |

## 12. HYBRID WORDS

A HYBRID WORD is one constructed from elements derived from more than a single language. For example:

*tele-*     (Greek, far off) plus *vis-* (Latin, see) = television.
*hyper*    (Greek, excessive) plus *irritabil-* (Latin, irritable) = hyperirritability.
*hom-*    (Greek, same) plus *later-* (Latin, side) = homolateral.
*micr-*    (Greek, small) plus *teeth* (English) = microteeth.
*acid-*     (Latin, acid) plus *phil-* (Greek, love) = acidophil.

CHAPTER II

# *Language: General and Scientific*

## General and Scientific Language

Language is man's chief medium of communication and makes possible the expression and preservation of a vast number of facts and ideas. Over the centuries many different languages have developed, so that human knowledge finds expression in many tongues. Ordinarily, however, a person acquires and transmits most of his knowledge through the use of his native language.

As knowledge and ideas increase and change, there is a corresponding increase in the number of words which a language contains. Every new discovery requires a name (*nomen*) as a mnemonic necessity, and minor changes are constantly being made in some of the words which already exist. Language is therefore vital and changing and is not a static phenomenon.

As an instrument of communication, the English language has adapted itself to diverse requirements. "Vernacular English" is the designation which has been applied to the ordinary speech used by the large majority of the population in dealing with the basic and elementary aspects of living. This branch of English is said to be largely the possession of the masses since they have made and continue to make that phase of the language what it is. No authoritarian controls are imposed upon the English language. The Oxford and the Webster dictionaries and scholars and teachers of language constitute the only court of appeal in regard to the sound, form, and meaning of English words. But dictionaries and scholars exercise only voluntary controls, so that English words undergo changes in spite of them. Changes in words can therefore be observed from one part of a country to another, from one period of time to another, and from one person to another, even at the same time and in the same place. And in the area of vernacular English, the spoken word is usually more influential than the written form in determining the character of the language.

The English used in specialized fields is sometimes called "technical English." But when that designation or others such as "the language of religion," "the language of psychology," and "the language of science" is used, it is not with the intent of conveying the idea that separate and distinct languages, in the strict sense, exist for the several areas of learning; all those "languages" are English and possess most of the characteristics of ordinary English. Nevertheless, the "languages" used in certain specialized areas do differ to some extent from ordinary English and from each other, in that each has developed some characteristics and proprieties of its own in matters of vocabulary, spelling, and usage.

The "technical English" used in certain areas of science, although manifesting most of the traits of ordinary English, differs from it in some respects. In the first place, "technical English" is largely the property of scholars and specialists who ordinarily are careful to preserve precedent and to seek accuracy and consistency in form and usage. Specialists rely on and are governed by the written word much more than by the spoken word. English technical words, therefore, because they have specialized and resticted uses, because they are so numerous, and because they are used by a small percentage of the population, are not likely to be admitted into the vocabulary of common English in any considerable number. For these reasons technical words of scientific English demonstrate greater stability and resistance to morphological and semantic change than do words of common English.[1] In the second place, technical English has more of an international character than does ordinary English.

---

1. Technical terms are not completely immune to change, however. Because of progress in scientific knowledge "atom" and "electron," for example, do not mean the same today as they did even a few years ago. Specialized terms, too, sometimes fall away from the protection of specialists and become part of the vocabulary of the masses. When this happens, the words are likely to suffer greater changes both in form and in meaning than if they had not come into general use. The following words illustrate such dialectic change: THEKE (Gk.: chest, box) has become TICK (mattress); ESCHARA (Gk.: pan of coals) has become SCAR; PHRENITIS (Gk.: condition of mind) has become FRENZY; KISTE (Gk.:

Many of the words used in technical English writing are identical or nearly identical in form and meaning with words used in scientific treatises written in other languages. The number of such words which are "common" to several languages is considerably larger in technical English than it is in ordinary English. This fact makes scientific writing approach the character of an international medium of communication. The amount of this "common" element will vary with the particular language involved and with the subject matter treated: in mathematics, physics, astronomy, and chemistry, for example, the amount is large; in some branches of the biological sciences the amount is only slightly less; in literature, economics, and politics, on the other hand, the amount of such "common" elements is much smaller than it is in most areas of the natural sciences. The two pairs of descriptive passages below will serve to illustrate this characteristic of technical English. The same information is recorded, first in French and then in English. It will be seen that technical words (in italics) constitute a high percentage of the total vocabulary and that they are almost identical in form in both languages.

> . . . la situation des différents territoire évolue profondément au cours de la *gastrulation:* le *chordo-mésoblaste* s'*invagine* complètement, ainsi d'ailleurs que l'*entoblaste*; du côté *dorsal,* le matériel *chordal* est étroitement appliqué contre le système *nerveux* présomptif; il forme le toit d'une *cavité,* l'*archenteron,* qui occupe le *centre* de l'*embryon.* Quant au *blastocèle,* il s'est réduit à l'état de *cavité* virtuelle. (Jean Brachet, *Embryologie Chimique,* pp. 358-59).

> . . . the location of the different areas changes profoundly during *gastrulation.* The *chorda-mesoderm invaginates* completely, as does the *entoderm.* On the *dorsal* side, the *notochord* material is in direct contact with the presumptive *nervous* system, and forms the roof of a *cavity,* the *archenteron,* which is *centrally* located. The *cavity* of the *blastocoel* is eventually obliterated. (Jean Brachet, *Chemical Embryology* [translated by Lester G. Barth] p. 345).

> L'étude de l'*acide ribonucléique* montre que les *spermatogonies* ont un *cytoplasme* beaucoup plus *basophil* que les *spermatocytes,* tandis que

box, chest) has become CHEST; PARALYSIS (Gk.: loosening, paralysis) has become PALSY; and KYNANCHE (Gk.: dog-collar) was heard as SYNANKE, which in Middle Latin became QUINANCIA, then SQUINANCHIA, and finally QUINSY.

les *spermatozoides* mûrs ne présentent qu'une faible *colorabilité* du *flagelle*. (*Ibid.*, p. 86).

The study of *ribonucleic acid* shows that the *spermatogonia* have a *cytoplasm* much more *basophilic* than the *spermatocytes*, while the mature *spermatozoa* show only a weak *coloration* of the *flagellum*. (*Ibid.*, p. 86).

## The Vernacular in Scientific Language

There have always been advocates of the view that scientific theory and fact should be expressed in the vernacular of the country, that is, in the ordinary language of the citizen whether that language happens to be English, German, French, Spanish, or any other. "Why," asks a person whose native tongue is English, "should a scientist say or write 'Quercus alba' instead of 'white oak,' or 'Apis mellifera' instead of 'honeybee,' or 'rubella scarlatinosa' instead of 'measles,' or 'hepaticolithotomy' instead of 'cutting out a liver stone,' or 'mesogaster' instead of 'mid-gut'? Is 'Pisum sativum' better than 'the cultivated pea,' or 'Rhizopus nigricans' better than 'black bread mold'? If the vernacular instead of the technical terms were used, scientific language would be greatly simplified and meanings could much more easily be conveyed to more people." The adovcates of this viewpoint usually point out that in the area of anatomy, for example, many unfamiliar and difficult technical terms have been substituted for common and familiar words (e.g., dactylus for finger; articulus for joint; gingiva for gum; ischium for hip), and from general medical language they cite such pairs of words as those below to illustrate how use of the technical instead of the popular terms results in concealment rather than in clarification of meaning.

| | | | |
|---|---|---|---|
| wristdrop | carpoptosis | midbrain | mesencephalon |
| eye tooth | upper canine cuspid | bridge (dentistry) | pontic |
| heart hurry | tachycardia | | |
| hindbrain | metencephalon | swimming bells | nectocalyxes |
| hindkidney | metanephros | needle holder | acutenaculum |
| heartometer | cardiometer | foregut | prosogaster, or protogaster |
| hairache | trichalgia | | |
| lousiness | pediculosis | squint | strabismus |

| | | | |
|---|---|---|---|
| overfeeding | superalimentation | thirst | dipsosis, or polydipsia |
| overgrowth | hypertrophy, or hyperplasia | windpipe | trachea |
| baldness | calvities, alopecia, or atrichia | | |

Sometimes single words combine technical and vernacular elements. Those who advocate a technical vocabulary for science say that such terms have "suffered only partial plebification"; for example:

| | | | |
|---|---|---|---|
| midcarpal | mesocarpal | megabladder | cystauxe |
| macroteeth | macrodontia | spontaneous generation | archegony, archebiosis, or archegenesis |
| fibro-fatty | fibro-adipose | | |
| lousicide | pediculicide | | |

Some of the reasons for objecting to the use of vernacular terms in scientific language will be made apparent in the discussions of the characteristics of scientific nomenclature and the use of Greek and Latin in the composition of technical terms (pp. 15-23; 26-29; 291). The most common objections may be stated briefly as follows:

1. A common word is usually less descriptive of the entity or concept which it names than a technical word is; compare, for example, the following pairs of synonymous words:

| | |
|---|---|
| atavism (**atavus,** ancestor) | throwing-back |
| epidermis (**epi,** upon; **derma,** skin) | scarf-skin |
| pachyderm (**pachys,** thick; **derma,** skin) | elephant |
| rhizodontropy (**rhiza,** root; **odont-,** tooth; **trope,** pivot) | crowning (a tooth) |
| fibula (**fibula,** brooch) | shank |

Occasionally, however, ordinary terms are just as descriptive as technical terms. In the following comparisons, for example, neither term has much advantage over the other if viewed only with respect to its descriptiveness and economy:

| | |
|---|---|
| cephalalgia (**kephalos,** head; **algos,** pain) | headache |
| Melanoplus femur-rubrum (**melano-,** black; **hoplon,** armor; **femur,** thigh; **ruber,** red) | red-legged grasshopper |
| pedodontia (**paid-,** child; **odont-,** tooth) | children's dentistry |

Geomys bursarius (**ge-,** earth; **mys,** mouse;     pocket-gopher
   **bursa,** pocket)
acutenaculum (**acus,** needle; **tenaculum,**    needle holder
   holder)

In the particular examples given above, the vernacular terms, in addition to being as descriptive as the technical terms, will also be more readily understood by English-speaking people. But this is not true of most vernacular terms. Moreover, when precise language is required for complex structures and processes, words of the vernacular English usually prove inadequate. For many important scientific entities common names do not even exist.

2. The vernacular term is usually less precise than the technical term and often has several meanings. "Hindbrain," for example, may refer to (a) the cerebellum, (b) the cerebellum and the pons, (c) the medulla oblongata, or (d) the rhombencephalon.

3. A term from the vernacular, or a folk-term, often carries with it an emotional meaning which may be inappropriate or even harmful; the corresponding technical term is free from this affective meaning. Compare, for example, cheiloschisis (CHEILOS, lip; SCHISIS, cleft) and harelip; rhizodontropy (RHIZA, root; ODONT-, tooth; TROPE, pivot) and peg-tooth; pediculous (PEDICULUS, louse; -OSUS, full of) and lousy. The many words used in ordinary language for phallus, anus, and flatus strikingly illustrate this character of popular language.[2]

4. Sometimes numerous popular names exist for the same entity; this results in vague and inconsistent language.

5. Words of popular speech are less stable than technica words and may vary in spelling and in meaning from place to plac , from period to period, and from person to person.

6. The acceptance of vernacular terms in scientific writing usually results in an unpleasant mixture of technical and nontechnical words. For example, a periodical article or a book may consistently use "wristdrop" instead of "carpoptosis" and yet never use "windpipe" instead of "trachea."

---

2. Cf. Edmund Andrews, *History of Scientific English*, Chap. 15.

7. Written treatises which use vernacular words for scientific concepts and phenomena lose much of their value to foreign readers. The words "Melanoplus femur-rubrum" and "Geomys bursarius," for example, (used as examples in (1) above) would have many advantages over their corresponding vernacular English words ("red-legged grasshopper" and "pocket-gopher") in that they are international and would be spelled exactly the same in Chinese, Hindi, Japanese, French, German, or Russian.

## Some Characteristics of Scientific Nomenclature

A nomenclature implies that some systematic scheme is employed in the naming of things. Viewpoints on whether any system of naming is necessary at all, or on what the system ought to be, vary widely from those favoring the use of random names to those demanding descriptive and carefully chosen euphonious terms. Some persons argue that a name is merely a name; that it is a tag by which something is identified and that it is unimportant what the tag is. Others argue, equally fervently, that the name applied to anything should be meaningful and appropriate. In such areas as mathematics, physics, and logic, satisfactory solutions to the problem of cumbersome terminologies have been found in the partial or almost exclusive use of symbols intead of words. For a while vitamins were identified by letter and number, but more recently the tendency is to use words.

Not all scientific fields have the same nomenclatural requirements; each field has peculiar needs of its own. The requirements in the concrete sciences which deal with material things are not the same as those for the abstract sciences. Sometimes specialties within the same field have differing requirements. In the field of biology an important nomenclatural problem has been to get a genus-species terminology that would differentiate and classify animals and plants. In medicine, on the other hand, the problem of classification has been less important than that of indicating causes, processes, procedures, and effects. In chemistry, as in biology, the primary function of the nomenclature is to differentiate kinds, whereas in dentistry it is to attach meaningful and correctly descriptive terms to concepts, anomalies, and processes. Most branches of the biological and medical sciences, however, in spite of some differences in their particular requirements, share several nomenclatural desiderata. Some of these desiderata are:

## Precise and Restrained Descriptiveness

A good scientific term will not be merely an arbitrary tag, but will suggest as clearly and as fully as possible the characteristics of the concept or thing to which it is applied. Seldom can a term fully describe a structure, anomaly, process, function, or effect, but it can generally supply a thumb-nail sketch or a shorthand description. The descriptiveness should be as precise as possible, suggesting the essential characteristic which differentiates the concept to which the word is applied from all other concepts; irrelevant or uncertain details should not be suggested. If, for example, the cause of a pathological condition is not known, the term used to describe that condition should not seek to make any etiological designation. And since there is no theoretical limit to the number of descriptive components that can be built into a compound word, restraint and moderation must be used. Attempting to make reference to too many characteristics, or to those which are not rather firmly established, will result either in cumbersome words or in terms which in a short time may prove to be ill-suited to the thing named.

Perhaps the most highly developed descriptive nomenclature in science is that used in chemistry and in pharmacology. Even without any previous knowledge about a particular compound, a chemist can, by observing the name of a compound, write out its chemical formula. The terms *butyl-para-aminobenzoate*, 17-*hydroxy-*11-*dehydrocortico-steronacetate*, and 2-*isobutyl-aminoethyl-para-aminobenzoate*, for example, are good names insofar as they are descriptive of the structures of the compounds to which they are applied. But the names lack restraint, economy, and convenience and are difficult to pronounce, and in recognition of these deficiencies, abbreviated or proprietary names are used: *butesin, cortisone*, and *butethamine. Sulfa* for *sulfanilamide* is another example of such shortening. Terms thus shortened are less precisely descriptive than the longer ones, but they gain much in economy, convenience, and ease of pronunciation. In effect, therefore, a nomenclature that is highly descriptive may become nondescriptive because of the necessity of adjustment to meet other nomenclatural desiderata.

The basis for naming a chemical compound is the content and structure of the compound. For that reason, a descriptive term which attempts to designate all the elements of a chemical compound may often be a long word. On the other hand, because all the word elements used in the construction of chemical terms uniformly refer to substances, the nomenclaure of chemistry is consistent and homogeneous — a situation which does not obtain in most of the other branches of science. In the medical and the biological sciences the entities and characteristics to be designated by descriptive terms range over a large number of heterogeneous factors such as size, color, movement, cause, effect, and degree. Under such conditions the difficulty of attaining a logical and precise descriptiveness in the nomenclature is much greater than it is in areas where fewer and more homogeneous factors have to be taken into account. Because of the large number of identified plants and because of the practice of cross-breeding genera and species, the problem of naming plants has become so complex that a different name has sometimes been procured for a species by the use of an anagram or by inverting some letters of the standard word (e.g., *Muilla* instead of *Allium*). Common or "fancy" names (i.e., words from the common or vernacular language) have been permitted for plants arising in cultivation through hybridization and not numerous enough in the wild to justify botanical recognition, (in "Sedum spectabile 'Brilliant'," for example the cultivar or "fancy" name is 'Brilliant')[3]. Since it is obvious that there are severe limitations to the descriptive power of a single word and since a very large number of factors may be involved in a structure or process for which a name is sought, it is sometimes impossible to get a single word that will possess the qualities of restrained and precise descriptiveness. In extremely complex structures, phenomena, or processes, only descriptive phrases using several words will suffice. In such cases scientists sometimes resort to acrostic, telescoped, or arbitrarily fabricated and meaningless words: ACTH, for example, is a sort of acrostic for "adrenocorticotropic hormone," and *Zdeac*, in dental

---

3. Cf., J. Lanjouw *et al.*, *International Code of Botanical Nomenclature* (Utrecht, Kemink en Zoon N. V., 1956), Article 28.

vocabulary, means "zone of disintegrating epithelial attachment cuticle." Such words are not descriptive at all, but they do possess certain other desirable nomenclatural qualities.

### Orientation to Its Own and Related Areas

A term is well oriented if it reveals readily its connection and relation with other concepts in its own area and in other closely related areas. In the binomial and trinomial nomenclature of the biological sciences, good orientation is achieved by the use of the two- or three-word designations of animals and plants. However, because orientation and classification are so important to the nomenclature of those areas, there is some danger that too little attention be given to other important factors in the naming process, such as to structure, process, quality, and procedure.

Even in areas where names are only single words, good orientation can be achieved through the use of a sort of "genus-species-variety" method of designation. By careful use in a word of one or more of the component elements used in other related words, the relationship between the several words as well as the special significance of each will be indicated. For example:

*occlusion* ("genus")

    mal*occlusion* ("species")

        neutr*occlusion*  
        mesi*occlusion*   } ("variety")  
        dist*occlusion*

Such words as those in the following groups may also be regarded as well oriented: (a) *gnathic*, pro*gnath*ism, eury*gnath*ic, micro*gnath*ia, pachy*gnath*ous; (b) leuko*penia*, glyco*penia*, chloro*penia*, thrombocyto*penia* (c) *cholecyst*itis, *cholecyst*ogram, peri*cholecyst*ic.

Good orientation of terms in a scientific area also requires careful observation of the terminology used in closely related branches of science so that words common to both areas may be harmonized in form and in meaning. If, for example, anatomists regularly use "deciduous premolars," it would seem questionable for dentists to use "deciduous molars" to identify the same teeth; or, if the regular term in anatomy for "broad-headed" is "eurycephalous," it would seem unwise for psychiatry to use (as it does) "brachycephalous" to designate the same condition.

A nomenclature which uses well-oriented terms is much more than a mere recording technique; it furnishes indications of important interrelationships and differences and thereby assists significantly in the organization of knowledge.

## Specificity

Specificity is a highly desirable quality for technical terms used in any area of science. Ideally, every entity should be so delimited by the name applied to it that all possibility of confusion would be removed. Technical words which have been carefully selected for their descriptive qualities will ordinarily possess the desirable quality of specificity. But occasionally and for valid reasons, short nondescriptive or partially descriptive terms are used. In such cases there is a risk of vagueness as, for example, in the word "maxilla." In ordinary circumstances the word may be satisfactory, but in those contexts where precision and exactness are imperative it is not satisfactory because of its lack of specificity. "Maxilla" is only partially descriptive, and it can convey the following four slightly different meanings: (a) the whole upper jaw, (b) the bone of the upper jaw, (c) one of the two parts of the upper jaw, and (d) either the upper or the lower jaw. If the attribute of precise descriptiveness does not impart specificity to a technical word, the only way in which the word can attain that desirable quality is for it to receive a careful definition either from the person who coined it or from the official body governing the nomenclature in the area where the word is used.

Folk-terms or words from the vernacular language generally lack specificity. For example, the terms "shin" ("the front part of the leg below the knee; the front edge of the tibia; the lower part of the leg." — Webster) and "shank" ("the lower part of the leg in man; the part between the knee and the ankle; the shin." — Webster) fail to make clear the difference between the inner (and larger) and the outer (and smaller) of the leg bones, whereas the words "tibia" and "fibula" are never ambiguous. To cite other examples, "cannabis" is not only "hemp," of which there are many varieties, but specifically and only "Indian hemp"; and "serpentaria" is "Virginia snakeroot," and not merely "snakeroot," which might be one of twelve different drugs.

## Linguistic Correctness

A good scientific word will conform both in its structure and its form to the best linguistic usage. In constructing the word, careful attention can be given to assure the use of correct roots, stems, prefixes, suffixes, combining vowels, terminations, and inflectional forms by making reference to the parent words from which the several elements of the technical term were derived, and by observing the rules of transliteration. Malformed terms and variations in the orthography of words cause annoying and unnecessary difficulties. (For examples, see pp. 265-271).

Coiners of scientific words are sometimes expected to explain the etymology of their terms. This is a sound practice because it not only reduces errors in word construction but also improves the quality of the terms chosen. The better scientific dictionaries supply (usually in the original alphabet and spelling) the words from which the technical terms have been derived.

## Purity

A word constructed from elements derived from a single language is usually preferable to a hybrid word, which combines elements derived from more than one language. Constructive elements derived from a single language ordinarily combine more easily and euphoniously than elements taken from different languages. (see pp. 274-280).

## Euphony

A word should have a pleasant sound. Complete agreement on exactly what constitutes pleasantness of sound is not easily attained, but in general it may be said that words such as "syzygy" and "psittacistic," which combine elements that are difficult for the tongue and vague to the ear of English-speaking people, should be avoided. In ordinary English a linguistic concession for the sake of euphony has been made in the word "pacifist" for "pacificist"; a similar concession, though not for reasons of euphony alone, has been made in "urinalysis" for "urinanalysis" and in "appendectomy" for "appendicectomy."

*Economy*

Words which are unduly long or which almost defy pronunciation should not be used unless absolutely necessary. Terms like "Brachyuropushkydermatogammarus," "pneumoultramicroscopicsilicovolcanokoniosis," and "hepaticocholangiocholecystenterostomy" offend good taste. A term like "laryngotracheobronchitis," however, might be justified in spite of its length because it so clearly describes the areas of inflammation and because its pronunciation is not excessively difficult.

*Functional Facility and Adaptability*

A good scientific term is one which is easy to use in normal situations and which enjoys or easily acquires general approval by adapting itself readily to the company of closely related words already in general use. For example, if a compound word must incorporate in its makeup a reference to the "blind" dilated intestinal pouch, a familiar word such as CAECUM or TYPHLOS would be a better choice for supplying the necessary constructive element than would an unfamiliar word such as AMAUROS or ALAOS even though all four of these words in the original language mean "blind"; or in constructing a compound term which must include "worm" in its meaning, it is ordinarily better to use a familiar word like HELMINS, SKOLEX, or VERMIS than some rare word like EULE because not only would the meaning of the latter word be unfamiliar but it would rarely, if at all, appear as an element in other compound words. MALAC-, for example, is a constructive unit frequently used in scientific terms to designate "soft" and is employed in compounds both before and after the noun it qualifies (e.g., *malac*osteon, chondro*malac*ia); it seems unwise, therefore, to have chosen the rarely-used constructive unit HAPAL- instead of the familiar MALAC- when a stem was needed for a compound word to describe "a soft condition of the nails." Such an unwise choice has made "hapalonychia" an "orphan" word, the only entry in Dorland's

*Medical Dictionary* which uses *hapal-* as the first component. "Ulotropsis," defined as "gum nourishment," is another example of a term which lacks the quality of functional facility. Even though *-tropsis* is in itself correct both in form and meaning, there is nevertheless no good justification why it, instead of *-trophy*, should have been used for "nourishment" in this word; *-trophy* is the usual element employed in scientific terminology to convey the meaning "nourishment" and is therefore more immediately meaningful than *-tropsis*. Similarly, MYKTER is not one of the words commonly used in anatomical or pathological language for designating "nose"; RHIS and NASUS are the most widely used. In Dorland's *Medical Dictionary* MYKTER has supplied the first element for only two compound terms, "mycteric" and "mycteroxerosis." It should be stated, however, that in both of these words an added notion may be conveyed by *mycter-* in that not only "nose" is meant, but "nasal passages." In such a situation the use of an uncommon word-element might be justified because it imparts to the compound term greater specificity than could be attained by the use of the more common word-element. As a general rule, however, a constructive element which possesses a helpful mnemonic signal and which through extensive use has acquired functional facility is superior to an element which, even though appropriate in meaning, is rarely used and therefore unfamiliar.

The degree to which the different words possess functional facility and adaptability can often be of help in making choices among synonymous terms. For example, on the basis of functional facility, "helminthology" would be preferred to "scolecology," and "dentistry" would be preferred to "odontology" or "stomatology"—although "stomatology" possibly describes the scope of the dental profession better than either "dentistry" or "odontology" does. Of course not only the quality of functional facility must be taken into account in making final choice among synonymous terms; other criteria of good scientific terms must also be considered.

To achieve functional facility a technical term has to satisfy the special requirements of the area in which the term will be chiefly used. The official *Codes* of nomenclature in a scientific field can be of valuable assistance in determining what those special requirements are.

*Stability*

A word, when once defined, should not without good cause be given new or additional meanings, nor should its spelling be altered. Unless technical terms can in general be relied upon to retain their specific forms and meanings, much uncertainty and confusion in terminology will result. For the purpose of protecting the form and meaning of technical terms, the so-called "Law of Priority" (see pp. 266 and 299) was imposed in some scientific areas. The paramount importance of a discriminating and intelligent first choice in naming things is therefore apparent. In spite of the desirability of retaining terms unchanged when they have once been introduced, a certain degree of refinement in existing scientific terms is nevertheless necessary, especially in instances where ill-chosen words have been introduced. Scientists also recognize that altered circumstances and new discoveries force upon some words a change in meaning even if the forms of the words do not change (e.g., "atom" and "electron"). It is partly due to an awareness of these facts that scientific organizations establish commissions on nomenclature and demand periodic revisions of dictionaries.

*Sanction*

Where choice among alternate terms may seem difficult to make on the basis of several valid criteria of a good term, that term should be given preference which has the recommendation of the official committee or agency on nomenclature in that scientific area. In the terminology of dentistry, for example, "denture" is preferable to "plate," "periodontitis" to "pyorrhea," and "endodontics" to "endodontia."[4]

Not many of the technical terms used in the biological and medical sciences can satisfy all of the requirements mentioned in the foregoing discussion; the best terms, however, will be those which satisfy the largest number of the desiderata.

---

4. Cf., *Report on Second Nomenclature Conference*, and *Report on Third Nomenclature Conference* (Bureau of Library and Indexing Service, American Dental Assn., 1953 and 1954). For a rather surprising example in hematology see Margaret E. Hughes, *Amer. Jour. Med. Tech.* XV, 1949, 264-72. For zoology, see the regularly published serial, *The Bulletin of Zoological Nomenclature*.

# CHAPTER III

# *The Latin and Greek Languages*

## Latin and Greek in Scientific Nomenclature

Many languages, both ancient and modern, have contributed to the English words and phrases in use today, but no language has supplied a larger part of these than have the ancient Greek and Latin languages. Of the ten thousand most common English words, approximately 46 per cent are derived directly or indirectly from the Latin and 7.2 per cent from the Greek; of the twenty thousand most common English words 52.5 per cent are of Latin and 10 per cent of Greek origin. These percentages rise even higher when the words considered are limited to those used in scientific fields. Most of the technical words used in medicine and dentistry have their origins in the Greek and Latin languages, and over two-thirds of present-day medical English is derived from Greek alone.[1] Anglo-Saxon, for example, from which is derived approximately one-third of the words in ordinary English, accounts for less than 5 per cent of the words in a medical dictionary. The traditional source for names of plants and animals has long been the classical languages. The more technical and highly specialized the terms are, the higher is the percentage of those which have their origins in Greek and Latin, especially in Greek. These two ancient languages can therefore be

---

1. Cf., M. J. Siefert, *Synthesis of Medical Terminology*, p. 1. Edmund Andrews in "Medical Terminology," *Annals of Medical History* X, 1928, 184-85, states that the percentage from Greek is 75. The Commission on Terminology of the Fédération Dentaire Internationale has declared: "The rapidly growing odonto-stomatology vocabulary shows that 90 per cent of its roots are derived from the ancient languages, more particularly from the Latin and the Greek." (*Internat. Dent. Jour.* III [March 1953], 438).

said to form the principal linguistic foundation of modern scientific terminology.

The three short samples of modern scientific writing given below, the first from an account of an experiment with the adrenocorticotropic hormone ACTH, the second from a description of a brain malformation, and the third a description of the chestnut oak, will reveal the pseudo-Greek-and-Latin aspect of the language. The words which have their origins in Greek and Latin are in italics.

In six of the ten *patients* in this group there was a *definite roentgenographic* or *operative evidence* of *pituitary chromophobe adenoma* or of *craniopharyngioma*, in *addition* to *clinical* findings *characteristic* of *hypopituitarism*. One *patient* had a *suprasellar tumor*, probably a *glioma* of the *optic chiasm*. In one *case*, the *major portion* of the *pituitary* had been *removed* or destroyed during *craniotomy* twelve years *prior* to the *study*. One *case represented* an *example* of *postpartum necrosis* of the *pituitary*. (*Jour. of Clin. Invest.* xxxiv, 1955, 899).

There were several bridges of grey *matter* crossing the *internal capsule*, linking the *caudate nucleus* with the *dorsal part* of the *putamen*. *Putamen, caudate nucleus* and *globus pallidus* showed an *apparently normal distribution* of small and large *cells*. The *intrastriatal fibres* were *normally myelinated*; although their arrangement was somewhat *irregular*, there was no *status marmoratus*. (*Jour. of Comparative Neurology* cii, 1955, 348).

Tree with furrowed bark; branchlets *glabrous* or *pilose* and soon *glabrate*; leaves heavy and *coriaceous*, *obvate* to *oblong* or *lanceolate*, often *abruptly acuminate*, with *acute* to *obtuse base*, yellow-green and *lustrous* above, *undulately crenate* with broad rounded teeth, pale and *minutely* downy or *glabrescent* beneath; *primary* ribs 10-16 pairs, straight, *prominent* beneath; fruiting *peduncle* shorter than *petioles* or almost *obsolete*; cup mostly *tuberculate* with hard and stout scales *united* at *base*; acorn *ovoid* or *ellipsoid*, broadly rounded above. (*Gray's Manual of Botany*, 8th Ed., 1950, p. 545).

Not only has the terminology of science up to the present been built largely on word-elements from Greek and Latin, but these so-called "dead languages" continue to supply the best word-stock from which new terms are formed. Word coinages, necessitated by the perennial advances in scientific fields, find their most suitable and frequent origins in the ancient languages of the Greeks and the Romans. The words added to medical dictionaries as they progress through new editions are largely of Greek origin.[2] The following reasons may be given why Greek and Latin have furnished and continue to furnish such a large proportion of the word-elements in our scientific nomenclature:

1. Although the Greeks were probably not the originators of science and technology, they nevertheless contributed more to knowledge and progress in those areas than any people up to the modern age. Hippocrates (5th century B.C.) and Galen (2nd century A. D.) were the founding fathers of western medicine and established Greek as the favored language of that science in Europe. For centuries throughout the Middle Ages and later, Latin was the language of science and medicine. For these reasons many of the words used in science today are found to have their origins in periods when the Greek and Latin languages were the standard vehicles of expression for scientific concepts. A historical study of many a branch of science will ultimately confront the student with ideas and theories which were expressed in the languages of the Greeks and the Romans. In fact, the nomenclature used in some sciences might fairly be said to constitute an epitome of their history. For these reasons alone, therefore, the balance of favor in scientific nomenclature quite naturally swings toward the Greek and Latin languages.

2. Since ancient Greek and Latin are no longer used as conversational languages, the meanings of the words in those languages have become established and stable. Greek and Latin words are no longer subject to the morphological and semantic changes which affect the words of currently spoken languages. For this reason, a scientific term constructed of elements taken from words whose meanings and forms have been stabilized will be likely to possess the same quality of stability in those respects. Precision of meaning and a lasting stability are highly desirable qualities of words used in the extensive and increasingly complex fields of science. Moreover, affective meanings and emotional overtones often adhere to words taken from currently spoken languages; such distracting qualities are avoided by the use of technical words whose constructive units have fixed and precise meanings. In ancient Greek and Latin the

2. Edmund Andrews, *A History of Scientific English*, pp. 269-70.

scientist can usually find word-elements enabling him to create a term exactly meeting his needs and one which will be likely to retain a preciseness of meaning and form.[3]

3. The synthetic nature, or affixing characteristic, of the Greek and Latin languages — especially the Greek — makes those languages particularly well suited for use in forming economical, descriptive, and euphonious compound terms. One or more Latin or Greek stems, prefixes, and suffixes can be synthesized into a single term that will furnish both a name and a definition and yet not seem harsh, artificial, or unwieldy. "Nephrolith" (NEPHR-, kidney; LITH-, stone), for example, is short, clear, and euphonious; even Latin requires two words, *renalis calculus* to express the idea. If further description is desired, another element can be added to the word without harming its desirable qualities, for example, "nephrolithotomy" (TOM-, cut "out"). "Gastralgokenosis" (GASTR-, stomach; ALG-, pain; KENOSIS, emptiness) is a succinct manner of saying "gastric pain when the stomach is empty"; "atelencephalia" (A-, not; TEL-, complete; EN-, in; KEPHAL-, head) is a neat term for "defective development of the brain"; "strephenpodia" (STREPH-, twist; EN-, in; POD-, foot) and "strephexopodia" (STREPH-, twist; EXO-, outward; POD-, foot) are words which in lucidity and in descriptive qualities surpass "club-foot" or even the common Latin loan phrases "talipes varus" and "talipes valgus." Since it is a normal characteristic of Greek and Latin words to be compounded of roots, stems, prefixes, and suffixes, new words coined in the same manner from Greek and Latin elements can be adapted to modern requirements and yet seem neither harsh nor artificial. It is generally difficult or impossible to determine from the structure of a technical term whether it is a word which was used by the Greeks or the Romans in their day or is one which has been coined in modern times.[4] The synthesis of several descriptive elements into one word, so desirable and almost

---

3. In general, words derived from the Greek are somewhat less susceptible to acquiring secondary meanings than words derived from the Latin.
4. *Diaphoresis* (perspiration, especially excessive) and *ecchymosis* (extravasation of blood; also discoloration of skin caused by it), for example, are native Greek words used by Hippocrates, Galen, and Celsus with essentially the same meanings as they carry today; *diathermy* and *ectopia*, on the other hand, are neologisms formed to meet the need for descriptive terms for new observations and developments. Yet all these words appear to be of equally good breeding.

necessary in the vocabulary of a complex and exact science, is greatly facilitated by the use of languages which themselves are synthetic and elastic in nature. Naturalness and pleasant euphony as well as economy and practical usefulness are the results of such a procedure.

4. Greek and Latin are universal languages. In almost any part of the world there are educated people who understand these ancient languages, especially Latin. If a scientist wishes international recognition of his researches, he writes the diagnoses and descriptive tracts in Latin; moreover, the codes of nomenclature in some scientific fields require that he do so. A prescription written in Latin can be interpreted by pharmacists in almost any country, and in some smaller countries it is still a requirement that prescriptions be written in Latin.[5] The universality of the two languages is further attested by the fact that treatises in foreign languages dealing with scientific subjects can be read more easily than material in the same tongue dealing with more general topics. The reason for this is that so many of the words used by scientists in different countries have a common source in Greek and Latin and therefore appear alike or nearly alike even though they have become naturalized in English, French, Spanish, German, Dutch, Italian, or other languages[6] (see pp. 11-12). The technical terminology of science has such a pronounced international aspect that some persons claim it comes nearer to being an international language than anything else yet devised.

5. Words constructed from Greek or Latin elements generally have the advantage of being immediately recognized as technical terms; their very appearance constitutes a recommendation for attention. The desire for this "foreignness," or departure from commonly used expressions, is so urgent that sometimes it accounts for the use of Greek-derived words instead of the somewhat less foreign appearing Latin-derived terms.

6. Certain terms constructed from Greek or Latin elements enable physicians, if they so wish, to conceal from the patient and others

---

5. Lists of the abbreviations of the common Latin phrases employed in medicine and pharmacy are available in such books as Lewis, *Medical Latin*; Beard, *Latin for Pharmacists*; and Dorfman, *Pharmaceutical Latin* — see Bibliography.

6. Portions of scientific tracts may actually on occasion seem to be pseudo-Latin; witness a phrase like the following used to describe certain animals: "the nigrescent maculation of their pristine niveous candour."

the nature of a disease. Such concealment may generally be regarded of minor importance, and yet some persons will argue conscientiously that in diagnosis and prescription writing the use of language which does not reveal to the patient the nature of his illness or the prescription may in some instances have a wholesome psychological effect and therefore be legitimate and wise.[7]

7. Extensive and continued use of Greek and Latin words as the main source for technical names has established in the nomenclature of the major sciences a cohesion and a unity not otherwise easily attainable. A modern scientific field can, therefore, by constructing its terminology on a Greek and Latin base, fruitfully ally itself with other scientific fields.

The reasons stated above explain why the Greek and Latin languages have been, and continue to be, the cornerstones on which scientific words are built. The choice of these two ancient languages was not a matter of accident or of sentimental yielding to tradition. Favoring their choice were compelling historical reasons as well as specific practical advantages that could be expected to accrue from the use of a common linguistic source which had a varied and extensive vocabulary but whose words were pliable in form and yet stable in meaning. A scientific vocabulary developed from such a linguistic source gave the scientists assurance that their technical terms would convey clearly and with negligible variation the same meanings everywhere.

## The Latin and Greek Languages. Transliteration

An understanding of the essential characteristics of the Latin and Greek languages is a most valuable asset for those who use and create scientific language: it enables them to refer with ease and understanding to the original words from which such a large percentage of scientific vocabulary has been derived; it enables them to use Greek and Latin dictionaries intelligently and to understand their system of word entries; it provides sound criteria for judging good and bad word formation; and since many scientific

---

7. Cf. *Jour. Mich. State Dental Assn.* XXXIII, 1951, 205.

dictionaries, nomenclatural codes, and descriptive tracts present Latin and Greek words in their original forms and refer to several of their inflectional aspects, it enables the student and the scientist to make maximum use of that information.

Latin and Greek are synthetic and rather highly inflected languages. Many Greek and Latin words were constructed by adding prefixes and suffixes to a comparatively small number of fundamental roots.[8] Words thus formed supplied stems which in turn were combined with other stems, prefixes, and suffixes in the construction of more words. In order to indicate their particular function in sentences, most Latin and Greek words were inflected, that is, systematically altered in spelling. The basic techniques and principles of word formation and inflection which were used in the Latin and Greek languages have long been employed in the construction of scientific vocabularies, and are still in use today.

The Latin and Greek languages may be studied systematically under three general headings: (1) *Vocabulary:* words, their construction, meaning and pronunciation. (2) *Inflections:* changes in the spelling of words to indicate changes in their function. Inflection is usually referred to as DECLENSION when applied to nouns, pronouns, and adjectives, and as CONJUGATION when applied to verbs. (3) *Syntax,* or *Grammar*: the rules of word usage in sentences. In this text, only those facts regarding these three aspects of the languages will be presented which are most directly applicable and helpful in attaining the stated objectives of the book. This means that most of the attention will be given to vocabulary, less to inflections, and very little to syntax.

## THE LATIN LANGUAGE

## A. LATIN ALPHABET AND PRONUNCIATION

The English and Latin languages use the same alphabet, except that the letters *w* and *j* are lacking in the Latin.

---

8. For a convenient and useful list of Latin roots see C. T. Lewis, *An Elementary Latin Dictionary*, pp. 935-52.

1. *Vowels:* The Latin vowels and their sounds are:

**a, ā**:   as in "*a*rch," and "f*a*ther"
**e, ē**:   as in "m*e*t," and "pr*e*y"
**i, ī**:   as in "p*i*t," and "mach*i*ne"
**o, ō**:   as in "*o*bey," and "h*o*le"
**u, ū**:   as in "f*u*ll," and "r*u*le"

2. *Diphthongs:* The Latin diphthongs and their sounds are:

**ae**:   as in "*ai*sle"
**au**:   as in "*ou*t"
**ei**:   as in "fr*ei*ght"
**eu**:   as in "f*eu*d"
**oe**:   as in "b*oi*l"

3. *Consonants:* The Latin consonants have the same sounds as they have in English except that:

**c**   is always hard, as in "cap"
**g**   is always hard, as in "gas"
**i**   (consonantal) is pronounced like *y* in "yet"
**v**   is pronounced like *w* in "window"
**s**   always has the sound it has in "son," not as in "wisdom"

4. *Syllables and Accent of Latin Words:* A Latin word has as many syllables as it has vowels and diphthongs. Final vowels are always pronounced. A syllable is long if it contains a long vowel or a diphthong or if it has a short vowel followed by two consonants or by *x* or *z*.

The last syllable (the ultima) is never accented. If the next to the last syllable (the penult) is long, it receives the accent; otherwise, the accent falls on the preceding syllable (the antepenult). For example: *arti' culus*; *axi' lla*; *impo' nere*; *ponderō' sus*.

## B. LATIN INFLECTIONS

The change in the spelling of a Latin word (usually in the ending) to indicate its grammatical function in a sentence is called INFLECTION. English also uses this device, but to a smaller extent than Latin does; for example: horse, horses, horse's, horses'; he, his, him; carry, carried; sing, sang, sung; fast, faster, fastest.

Latin nouns, pronouns, and adjectives have GENDER (masculine, feminine, or neuter), NUMBER (singular or plural), and CASE (nominative, genitive, dative, accusative, ablative, or vocative). Adjectives and adverbs also have DEGREE (positive, comparative, or superlative). Gender, number, case, and degree of a Latin word are usually indicated by the spelling of the terminal suffixes.

Latin verbs have VOICE (active and passive); MOOD (indicative, subjunctive, imperative, infinitive); TENSE (present, imperfect, future, perfect, pluperfect, future-perfect); NUMBER (singular and plural); PERSON (first, second, third). Voice, mood, tense, number, and person are also indicated in Latin by infixes, suffixes, or other changes in spelling.

Latin prepositions and conjunctions are not inflected.

## 1. Declension of NOUNS

A Latin noun falls into (or "belongs to") one of five categories, generally called "declensions." That which determines into which of the five declensions a noun falls is its spelling in the genitive case, singular number. For this reason Latin dictionaries and vocabularies give, in addition to the NOMINATIVE (the "name" case, used as the entry form in dictionaries and vocabularies), also the GENITIVE (corresponding to the "possessive" case in English) singular form of Latin nouns. This information is valuable because the genitive case form is frequently used in descriptive phrases of scientific writing and in binomial names in biology (e.g., *musculus oculi*, "muscle of the eye"; *flexor digiti*, "flexor of the finger"; *species incertae sedis*, "a species of uncertain location"; *forma foliarum*, "shape of the leaves"; *streptococcus bovis*, "streptococcus of cattle"). But the genitive case is of special importance because it reveals the BASE of the word, that is, that part of the word which remains after removing the terminal suffix of the genitive case, and which furnishes the particular constructive element that is necessary for correct word formation.

The ACCUSATIVE case in Latin corresponds to the "objective" case in English. Its most common use is as direct object of a verb or of a preposition (e.g., *adde aquam:* "add water"; *recipe sulfuris grammata quattuor:* "take four grams of sulphur"; *ante cibum:* "before (food) meals"; *in pilulas duas:* "into two pills").

Words in the ABLATIVE case appear often in scientific descriptive tracts written in Latin. The ablative has a number of uses in Latin sentences, but two of its most important functions in the context of scientific writing are to make a word descriptive (e.g., *erecta cauda:* "with erect tail"; *pedibus nitidis* "with glistening feet"; *lateribus convergentibus:* "with its side converging") or to designate the "respect in which" a descriptive adjective applies to the thing being described (e.g., *apice acuta:* "pointed *at the tip,*" i.e. "*in respect to its tip,* pointed"; *colore violaceae vel albescentes:* "violet or whitish *in color*").

Only the nominative, genitive, accusative, and ablative cases will be given consideration in this text. The characteristic endings (terminal suffixes) of these cases in each of the five declensions are shown in the following table:

(The five declensions are designated by I, II, III, IV, V. Genders are designated by *M* (masculine), *F* (feminine), and *N* (neuter). The nominative singular in Declension III has various endings.)

### SINGULAR

| | I<br>F | II<br>M | II<br>N | III<br>M & F | III<br>N | IV<br>M & F | IV<br>N | V<br>M & F |
|---|---|---|---|---|---|---|---|---|
| *Nom.* | -a | -us, -er | -um | (various) | | -us | -ū | -ēs |
| *Gen.* | -ae | -ī | | | -is | | -ūs | -ēi |
| *Acc.* | -am | -um | | -em | | -um | -ū | -em |
| *Abl.* | -ā | -ō | | | -e (-i) | -ū | | -ē |

### PLURAL

| | I<br>F | II<br>M | II<br>N | III<br>M & F | III<br>N | IV<br>M & F | IV<br>N | V<br>M & F |
|---|---|---|---|---|---|---|---|---|
| *Nom.* | -ae | -ī | -a | -ēs | -a | -ūs | -ua | -ēs |
| *Gen.* | -ārum | -ōrum | | -um | | -uum | | -ērum |
| *Acc.* | -ās | -ōs | -a | -ēs | -a | -ūs | -ua | -ēs |
| *Abl.* | -īs | -īs | | -ibus | | -ibus | | -ēbus |

From the above table observe that:

1. The endings of the nominative singular vary, but *-a, -us, -um* are very common.
2. Common nominative plural endings are *-ae, -ī, -a, -ēs.*
3. Genitive plural endings are *-ārum, -ōrum, -um, -ērum.*
4. Common accusative singular endings are *-am, -em, -um.*
5. Common accusative plural endings are *-ās, -ōs, -ēs.*

6. Ablative plural endings are *-īs, ibus (-ēbus)*.

7. The nominative and accusative of neuter nouns are spelled alike, and in the plural always end in *-a*.

8. The gender of a noun is often indicated by the ending of the nominative singular:

   *-a* indicates feminine gender (e.g., *aqua, alga, lingua, vena*).
   *-us* most often indicates masculine gender (*locus, digitus, fungus*), but not always (e.g., *corpus* is neuter).
   *-um* indicates neuter gender (e.g., *cilium, oleum, sputum*).

9. If the nominative plural ends in *-a*, the gender of the word is neuter (e.g., *corpora, genera, cornua, foramina*).

A Latin noun can "belong to" only one of the five declensions and uses the endings of that declension only. The endings shown in the preceding table are attached to the BASE of nouns, as illustrated in the sample nouns declined below.

### SINGULAR

|      | I        | II          |            |           |
|------|----------|-------------|------------|-----------|
| *Nom.* | aqu**a**   | fung**us**    | canc**er**   | cili**um**  |
| *Gen.* | aqu**ae**  | fung**ī**     | canc**rī**   | cil**iī**   |
| *Acc.* | aqu**am**  | fung**um**    | canc**rum**  | cili**um**  |
| *Abl.* | aqu**ā**   | fung**ō**     | conc**rō**   | cili**ō**   |

### PLURAL

|      |          |             |            |           |
|------|----------|-------------|------------|-----------|
| *Nom.* | aqu**ae**  | fung**ī**     | canc**rī**   | cil**ia**   |
| *Gen.* | aqu**ārum**| fung**ōrum**  | canc**rōrum**| cili**ōrum**|
| *Acc.* | aqu**ās**  | fung**ōs**    | canc**rōs**  | cil**ia**   |
| *Abl.* | aqu**īs**  | fung**īs**    | canc**rīs**  | cili**īs**  |

### SINGULAR
### III

|      |          |             |           |
|------|----------|-------------|-----------|
| *Nom.* | cortex    | extensor     | ligatio    |
| *Gen.* | cortic**is**| extensor**is** | ligation**is**|
| *Acc.* | cortic**em**| extensor**em** | ligation**em**|
| *Abl.* | cortic**e** | extensor**e**  | ligation**e** |
| *Nom.* | fin**is**   | foramen      | genus      |
| *Gen.* | fin**is**   | foramin**is**  | gener**is**  |
| *Acc.* | fin**em**   | foramen      | genus      |
| *Abl.* | fin**e**    | formin**e**    | gener**e**   |

## PLURAL

| Nom. | cortic**ēs** | extensor**ēs** | ligation**ēs** |
| Gen. | cortic**um** | extensor**um** | ligation**um** |
| Acc. | cortic**ēs** | extensor**ēs** | ligation**ēs** |
| Abl. | cortic**ibus** | extensor**ibus** | ligation**ibus** |
| Nom. | fin**ēs** | foramin**a** | gener**a** |
| gen. | fin**ium** | foramin**um** | gener**um** |
| Acc. | fin**ēs** | foramin**a** | gener**a** |
| Abl. | fin**ibus** | foramin**ibus** | gener**ibus** |

## SINGULAR

|  | IV | | V |
|---|---|---|---|
| Nom. | sin**us** | corn**u** | rabi**es** |
| Gen. | sin**ūs** | corn**ūs** | rabie**ī** |
| Acc. | sin**um** | corn**ū** | rabi**em** |
| Abl. | sin**ū** | corn**ū** | rabi**ē** |

## PLURAL

| Nom. | sin**ūs** | corn**ua** | rabi**ēs** |
| Gen. | sin**uum** | corn**uum** | rabi**ērum** |
| Acc. | sin**ūs** | corn**ua** | rabi**ēs** |
| Abl. | sin**ibus** | corn**ibus** | rabi**ēbus** |

The STEMS of Latin nouns belonging to Declensions I, II, IV, and V (and some of those belonging to Declension III) end respectively in the vowels *a*, *o*, *u*, and *e*. Accordingly, those declensions are often referred to as the A-Declension, the O-Declension, the U-Declension, and the E-Declension.

| *DECLENSION* | | *EXAMPLE* |
|---|---|---|
| I, | or A-Declension | *aqua* (stem *aqua-*; base *aqu-*) |
| II, | or O-Declension | *fungus* (stem *fungo-*; base *fung-*) |
| (III) | | *tussis* (stem *tussi-*; base *tuss-*) |
| IV, | or U-Declension | *fructus* (stem *fructu-*; base *fruct-*) |
| V, | or E-Declension | *facies* (stem *facie-*; base *faci-*) |

## 2. *Declension of ADJECTIVES*

An adjective must agree in gender, number, and case with the noun it modifies. Latin dictionaries and vocabularies, therefore, present the nominative singular forms of adjectives in all three genders.

Latin adjectives use the same inflectional endings as those used by Latin nouns of Declensions I, II, and III; they never use the endings of Declensions IV or V. Adjectives may therefore be classified into two general groups according to the system of declension which they use:

(1) *Those adjectives which use the endings of Declensions I and II*

Adjectives using the endings of Declensions I and II are usually entered in dictionaries as follows: *albus, -a, -um* (sometimes *ruber, rubra, rubrum*). This means that the nominative singular in the masculine is *albus* (or *ruber*), in the feminine *alba* (or *rubra*), and in the neuter *album* (or *rubrum*), and that *albus* and *album* are inflected according to Declension II and *alba* according to Declension I.

(2) *Those adjectives which use the endings of Declension III*

An adjective belonging to Declension III is usually entered in dictionaries in one of three ways: (a) *facilis, -e*, which means that the nominative singular in both masculine and feminine is *facilis* and in the neuter is *facile* and that the genitive singular in all genders is *facilis*. (b) *ingens, -ntis* which means that the same form is used for all genders and that the genitive singular is *ingentis*. (c) *acer, acris, acre*, which means that the forms in the nominative singular differ in the three genders and that the genitive singular in all genders is *acris*.

The adjectives of this group are declined like the nouns of Declension III, but it is important to keep in mind that the NOMINATIVE AND THE ACCUSATIVE CASES IN THE NEUTER are alike, both in the singular and the plural; that the ABLATIVE SINGULAR usually ends in *-ī* instead of in *-e*; that the NEUTER PLURAL IN THE NOMINATIVE AND THE ACCUSATIVE ends in *-ia* instead of *-a*; and that the GENITIVE PLURAL ends in *-ium* instead of in *-um*. Observe these points in the declension of the sample adjectives *facilis, -e* and *ingens*.

## SINGULAR

|  | M & F | N | M & F | N |
|---|---|---|---|---|
| *Nom.* | facilis | facile | ingens | ingens |
| *Gen.* | facilis | facilis | ingentis | |
| *Acc.* | facilem | facile | ingentem | ingens |
| *Abl.* | facilī | facilī | ingentī | |

## PLURAL

|  | M & F | N | M & F | N |
|---|---|---|---|---|
| *Nom.* | facilēs | facilia | ingentēs | ingentia |
| *Gen.* | facilium | facilium | ingentium | |
| *Acc.* | facilēs | facilia | ingentēs | ingentia |
| *Abl.* | facilibus | facilibus | ingentibus | |

Latin adjectives have three degrees of comparison: (1) the positive, (2) the comparative, and (3) the superlative, and these degrees are indicated by special terminal suffixes. For example:

| Positive | Comparative | Superlative |
|---|---|---|
| longus, -a, -um | longior, longius | longissimus, -a, -um |
| brevis, -e | brevior, brevius | brevissimus, -a, -um |
| velox, -ocis | velocior, velocius | velocissimus, -a, -um |
|  | (or) | |
| celer, celeris, celere | celerior, celerius | celerrimus, -a, -um |
|  | (or) | |
| facilis, -e | facilior, facilius | facillimus, -a, -um |
|  | (or, irregularly) | |
| bonus, -a, -um | melior, melius | optimus, -a, -um |
| magnus, -a, -um | maior, maius | maximus, -a, -um |

Adjectives in the comparative degree are declined in Declension III; for example:

## SINGULAR    PLURAL

|  | M & F | N | M & F | N |
|---|---|---|---|---|
| *Nom.* | brevior | brevius | breviorēs | breviora |
| *Gen.* | brevioris | | breviorum | |
| *Acc.* | breviorem | brevius | breviorēs | breviora |
| *Abl.* | breviore | | brevioribus | |

For purposes of illustraton and review of Latin declensions, a few nouns and adjectives together have been declined through the four cases in the singular and the plural. Observe that the endings of the adjectives are sometimes, but not always, the same as those of the nouns. Although an adjective must agree with the noun it modifies in gender, number, and case, the endings of the noun and adjective need not be alike in spelling because the two words may belong to different declensions.

SINGULAR

|  | (a yellow corolla) | (the trigeminal nerve) | (a very high tree) |
|---|---|---|---|
| *Nom.* | corolla flava | nervus trigeminus | arbor altissima |
| *Gen.* | corollae flavae | nervi trigemini | arboris altissimae |
| *Acc.* | corollam flavam | nervum trigeminum | arborem altissimam |
| *Abl.* | corolla flava | nervo trigemino | arbore altissima |

PLURAL

|  |  |  |  |
|---|---|---|---|
| *Nom.* | corollae flavae | nervi trigemini | arbores altissimae |
| *Gen.* | corollarum flavarum | nervorum trigeminorum | arborum altissimarum |
| *Acc.* | corollas flavas | nervos trigeminos | arbores altissimas |
| *Abl.* | corollis flavis | nervis trigeminis | arboribus altissimis |

SINGULAR

|  | (a fixed flower) | (an outlet duct) |
|---|---|---|
| *Nom.* | flos sessilis | ductus efferens |
| *Gen.* | floris sessilis | ducti efferentis |
| *Acc.* | florem sessilem | ductum efferentem |
| *Abl.* | flore sessili | ducto efferenti |

PLURAL

|  |  |  |
|---|---|---|
| *Nom.* | flores sessiles | ducti efferentes |
| *Gen.* | florum sessilium | ductorum efferentium |
| *Acc.* | flores sessiles | ductos efferentes |
| *Abl.* | floribus sessilibus | ductis efferentibus |

SINGULAR

|  | (the large occipital opening) | (a larger leaf) |
|---|---|---|
| *Nom.* | foramen occipitale magnum | folium maius |
| *Gen.* | foraminis occipitalis magni | folii maioris |
| *Acc.* | foramen occipitale magnum | folium maius |
| *Abl.* | foramine occiptali magno | folio maiore |

## PLURAL

| | | |
|---|---|---|
| *Nom.* | foramina occipitalia magna | folia maiora |
| *Gen.* | foraminum occipitalium magnorum | foliorum maiorum |
| *Acc.* | foramina occipitalia magna | folia maiora |
| *Abl.* | foraminibus occipitalibus magnis | foliis maioribus |

### 3. *Gender and Agreement*

The gender of a Latin noun is not always determined by sex (i.e., natural gender) or by what seems appropriate to a sex; it is most often indicated by the ending which the noun has in the nominative case (i.e., grammatical gender) or by its signification. For example:

*hortus* (garden) is masculine because it ends in *-us*.
*ager* (field) is masculine because it ends in *-er*.
*aqua* (water) is feminine because it ends in *-a*.
*species* (appearance) is feminine because it ends in *-es*.
*lutum* (mud) is neuter because it ends in *-um*.
*cornu* (horn) is neuter because it ends in *-u*.

Not every Latin noun ending in *-us* is masculine; a few, such as *manus* (hand) and the names of trees (e.g., *quercus*, oak), are feminine, and a few are neuter (e.g., *corpus, corporis*, body).

It is a common practice in science to use many technical words, whatever their origin, in their latinized forms. In a binomial nomenclature such as is used in the biological sciences, in descriptive tracts written entirely in Latin or using numerous Latin phrases, and in other circumstances where technical terms are used more than singly, the matter of Latin gender and agreement, as illustrated above, is very important.[9]

### 4. *Conjugation of VERBS*

Latin dictionaries and vocabularies usually list verbs as follows:

*ligo, ligare, ligavi, ligatum*, to tie, bind.
*misceo, miscere, miscui, mixtum*, to mix.
*scribo, scribere, scripsi, scriptum*, to write.
*facio, facere, feci, factum*, to do, make.
*audio, audire, audivi, auditum*, to hear.

---

9. It is also at times a vexing question. See R. E. Blackwelder, "The Gender of Scientific Names in Zoology," *Jour. Washington Acad. of Sci.* XXXI, 1941, 135-40; R. W. Brown, *The Composition of Scientific Words*, pp. 50-54.

Forms such as those above, some of which are abbreviated when there is no risk of ambiguity (e.g., *ligo, -are, -avi, -atum*), are called PRINCIPAL PARTS and furnish the basis for the many inflected verb forms. For our purposes the most important of a verb's principal parts are the second, that is, the PRESENT INFINITIVE (*ligare, miscere, scribere, facere, audire*), and the fourth, that is, the PERFECT PASSIVE PARTICIPLE (*ligatum, mixtum, scriptum, factum, auditum*). Only these two principal parts will therefore be given for the verbs included in the General Latin Vocabulary list (pp. 87-131), and verbs will be referred to by their present infinitive form.

Scientific terms use extensively the following Latin verb stems and bases:

(a) The PRESENT STEM. This stem is found by dropping the final *-re* of the present infinitive: *liga-*; *misce-*; *scribe-*; *face-*; *audi-*.[10] Such words as *liga*ment, *misce*genation, pre*scribe*, *audio*gram illustrate how the present stem has been used in the construction of compound terms.

(b) The PRESENT PARTICIPIAL STEM. The present participle of a Latin verb is formed by attaching the suffix *-ns* to the present stem (if the first-listed form of the verb ends in *-io*, the letters *-ie* will appear before the *-ns* suffix). All present participles are declined in Declension III, like the adjective *ingens* (see p. 37). The stem is found by dropping the case ending *-is* from the genitive singular form. The present participles and their stems of the sample verbs given above are as follows:

|      | (tying)   | (mixing)   | (writing)   | (making)   | (hearing)  |
|------|-----------|------------|-------------|------------|------------|
| *Nom.* | ligans    | miscens    | scribens    | faciens    | audiens    |
| *Gen.* | *ligan*tis | *miscen*tis | *scriben*tis | *facien*tis | *audien*tis |

Present participial stems are used extensively in words like al*ligant*, rube*facient*, trans*audient*.

(c) The BASE of the PERFECT PASSIVE PARTICIPLE. The passive participial base is found by dropping the nominative case ending *-us, -a,* or *-um* from the participle, for example:

---

10. If the present infinitive ends in *-ari, -eri,* or *-iri,* drop the final *-ri*; if it ends in *-i* only, change the *i* to *e* to form the present stem.

| Participle | Base | Derivative |
|---|---|---|
| ligatus, -a, -um | ligat- | colligation |
| mixtus, -a, -um | mixt- | commixture |
| scriptus, -a, -um | script- | prescription |
| factus, -a, -um | fact- | olfactory |
| auditus, -a, -um | audit- | auditorium |

It will be useful to note from the examples given that the participial base very frequently ends in -t. The other common ending of the participial base is -s (occasionally, -x). For example:

| Infinitive | Perfect Participle | Base | Derivative |
|---|---|---|---|
| haerere (stick) | haesum | haes- | adhesion |
| fundere (pour) | fusum | fus- | suffusion |
| fluere (flow) | fluxum | flux- | defluxion |
| flectere (bend) | flexum | flex- | semiflexion |

For derivative study and for construction of scientific terms the participial base is the most important single form of the Latin verb.

There are three special Latin verbal forms, all expressing a command or instruction, which are not infrequently used in scientific writing; they are the following:

(1) *Present imperative* (issuing an order):

| Verb | Present Imperative | Meaning |
|---|---|---|
| recipere | recipe | take! |
| miscere; dividere | misce et divide | mix and divide! |
| solvere | solve | dissolve! |
| signare | signa | mark! |

Note that the present imperative form of a Latin verb is identical with its present stem.

(2) *Present subjunctive*, third person (another method of expressing a command):

| Verb | Present Subjunctive | Meaning |
|---|---|---|
| stare | stet; stent | let it stand; let them stand |
| agitare | agitetur | let it be shaken |
| capere | capiat | let him (her) take |
| solvere | solvantur | let them be dissolved |
| siccare | siccentur | let them be dried |

Note that the singular endings are *-t* in the active voice and *-tur* in the passive voice; in the plural they are *-nt* and *-ntur*. Also note that these endings are attached to the present stem after the final vowel of the stem has been changed.

(3) *Gerundive*, formed by adding the suffix *-ndus, -a, -um* to the present stem. This suffix conveys the meaning of obligation or necessity:

nomen conserva*ndum* (*conservare*): "a name to be preserved."
nomen inquire*ndum* (*inquirere*): "a name to be investigated."
massa in tres pilulas forma*nda* (*formare*): "shape the mass into three pills."

## C. VOWEL AND CONSONANT CHANGES IN LATIN

1. *Vowel Gradation* (*ablaut*). The most common occurrence of vowel gradation in Latin words takes place *when a prepositional prefix is attached to a root or stem*. These changes in the spelling of a Latin root or stem are of course reflected in its English derivatives. The most important vowel changes are the following:

(a) Before a single consonant (except *r*), a short *a* or *e* in the root is usually changed to *i*. For example:

| Latin Word | English Derivative | Prefixed Latin Word | English Derivative |
|---|---|---|---|
| cadere (fall) | caducous | decidere | deciduous; coincidence |
| caput (head) | capital | sinciput occipitium | occipital; precipitate |
| facere (do) | rubifacient | deficere | deficient; calcification |
| habere (hold) | habenula | inhibere | inhibitory |
| sedere (sit) | sediment | insidere | insiduous |
| tenere (hold) | tenaculum | continere | continent |

(b) Before two consonants, a short *a* in the root usually changes to *e*. For example:

| Latin Word | English Derivative | Prefixed Latin Word | English Derivative |
|---|---|---|---|
| ager (field) | agriculture | peregrinus | peregrination |
| annus (year) | annual | perennius | perennial |
| arma (weapons) | armiger | inermis | inerm |
| barba (beard) | barbate | imberbis | imberbe |
| factus (done) | factual | infectus | infection |

(c) *ae* becomes *i*, and *au* becomes *u*; for example:

| Latin Word | English Derivative | Prefixed Latin Word | English Derivative |
|---|---|---|---|
| caesum (cut) | caesura | incisus | incision, excise |
| clausum (closed) | claustrum | inclusus | inclusion, occlusion |

2. *Consonant Changes.* When certain prefixes ending in a consonant are attached to words beginning with a consonant, the final consonant of the prefix is assimilated, fully or partially, to the other consonant; for example:

> *ad* (to) plus *ligare* (to bind) becomes **al**ligare.
> *com* (with) plus *ligare* (to bind) becomes **col**ligare.
> *in* (in) plus *radiare* (to shine) becomes **ir**radiare.
> *in* (not) plus *percipere* (to perceive) becomes **im**percipere.
> *ob* (against) plus *ponere* (to place) becomes **op**ponere.
> *per* (throughout) plus *lucidus* (clear) becomes **pel**lucidus.
> *sub* (under) plus *flavus* (yellow) becomes **suf**flavus.

## D. TRANSLITERATION OF LATIN

Since English and Latin use the same alphabet, transliteration of words from Latin to English presents no difficulties. The only changes in spelling to be observed are the following:

1. The Latin diphthongs *ae* and *oe* generally become *e* in English words; for example:

| Latin | English | Latin | English |
|---|---|---|---|
| adhaesio | adhesion | aequilibrium | equilibrium |
| caeruleus | ceruleous | oesophagus | esophagus |
| saeptum | septum | foetidus | fetid |
| caecum | cecum | | |

2. The letter *i* is sometimes a consonant in Latin; if so, it is transposed into English as *j*. For example:

| Latin | English |
|---|---|
| maior (larger) | major |
| iacere, iactum (to throw) | jactation |
| iungere, iunctum (to join) | juncture |

3. Minor changes are made in the terminations of some Latin words when they are brought over into English. These changes are indicated in the section on suffixes (see pp. 75-81). In general, there is a tendency to drop the inflectional endings since in English they rarely serve, as they do in Latin, to indicate the grammatical function of the word in a sentence. It should be emphasized, however, that in the scientific names of plants and animals and wherever Latin is used in diagnoses and descriptions, the exact Latin spelling is retained.

## THE GREEK LANGUAGE

## A. GREEK ALPHABET AND PRONUNCIATION

The Greek alphabet is the parent of our English alphabet. In its most common version the Greek alphabet had 24 letters, each with its own name and fixed phonetic value, as follows:

| Name of Letter | Capital | Small | Sound | Latin and English Equivalent* |
|---|---|---|---|---|
| alpha | A | α | father | a |
| beta | B | β | bug | b |
| gamma | Γ | γ | gum | g (or n) |
| delta | Δ | δ | do | d |
| epsilon | E | ε | let | e |
| zeta | Z | ζ | gaze | z |
| eta | H | η | fête (French) | e |
| theta | Θ | θ | thin | th (occasionally t) |
| iota | I | ι | machine | i |
| kappa | K | κ | kin | c (or k) |
| lambda | Λ | λ | log | l |
| mu | M | μ | men | m |
| nu | N | ν | now | n |
| xi | Ξ | ξ | ax | x |
| omicron | O | o | optic | o |
| pi | Π | π | put | p |
| rho | P | ρ | run | r (or rh) |
| sigma | Σ | σ, ς | sat | s |
| tau | T | τ | tap | t |
| upsilon | Υ | υ | über (German) | y (or u) |
| phi | Φ | φ | graph | ph (or f) |
| chi | X | χ | chord | ch |
| psi | Ψ | ψ | ships | ps |
| omega | Ω | ω | go | ō |

* Where alternates are given, see below under Transliteration.

The small letters are in more general use than the capital letters.
The VOWELS are α, ε, η, ι, ο, υ, and ω. Note that both ε and
η come over as *e* into Latin and English, and that both ο and ω come
over as *o*. η and ω are always long in quantity.

The DIPHTHONGS and their sound values are as follows:

αι  as in *ai*sle                  οι  as in *oi*l.
αυ  as *ow* in cow.                ου  as in b*ou*quet.
ει  as in *ei*ght.                 υι  as in q*ui*t.
ευ  as "eh-oo."

The improper diphthongs ᾳ, ῃ, and ῳ (the "ι" under the letters
is called the iota-subscript) are pronounced the same as α, η, and ω.

The CONSONANTS have the sound values indicated above in
the table of the alphabet. Special attention should be given to the
following consonants:

1. A γ before γ, κ, χ, or ξ is called a "nasal gamma" and in Greek
has the sound of the "n" in the English word "ink"; for example:
ἀγγεῖον = a*n*geion; ἀγκών = a*n*kon; βρόγχος = bro*n*chos; φάρυγξ =
phary*n*x.

2. The DOUBLE CONSONANTS are ζ (dz), ξ (ks), and ψ (ps).

3. The MUTES are as follows, arranged into *Classes* and *Orders:*

CLASSES:                           ORDERS:
Labials: π, β, φ                   Smooth: π, κ, τ
Palatals: κ, γ, χ                  Middle: β, γ, δ
Dentals: τ, δ, θ                   Rough:  φ, χ, θ

## ACCENTS

The accented syllable of a Greek word is always marked. The
ACUTE accent ( ΄ ) may stand on any one of the last three syllables
(e.g., καθαρτικός, κρανίον, γράμματα), the CIRCUMFLEX accent
( ⌢ ) on a long syllable only and on the last (ultima) or on the next
to the last (penult) syllable (e.g., σκοπῶ, νεῦρον, γλῶσσα), and the
GRAVE accent ( ` ) on the last syllable only. The grave accent is
used only in composition when a word with an acute on the ultima
is followed by another word (e.g., καθαρτικὸς ἀλλήλων); it will
therefore rarely appear on words as used in this text.

The kind and the position of the accents will occasionally assist in distinguishing the meanings of two words which, except for the accent, are spelled alike; for example:

ἀραῖος : prayed to, cursed; ἄραιος: thin, light.
θερμός : hot; θέρμος: bean.
θυμός : soul; θύμος: warty excrescence.
δῆμος : people; δημός: fat.
ὦμος : shoulder; ὠμός: raw.
βίος : life; βιός: bow.
βυσσός : bottom; βύσσος: fine flax.

When a Greek word is latinized or anglicized, the accent is not transferred to the Latin or the English word.

## BREATHING MARKS

Every Greek word beginning with a vowel or a diphthong has either a SMOOTH (') or a ROUGH (') breathing mark over the initial syllable. The rough breathing mark signifies that "h" is sounded before the vowel; the smooth breathing mark signifies that the vowel is sounded without the "h". All Greek words beginning with rho (ῥ) or upsilon (ὑ) have rough breathing. For example:

ἄνθος  = anthos          ἵππος  = hippos
αὐτός  = autos           ῥεῦμα  = hreuma
                         ὕδωρ  = hydor

## PRONUNCIATION

Each Greek letter, except γ, and each Greek diphthong represents one sound only (see pp. 44-45). The Greek language has no silent letters. A Greek word contains as many syllables as it has vowels and diphthongs.

Pronounce the following words, observing the letter sounds (including the nasal-gamma), the accent, and the breathing marks:

ἄλγος        γάγγλιον      ἐγκέφαλος     ῥεῦμα
νέκταρ       ὦμος          θρίξ          τραχύς
πῦρ          κόνδυλος      ῥόδον         μικρός
καρδία       ῥίζα          δῆμος         σπλάγχνον

| | | | |
|---|---|---|---|
| γυμνός | ζῷον | πνεῦμα | δέρμα |
| δρόμος | ζώνη | ἄνθρωπος | ῥάχις |
| χρόνος | ἕλκος | φάρυγξ | ψυχή |
| ὀξύς | ἀγγεῖον | ὕπνος | ἥλιος |
| ῥίς | σφυγμός | ξηρός | ἑτερογενής |
| σπεῖρα | ξανθός | ἱστός | ἠχώ |

## B. GREEK INFLECTIONS

The inflectional characteristics of Greek words are about the same as those which have been given for Latin (see pp. 31-33).

1. *The GENDER* of a Greek noun is usually indicated by its ending and less often by its meaning or natural sex. Briefly, it may be said that

(a) nouns ending in -ης or -ος are most likely masculine in gender. (Some nouns ending in -ος are neuter, and a few are feminine)

(b) nouns ending in -α or -η are most likely feminine.

(c) nouns ending in -ον or -μα are neuter.

To a considerable degree, however, the gender of Greek nouns has to be learned by observation. Dictionaries usually indicate the gender of a noun by inserting immediately after it the definite article ("the") of the appropriate gender: ὁ for masculine, ἡ for feminine, and τό for neuter (e.g., φόβος, ὁ, fright; χαίτη, ἡ, hair; ὀστέον, τό,, bone; δέρμα, -ατος, τό, skin.) In composition, however, the definite article normally precedes the noun, as it does in English. The following examples illustrate how the gender of a noun is revealed by the definite article, even in instances where the inflectional endings do not indicate it:

| | | | |
|---|---|---|---|
| ὁ βλαστός, | the sprout, shoot | ἡ φλέψ, | the vein |
| ὁ σφιγκτήρ, | the band | τὸ ἰσχίον, | the hip-joint |
| ἡ αἰτία, | the cause | τὸ στόμα, | the mouth |
| ἡ φωνή, | the sound | τὸ μέλος,, | the limb |
| ἡ γάστηρ, | the belly | τὸ ἧπαρ, | the liver |

### 2. *Declension of NOUNS*

Greek nouns are declined in five cases: the nominative, genitive, dative, accusative, and vocative. In this text we shall consider only the NOMINATIVE (singular and plural) and the GENITIVE (singular) cases. These two cases are important in word-formation for the same reasons that were given for their importance in Latin nouns, namely: (1) the nominative (singular) is the "name" case and is the entry-form used in Greek lexicons and vocabularies; (2) the genitive (singular) reveals the BASE of the word.

Greek has only three declensions. A noun can "belong to" only one of the three declensions, and the characteristic endings of that declension are attached to the BASE of the noun. The characteristic endings of each declension in the nominative (singular and plural) and the genitive (singular) cases are as follows:

### SINGULAR

|  | I (α-declension) | | II (o-declension) | | III (consonant declension) | |
|---|---|---|---|---|---|---|
|  | M | F | M | N | M & F | N |
| *Nom.* | -ης | -η -α | -ος | -ον | (-ς, or none) | |
| *Gen.* | -ου | -ης -ας | -ου | | -ος | |

### PLURAL

|  |  |  |  |  |  |  |
|---|---|---|---|---|---|---|
| *Nom.* | -αι | | -οι | -α | -ες | -α |

The following observations will prove helpful:

(a) Most nouns of Declension I end in -η or -α and are feminine. The corresponding nouns in Latin are those of Declension I ending in -a (feminine).

(b) Nouns of Declension II are masculine if they end in -ος, and neuter if they end in -ον. The corresponding nouns in Latin are those of Declension II ending in -us (masculine) and -um (neuter).

(c) The nominative plural endings in Declension III (-ες and -α) are the same as those of Latin in Declension III (-ēs and -a).

(d) All nouns of neuter gender end in -α in the nominative plural. All neuter nouns in Latin also end in -a in the nominative plural.

(e) As noted before, the base of Greek nouns is found by removing the case ending from the genitive singular form.

Sample nouns from each of the three declensions are declined in the nominative and genitive cases as follows:

## SINGULAR
### I

|  | M | F | |
|---|---|---|---|
| *Nom.* | ἀθλητής, athlete | γλῶσσα, tongue | ἀκμή, summit |
| *Gen.* | ἀθλητοῦ | γλώσσης | ἀκμῆς |

## PLURAL

|  | | | |
|---|---|---|---|
| *Nom.* | ἀθληταί | γλῶσσαι | ἀκμαί |
|  | (*Stem:* ἀθλητα- | γλωσσα- | ἀκμα-) |
|  | (*Base:* ἀθλητ- | γλωσσ- | ἀκμ-) |

## SINGULAR
### II

|  | M | N |
|---|---|---|
| *Nom.* | βλαστός, sprout | ἄρθρον, joint |
| *Gen.* | βλαστοῦ | ἄρθρου |

## PLURAL

|  | | |
|---|---|---|
| *Nom.* | βλαστοί | ἄρθρα |
|  | (*Stem:* βλαστο- | ἄρθρο-) |
|  | (*Base:* βλαστ- | ἄρθρ-) |

## SINGULAR
### III

|  | M | F | N | |
|---|---|---|---|---|
| *Nom.* | φῶς, light | σάρξ, flesh | στόμα, mouth | ἄνθος, flower |
| *Gen.* | φωτός | σαρκός | στόματος | ἄνθους (ἄνθεσος) |

## PLURAL

|  | | | | |
|---|---|---|---|---|
| *Nom.* | φωτές | σάρκες | στόματα | ἄνθεα |
|  | (*Stem:* φωτ- | σάρκ- | στόματ- | ἄνθεσ-) |
|  | (*Base:* φωτ- | σάρκ- | στόματ- | ἄνθε-) |

*Memoranda:*

(a) For nouns of Declension III, the BASE becomes apparent in the genitive singular; it is not often apparent in the nominative singular. For nouns of Declension I and II the BASE can be observed in the nominative singular form as well as in the genitive.

(b) Nouns ending in -μα in the nominative singular (e.g., δέρμα, σπέρμα, χρῶμα) constitute an important group. These are neuter in gender and are declined like στόμα (the nominative plurals therefore end in -ματα).

(c) Although a noun ending in -ος is likely to be masculine and belong to Declension II, some important Greek nouns ending in -ος are neuters belonging to Declension III (e.g., χεῖλος, lip; ἔθνος, tribe, nation; ῥάμφος, beak, bill) and are declined like ἄνθος.

## 3. *Declension of ADJECTIVES*

Adjectives must agree in gender, number, and case with the noun they modify. Greek adjectives use the same inflectional endings as Greek nouns. Two of the more common patterns for Greek adjectives are the following:

(a) The use of the endings -ος, -η (or -α), -ον in the masculine, feminine, and neuter genders respectively. These adjectives are entered in dictionaries in this fashion: μόνος, -η, -ον. The masculine and neuter genders are declined in Declension II and the feminine in Declension I. A few adjectives of this class use -ος as the ending for both masculine and feminine; for example, ἄλογος (masc. and fem.), ἄλογον (neut.). The following sample words will illustrate:

SINGULAR

| | M | F | N |
|------|--------|--------|------------------|
| *Nom.* | μιχρός | μιχρά | μιχρόν, small |
| *Gen.* | μιχροῦ | μιχράς | μιχροῦ |

PLURAL

| | | | |
|------|--------|--------|--------|
| *Nom.* | μιχροί | μιχραί | μιχρά |

SINGULAR

| | | | |
|------|--------|--------|------------------------|
| *Nom.* | μόνος | μόνη | μόνον, alone, one |
| *Gen.* | μόνου | μόνης | μόνου |

PLURAL

| | | | |
|------|--------|--------|--------|
| *Nom.* | μόνοι | μόναι | μόνα |

(b) The use of Declension III endings in the masculine and neuter, and Declension I endings in the feminine gender. These adjectives are usually entered in dictionaries in either one of the two following fashions: (a) γλυκύς, -εῖα, -ύ or (b) μέλας, μέλαινα, μέλαν. Their declensions in the nominative and genitive are as follows:

### SINGULAR

|       | M | F | N |
|-------|---|---|---|
| *Nom.* | γλυκύς | γλυκεῖα | γλυκύ, sweet |
| *Gen.* | γλυκέος | γλυκείας | γλυκέος |

### PLURAL

|       | M | F | N |
|-------|---|---|---|
| *Nom.* | γλυκεῖς | γλυκεῖαι | γλυκέα |

### SINGULAR

|       | M | F | N |
|-------|---|---|---|
| *Nom.* | μέλας | μέλαινα | μέλαν, black |
| *Gen.* | μέλανος | μελαίνης | μέλανος |

### PLURAL

|       | M | F | N |
|-------|---|---|---|
| *Nom.* | μέλανες | μέλαιναι | μέλανα |

## 4. *Conjugation of VERBS*

The Greek VERB is elaborately inflected. Dictionaries and vocabularies ordinarily list for each verb its principal parts (six for a regular verb), beginning with the first person singular, present indicative. This first form usually exhibits the endings -ω, -ομαι, or -μι (signifying "I"); the VERBAL STEM can then be determined by the removal of these endings. Scientific dictionaries which give the orignal Greek words from which a technical term is derived often present the Greek verbs in their present infinitive form. The most common terminal suffixes used to designate the present infinitive are -ειν, -εσθαι, and -ναι, and these are attached to the VERBAL STEM.

| *First Person, Singular, Present* (the usual entry form used in dictionaries) | *Present Infinitive* (the usual form given in scientific dictionaries) | *Verbal Stem* |
|---|---|---|
| γράφω, I write | γράφειν, to write | γράφ- |
| σχίζω, I split | σχίζειν, to split | σχίζ- |
| βούλομαι, I wish | βούλεσθαι, to wish | βούλ- |

Because of the nature of some Greek verbs, their true stems appear neither in the dictionary entry forms nor in their present infinitive forms; in such instances, the dictionary generally gives in parentheses the true stem or the root of the verb. For example:

| Entry Form: first person, singular | Present Infinitive | Present Stem | True Stem or Root |
|---|---|---|---|
| γίγνομαι | γίγνεσθαι | γίγν- | γεν-, become |
| πράσσω | πράσσειν | πράσσ- | πραγ-, do |
| σκέπτομαι | σκέπτεσθαι | σκέπτ- | σκεπ-, look at |
| δίδωμι | διδόναι | δίδο- | δο-, give |
| δείκνυμι | δεικνύναι | δείκνυ- | δεικ-, point out |

In analyzing or constructing scientific words, identity of the true stem of a Greek verb is of prime importance because it is to this stem that several of the suffixes used in forming nouns and adjectives are attached (see *Suffixes*, pp. 140-44).

## C. VOWEL AND CONSONANT CHANGES IN GREEK

1. An important VOWEL CHANGE (ABLAUT) is that of ε to o when a verbal stem becomes a noun stem or an adjective stem; for example:

| Verb and Verb Stem | Noun and Noun (or Adj.) Stem | Derivatives |
|---|---|---|
| τρέπειν, to turn (τρεπ-) | τροπή, a turning (τροπ-) | *trep*onema, *trep*opnea allo*trop*ic, helio*trop*e |
| τείνειν, to stretch (τειν-) | τόνος, a stretching (τον-) | *ten*esmus, *ten*odesis dys*ton*ic, peri*ton*eum |
| τέμνειν, to cut (τεμν-) | τόμος, a cut (τομ-) | *Temn*odon, A*temn*us a*tom*, dicho*tom*y |
| φέρειν, to carry, bear (φερ-) | φορητός, carried φόρος, that brought (φορ-) | peri*pher*y, tel*pher* dia*phor*esis, sporo*phor*e |
| λέγειν, to speak (λεγ-) | λόγος, word λογικός, pertaining to speech (λογ-) | pro*leg*omena, a*lex*ia (*leg*- plus *sia* = *lexia*), bio*log*y, neo*log*ism |
| ἐργάζεσθαι, to work (ἐργ-) | ὄργανον, instrument (ὀργ-) | all*ergy*, syn*erg*istic *organ*onomy, micro*organ*ism |

2. ELISION occurs when a prefix or a stem ending in a vowel is prefixed to a word beginning with a vowel; the first element of the compound usually loses its final vowel. For example:

ἐπί  plus  ὀνομάζειν = ἐπονομάζειν
ὑπό  plus  ἀκούειν = ὑπακούειν

Further illustrations may be found on pages 133-34.

3. CONSONANT CHANGES. Important consonant changes take place when joining word elements which begin or end with MUTES.

a. No mute (except κ) can stand before σ because:

π, β, or φ before σ = ψ
$$\left\{\begin{array}{ll} σῆπ\text{-}σις & = σῆψις \\ τρίβ\text{-}σις & = τρίψις \\ στρέφ\text{-}σις & = στρέψις \end{array}\right.$$

κ, γ, or χ before σ = ξ
(except wth prefix ἐκ; e.g., ἐκστάς)
$$\left\{\begin{array}{ll} πρῆκ\text{-}σις & = πρῆξις \\ λέγ\text{-}σις & = λέξις \\ θρίχ\text{-}ς & = θρίξ \end{array}\right.$$

τ, δ, or θ before σ = σ
(the mute disappears)
$$\left\{\begin{array}{ll} χάριτ\text{-}ς & = χάρις \\ σχίδ\text{-}σις & = σχίσις \\ ὄρνιθ\text{-}ς & = ὄρνις \end{array}\right.$$

b. A mute before μ changes as follows:

π, β, or φ before μ becomes μ: γράφ-μα = γράμμα
κ, γ, or χ before μ becomes γ: πλέκ-μα = πλέγμα
τ, δ, or θ before μ becomes σ (or remains unchanged):
    κλύδ-μα = κλύσμα

c. When a labial or a palatal mute stands before another mute, it must be coordinate with the other mute (that is, of the same ORDER; see above, p. 45). For example:

| | | |
|---|---|---|
| ἐλλιπ-τικός | remains | ἐλλιπτικός |
| ἐπιληβ-τικός | becomes | ἐπιληπτικός |
| τριβ-τικός | becomes | τριπτικός |
| στρεφ-τικός | becomes | στρεπτικός |
| πραγ-τικός | becomes | πρακτικός |
| πεγ-τικός | becomes | πεκτικός |

d. When another dental mute (τ, δ, θ) comes before τ, it is changed to σ; for example:

πλατ-τικός    becomes    πλαστικός
κλυδ-τικός    becomes    κλυστικός

e. Whenever a smooth mute (π, κ, τ) immediately precedes a word beginning with rough breathing, it is changed to the rough mute of the same class; for example:

(1) κατά plus αἵρεσις = καθαίρεσις (the final -α of κατά elides before the diphthong αι, which brings the smooth mute τ before rough breathing. The mute is then aspirated to θ. The rough breathing mark disappears on the resultant compound term.)

(2) ἐπί plus ἵππιον = ἐφίππιον (the final -ι of ἐπί elides before the initial vowel of ἵππιον; the smooth mute π becomes aspirated to φ).

(3) ἐκ plus αἱμάσσω = ἐξαιμάσσω (the smooth mute κ becomes aspirated before the rough breathing of αἱμάσσω).

f. The consonant ν changes as follows:

(1) Before a labial mute (π, β, or φ) it becomes μ; for example:

ἐν-πάθη     becomes    ἐμπάθη
συν-βίος    becomes    σύμβιος
συν-φύσις   becomes    σύμφυσις

(2) Before a palatal mute (κ, γ, or χ) it becomes γ (nasal); for example:

συν-κοπή    becomes    συγκοπή
συν-γενής   becomes    συγγενής
συν-χρόνος  becomes    σύγχρονος

(3) Before a σ it is dropped; for example:

συν-στολή     becomes    συστολή
συν-στρεπτός  becomes    συστρεπτός

(4) Before a λ or a μ it is assimilated; for example:

ἐν-λόβιον    becomes    ἐλλόβιον
συν-μετρία   becomes    συμμετρία

g. The initial ῥ of a word is doubled whenever another word ending in a vowel is prefixed; but if the prefix ends in a diphthong, the ῥ remains single. For example:

| κατα-ῥέω | becomes | καταρρέω |
| παρα-ῥυθμός | becomes | παράρρυθμος |
| εὐ-ῥυθμός | remains | εὔρυθμος |

## D. TRANSLITERATION OF GREEK

Many Greek words (although only a small percentage of the total number in the language) were adopted by the Romans, who transcribed them into Latin by using the letters of their own alphabet. The pattern which the Romans set has ever since been generally followed in the transliteration of Greek words into languages which use the Latin alphabet.[11] In transcribing Greek words into English, only minor deviations from the Latin system have been introduced. As may be seen from the table on page 44, the Latin and the English equivalents of the individual Greek letters are the same (except that Greek κ sometimes comes over as *k* into English, never so into Latin). In the examples given below of Greek words adopted into both Latin and English, it will be seen that there are differences between the Latin and the English versions, but that these differences are not extensive.

| Greek | Latin | English |
|---|---|---|
| σφαῖρα | sphaera | sphere |
| ἀμοιβή | amoeba | ameba |
| κόγχη | concha | conch |
| βραχίων | brachium | brachium |
| στόμαχος | stomachus | stomach |
| σύριγξ | syrinx | syringe |
| ἄντρον | antrum | antrum |
| ῥόμβος | rhombus | rhomb |
| ἕλιξ | helix | helix |

11. In 1737 Linnaeus, who introduced the binomial system of scientific nomenclature, wrote in his *Critica Botanica:* "When Greek names are transliterated into Latin, the equivalents used by the Romans from all time must be adopted in representing the Greek letters" (Hort translation). This viewpoint still has general support; see *Science* CXV (Jan. 18, 1952), 63-64. In the area of biology, only the microbiologists (who coordinate their principles of terminology closely with those in botany and zoology) have officially adopted an outline, with illustrations, of the accepted usages in the transliteration and latinization of Greek words. This outline is printed as Appendix A in the *International Code of Nomenclature*

Many of our scientific terms have been constructed directly from the Greek words without first latinizing them. But since the Latin has exerted greater influence than the Greek in determining the form (especially the endings) of words in many scientific fields, it is advisable to adhere to the following general rule in transcribing Greek words into English: *Transliterate the Greek word into Latin first and then into English.*

In the transliteration of Greek words or word-elements into Latin or English, the following matters deserve special attention:

1. The Greek case-endings are usually changed to the corresponding case-endings of Latin. This is regularly done if a Greek word is made Latin and *used as such* (e.g., in the scientific names of plants and animals). For this reason, the Greek feminine endings -η and -α of Declension I are both transcribed *-a* (i.e., the feminine ending of Latin words belonging to Declension I), and the masculine -ος and the neuter -ον of Declension II are transcribed *-us* and *-um* (i.e., the masculine and the neuter endings of Latin words belonging to Declension II). For example:

| | |
|---|---|
| θήκη (case) = thec*a*. | γῦρος (ring) = gyr*us*. |
| κόμη (hair) = com*a*. | σπόνδυλος (vertebra) = spondyl*us*. |
| κόγχη (shell) = conch*a*. | στραβισμός (squint) = strabism*us*. |
| ἀορτή (artery) = aort*a*. | στέρνον (chest) = stern*um*. |
| φιάλη (flask) = phial*a*. | ἄντρον (cave) = antr*um*. |
| ἄκανθος (thorn) = acanth*us*. | κράνιον (skull) = crani*um*. |
| βῶλος (lump) = bol*us*. | γεράνιον (a flower) = Gerani*um* |

(a) In some English words, however, the Greek endings, especially -η and -ον, have been retained; for example:

| | |
|---|---|
| ἀκμή (point) = acm*e*. | κόσμος (order) = cosm*os*. |
| φωνή (sound) = phon*e*. | κόλον (colon) = col*on*. |
| ψυχή (soul) = psych*e*. | νεῦρον (nerve) = neur*on*. |
| συγκοπή (a cutting) = syncop*e*. | σκελετόν (dried) = skelet*on*. |
| ἄσβεστος (unquenchable) = asbest*os*. | μικρόν (small) = micr*on*. |

---

*of Bacteria and Viruses* (1958), pp. 137-40; also in *International Bulletin of Bacteriological Nomenclature and Taxonomy* III (June 1, 1953), 63-69. Very helpful in this matter is R. E. Buchanan's treatise in Breed, Murray, and Smith's *Bergey's Manual of Determinative Bacteriology*, 7th Ed., 1957, pp. 15-28. See also "Fundamentals of Medical Etymology" in *Dorland's Medical Dictionary*, 23rd Ed., pp. 1583-98.

(b) Some Greek words taken into English have dropped their inflectional suffixes altogether, or substituted an English suffix; for example:

στόμαχος (gullet) = stomach.  τόνος (stretching) = tone.
πέταλον (petal) = petal.  κῶνος (cone) = cone.
ὄργανον (instrument) = organ.  λοβός (lobe) = lobe.
κόγχη (shell) = conch.  σφαῖρα (ball) = sphere.

(c) When Greek words of Declension III are transcribed into Latin and *used as Latin words*, they take the case endings of Declension III in Latin. In the nominative singular and plural, and in some of the other cases, these endings are the same in Latin as they are in Greek, as will be noted in the following examples:

## SINGULAR

| | *Masculine* | | *Feminine* | | *Neuter* | |
|---|---|---|---|---|---|---|
| *Nom.* | κάλυξ | calyx | χλαμύς | chlamys | χάσμα | chasma |
| *Gen.* | κάλυκος | calycis | χλαμύδος | chlamydis | χάσματος | chasmatis |
| *Dat.* | κάλυκι | calyci | χλαμύδι | chlamydi | χάσματι | chasmati |
| *Acc.* | κάλυκα | calycem | χλαμύδα | chlamydem | χάσμα | chasma |
| *Abl.* | | calyce | | chlamyde | | chasmate |

## PLURAL

| | *Nom.* | | *Feminine* | | *Neuter* | |
|---|---|---|---|---|---|---|
| *Nom.* | κάλυκες | calyces | χλαμύδες | chlamydes | χάσματα | chasmata |
| *Gen.* | καλύκων | calycum | χλαμύδων | chlamydum | χασμάτων | chasmatum |
| *Dat.* | χάλυξι | calycibus | χλαμύσι | chlamydibus | χάσμασι | chasmatibus |
| *Acc.* | κάλυκας | calyces | χλαμύδας | chlamydes | χάσματα | chasmata |
| *Abl.* | | calycibus | | chlamydibus | | chasmatibus |

2. A γ before κ, γ, χ, or ξ is a nasal-gamma and is transcribed *n:* ὄγκος = o*n*cos; ἀγκών = a*n*con; συγγένης = sy*n*genes; ἀγγεῖον = a*n*geion; σύγχρονος = sy*n*chronos; ῥύγχος = rhy*n*chos; χόγχη = co*n*che; φαρύγξ = phary*n*x; σάλπιγξ = salpi*n*x.

3. A κ is regularly transcribed into Latin as *c*, and usually so into English also. In some English words, however, where the hard sound is desired, and especially in newer coinages in medical areas, the *k* is retained. κυμ-: *c*ymograph, *k*ymograph; κακ-: *c*acosmia, *k*akosmia; κινε-: acro*c*inesis, oo*k*inesis.

4. A θ was occasionally transcribed *t* in Latin, and English kept the Latin spelling; for example, σπάθη (base, σπάθ-) was used in the formation of Latin SPATULA (*-ula*, a diminutive suffix) and English adopted the Latin word without change.

5. The iota subscript is disregarded in transliteration; for example: ᾠόν = oon; ᾠδή = ode.

6. An υ is transliterated *y*, except when it forms part of a diphthong: υ = *y*; αυ = *au*; ευ = *eu*; ου = *ou* or *u*; for example:

> ἀνάλυσις: anal*y*sis; κρύπτ-: cr*y*ptogenesis.
> αὐτό: *au*tomatic; σαύρ-: dinos*au*r.
> λευκ-: le*u*cocyte; εὐγεν-: *eu*genics.
> ἀκου-: ac*ou*stic; οὐραν-: *u*ranoschisis.
> βουλ-: hyperb*u*lia.

The final -υ of adjectival stems does not elide before an initial vowel of the next component (γλυκύς is an exception, its most common combining form in English words being *glyco-*); for example:

> ἀμβλύ- plus ὤψ (ὠπ-) = ambl*y*opia.
> πολύ- plus ἄλγος = pol*y*algesia.
> παχύ- plus ὄστεον = pach*y*ostosis.

7. The Greek diphthongs αι, ει, and οι are transcribed into Latin as *ae*, *ei*, and *oe*. In English words constructed from the Greek, the Latin spellings of these diphthongs are sometimes retained (especially in British English), but more often they are reduced to *e*, *i*, and *e*. In some scientific terms the exact spellings of the Greek diphthongs are retained (*ai*, *ei*, and *oi*). For example:

| Gk. | Lat. | English | Examples |
|---|---|---|---|
| αι | *ae* | ae, or e | αἴσθε-: *ae*sthetic, *e*sthetic. |
| | | | παιδ-: p*ae*diatric, p*e*diatrics. |
| ει | *ei* | ei, or i | εἰκών: *ei*conometer, *i*conomania. |
| | | | χειρ-: ch*ei*romegaly, ch*i*ropodist. |
| οι | *oe* | oe (rarely), or e | οἰκ-: (o)*e*cology. |
| | | | ὅμοι-: hom(o)*e*omorphous. |
| | | | κοῖλ-: c*oe*lenterate. |

The tendency of English to reduce both the αι and the οι of Greek to *e* (instead of retaining the latinized *ae* and *oe*, or even the Greek *ai* and *oi*) sometimes causes uncertainty about the meaning of words. If, for example, καινός (new), κενός (empty), and κοινός (common) are all transliterated CENOS (or KENOS), a valuable key to meaning is lost; should "cenobium" (βίος, life), for example, be interpreted to mean "new life", "empty life," or "common life?" Possibly it is for the sake of clarity that there is a tendency in some of the more recent coinages to retain the exact Greek spelling of the diphthongs instead of following either the Latin or the English pattern; for example:

*kai*nophobia (καινός, new; φόβος, fear) instead of c(*a*)*e*nophobia.
*koi*lonychia (κοῖλος, hollow; ὄνυξ, nail) instead of c(*o*)*e*lonychia.
brachych*ei*lia (βραχύς, short; χεῖλος, lip) instead of brachych*i*lia.
*koi*notropic (κοινός, common; τρόπος, turning) instead of c(*o*)*e*notropic.
*loi*mology (λοιμός, plague; λόγος, word) instead of *le*mology.
*oi*kophobia (οἶκος, home; φόβος, fear) instead of *e*cophobia.

8. Rough breathing (ʿ) on an initial vowel or diphthong of Greek words is represented in Latin and in English by the letter *h* placed before the vowel or diphthong; for example: ἥλιος = helios; ὁμόλογος = homologos; ὁδός = hodos; αἷμα = haema.

Rough breathing on an initial ῥ of Greek words is represented in Latin and in English by an *h* following the *r*; for example: ῥεῦμα = rheuma; ῥάχις = rhachis.

In the Greek language, the rough breathing on an initial vowel or diphthong of a word disappeared whenever another word-element was prefixed to the original word; for example:

δύς (bad) plus ἥλιος (sun) became δυσήλιος.
ἀν (not) plus ὁμόλογος (agreeing) became ἀνομόλογος.
μακρός (long) plus ἡμέρα (day) became μακρημερία.
εἰς (into) plus ὁδός (road) became εἴσοδος.
ἀν (not) plus αἷμα (blood) became ἀναιμία.

When the resultant compound Greek words in the foregoing examples are transliterated into Latin letters, no *h* will appear (dyselios, anomologos, macremeria, eisodos, anaemia).

Such loss of the original aspiration of a Greek word element as illustrated above in Greek words has, however, been irregularly observed both in Roman and in modern usage. Because of famili-

arity with the Greek words in their simple form (i.e., not compounded), the aspirate *h* was always felt to be present and therefore
an *h* was included in the Greek stem regardless of whether it was used
as the first or as a later component of a compound term. In modern
scientific terminology, therefore, no consistency can be observed in
the retention or the omission of the aspirate on Greek stems which
are used as middle or end components of compound words. Often
two versions of a compound are in use, one with and the other
without the *h*, while in other similar compounds employing the same
aspirated Greek stem, only one version is in use.[12] For example:

(a) ἱδρώς (perspiration) with:
    χρῶμα (color): both chromhidrosis and chromidrosis.
    ὑπέρ (excessive): both hyperhidrosis and hyperidrosis.
    αἷμα (blood): both hemathidrosis and hematidrosis.
    ὀσμή (smell): only osmidrosis (without *h*).
    κύανος (blue): only cyanohidrosis (with *h*).

(b) ἕλκος (ulcer) with:
    δάκρυον (tear): both dacryohelcosis and dacryelcosis.
    γαστήρ (belly): only gastrohelcosis (with *h*).
    ὠτ- (ear): only othelcosis (with *h*).
    κύστις (bladder): only cystelcosis (without *h*).
    ἔντερον (intestine): only enterelcosis (without *h*).

(c) αἷμα (blood) with:
    νέφρος (kidney): both nephrohemia and nephremia.
    γλυκύς (sweet): both glycohemia and glycemia.
    δέρμα (skin): only dermathemia (with *h*).
    ἀν (without): only anemia (without *h*).

d) ἱστός (tissue) with:
    γλυκύς (sweet) and ἔχειν (hold): only glycohistechia (with *h*).
    ὑπέρ (excessive) and γλυκύς (sweet): only hyperglycistia (without *h*).

Since long-standing practice in word construction has retained from
classical Greek (with sound precedent and only rare exceptions) the
*h* on initial syllables, and since it has also (but without sanction of
precedent from classical Greek) used it extensively within compounds,
a Greek stem in modern terminology has come to be more easily
recognized if the *h* is retained than if it is omitted. For example, both

---

12. According to Dorland's *Medical Dictionary*.

"icterohepatitis" and "icterepatitis" (ἴκτερος, jaundice; ἧπαρ, liver) occur in current usage, but the former version is more quickly recognized and understood than the latter. "Metrypercinesis" (μήτρα, uterus; ὑπέρ, excessive; κίνεσις,, movement) and "metryperesthesia" (αἴσθεσις, feeling) present rather strange appearances because of the omission of the familiar *h* on "hyper"; and "neurypnology" is not as immediately clear as its full form "neurohypnology" (νεῦρον, nerve; ὕπνος, sleep; λόγος, word). Because it contributes to easier recognition of stems and their meanings, even more frequent use of *h* within compound words can be expected in future word coinages, whether these be Latin names for microorganisms, plants, and animals or scientific names in English.[13] In instances of this kind, a slight deviation from the best historical and linguistic precedents in the composition of scientific terms can be justified by the practical advantage gained in functional facility and clarity of meaning.

9. An INITIAL ῥ of a Greek stem should, according to classical Greek usage, be doubled when preceded by a vowel and remain single when preceded by a diphthong (see above, p. 55); for example:

πλατύς (wide) plus ῥίς, ῥινός (nose) = πλατύρρινος.
γλυκύς (sweet) plus ῥίζα (root) = γλυκύρριζα.
εὐ (good, easy) plus ῥηκτός (breakable) = εὔρηκτος.

Latin scientific names which have been derived from the Greek should, and generally do, conform to the classical usage. But in the construction of English scientific terms the practice of using a single or double *r* after vowels has been very irregular, with a marked tendency not to double the *r* except in such well-established forms as -rrhea, -rrhagia, -rrhaphy. The irregularity is illustrated by the following words which are in current use:

macrorhinia (μακρός large; ῥίς, ῥινός, nose).
microrrhinia (μικρός, small; ῥίς, ῥινός, nose).
leptorhine (λεπτός, thin; ῥίς,, ῥινός, nose).
bradyrhythmia (βραδύς, slow; ῥυθμός, rhythm).
koilorrhachic (κοῖλος, hollow; ῥάχις, spine).

---

13. Cf., Frederick E. Clements, "Greek and Latin in Biological Nomenclature," *University Studies of the University of Nebraska* III, 1902, 58-60; and Roland W. Brown, *Composition of Scientific Words*, p. 21.

# CHAPTER IV

# *Word Lists*

## Introduction to the Word Lists

In order to attain proficiency in word analysis and to develop an appreciation of the linguistic, historical, and practical aspects of a scientific nomenclature, an abundant and convenient supply of scientific terms must be available for study and practice. The word lists in this Chapter supply those necessary "laboratory" materials.

Those Latin and Greek words which have furnished the elements most frequently used in the construction of medical and biological terms have been classified separately under each language into four groups: (1) PREFIXES, (2) SUFFIXES, (3) NUMERALS, and (4) GENERAL VOCABULARY.[1] Except for the numerals and the suffixes, all the Latin and Greek entry words as well as their English derivatives have been listed alphabetically in order to make the location of individual words as easy as possible.

Greek words have been written in English letters, disregarding vowel and consonant changes usually made in transliteration.

The derivatives listed under the entry words have been drawn from the vocabularies of various areas of biology and medicine and

---

1. Words have not been grouped into separate lists for the several specialized areas of biology and medicine. If such specialized lists are desired, a number are already available in such books as E. J. Field and R. J. Harrison, *Anatomical Terms: Their Origin and Derivation*; John H. Hough, *Scientific Terminology*; Edmund C. Jaeger, (a) *A Source Book of Biological Names and Terms*; (b) *A Dictionary of Greek and Latin Combining Forms Used in Zoological Names*; (c) *A Source-Book of Medical Terms*; Axel L. Melander, *A Source Book of Biological Terms*; O. H. Perry Pepper, *Medical Etymology*; T. H. Savory, *Latin and Greek for Biologists*; Robert S. Woods, *The Naturalist's Lexicon*; and glossaries of standard classroom texts in the separate fields (see Bibliography).

have been chosen because of their value as "laboratory material." As good "laboratory material" these words illustrate the use of a particular word element in a variety of combinations, they offer a challenge to diagnosis and interpretation, they illustrate the important principles of word formation and the variations thereof, and whenever possible, they provide mnemonic "handles" whereby the forms and meanings of one or more important word elements can be recalled when these appear in other combinations. If a word meets most of the above requirements, it has been included among the derivatives whether it happens to be a familiar and widely used term or not.

Most of the derivatives throughout the word lists are English words. In the section on Latin Suffixes, however, the examples used are Latin words. The reason for using Latin words in that section is to illustrate clearly the exact and full endings which Latin scientific names using those suffixes will have. (Modern Latin scientific names are Latin largely in endings only). By using the illustrative words in that section as models, the large number of English derivatives in the word lists which have used those Latin suffixes in their construction can easily be converted, if so desired, into classical or modern Latin words.

Except in some instances where only a few scientific terms derived from an entry word exist (more common in the Latin lists than in the Greek), space has not been given in the lists to derivatives which differ only in minor detail from a word already listed and which therefore would present no new challenge to diagnosis. Such exclusions help to avoid tedious listing of such slightly variant forms as, for example, "retrograde, retrogradation, retrogress, retrogression, retrogressive," or "synergetic, synergia, synergism, synergist, synergistic, synergy."

Very few hybrid terms are included among the derivatives in the Latin lists; in the Greek lists there are more, although their number is considerably below that which would be required for a true representation of the proportion of hybrid to "purebred" words in the terminology of medicine and biology.

No definitions are furnished for the derivative words in the lists. In choosing between the alternatives of listing a generous number of derivative words without definitions and a much smaller number of words with definitions, the former seemed the sounder procedure.

Ordinarily, the definition of a term can easily be found, but to find additional derivatives of a foreign word when they are needed is generally not easy. Moreover, the larger the number of derivatives given for a word is, the greater is the likelihood that among those derivatives will appear one or more fairly familiar terms by which the meaning of that foreign word element can be remembered. Another important consideration was conservation of space, because definitions of technical terms are seldom brief. Furthermore, to supply a definition for a word would generally disqualify that word as a challenging exercise in analysis and interpretation—a factor of considerable importance. Throughout this text the viewpoint is maintained that the student can develop the ability to formulate a fairly accurate and meaningful definition of a scientific term by observing its makeup. Although the student's tentative definition will usually appear inadequate when compared with the precise dictionary definition, it can, nevertheless, "put him on the right track" and supply him with the basic notion involved so that when he meets the word in context and thereby receives further illumination regarding its probable meaning he will rarely need the aid of a dictionary.

To learn words in isolation or largely outside of any context is unnatural and somewhat difficult. In any language, words derive their full meaning and tone from the contexts in which they appear; if they are removed from the "society" in which they normally move, their "personality" becomes rather colorless. Context not only casts a play of light and shadow on a word, but frequently suggests its primary meaning. The problem in learning the meaning of words largely without the benefit of context is therefore one of finding some "handles" by which forms and meanings can be remembered. In such learning, the effectiveness of different techniques varies greatly from person to person. Each student will have to rely largely on whatever mnemonic device proves effective for him, and in most cases that will be the association of the foreign word-element with some word which is already part of his vocabulary.[2] It is therefore suggested that in studying the words in the lists, most attention be given to the combining form of a word as it clearly appears in an

---

2. The best road to a genuine appreciation of the meaning and form of words is to study the language and literature in which those words find their native habitat.

already familiar or easily learned derivative, whether that derivative happens to be a scientific term of not. That term can then become the key by which the basic meaning of the new word-element can be recalled when it is seen in combination with other stems and affixes. The inclination to memorize the entry form of the Latin or Greek word in the lists should be resisted in favor of the procedure suggested. Furthermore, careful attention to technical terms while reading scientific texts and listening to lectures will not infrequently furnish the student with contexts for many of the words in the list. In any case, it is imperative to proceed systematically and persistently in the acquisition of a good working stock of high-yielding word-elements. The word lists that follow, with their generous supply of derivatives, furnish working materials necessary to achieve that end. The more "meaning-units" a person comes to recognize in compound terms, the less likely will he be to shun long words or fall into error in ascertaining their meanings. The recognition in "visceroptosis," for example, of *viscero-* and *-ptosis* as common combining forms meaning, respectively, "bowels" and "a condition of sagging" will prevent such excessive, but seemingly reasonable, dissection of the word as *vis-* (power), *cer-* (wax), and *opt-*( vision); "ultrasetaceous" will not be thought to be a compound of *ultra-* (excessive), *se-* (apart), and *tac-* (touch) instead of one made from the familiar elements *ultra-* (excessive), *set-* (hair, bristle), and *-aceous* (having the quality of); and "malacosteon" will immediately be recognized as made up of *malaco-* (soft) and *osteon* (bone), and not of *mala-* (bad) and *costa* (rib).

When more than one meaning is given for an entry word, the first is usually the more basic one and in the majority of instances the most important to remember. From the basic meaning, secondary and metaphorical meanings develop. For example, POIKILOS in the Greek language meant "many-colored, spotted, mottled" as of leopards, fawns, etc., and from that basic meaning developed secondary meanings like "changeful, various, diversified, manifold, and intricate." In using this adjective in the construction of scientific words, sometimes one meaning is intended and sometimes another.[3] The best procedure,

---

3. It may be stated that in general the primary meaning of a word element is more often intended in zoological, botanical, and bacteriological terms than in medical terms.

therefore, is to learn first the basic meaning of a word and from that to make transitions to the metaphorical meanings it may have as these are suggested in each instance by the other constructive units used with it in a particular term. In cases where a word is extensively used in a specialized sense in medical or biological nomenclature, that specialized meaning will be given even though it was not a meaning associated with the word in the original language. Moreover, even in those instances where for modern terminology it is less important to remember the primary meaning of a word than it is to recall one of its specialized applied meanings (e.g., **acetabul**um: vinegarcup; socket of the hipbone; **labyrinth**os: a maze of passages; the internal ear; **mys, my**os: mouse; muscle), the primary meaning is nevertheless of considerable value because it casts interesting sidelights on the history of certain terms and contributes considerably to an understanding of the processes and factors involved in the development of scientific terminology.

## Latin Prefixes

Prefixes were used extensively as constructive elements in the formation of words in the Latin language, and they have continued to be used widely in the building of vocabulary in many languages. The following observations about Latin prefixes are worth noting.

A. Most of the prefixes used in the Latin language were prepositions and adverbs which in that language could be used as independent and separate words. These are known as SEPARABLE PREFIXES. Other prefixes were not used as separate words but adhered to some following noun or verbal stem. These are known as INSEPARABLE PREFIXES. For example:

**Ad**renal: *near* the kidney; cf. Latin *ad urbem*, "near the town."
**Sub**costal: *under* the ribs; cf. Latin *sub terra* "under the ground."
**Trans**ocular: *across* the eye; cf. Latin *trans flumen*, "across the river."
**Intus**susception: accepting *within*; cf. Latin *intus relictus*, "left within."
**Retro**flexion: a bending *backward*; cf. Latin *retro respicere*, "to look back."
**Ambi**dextrous: *both*-handed: *ambi* was not used alone in Latin.
**Dis**crete: separate *apart*; *dis* was not used alone in Latin.
**Re**version: turning *back*; *re* (adverb) was not used alone in Latin.
**Se**gregation: *apart from* the crowd; *se* (adverb) was not used alone in Latin.

B. The force of a prefix when it is attached to a word may vary. It may convey (a) its literal physical meaning, (b) a metaphorical or figurative meaning, or (c) an intensive or perfective force. Occasionally, a prefix adds no perceptible meaning. For example:

**Per**oral: *through* the mouth.
**Per**acid: *very* (through-and-through; thoroughly) acid.
**Sub**cutaneous: *under* the skin.
**Sub**febrile: *somewhat* feverish.
**In**cisor: that which cuts *in*.
**In**ebriety: *habitual* (i.e., verily) drunkenness.
**Co**hesion: sticking *together*.
**Cor**rugate: to wrinkle thoroughly; practically equivalent to "rugate."
**De**salination: *absence* of salt.
**De**lacrimation: *excessive* flow of tears.
**De**nigration: process of becoming black (same as "nigration").
**De**gustation: the act of tasting (same as "gustation").

C. More than one prefix may be attached to a single stem. This means that prefixes will appear within as well as at the beginning of words. (Latin prefixes, however, are more likely to constitute the first component of Latin compound words than Greek prefixes are to constitute the first component of Greek compound words). For example:

superdistension (**super-**, **dis-**).
concomitant (**con-**, **com-**).
predelineate (**prae-**, **de-**).
intussusception (**intus-**, **sub-**).
irresuscitable (**in-**, **re-**, **sub-**).
decompression (**de-**, **com-**).
preperception (**prae-**, **per-**).
coadunate (**co-**, **ad-**).

D. When certain prefixes ending in a consonant are attached to words beginning with a consonant, the consonant of the prefix is often changed either (a) to the same consonant with which the word to which it is attached begins, or (b) to another consonant more easily pronounced in combination with the first consonant of the attached word. This change is called ASSIMILATION, and the word "assimilation" is itself an example of the process. For example:

**Ad**-similis becomes *as*similis.
**Con**-rugator becomes *cor*rugator.
**In**-pression becomes *im*pression.
**Sub**-pensor becomes *sus*pensor.

E.  In the Latin prefix *ex-*, the *s* sound is contained in the *x*; therefore, when *ex-* is prefixed to words beginning with *s*, the *s* is dropped. For example:

**Ex**-stirpation becomes extirpation.
**Ex**-sudation becomes exudation.
**Ex**-spiration becomes expiration.

F. The final vowel of a Latin prefix usually does *not* elide before another vowel; for example:

**Antero**inferior                    **Re**agent
**Infra**occlusion                    **Pre**operative
**De**albation

* * * * * * * * * *

1. **A-**, **ab-**, **abs-**: away from, off.

abaxial (*axis, axis,* axis)
aberrant (*errare, erratum,* to wander, stray)
abscission (*scindere, scissum,* to cut, split)
abstergent (*tergere, tersum,* to wipe)
abterminal (*terminus,* limit, end)
aversive (*vertere, versum,* to turn)
avulsion (*vellere, vulsum,* to tear)

2. **Ad-**: (often assimilated to a following consonant): to, toward, near.

accommodation (*commodare, commodatum,* to adjust, adapt)
adhesion (*haerere, haesum,* to stick to, cling)
afferent (*ferre, latum,* to bear, carry)
agglutinant (*glutinare, glutinatum,* to glue, bind)
alligation (*ligare, ligatum,* to bind, attach)
annectent (*nectere, nexum,* to tie, join)
appetition (*petere, petitum,* to seek)
assimilation (*similis, similis,* like, similar)
atterminal (*terminus,* limit, end)
attollens (*tollere, sublatum,* to lift)

3. **Ambi- (ambo-, amb-, am-, an-)**: around, on both sides, both.

> ambiens; ambitus (*ire, itum,* to go)
> ambivert (*vertere, versum,* to turn)
> amboceptor (*capere, captum,* to take)
> ambosexual (*sexus, sexus,* sex)
> amplexation (*plectere, plexum,* to braid, interweave)
> ancipital (*caput, capitis,* head)

4. **Ante-**: before, forward.

> antebrachium (*brachium, brachi,* arm)
> antefebrile (*febris, febris,* fever)
> antepartum (*parere, partum,* to give birth)

5. **Antero-, anterior**: before, front or forward part of.

> anteroinferior (*inferior, inferioris,* lower, below)
> anterolateral (*latus, lateris,* side)
> anteroventral (*venter, ventris,* belly)
> inferoanterior (*inferus,* below)

6. **Bi- (bis-, bin-)**: twice, twofold.

> biciliate (*cilium, cili,* eyebrow, cilium)
> binaural (*auris, auris,* ear)
> binocular (*oculus, oculi,* eye)
> biramous (*ramus, rami,* branch)
> bisaxillary (*axilla, axillae,* small axis, armpit)
> bisiliac (*ilium, ili,* flank bone)

7. **Circum-**: around.

> circumduction (*ducere, ductum,* to lead)
> circumoral (*os, oris,* mouth)
> circumrenal (*ren, renis,* kidney)

8. **Co- (col-, com-** before b, m, p, **con-, cor-)**: with, together, completely, (perfective).

> cohesion (*haerere, haesum,* to cling, stick)
> colligate (*ligare, ligatum,* to tie)
> commensal (*mensa, mensae,* table)
> conconsciousness (*conscius, -a, -um,* knowing well)
> concretion (*crescere, cretum,* to grow, increase)
> convolvent (*volvere, volutum,* to roll, turn)
> corrugator (*rugare, rugatum,* to wrinkle)

9. **Contra-** (**counter-** often before vowels): against, opposite.

> counterirritant (*irritare, irritatum,* to irritate)
> contralateral (*latus, lateris,* side)
> contratussin (*tussis, tussis,* cough)
> contravolitional (*vol-, velle,* to wish, desire)

10. **De-**: down from, from, undoing, (intensive).

> dealbation (*albus, -a, -um,* white)
> defatigation (*fatigare, fatigatum,* to tire, become weary)
> deferent (*ferre, latum,* to bear, carry)
> degustation (*gustare, gustatum,* to taste)
> delactation (*lac, lactis,* milk)
> delacrimation (*lacrima, lacrimae,* tear)
> deligation (*ligare, ligatum,* to tie)
> dementia (*mens, mentis,* mind)
> denigration (*niger, nigra, nigrum,* black)
> desalination (*sal, salis,* salt)
> desiccant (*siccare, siccatum,* to dry)

11. **Demi-**: half, part.

> demifacet (*facies, faciei,* face)
> demilune (*luna, lunae,* moon)
> deminatured (*natura, naturae,* nature)
> demipenniform (*penna, pennae,* wing; *forma, formae,* form)

12. **Dis-** (**dif-, di-**): apart from, asunder, separation, removal.

> diffluent (*fluere, fluxum,* to flow)
> digestant (*gerere, gestum,* to carry, bear)
> dilaceration (*lacerare, laceratum,* to tear to pieces)
> discission (*scindere, scissum,* to cut, split)
> discrete (*cernere, cretum,* to separate)

13. **E-, ef-** (before f), **ex-**: out of, forth, off.

> edentata (*dens, dentis,* tooth)
> efferent (*ferre, latum,* to bear, carry)
> emaculation (*macula, maculae,* spot, blemish)
> eviscerate (*viscus, visceris,* bowels)
> expectorant (*pectus, pectoris,* breast, chest)
> extirpation (*stirps, stirpis,* stalk, lineage)
> exudation (*sudare, sudatum,* to sweat)

14. **Extra-, extro-**: on the outside, beyond, outer.

   extraligamentous (*ligamentum, ligamenti,* ligament)
   extrapulmonary (*pulmo, pulmonis,* lung)
   extravasate (*vas, vasis,* vessel)
   extrospection (*spectare, spectatum,* to look)

15. **In-, (im-, ir-)**: in, into, on, against, (intensive).

   immersion (*mergere, mersum,* to dip)
   incisor (*caedere, caesum, (cid-, cis-),* to cut)
   inebriety (*ebrietas, ebrietatis,* drunkeness)
   ingestation (*gerere, gestum,* to bear, carry)
   intumescence (*tumescere,* to swell up)
   irradiation (*radiare, radiatum,* to shine)

16. **In- (il-, im-, ir-)**: not.

   illorica (*lorica, loricae,* breastplate)
   imberbis (*barba, barbae,* beard)
   immiscible (*miscere, mixtum,* to mix)
   imperception (*percipere, perceptum,* to perceive)
   inermis (*arma, armorum,* weapons)
   irresuscitable (*resuscitare, resuscitatum,* to arouse again)

17. **Infra-**: below, lower.

   infracostal (*costa, costae,* rib)
   infrascapular (*scapula, scapulae,* shoulder blade)
   infraocclusion (*occludere, occlusum,* to close)

18. **Inter-**: between.

   interdentium (*dens, dentis,* tooth)
   internatus (*nasci, natum,* to be born, grow)
   interosseous (*os, ossis,* bone)
   intervascular (*vas, vasis,* vessel)

19. **Intra-**: within, inside, during.

   intrabuccal (*bucca, buccae,* cheek)
   intracervical (*cervix, cervicis,* neck)
   intrafebrile (*febris, febris,* fever)
   intravesical (*vesica, vesicae,* bladder)

20. **Intro**-: within, inward.

> introjection (*iacere, iactum*, to throw, cast)
> introsusception (*suscipere, susceptum*, to receive)
> introvision (*videre, visum*, to see)

21. **Intus**-: within.

> intussusception (*suscipere, susceptum*, to receive)

22. **Juxta**-: beside, near to.

> juxtarticular (*articulus, articuli*, joint)
> juxtaspinal (*spina, spinae*, spine)

23. **Non**-: not.

> nonconductor (*conducere, conductum*, to lead together)
> nonocclusion (*occludere, occlusum*, to close)
> nonparous (*parere, partum*, to give birth)
> nonseptate (*saepire, saeptum*, to hedge in)
> nonvalent (*valere*, to have strength)

24. **Ob**- (**o**-, **oc**-, **op**-): against, in the way, facing, (intensive).

> obmutescence (*mutescere, mutum*, to grow dumb, mute)
> obnubilation (*nubila, nubilae*, cloud)
> obovate (*ovum, ovi*, egg)
> occiput (*caput, capitis*, head)
> opplete (*plere, pletum*, to fill)

25. **Per**- (**pel**-): throughout, thoroughly, excessively, (intensive).

> pellucid (*lucidus, lucidi*, clear)
> peracetate (*acetum, aceti*, vinegar)
> percurrent (*currere, cursum*, to run)
> pernasal (*nasus, nasi*, nose)
> perniger (*niger, nigri*, black)

26. **Post**-: after, behind.

> postcerebral (*cerebrum, cerebri*, brain)
> postnatal (*nasci, natum*, to be born)
> postpubescent (*pubescere*, to reach puberty)

27. **Postero**-: behind.

> posterolateral (*latus, lateris*, side)
> posterosuperior (*superior, superioris*, upper)

28. **Prae-** (**pre-**): before, in front of.

>   precordium (*cor, cordis,* heart)
>   predormitium (*dormire, dormitum,* to sleep)
>   premaxillary (*maxilla, maxillae,* jaw)
>   prenatal (*nasci, natum,* to be born).

29. **Praeter-** (**preter-**): beyond, past, more than.

>   pretergress (*gradi, gressum,* to go, walk)
>   preterhuman (*humanus, -a, -um,* human)
>   preterlethal (*lethum, lethi,* death)
>   preternatural (*natura, naturae,* nature)

30. **Pro-**: before, in front of, forth, front part of.

>   procumbent (*cumbere, cubitum,* to lean, recline)
>   progenia (*gena, genae,* chin)
>   prolabium (*labium, labii,* lip)
>   protuberance (*tuber, tuberis,* bulge, swelling)

31. **Re-** (**red-**): again, back, (intensive).

>   redolent (*olere,* to emit a smell)
>   reflorescence (*florescere,* to blossom)
>   refraction (*frangere, fractum,* to break)
>   refrigerant (*frigerare,* to make cool)
>   renascent (*nasci, natum,* to be born, grow)

32. **Retro-**: backward, behind.

>   retroflexed (*flectere, flexum,* to bend, flex)
>   retronasal (*nasus, nasi,* nose)
>   retroversion (*vertere, versum,* to turn)

33. **Se-**: apart, free from.

>   secretion (*cernere, cretum,* to divide, separate)
>   segregation (*grex, gregis,* herd, crowd)

34. **Semi-**: half, somewhat.

>   semiorbicular (*orbis, orbis,* orb, circle)
>   semirecumbent (*recumbere, recubitum,* to recline)
>   semisomnus (*somnus, somni,* sleep)

35. **Sub-** (**suc-**, **suf-**, **sup-**, **sus-**): under, below, near, somewhat, moderately.

    subauratus (*aurum, auri,* gold)
    subcutis (*cutis, cutis,* skin)
    subdorsal (*dorsum, dorsi,* back)
    succavus (*cavus, cavi,* hollow, concave)
    suffix (*figere, fixum,* to fasten, fix)
    suffrutescent (*frutex, fruticis,* a shrub)
    suppuration (*pus, puris,* pus)
    suspensor (*pendo, pensum,* to hang)

36. **Super-** (**sur-**): over, above, excessively.

    superciliary (*cilium, cilii,* eyebrow)
    superdistention (*distendere, distentum,* to stretch)
    supergenual (*genu, genus,* knee)
    supernatant (*natare, natatum,* to swim, float)
    suralimentation (*alimentare, alimentatum,* to nourish)
    surexcitation (*excitare, excitatum,* to arouse)

37. **Supra-**: above, upon, upper.

    supra-axillary (*axilla, axillae,* armpit)
    suprapelvic (*pelvis, pelvis,* basin, pelvic region)
    suprarenal (*ren, renis,* kidney)

38. **Trans-** (often **tran-** before s): across, through.

    transaudient (*audire, auditum,* to hear)
    transforation (*forare, foratum,* to pierce, drill)
    translucent (*lux, lucis,* light)
    transpinalis (*spina, spinae,* spine)
    transpiration (*spirare, spiratum,* to breathe, exhale)
    transseptal (*saeptum, saepti,* division, barrier)
    transude (*sudare,* to sweat)

39. **Ultra-**, **ultro-**: beyond, excessive.

    ultraligation (*ligare, ligatum,* to bind, tie)
    ultrasetaceous (*seta, setae,* bristle, hair)
    ultrastellar (*stella, stellae,* star)
    ultromotivity (*motio, motionis,* movement)

## LATIN SUFFIXES

Suffixes are among the most important formative elements of Latin words. Except in rare instances, suffixes did not exist as separate words in the Latin language, but were used as additions to roots and stems to impart changes in meaning and to create new words. Their number and use grew enormously from the relatively few primary suffixes which were first attached to basic Latin roots. Words thus formed furnished stems to which secondary suffixes were attached to create other words. A Latin word may therefore have more than one suffix.

Because Latin suffixes are so numerous and because their functions are sometimes quite intricate and overlapping, only a selected list is given below. They are grouped under: A. Substantival (Noun) Suffixes, B. Adjectival Suffixes, C. Verbal Suffixes, and D. Adverbial Suffix. The numbering of the groups will aid in associating those suffixes which are closely related in meaning. The illustrative words used in this section are Latin for the reason stated on page 63.

## A. SUBSTANTIVAL (NOUN) SUFFIXES

| Suffix | Meaning | Stem or base to which attached | Examples |
|---|---|---|---|
| 1. **-or*** | the agent; he or that which does | participial base | extensor (*extendere, extensum,* to draw out) flexor (*flectere, flexum,* to bend) infusor (*infundere, infusum,* to pour in) vector (*vehere, vectum,* to carry) |

When taken into English, Latin nouns ending in **-or** usually retain their exact Latin form, for example: flexor, vector, incisor, auditor, generator.

| Suffix | Meaning | Stem or base to which attached | Examples |
|---|---|---|---|
| 2. **-io*** **-ura*** | action, or condition resulting from an action | participial base | adhaesio (*adhaerere, adhaesum,* to stick to) ligatio (*ligare, ligatum,* to tie) purgatio (*purgare, purgatum, to* cleanse) |

| Suffix | Meaning | Stem or base to which attached | Examples |
|--------|---------|-------------------------------|----------|
|        |         |                               | tensio (*tendere*, *tensum*, to stretch) |
|        |         |                               | fissura (*findere*, *fissum*, to split) |
|        |         |                               | junctura (*iungere*, *iunctum*, to join) |
|        |         |                               | ligatura (*ligare*, *ligatum*, to tie) |

The English version of the suffix **-io** is *-ion*; for example: adhesion, ligation, purgation, tension, excision, fission, articulation.

The English version of **-ura** is usually *-ure*; for example: fissure, juncture, ligature, flexure, fracture, aperture.

*NOTE: The suffixes are actually **-tor, -tio,** and **-tura,** which are attached to the word root. But since the participial suffix is **-to,** the net result is the same as if **-or, -io,** or **-ura** are attached to the participial base. Since Latin participial bases end in **-t, -s,** or **-x,** nouns using these three suffixes will always end in **-tor, -sor, -xor**; **-tio, -sio, -xio**; and **-tura, -sura, -xura.**

| Suffix | Meaning | Stem or base to which attached | Examples |
|--------|---------|-------------------------------|----------|
| 3. **-men** **-mentum** | action, or condition resulting from an action | present stem | foramen (*forare*, to bore) |
|        |         |                               | semen (*serere* [*se-*], to sow) |
|        |         |                               | specimen (*specere*, to look at) |
|        |         |                               | stamen (*stare*, to stand) |
|        |         |                               | tegmen (*tegere*, to cover) |
|        |         |                               | fragmentum (*frangere*, to break) |
|        |         |                               | nutrimentum (*nutrire*, to nourish) |
|        |         |                               | sedimentum (*sedere*, to sit) |

English retains the Latin forms of nouns ending in **-men**; for example: foramen, semen, specimen, stamen, tegmen.

The suffix **-mentum** usually appears as *-ment* in English words; for example: fragment, nutriment, sediment, ligament, segment.

| Suffix | Meaning | Stem or base to which attached | Examples |
|---|---|---|---|
| 4. **-ulum** (**-ula**) **-bulum** (**-bula**) **-culum** **-brum** **-crum** **-trum** | instrument; means of an action; place | verb root or stem | cingulum (*cingere*, to girdle) coagulum (*co-agere*, to bring together) vinculum (*vincire*, to tie) pabulum (*pascere* [*pa-*], to feed) infundibulum (*infundere*, to pour into) mandibula (*mandare*, to chew) retinaculum (*retinere*, to hold back) vehiculum (*vehere*, to carry) cribrum (*cernere* [*cri-*], to separate) claustrum (*claudere*, to close) |

| Suffix | Meaning | Stem or base to which attached | Examples |
|---|---|---|---|
| 5. **-ia** (**-tia**) **-itas** **-tudo** | quality, condition, state | adjective, or present participial stem. | dementia (*demens*, out of one's senses) nigritia (*niger*, black) patientia (*patiens*, suffering) sequentia (*sequens*, following) |
| **-or** | | verb stem | aciditas (*acidus*, sour) loquacitas (*loquax*, talkative) senilitas (*senilis*, old) altitudo (*altus*, high) lassitudo (*lassus*, weary) magnitudo (*magnus*, large) calor (*calere*, to be warm) tremor (*tremere*, to tremble) tumor (*tumere*, to swell) |

In English the Latin suffix **-tia** remains unchanged or becomes -*ce*; for example: dementia, patience, sequence. **-itas** becomes -*ity*, and **-tudo** becomes -*tude* in English; for example: acidity, loquacity, senility, altitude, lassitude, magnitude. Words in **-or** remain unchanged in English; for example: calor, tremor, tumor, odor, pallor.

| Suffix | Meaning | Stem or base to which attached | Examples |
|--------|---------|-------------------------------|----------|
| 6. **-arium** **-orium** **-ium** | place; space (of time); area for work; apparatus | verb and noun | aquarium (*aqua*, water) solarium (*sol*, sun) herbarium (*herba*, plant) aviarium (*avis*, bird) instrumentarium (*instrumenta*, tools) sanatorium (*sanare*, to heal) auditorium (*audire*, to hear) compressorium (*compremere*, to press) palpatorium (*palpare*, to feel) preventorium (*prevenire*, to prevent) sensorium (*sentire*, to feel) interdentium (*inter*; *dens*, tooth) puerperium (*puer*; *parere*, to give birth) predormitium (*prae*; *dormire* to sleep) interscapilium (*inter*; *scapula*, shoulder) |

These suffixes are properly adjectival, but in their neuter forms have been used substantively. Their English versions are the same as the Latin, or they change to *-ry*; for example: aviary, mortuary, apothecary, laboratory.

| Suffix | Meaning | Stem or base to which attached | Examples |
|--------|---------|-------------------------------|----------|
| 7. **-ulus** (**olus** after a vowel) **-culus** **-illus** **-unculus** **-ellus** | small; (diminutives) | noun (occasionally adjective) base | globulus (*globus*, sphere) calculus (*calx*, stone) nucleolus (*nucleus*, kernel) alveolus (*alveus*, cavity) petiolus (*pes*, foot) capsula (*capsa*, box) ramulus (*ramus*, branch) lunula (*luna*, moon) auricula (*auris*, ear) ventriculus (*venter*, belly) radiculus (*radix*, root) geniculum (*genu*, knee) |

| Suffix | Meaning | Stem or base to which attached | Examples |
|--------|---------|-------------------------------|----------|
|        |         |                               | palpaculum (*palpus*, feeler) |
|        |         |                               | corpusculum (*corpus*, body) |
|        |         |                               | cuticulus (*cutis*, skin) |
|        |         |                               | pupilla (*pupa*, doll) |
|        |         |                               | lapillus (*lapis*, stone) |
|        |         |                               | fibrilla (*fibra*, fiber) |
|        |         |                               | carbunculus (*carbo*, coal) |
|        |         |                               | pedunculus (*pes*, foot) |
|        |         |                               | ocellus (*oculus*, eye) |
|        |         |                               | flagellum (*flagrum*, whip) |
|        |         |                               | lamella (*lamina*, thin plate) |

In English words the Latin spelling of these suffixes is either retained, or the final syllable is shortened to *-e*; **-culus** in often syncopated to *-cle*; for example: globule, capsule, ventricle, cuticle, palpacle, peduncle. Words ending in *-illa* often drop the final syllable; for example: pupil, fibril.

More than one diminutive suffix may be used in a single word; for example: maxillula (*mala*, cheek); petiolula (*pes*, foot).

Some of the instrumental suffixes (4, above) resemble these diminutive suffixes, but note that the former are attached to *verb stems* and the latter to *noun stems*.

## B. ADJECTIVAL SUFFIXES

| Suffix | Meaning | Stem or base to which attached | Examples |
|--------|---------|-------------------------------|----------|
| 1. **-ilis** | ability, | verb | facilis (*facere*, to do) |
| **-bilis** | capability, | | fissilis (*findere*, to split) |
| | capacity | | fragilis (*frangere*, to break) |
| | | | sessilis (*sedere*, to sit) |
| | | | volatilis (*volare*, to fly) |
| | | | audibilis (*audire*, to hear) |
| | | | flexibilis (*flectere*, to bend) |
| | | | solubilis (*solvere*, to loosen) |

In English these suffixes usually appear as *-ile* and *-ble*; for example: facile, fissile, fragile, sessile, volatile, audible, flexible, soluble.

| Suffix | Meaning | Stem or base to which attached | Examples |
|--------|---------|-------------------------------|----------|
| 2. **-idus** | in a state or condition of | verb | aridus (*arere*, to be dry) |
| | | | flaccidus (*flaccere*, to droop) |
| | | | fluidus (*fluere*, to flow) |
| | | | frigidus (*frigere*, to be cold) |
| | | | rigidus (*rigere*, to be stiff) |
| | | | torridus (*torrere*, to be hot) |
| | | | turgidus (*turgere*, to swell up) |

In English words these suffixes appear as *-id*; for example: arid, flaccid, fluid, frigid, rigid, torrid, turgid.

| Suffix | Meaning | Stem or base to which attached | Examples |
|--------|---------|-------------------------------|----------|
| 3. **-eus** | made of; | noun | aureus (*aurum*, gold) |
| **-ius** | having the | | ferreus (*ferrum*, iron) |
| **-aceus** | quality or | | igneus (*ignis*, fire) |
| **-aneus** | nature of; like | | ligneus (*lignum*, wood) |
| | | | noxius (*noxa*, harm) |
| | | | farinaceus (*farina*, flour) |
| | | | capillaceus (*capillus*, hair) |
| | | | crustaceus (*crusta*, shell) |
| | | | cutaneus (*cutis*, skin) |
| | | | calcaneus (*calx*, heel) |

In English these suffixes usually end in *-ous*; for example: ferrous, igneous, noxious, farinaceous, capillaceous, cutaneous.

| Suffix | Meaning | Stem or base to which attached | Examples |
|--------|---------|-------------------------------|----------|
| 4. **-alis** | having a | noun | abdominalis (*abdomen*, abdomen) |
| **-aris** | connection | | corticalis (*cortex*, bark) |
| **-ilis** | with; pertaining to | | dorsalis (*dorsum*, back) |
| | | | lactealis (*lac*, milk) |
| | | | alveolaris (*alveolus*, small hollow) |
| | | | iugularis (*iugulum*, throat) |
| | | | ocularis (*oculus*, eye) |
| | | | scapularis (*scapula*, shoulder) |
| | | | virilis (*vir*, man) |
| | | | senilis (*senex*, old man) |
| | | | infantilis (*infans*, infant) |

In English these suffixes appear as *-al*, *-ar*, or *-ile*; for example: abdominal, cortical, dorsal, lacteal, digital, cerebral, caudal, alveolar, jugular, ocular, scapular, fibular, virile, senile, infantile.

| | Suffix | Meaning | Stem or base to which attached | Examples |
|---|---|---|---|---|
| 5. | **-anus** | place, or | noun | Americanus (*America*, |
| | **-enus** | origin; | | America) |
| | **-aneus** | belonging to | | Darwinianus (*Darwin*) |
| | **-(i)ensis** | | | montanus (*mons*, mountain) |
| | **-(e)stris** | | | meridianus (*meridies*, midday) |
| | | | | terrenus (*terra*, earth) |
| | | | | subterraneus (*sub*; *terra*, earth) |
| | | | | Iowensis (*Iowa*) |
| | | | | Parisiensis (*Paris*) |
| | | | | hortensis (*hortus*, garden) |
| | | | | pratensis (*prata*, meadow) |
| | | | | silvestris (*silva*, forest) |
| | | | | rupestris (*rupes*, cliff) |
| 6. | **-osus** | full of | noun | fibrosus (*fibra*, fiber) |
| | **-lentus** | | | fructuosus (*fructus*, fruit) |
| | | | | pilosus (*pila*, hair) |
| | | | | rimulosus (*rimula*, small crack) |
| | | | | rugosus (*ruga*, wrinkle) |
| | | | | venosus (*vena*, vein) |
| | | | | corpulentus (*corpus*, body) |
| | | | | lutulentus (*lutum*, dirt) |
| | | | | pestilentus (*pestis*, pest) |
| | | | | somnolentus (*somnus*, sleep) |
| | | | | succulentus (*succus*, juice) |

In English words the suffix **-osus** usually appears as *-ose* or as *-ous*; **-lentus** appears as *-lent*; for example: fibrous, adipose, cellulose, pilous, rugose, venose, corpulent, pestilent, succulent, somnolent, virulent.

## C. VERBAL SUFFIXES

| Suffix | Meaning | Stem or base to which attached | Examples |
|--------|---------|-------------------------------|----------|
| 1. **-ate** | to put into action; perform | noun or adjective | attenuate (*tenuis*, thin) <br> elaborate (*labor*, toil) <br> radiate (*radius*, ray, spoke) <br> stimulate (*stimulus*, a goad) |
| 2. **-sc-** | to begin an action (inceptive) | verb stem (derived from noun or adjective) | calescence (*calor*, heat) <br> deliquesce (*liquor*, fluid) <br> putrescence (*putris*, rotten) <br> arborescent (*arbor*, tree) <br> flavescent (*flavus*, yellow) <br> florescent (*flos*, flower) <br> rubescent (*ruber*, red) |

The *-ent* which is often attached to the **-sc-** suffix is the present participial stem (see page 40).

## D. ADVERBIAL SUFFIX

| Suffix | Meaning | Stem or base to which attached | Examples |
|--------|---------|-------------------------------|----------|
| 1. **-ad** | in the direction of; toward | noun, adjective, adverb | apicad (*apex*, top) <br> caudad (*cauda*, tail) <br> cephalad (*kephalos*, head) <br> dextrad (*dexter*, the right) <br> dorsoventrad (*venter*, belly) <br> ectad (*ecto*, outside) <br> retrad (*retro*, back) |

This suffix has been developed in modern times from the Latin preposition and prefix *ad*.

\* \* \* \* \* \* \* \* \* \*

Occasionally a scientific field establishes its own system of suffixes. Chemistry, for example, has chosen to designate particular combinations of substances by the use of such suffixes as the following:

| Suffix | Assigned Meaning | Example |
|---|---|---|
| **-ase**: | enzyme | oxidase |
| **-ose**: | carbohydrate | dextrose |
| **-ate**: | salt formed from acid whose name ends in *-ic* (with a few exceptions) | sulphate |
| **-ite**: | salt formed from acid whose name ends in *-ous* | sulphite |
| **-id** (**ide**): | a compound of two elements | ferric oxide |
| **-ol** | alcohol or phenol | glycerol |

## Latin Numerals

The cardinals and the ordinals are listed together. The list includes only those numbers which appear most frequently in compound terms; for others, consult a Latin dictionary or textbook.

When used in compound words, most Latin cardinals appear in their full form; for example: **quinque**folius, **septem**nervia, **octo**guttata, **decem**plex.

**Un**us: one.    **Prim**us: first.

| | | |
|---|---|---|
| adunatus | unilateral | primary |
| coadunate | union | primates |
| malunion | unipenniform | primipara |
| reunient | uniseptate | primogeniture |
| unifilar | univalent | primordial |
| unilaminar | primacy | |

**Duo** (Gk. δύο): two. **Secund**us: second.

| | | |
|---|---|---|
| dualis | reduplicate | secundigravida |
| duplex | secund | secundines |
| duoparental | secundiflorus | secundiparous |

**Tres** (combining form is **Tri-** from Gk. τρεῖς): **Terti**us: third. (see **Treis** in Greek list)

| | | |
|---|---|---|
| triangle | trident | tertiary |
| triceps | tertian | |

**Quattuor, quadri-, quadru-**: four. **Quart**us: fourth. **Quadr**us: fourfold

| | | |
|---|---|---|
| quadrifid | quadrumanous | quadrisection |
| quadrilateral | quadruped | quartan |
| quadriparous | quadrangle | quartile |
| quadrivalent | quadriceps | quartos |
| quadrimaculate | quadrifidus | |

**Quinque**, (**quin-**): five. **Quint**us: fifth.

| | | |
|---|---|---|
| quinary | quinquefoliolate | quintisternal |
| quincuncial | quinquevalent | quintuplet |
| quinquecostate | quintan | |

**Sex** (**se-**): six. **Sext**us: sixth.

| | | |
|---|---|---|
| sejugous | sexfid | sextan |
| sexdigitate | sexivalent | sextipara |
| sexennial | sexpartite | sextuplet |

**Septem**: seven. **Septim**us: seventh.

| | | |
|---|---|---|
| septan | septennial | septuplet |
| septempartite | septigravida | septimal |
| septenate | septivalent | |

**Octo** (Gk. ὀκτώ): eight. **Octav**us: eighth.

| | | |
|---|---|---|
| octarius | octennial | octave |
| octavalent | octipara | octavo |

**Novem**: nine. **Non**us: ninth.

| | | |
|---|---|---|
| November | nonagon | nonillion |
| novennial | | |

**Decem** (Gk. δέκα): ten. **Decim**us: tenth. **Decuss**is: a Roman coin worth 10 units and marked **X**; hence, crossed; a chiasm.

| | | |
|---|---|---|
| decemfid | decempartite | decimate |
| decemfoliate | decennary | decussate |
| decemjugate | decimal | |

**Undecim**: eleven. **Undecim**us: eleventh.

| | |
|---|---|
| undecagon | undecifilus |

**Duodecim** (**Duodeni**): twelve. **Duodecim**us: twelfth.

| | | |
|---|---|---|
| duedenohepatic | duodenum | transduodenal |
| duodenojejunostomy | gastroduodenal | duodecimal |

**Viginti**: twenty. **Vicesim**us: twentieth.

| | | |
|---|---|---|
| vigintiangular | vigintilobus | vicennial |

**Centum**: one hundred. **Centesim**us: hundredth.

| | | |
|---|---|---|
| centipede | tercentenary | centesimal |

**Mille**: one thousand. **Millesim**us: thousandth.

| | | |
|---|---|---|
| micromilligram | millimeter | millesimal |
| millefolius | milliped | |

# GENERAL LATIN VOCABULARY

Many Latin words have come into English as loan words, that is, without undergoing any change whatever. A few examples of such words are the following:

| | | | | |
|---|---|---|---|---|
| abdomen | arbor | cortex | irrigator | species |
| antenna | axis | cumulus | labium | stimulus |
| anterior | bacillus | femur | locus | terminus |
| antrum | cadaver | focus | pallor | vertebra |
| apparatus | color | fungus | rabies | vertex |
| appendix | conifer | genus | sinus | viscera |

In a few instances, English has adopted certain specific inflected forms of Latin words. Examples of such words are the following:

| | | | | |
|---|---|---|---|---|
| habitat | recipe | interest | proviso | vim |

The largest contribution of Latin to scientific English, however, is in supplying the constructive elements from which derivative words are formed. Many of these derivative words are only slightly changed from their original Latin forms; many more of them, however, are neologisms which did not exist in Latin but which have been constructed out of Latin word elements to meet specific needs. For example:

| *Slightly Changed* | *Neologisms* |
|---|---|
| adjuvant (*adiuvans*) | alveolodental (*alveolus, dens, -alis*) |
| aperture (*apertura*) | axiolinguoocclusal (*axis, lingua, occlusus, -alis*) |
| capsule (*capsula*) | brevipennate (*brevis, penna, -atus*) |
| expel (*expello*) | costotransverse (*costa, trans, versus*) |
| furcate (*furcatus*) | equibiradiate (*aequus, bi-, radius, -atus*) |
| lacrimose (*lacrimosus*) | ferrocalcite (*ferrum, calx; lithos*) |
| ocular (*ocularis*) | mollipilose (*mollis, pilus, -osus*) |
| pistil (*pistillum*) | seroflocculation (*serum, floccus, -ulus, -io*) |
| prime (*primus*) | silicotuberculosis (*silex, tuber, -culus; osis*) |
| putrid (*putridus*) | vasoligature (*vas, ligatura*) |

The entry forms in the word lists are Latin words in their original spelling. For NOUNS and ADJECTIVES, only the nominative case is given unless the genitive case form is also necessary in order to reveal the base of the word. ADJECTIVES have been entered in their masculine singular form only. For VERBS, only the present infinitive and the perfect participle are given. The base or stem of the Latin word is indicated by printing that part of the word in bold type.

A few inconsistencies may be noticed in the method of listing. For example, the words **acer, acerb**us, **acetabul**um, **acet**um, **acid**us, **ac**us, and **acut**us have been given separate entries rather than included under a single entry as might be suggested by the fact that all these words are built on the same Latin root (**ac-**) and are therefore closely related in meaning; on the other hand, the words **lux** and **lucid**us have been included with the entry-word **luce**re, **nocu**us has been entered with **noce**re, **nucle**us with **nux,** and **rabid**us with **rabe**re. Further, cingulum and claustrum (loan words), for example, have been included among the derivatives under **cinge**re and **claude**re respectively, even though these same words in Latin are not inserted on the entry line. In the listing of related words such as those mentioned the procedure used in each instance has been determined solely on the basis of which method of presentation has proved in classroom instruction to be the most effective and economical.

Occasional differences between the spelling of a base as it appears in the original Latin word and in a derivative (e.g., imberbis under **barb**a; cingulum under **cinge**re; biceps and precipitate under **caput**) will generally be made clear by referring to the explanation of vowel changes (pp. 42-43).

Greek words adopted by the Romans do not appear in the Latin lists unless significant differences in spelling or some other special factor warrant their inclusion: **arteri**a (Greek, ἀρτερία) and **brachi**um (Greek, βραχίων), for example, will be in the Greek lists only; **fer**re (Latin) and **pher**ein (Greek, φέρειν), however, will appear in their respective lists.

The general word list that follows contains about 725 Latin entry words. The more important of these words (approximately 378) have been designated by asterisks.

\* \* \* \* \* \* \* \* \* \* \*

**\*Abdomen, abdomin**is: body cavity, paunch.

| | | |
|---|---|---|
| abdomen | abdominous | subadominal |
| abdominal | postabdomen | thoracico-abdominal |
| abdominoposterior | | |

**Acer, Acr**is: sharp, pungent, bitter.

| | | | |
|---|---|---|---|
| acescence | acrid | acridine | acrimony |

**Acerb**us: harsh, bitter, severe.

| | | |
|---|---|---|
| acerbate | acerbity | exacerbation |

**\*Acetabul**um: vinegar cup; the cup-shaped socket of the hipbone.

| | | |
|---|---|---|
| acetabulectomy | acetabuloplasty | postacetabular |
| acetabulifera | acetabulum | subacetabular |

**Acet**um: vinegar, acetic acid.

| | | |
|---|---|---|
| acetic | acetolysis | acetum |
| acetimeter | acetosus | subacetal |

**\*Acid**us: sour; acid.

| | | | |
|---|---|---|---|
| acidifiable | acidogenic | antacid | subacid |
| acidify | acidophil | monacid | superacid |
| acidimeter | acidosis | peracidity | |

**\*Ac**us: needle, needlelike process. **Acule**us: small point; sting. **Acumen, acumin**is: point.

| | | | |
|---|---|---|---|
| acicular | aculeiform | acupression | acutorsion |
| aciculum | acuminate | acupuncture | biacuminate |
| aciform | acuminiferous | acusector | pentacula |
| acuclosure | acuminifolius | acutenaculum | subacuminate |
| aculeate | | | |

**Acut**us: sharp, pointed.

| | | |
|---|---|---|
| acutilingual | peracute | superacute |
| acutipennate | subacute | |

**\*Adeps, adip**is: fat.

| | | |
|---|---|---|
| adipocellular | adipofibroma | adiposity |
| adipocere | adipohepatic | |

**Adolesce**re, **adult**um: to grow up.

| | | |
|---|---|---|
| adolescent | adult | preadult |

**\*Aequ**us: equal, even.

| | | |
|---|---|---|
| equiangular | equilibrium | equivalence |
| equibiradiate | equimolecular | inequivalve |

**Aestiv**us: pertaining to summer.

| | |
|---|---|
| aestivate | estivoautumnal |

**Ager, agr**i: field, land.

| | | |
|---|---|---|
| agrestal | agromania | peregrination |
| agriculture | agronomy | |

**\*Age**re, **act**um: to do, set in motion, function.

| | | |
|---|---|---|
| activator | coagulate | reaction |
| agent | counteract | seroreaction |

**Agita**re, **agitat**um: to shake, excite, hurry.

agit(ata) vas(e)    agitographia    agitosus
agitation    agitolalia

*****Al**a: wing, winglike process.

alar    aliped    alula    exalate
alate    alisphenoid    basalar

**Albumen, albumin**is: white of an egg; a common protein.

albumen    albuminoreaction    exalbuminous
albuminiferous    albuminuria    lactalbumin

*****Alb**us: white.

albefaction    albicant    superalbal
albescent    albino

*****Alg**a: seaweed.

algae    algicide    algoid    algophagus
algal    algivorous    algology

*****Algor, algor**is: cold, coldness. **Alge**re: to feel cold.

algefacient    algid    algogenin
algoscopy    algogenic    algor (mortis)

*****Aliment**um: nourishment, food.

aliment    inalimental    superalimentation
alimentotherapy    subalimentation

**Alt**us: high.

alticola    altimeter    altitude    altofrequent

*****Alveol**us: small hollow, cavity, pit; socket of root of a tooth; sac or cell.

alveolodental    alveolus    basialveolar    bialveolar
alveololabial

**Alv**us: belly, abdomen with intestines.

alveus    alvine    alvinolith    alvus

*****Ambula**re, **ambulat**um: to walk about.

adambulacral    ambulatorium    noctambulation somnambulate
ambulant    interambulacrum    pseudambulacrum

**Amplex**us: an embracing, encircling.

amplexation    amplexicaul    semiamplexicaul

**Ampull**a: bottle; flask-like dilation.

ampule    ampullaceal    ampullula    juxta-ampullar
ampulla

**Amyl**um: starch.

amylase    amylin    amylolytic    amylose

**Angin**a: a choking, strangling.

angina pectoris    anginal    anginiform    anginophobia

**Angul**us: angle.

angulosplenial    quadrangle    surangular    triangle
multangular

**Angust**us: narrow.
 angustifolia    angustirostrate   angusty

*****Anim**a: air, breath, life.
 animalculum  animality   exanimation  transanimation

*****Annul**us: a ring.
 annular    annulose   exannulate   interannular
 annulet

*****Ann**us: year.
 annual    perennial   pseudannual  superannuate

*****Antenn**a: sailyard; a feeler of an arthropod.
 antenna    antennary   antennifer   antennule

*****An**us: the seat, fundament, the lower opening of the alimentary canal.
 anorectal   anus     postanal    subanal
 anovesical   circumanal   preanal    supra-anal

**Aperi**re, **apert**um: to open.
 aperient    aperitive   apertometer  aperture

*****Apex**, **apic**is: tip, summit, end.
 abapical    apicoectomy    apiculale
 apex     apicolocator    subapical

**Ap**is: bee.
 apiculture   apiphobia    apitoxin
 apiotherapy   apisination   apivorous

**Apta**re, **aptat**um: to fit, fasten.
 aptitude    coaptation    maladaptation

*****Aqu**a: water.
 aquapuncture  aqueous    aquosity
 aquatic    aquiparous   terraqueous

**Ara**re, **arat**um: to plow.
 arable     exarate     inarable

*****Arbor**, **arbor**is: tree.
 arboretum   arborization  arboroid   subarborescent
 arboriculture

*****Arc**us: bow, arch.
 arc      arciform    arcuate
 arcade    arcocentrum   subarcuate

**Are**a: space.
 area     areola    areolate   areolitis

**Aren**a: sand.
 arenaceous   arenation   arenicola   arenoid

**Argent**um: silver.
 argentation   argentiferous  argentophil   argentous

**\*Articul**us: knuckle, joint.
    abarticular           biarticular            monoarticular
    articulata            disarticulation        perarticulation

**Atav**us: ancestor.
    atava                 atavic                 atavism

**\*Ater, atr**a, **atr**um: black.
    aterrimus             atrament        atricapillus        atropunctatus
    atrabiliary

**\*Atri**um: entrance-hall, room; auricle of the heart.
    atriopore             atrium                 interatrial
    atrioventricular      atrium sinistrum

**\*Audi**re, **audit**um: to hear.
    audiogram         audiphone         auditory           transaudient
    audiometry

**Aur**a: air, breath; sensation preceding an attack of epilepsy.
    aura                  aural             aurophysa          aurula

**\*Aur**is: ear.
    auricle           auripuncture       postaural          subaural
    auriculate        aurophore          preauricular
    aurilave          biauricular        sinistraural

**Aur**um: gold. **Auranti**um: an orange.
    aurantia          auriasis                 aurococcus
    aurantiasis       auriferous               aurotherapy

**\*Ausculta**re, **auscultat**um: to listen to.
    auscultation          auscultatory           auscultoplectrum

**Av**is: bird.
    avian             avicula           avicularium        avifauna

**\*Axill**a: armpit.
    axillar               infra-axillary         subaxillary
    circumaxillary        primaxil

**\*Ax**is: axle, axis.
    axial             axiolinguoclusal   epaxial            postaxial
    axiobuccal        axipetal           pluriaxial         subaxial


# B

**Bacc**a: berry.
    baccate           bacciferous        bacciform          baccivorous

**\*Bacill**um (**bacul**um): little rod or staff; rod-shaped bacteria.
    bacillemia        bacilliform        baculiform         prebacillary

**Barb**a: beard.
    barbate           barbicel           barbule            imberbis
    barbel

**\*Bibe**re: to drink.
    bibacious       bibulous       imbibition       subimbibitional

**\*Bil**is: bile.
    atrabilious       bilin       bilirubin       biliuria
    bilification

**Bracte**a: thin metal plate.
    bract       bracteole       ebracteolate       tribracteate

**\*Brev**is: short.
    brevicollis       breviflexor       brevipennate
    breviductor       brevilingual       brevirostrate

**\*Bucc**a: cheek; mouth.
    axiobuccal       cervicobuccal       nasobuccal
    buccolabial       extrabuccal       postbuccal
    bucculent       intrabuccal       suprabuccal

**Buccin**a: horn, trumpet; muscle of the cheek.
    buccina       buccinator       buccinulum

**Bulb**us: bulb.
    bulbiferous       bulbil       pseudobulbous       retrobulbar

**\*Bulli**re, **bullit**um: to boil. **Bull**a: bubble, blister.
    bulla       bullation       bullous       ebullition
    bullate       bulliopsis       ebullient

**\*Burs**a: bag, pouch, sac (between parts moving upon one another).
    bursa       bursicule       bursitis       bursula
    bursal       bursiform       bursolith

## C

**\*Cade**re, **cas**um (**cid**-): to fall, befall. **Caduc**us, -a, -um: falling, fallen.
    cadaver       casual       deciduous       intercadence
    caducous       coincident       indeciduate       recidivism

**\*Caec**us: blind.
    caecostomy       ileocaecal       retrocecal
    caecum       postcecal       subcecal

**\*Caede**re, **caes**um (-**cid**, **cis**-): to cut; kill.
    caesural       excise       loculicidal       suicide
    circumcision       incisor       subincision       vermicide

**\*Cale**re: to be warm.
    calefacient       calory       subcalorism
    calenture       decalescence       transcalent

**Call**um: hard or thick skin.
    callosity       corpus callosum       supracallosal

**Calv**us: hairless, bald.
    calvarium       calvities       decalvant

**\*Calx, calc**is: heel. **Calcar**: spur.
  calcaceous          calcariferous       ecalcarate          subcalcarine
  calcaneofibular     calcarine           recalcitrant

**\*Calx, calc**is: limestone, lime concretion.
  calcareous                calcification               decalcify
  calcibilia                calciphilia                 ferrocalcite
  calcicole                 calculus                    subcalcareous

**Cambi**um: exchange.
  cambiform         cambiogenetic       cambium            procambium

**Canal**is: channel, canal.
  canal                    canaliculus                 canalization
  canalicular              canaliform

**Cancell**i: lattice, grating.
  cancellated             cancellous

**\*Cancer, cancr**i, (French, **Chancre**): crab; cancer, tumor.
  cancer             cancroid            chancre            precancerous
  cancrisocial       cancrum oris        chancriform

**Cand**ere: to shine, glitter, be hot. **Candid**us: white, bright.
  candescent              candida                     incandescence

**\*Cap**ere, **capt**um (**cip(i)-, cept-**): to take, seize, grasp.
  amboceptor         inception           nociceptive        receptor
  exciple            intrasusception     preperception      susceptibility
  exteroceptive      intussusception     proprioceptor

**\*Capill**us: hair; a minute bodily vessel.
  capillaceous       capillary           capillitium        precapillary
  capillariomotor    capilliculture      intercapillary

**\*Caps**a: box.
  capsicum                capsuliferous               pentacapsular
  capsule                 intracapsular

**\*Caput, capit**is (**cep-, cip-**): head.
  basioccipital      capitulum           occipital          sinciput
  biceps             centriciput         precipitate        subcapital
  bicipital          decapitation        quadriceps         suboccipital
  capitellum         janiceps

**Carbo, carbon**is: charcoal, carbon; carbon dioxide.
  carbogaseous            carbonate                   carbonize
  carbohydrate            carboniferous

**Cari**es: decay, rot.
  anticarious             caries                      cariosity

**Carin**a: keel, keel-shaped structure.
  carina             ecarinate           subcarinate
  cariniform         multicarinate

**\*Caro, carn**is: flesh.

| | | | |
|---|---|---|---|
| carneous | carnification | carnucula | incarnant |
| carniferrin | carnivorous | excarnation | |

**\*Cartilago, cartilagin**is: gristle, cartilage.

| | | | |
|---|---|---|---|
| cartilage | fibro-cartilage | intercartilaginous | procartilage |

**\*Case**us: cheese.

| | | | |
|---|---|---|---|
| caseate | caseification | casein | caseinogen |

**Caten**a: chain.

| | | |
|---|---|---|
| catenoid | catenulate | concatenate |

**\*Caud**a: tail.

| | | | |
|---|---|---|---|
| acaudal | caudad | caudiduct | nudicaudate |
| bicaudal | caudicle | ecaudate | planicaudate |

**\*Caul**is: stalk.

| | | | |
|---|---|---|---|
| amplexicaul | caules | caulicolous | triplocaulescent |
| anthocaulis | caulescent | nudicaulous | |

**\*Cav**us: hollow.

| | | |
|---|---|---|
| biconcave | cavicorn | excavation |
| cavernosus | concave | precava |

**\*Cede**re, **cess**um: to go, move.

| | | |
|---|---|---|
| abscess | antecedent | retrocession |
| accessorius | intercede | succedaneum |

**\*Cell**a: room, cell.

| | | |
|---|---|---|
| bicellular | cellipetal | heterocellular |
| cell | cellulose | lignocellulose |

**\*Cer**a: wax. **Cerumen, cerumin**is: earwax.

| | | | |
|---|---|---|---|
| adipocere | cerate | ceriferous | ceruminous |
| ceraceous | cere | ceromel | |

**\*Cerebr**um: the brain.

| | | | |
|---|---|---|---|
| archicerebrum | cerebrifugal | decerebrate | pleurocerebral |
| cerebellum | cerebropedal | intracerebral | subcerebellar |

**\*Cerne**re, **cret**um (**cre-**): to separate, sift, distinguish; secrete.

| | | | |
|---|---|---|---|
| discernment | excernant | incretion | secretion |
| discrete | excreta | prosecretin | supersecretion |

**\*Cervix, cervic**is: neck.

| | | | |
|---|---|---|---|
| cervical | cervicodorsal | costicervical | endocervicitis |

**Cib**us: food.

| | | | |
|---|---|---|---|
| cibation | cibomania | cibophobia | postcibal |

**\*Cicatrix, cicatric**is: scar.

| | | | |
|---|---|---|---|
| cicatrices | cicatricose | cicatricula | cicatrize |

**\*Cili**um: eyelid; hairlike process.

| | | | |
|---|---|---|---|
| biciliate | ciliola | intercilium | palpocil |
| cilia | cilograde | nasociliary | superciliary |

**Cing**ere, **cinct**um: to bind about, gird.

cinctoplanular      cincture      cingulum

**Cirr**us (sometimes wrongly spelled **cirrh**us): lock, curl, ringlet.

cirrhobranchiate      cirrocumulus      neurocirrus
cirriped      cirrose      notocirrus

*****Cita**re, **citat**um (**cie**-, **cit**-): to rouse, put in motion, stir up.

excitation      excitor      superexcitation
excitonutrient      resuscitation

*****Claud**ere, **claus**um (**clus**-): to close, shut.

abocclusion      claudent      claustrophobia
circumclusion      claudiconchi      occlusion

**Clav**a: club; a structure thickened at the end.

clavate      clavicornia      subclavate
claviceps      clavola

*****Clav**is: key; collarbone.

clavicle      interclavicular      subclavian
costoclavicular      preclavicular

**Clype**us: shield.

anteclypeus      clypeola      frontoclypeus
clypeiform      clypeus

*****Cole**re, **cult**um: to till, care for; inhabit.

arenicolous      cellicolous      saxicoline
capilliculture      petricola      seroculture
caulicolous      pratincole      subculture

*****Coll**um: neck.

brevicollis      decollation      torticollis
colliform      retrocollic

**Columen, columin**is; **Column**a: column.

column      columella      extracolumellar    intercolumnar

**Coque**re, **coct**um: to cook; ripen, mature.

coctolabile      concoct      dementia praecox
coctostable      decoction      precocial

**Copul**a: a bond, union.

copula      copularium      copulate

*****Cor, cord**is: heart.

cordate      intracordal      obcordate
cordiform      misericord      postcordial

**Cori**um: skin, vascular layer beneath the epidermis.

coriaceous      corium      excoriation

*****Cornu**: horn, hornlike projection.

antecornu      cavicorn      interramicorn      postcornu
bicorn      circumcorneal      longicorn      (tunica) cornea

**Coron**a; **coroll**a: crown.

| corolla | corona | coronet |
| corolliferous | coronary | paracorolla |

**\*Corpus, corpor**is: body.

| bicorporate | corpulent | corpuscle |
| corporeal | corpus alienum | intracorporal |

**\*Cortex, cortic**is: bark, outer layer.

| cortiadrenal | corticipetal | decortication | subcortical |
| cortices | corticotropic | infracortical | transcortical |

**\*Cost**a: rib.

| costoscapular | precostal | subcostal | tricostate |
| intracostal | sternocostal | supracostal |

**\*Cox**a: hip, hipjoint.

| coxae | coxofemoral | coxotuberculosis |
| coxalgia | coxopodite | intercoxal |

**Crepa**re, **crepita**re, **crepitat**um: to rattle, creak, crackle.

| crepitation | crepitus | decrepitate | subcrepitant |

**\*Cresce**re, **cret**um (**cre-**): to increase, grow.

| accretion | concretion | decrement | increment |
| circumcrescent | crescent | excrescence |

**Crus, crur**is: leg, leglike part.

| crura | inguinocrural | tricrural |
| crural | subcrureus |

**Crux, cruc**is: cross.

| cruciate | cruciform | excruciating |

**\*Cuba**re, **cubat**um (**-cumbe**re, **cubit**um): to lie down. **Cubit**us: elbow, forearm.

| antecubital | decubitus | postcubital | succubus |
| brachiocubital | incubation | procumbent | ventricumbent |
| cubitocarpal | incubus | semirecumbent |

**Cune**us: wedge.

| cuneate | intercuneiform | praecuneus |
| cuneus | obcuneate |

**Cupr**um: copper.

| cupremia | cupreous | cupriferous | electrocuprol |

**\*Curre**re, **curs**um: to run.

| concurrent | incurrent | recur |
| excursion | precursive |

**Cuspis, cuspid**is: point, end.

| cuspid | multicuspid | tricuspid |

**\*Cute**re, **cuss**um: to shake, strike.

| concussion | discutient | percussion | succussion |

**\*Cut**is: skin.

| cutaneous | cuticolor | mucocutaneous | transcutaneous |
| cuticle | intracutaneous | subcuticular | |

# D

**Decuss**is: see **Decem,** in numerals list.

**Deglut**ire: to swallow.

| deglutible | deglutition |

**\*Dens, dent**is: tooth.

| bidentate | dentifrice | interdental | subdental |
| dedentition | dentin | labiodental | |
| denticle | edentate | serratodenticulate | |

**\*Dexter, dextr**a, **dextr**um: right (hand or side).

| ambidextrous | dextraural | dextrocular |
| dextrad | dextrin | dextrorse |

**\*Digit**us: finger, toe.

| digit | digitipinnate | imparidigitate |
| digitigrade | digitule | interdigitation |

**\*Dole**re: to feel pain, give pain.

| dolores vagi | dolorific | dolorogenic | indolent |

**\*Dormi**re, **dormit**um: to sleep.

| dormant | dormoron | obdormition | predormitium |

**\*Dors**um: the back, upper part.

| cervicodorsal | dorsigrade | dorsulum | subdorsal |
| dorsad | dorsonasal | mediodorsal | |

**\*Duce**re, **duct**um: to lead, draw.

| abducent | duct | intraduct | preinduction |
| adductor | ductile | levoduction | subduct |
| conductor | ductule | oviduct | superabduction |

**\*Dur**us: hard.

| dura mater | durilignosa | induration |
| duramen | extradural | superdural |

# E

**Ebrietas, ebrietat**is: drunkenness.

| ebriecation | ebrietas | inebriety |

**Ebur, ebor**is: ivory. **Eburne**us: of ivory.

| eburifera | eburnation | eburneola | eburneous |

**Ede**re (**es-**): to eat.

| comestible | edacious | edible | obesity |

**\*Ego**: I, the self.

alter ego         egocentric         egomania         superego

**\*Erra**re, **errat**um: to wander, deviate.

aberration         aberrometer         erratum

**\*Exter, extern**us, **exterior, extrem**us: on the outside, outermost. **Extrinsec**us: from the outside.

exteriorize         exterofection         extremity
externalism         extine            extrinsic
exteroceptive       extremism          extrorse

**Exuvi**ae: that which is shed or cast off, molt.

exuviae            exuvial            exuviate

# F

**\*Face**re, **fact**um (**facie-, fic-, fect-**): to do, make, cause.

artifact        effector        mellifica        petrifaction
calcification   fructification   mucific         rubefacient
dolorific       infection       olfactory

**\*Faci**es (**fici-**): form, figure; face; outer surface.

bifacial        facies          interfacial      superficies
facet           faciolingual     nervus superficialis

**Faex, faec**is: sediment, dregs, excrement.

defecation      feces           feculent

**Falx, falc**is: sickle, pruning-hook.

falcate         falcipedius      falx
falciform       falcula

**\*Fasci**a: band, bundle; a band of tissue investing muscles or organs; a bandage.

extrafascial    fasciation       fasciola
fascia          fasciculus       subfascial

**\*Fatiga**re, **fatigat**um: to grow weary.

defatigation    fatigability     fatigue          indefatigable

**Fauces**: throat.

fauces          faucial          suffocate

**Faun**a: gods of the grove; animals.

avifauna        fauna            faunal

**\*Febr**is: fever.

antefebrile     febricula        febrifugal       postfebrile
febricide       febrifacient     intrafebrile     subfebrile

**Fecund**us: fertile, fruitful. (see **Fet**us).

fecundate       fecundity        superfecundation

**\*Femur, femor**is: thigh, thighbone.
  femoral                 femur                    interfemoral
  femorotibial            ileofemoral
**Fenestr**a: window, opening.
  defenestration     fenestra            fenestrated          fenestrule
**\*Fer**re, **lat**um: to bear, carry, produce.
  ablation           circumferential   Porifera            sublation
  acuminiferous      coniferous        seminiferous        transference
  afferent           efferent          somniferous
**\*Ferr**um: iron.
  ferric                 ferrocalcite             ferrotherapy
  ferriferous            ferrometer               ferruginous
**Fertil**is: fertile.
  fertile            fertility          fertilization        infertile
**\*Ferve**re: to boil, be hot, glow.
  defervescence          ferment                  fervid
  effervescent           fervescence
**Fetor, (fetid**us): stench, offensive odor.
  asafetida              fetid                    fetor
**Fet**us **(fe-)**: a bringing forth, offspring, unborn offspring.
  effete                 feticulture              superfetation
  feticide               fetus
**\*Fibr**a: fiber, filament.
  fiber                  fibrillate               fibrinogen
  fibril                 fibrillose               myofibrillae
**\*Fibul**a: pin, brooch; outer bone of the leg.
  calcaneofibular    fibula             parafibula          tibiofibular
**Fige**re, **fix**um: to fix, fasten, pierce.
  basifixed              fixation                 transfixation
  dorsifixed             fixative
**Filix, filic**is: fern.
  filicifolia        filiciform         filicoid            quercifilix
**\*Fil**um: thread.
  filament           filicauline        filum               unifilar
  filaria            filiform           interfilamentar
  filaricide         filoplume          interfilar
**\*Finde**re, **fiss**um **(fid-)**: to split, cleave.
  contrafissure      fissiparous        multifid            superfissure
  fissilingual       fissipedia         pinnatifid          trifid
  fission            fissure            subfissure
**Fistul**a: reed, pipe; pipelike ulcer.
  fistula            fistulatomy        fistulization       gastric fistula

**Flabell**um: small fan.

| | | | |
|---|---|---|---|
| biflabellate | flabellifoliate | flabelliform | flabellum |

**Flacc**us: flabby, hanging down.

| | |
|---|---|
| flaccid | flaccidity |

\***Flagell**um: whip, scourge; whiplike appendage.

| | | |
|---|---|---|
| biflagellate | flagelliform | flagellum |
| exflagellate | flagellula | hemoflagellate |

**Flamm**a: flame; flame-red.

| | | | |
|---|---|---|---|
| flamiceps | flammula | flamosus | inflammation |

\***Fla**re, **flat**um: to blow, distend with gas.

| | | |
|---|---|---|
| conflation | flatus | insufflate |
| flatulence | inflation | perflation |

\***Flav**us: yellow.

| | | |
|---|---|---|
| flavella | flavin | Flavobacterium |
| flavescens | flavism | subflavous |

\***Flecte**re, **flex**um: to bend, turn.

| | | | |
|---|---|---|---|
| anteflexion | flexor | reflection | semiflexion |
| circumflex | flexure | retroflex | superflexion |
| flexion | | | |

**Flocc**us: lock (of wool), tuft.

| | | |
|---|---|---|
| floccifera | floccose | flocculent |
| floccilation | floccule | seroflocculation |

\***Flos, flor**is: flower, blossom.

| | | | |
|---|---|---|---|
| calyciflorous | floret | geminiflorous | semiflosculus |
| cauliflory | floriculture | inflorescence | |
| efflorescence | florid | passiflora | |

\***Flue**re, (**flux**-), **fluct**um: to flow. **Fluvi**us: river.

| | | | |
|---|---|---|---|
| confluent | effluvium | flux | reflux |
| defluxion | fluviomarine | ossifluence | semifluctuation |
| diffluent | fluvioterrestrial | profluvium | |

\***Foli**um: leaf.

| | | | |
|---|---|---|---|
| angustifoliate | exfoliation | foliole | subfoliar |
| defoliate | foliferous | foliose | unifoliolate |

**Foll**is: bag, bellows.

| | | | |
|---|---|---|---|
| follicle | folliculina | folliculitis | folliculose |

\***Fora**re, **forat**um: to bore, drill.

| | | | |
|---|---|---|---|
| biforate | foraminate | imperforation | postperforatum |
| foramen | foraminiferous | perforation | transforation |

\***Form**a: shape, form.

| | | | |
|---|---|---|---|
| amoebiform | bacciform | ensiform | guttiform |
| arciform | bipenniform | flagelliform | laminiform |

\***Foss**a: something dug, ditch; depression.

| | | |
|---|---|---|
| fossa | fossiliferous | fossula |
| fossil | fossor | infossate |

**\*Frange**re, (**frag**-), **fract**um: to break.
anfractuous (*ambi*-)   effraction        fragment          ossifraga
diffraction              fracture          infraction        refrangible

**\*Frons, frond**is: leaf, leafy branch.
albifrons                frond             frondescence      frondiculus

**\*Frons, front**is: forehead, front.
adfrontal                frontoclypeus     oculofrontal
frontal                  frontomalar       sectifrontes
frontipetal              nasofrontal       subfrontal

**\*Frux, frug**is; **fruct**us: fruit (of the earth).
fructify                 frugilegus        frutescent        suffruticose
fructose                 frugivorous       fruticulose

**\*Fuge**re (**fuga**re): to flee, shun, put to flight.
basifugal                centrifugal       fugacious         vermifugal
calcifuge                febrifuge         nidifugous

**Fulge**re: to shine, flash, glitter.
effulgent                fulgent           fulgurating

**Fulmina**re: to flash like lightning; develop suddenly.
fulminant                fulmination

**\*Funde**re, **fus**um: to pour, melt.
effusion                 infundibulum      perfusion         transfusion
funnel                   infusoriform      suffusion

**\*Fung**us: mushroom, fungus.
fungicide                fungicolous       fungiferous       fungivorous

**Fun**is: rope, cord.
funic                    funicle           funicular         funiform

**\*Furc**a: fork, prong.
bifurcate                furciferous       furculum
furcal                   furcipus          postfurca

**Fuscare**, **fuscat**um: to darken, make dusky.
fuscin                   haemofuscin       infuscate         obfuscation

## G

**\*Gemin**us: twin, paired, born together. **Gemell**i: twins.
bigeminal                gemellipara       geminidens        postgeminum
gemellary                geminate          geminiflorous     tergeminate

**\*Gemm**a: bud, gem.
gemmaceous               gemmiparous       gemmule           subgemmal
gemmation                gemmulation       intergemmal

**Gen**a: cheek.
gena                     genal             postgena

**\*Genu**: knee, kneelike bend or protuberance.
geniculated     genuflection     postgeniculatum   supergenual
genucubital     genupectoral     pregeniculum     supragenual

**\*Genus, gener**is: origin, kind, race; class.
bigeneric     gene     genotype
congenerous     genera     miscegenation
degeneration     generic     propriogenic

**\*Gere**re, **gest**um: to carry, bear.
congestive     gestation     penniger     veliger
decongestive     ingesta     predigestion
egest     palpiger     setigerous

**\*Germen, germin**is: sprout, germ.
germarium     germiculture     germinate     subgerminal
germicide     germifuge     germiparity

**\*Gigne**re, **genit**um: to beget.
congenital     gignimentum     primogenitor     vitelligenous
genitocrural     indigenous     ultimogeniture

**\*Gingiv**a: the gum.
buccogingival     gingivitis     subgingival
gingival     gingivolabial

**Glaber, glabr**is: smooth, hairless.
glabella     glabrate     glabriscala
glabellad     glabrificin     glabrous

**Gladi**us: sword.
gladiate     gladiformis     gladiolus     gladiomanubrial

**\*Glans, gland**is: acorn; gland.
gland     glanders     glandula     glandulose

**\*Glob**us: ball, sphere.
conglobate     globule     hemoglobin
globous     globuliferous     lactoglobulin

**Glomera**re: to wind or gather into a ball. **Glomus, glomer**is: a ball.
conglomerate     glomeruliferous     glomiform     glomus
glomeronephritis     glomerulus     glomospira

**Glum**a: hull, husk.
glumaceous     glumiferous     latiglumis
glume     glumiflorous

**\*Gluten, glutin**is: glue, gelatin(ous).
agglutinative     glutinous     isoagglutination
conglutinant     heteroagglutinin

**\*Grad**i, **gress**um: to step, walk, go.
ciliograde     gradient     progressive     saltigrade
degradation     ingredient     pronograde     tardigrade
digitigrade     intergrade     retrograde

**Gran**um: grain, seed.
granellae  granose  granulite
granellarium  granular

**\*Grav**is: heavy, laden, severe; pregnant.
aggravate  gravitational  ingravescent  primigravida
gravid  gravity  pregravidic

**Grex, greg**is: flock, herd.
aggregate  gregarious  segregation
disaggregation  locogregiform

**Grum**us: a small heap.
grume  grumose  grumous

**Gul**a: throat.
flavigularis  gulamentum  gullet
gula  gular

**Gurgita**re, **gurgitat**um: to flood, engulf, flow, whirl.
gurgitation  ingurgitate  regurgitate

**\*Gusta**re, **gustat**um: to taste.
degustation  gustatism  gustometry
gustation  gustatorius

**Gutt**a: a drop.
gutta  guttation  guttiform  guttulate

**\*Guttur, guttur**is: throat.
guttural  gutturonasal  gutturotetany

## H

**Habe**re, **habit**um: to have, hold.
adhib(endus)  habena  habenula  inhibitory

**\*Habita**re: to inhabit, dwell.
cohabitation  habitat  inhabited

**Habit**us: condition, state, habit, physique.
habit  habituation

**\*Haere**re, **haes**um: to stick, cling.
adhesion  incoherent  nonadherent
cohesion  inherent

**\*Hala**re, **halit**um: to breathe. **Halit**us: breath.
exhalation  halituous  inhalant
halitosis  halitus

**Hallucina**ri, **hallucinat**um: to wander in mind.
hallucination  hallucinotic

**Hallux, halluc**is: the big toe.
hallucal  halluces  hallux  prehallux

**Ham**us: hook.
    hamate              hamulus            rostrohamus
    hamular           pisohamate

**Hauri**re, **haust**um: to draw out, drink.
    exhaustion        haustorium        prehaustorium
    haustellum       haustral

\***Hia**re, **hiat**um: to stand open, yawn, gape. **Hiat**us: an opening, gap, fissure.
    dehiscence        hiatal            indehiscent
    hiant              hiatus

\***Homo, homin**is: man, human being.
    homicidal         hominal          homunculus

\***Hor**a: hour. (Used mainly in abbreviations).
    *hor(a) decub(itus)*    *hor(ae) un(ius) spatio*    *q(uaque) h(ora)*

\***Hort**us: garden.
    horticola      horticulture     hortulanus     hortulia

\***Humer**us: shoulder, upper arm.
    humeral         scapulohumeral     xiphihumeralis
    humerus        subhumeral

\***Humor**: liquid, moisture. **Humid**us: damp, moist.
    humectant      humidity      **humor**        humoral

\***Hum**us: earth, soil.
    humic           humus          posthumous
    humistratus     inhumation

# I

\***I**re, **it**um: to go.
    abient         ambient       comitalia     introitus
    aditus         coition       concomitant    transitory

**Ict**us: stroke, blow.
    ictometer    ictus paralyticus    ictus sanguinis    ictus solis

\***Ili**um: flank, the wide upper portion of the hipbone. **Ile**um: the distal portion of the small intestine.
    ileocecal      ileotransverstomy    iliocaudal    iliotibial
    ileofemoral   iliac            iliolumbar    sacroiliac

**Incus, incud**is. anvil; a small bone of the ear.
    incudal        incudectomy    incudes       incudiform
    incudate

**Indue**re: to put on. **Indusi**um; **Induvi**ae: clothes, garments; enveloping membrane.
    indusiate       indusium        induviate
    indusiform     induviae

**\*Inguen, inguin**is: groin.

exinguinal            inguinal              suprainguinal
ilioinguinal          inguinoscrotal

**\*Intestin**us: internal; intestine.

gastrointestinal      intestival            intestiniform

**Irrita**re, **irritat**um: to excite, stir up.

abirritate            counterirritant       irritability

## J

**Jace**re: to lie, be recumbent.

adjacent        interjacent        subjacent         superjacent

**\*Jace**re, **jact**um, (**jacta**re; **jacul**-): to cause to lie, throw.

dejection             injection             projection
ejaculation           jactation             projicient
ejecta                jaculator             trajectory

**Jejun**us: empty, fasting; dry.

jejunal               jejunectomy           jejunum (intestinum)

**\*Junge**re, (**juge**re), **junct**um: to join. **Jug**um: yoke; a depression or
ridge connecting two structures.

adjunction     disjunction     junctional       subconjunctival
biconjugate    jugal           juncture         subjugal
conjunctive    jugum           quadratojugal

**Jugul**um: the collarbone, neck of throat.

intrajugular          jugular               jugulation           subjugular

## L

**\*Lab**i, **laps**um: to glide, slip, fall. **Laps**us: a slip, a falling.

collapse              labile                relapse
frigolabile           prolapse

**\*Labi**um; **labr**um: lip, lip-like structure.

antelabrum     dentilabial     labial          labioversion
bilabiate      epilabrum       labiatiflorus   labral
cervicolabial  labellum        labiose         prolabium

**\*Lac, lact**is: milk.

ablactation           lactiferous           prelacteal
delactation           lactimorbus           serolactescent
lactase               lactose               superlactation

**Lacera**re, **lacerat**um: to tear to pieces, mangle.

dilacerate            laceration

**Lacini**a: flap, fringe.

lacinia         laciniate       laciniosus       lacinula

**\*Lacrim**a: tear.

delacrimation    lacrimal    lacrimose    prelacrimal
illacrimation    lacrimator    nasolacrimal

**Lacun**a: small pit, gap.

lacuna    lacunose    lacunosorugose    lacunule

**\*Laede**re, **laes**um: to hurt, strike, injure.

collision    elision    lesion

**Laev**us: left.

laevulose    levorotatory    levoversion
levoduction    levotorsion

**\*Lamin**a; **Lamell**a: thin plate, layer.

bilamellar    interlaminate    lamella    laminated
delamination    intralamellar    lamellirostral    laminiplantar

**Lan**a: wool. **Lanugo, lanugin**is: fine hair, down.

lanate    lanolin    lanugo
laniferous    lanuginose

**Lance**a: spear, lance.

lancelet    lancet    sublanceolate
lanceolate    oblanceolate

**Lapis, lapid**is: stone.

lapidicolous    lapidify    lapillus    lapis lunaris

**\*Larv**a: ghost; mask; early stage of some animals when unlike the parent, i.e., "masked."

larvae    larviform    larvivorous
larval    larviparous    larvule

**Late**re: to lie hidden.

delitescence    latebricole    latescent
latebra    latent

**\*Lat**us: wide, broad. **Dilatat**us: expanded.

dilatation    latirostral    m. latissimus
dilator    latiseptate

**\*Latus, later**is: side.

ambilateral    collateral    latericumbent    lateroflexion
bilateral    inferolateral    laterigrade    superolateral

**\*Lava**re, **lot**um (**lue-,lut-**): to wash.

ablutomania    diluent    lavage    lotion
alluvial    dilution    lavation

**Len**is: soft, mild.

leniceps    lenient    lenify    lenitive

**Lens, lent**is: lentil; lens. **Lentigo, lentigin**is; **Lenticul**a: lentil-shaped spot; a freckle.

lenticel    lentigerous    lentigo
lenticonus    lentiginose    lentil
lentiform    lentiglobus    sublenticular

**\*Let(h)um**: death.
lethal                    preterlethal              superlethal
lethiferous               sublethal

**\*Levare, levatum**: to lighten, raise. **Levis**: light.
alleviate                 elevate                   levator                   levitation

**Libet**: it pleases. **Libido, libidinis**: pleasure, desire.
ad libitum                libidinal                 libidinous                libido

**Lien**: spleen.
gastrolienal              lienculus                 perilienal
lienal                    lienorenal

**\*Ligare, ligatum**: to bind, tie. **Ligamentum**: ligament.
bicolligate               intraligamentous          superligamen
colligation               ligation                  ultraligation
deligation                ligature                  vasoligature

**\*Lignum**: wood.
liberoligneous            lignescent                ligniform                 lignivorous
ligneous                  lignification             lignite                   lignocellulose

**Limen, liminis**: lintel, threshold.
elimination               liminal                   subliminal                supraliminal

**Limus**: mud.
limicoline                limicolous                limose                    limosella

**Linea**: line.
collinear                 linellae                  predelineation
linear                    lineolate

**\*Lingua**: tongue. **Ligula**: small tongue, shoe-tongue or latchet; strap.
breviligulata             fissilingual              linguodental              perlingual
cervicolingual            liguliflorous             linguoversion             retrolingual
elinguation               lingula                   longiligula               sublingual

**\*Liquare**: to melt. **Liquescere**: to become fluid.
colliquative              liquefaction              liquidambar
deliquesce                liquid                    liquidity

**\*Locus**: place.
antelocation              localize                  loculus                   trilocular
dislocation               locellus                  prelocomotion
intralocular              loculicidal               translocation

**\*Longus**: long.
elongation                longicorn                 longipennate              longirostrate
longicaudal               longimanous               longiradiate              longitude

**Lorum**: strap, thong. **Lorica**: a corselet of thongs.
loral                     lore                      loricate                  loripes
lorate                    lorica                    lorigera                  supraloral

**\*Lucere**: to shine. **Lux, lucis**: light. **Lucidus**: clear, lucid.
lucid                     luciferin                 luculent                  relucent
lucidity                  lucifugal                 noctilucent               translucent

**\*Lumb**us: loin.

dorsolumbar    lumbago    lumbocostal    supralumbar
intralumbar    lumbar    sacrolumbar

**\*Lumen, lumin**is: light; space between walls of a tubular organ.

bioluminescence    lumen    luminiferous    triboluminescence
intraluminal    luminescence    transillumination

**Lun**a: moon.

lunacy    lunifrons    lunulet
lunate    lunula    semilunar

**Lute**us: orange-yellow.

illutation    luteal    lutein    luteinization

**\*Luxa**re, **luxat**um: to dislocate.

luxation    reluxation    semiluxation    subluxation

**Lymph**a: clear water, liquid; yellowish fluid of the body.
(See Greek **Lymph**a).

## M

**\*Macul**a: spot, stain.

bimaculate    macula    maculation    palpimacula
immaculate    macular    maculose    papillomacular

**\*Magn**us: large, great.

magna-glans    magnicaudate    magnification    magnirostrate

**\*Mal**a: cheek, cheekbone, jaw.

deutomalae    malar    orbitomalar
frontomalar    maloplasty

**Malle**us: hammer, club; one of the small bones of the ear.

ambomalleal    malleoincudal    malleoramate    supramalleolar
extramalleolar    malleolus    malleus

**\*Mal**us: bad, faulty.

malformation    malinterdigitation    malocclusion
malignant    malnutrition    malposition

**\*Mamm**a: breast, the mammary gland, pap.

inframammary    mammectomy    mammilliform
mammal    mammilla    premammary

**\*Mandibul**a (**mande**re: to chew): jaw, bone of lower jaw.

basimandibula    mandible    stylomandibular
ceratomandibular    mandibulopharyngeal    submandibular

**\*Man**us: hand. **Manubri**um: handle.

bimanous    longimanous    maniluvium    quadromanous
dextromanual    maniculated    manubrium

**Margo, margin**is: edge, border.

emarginate    margin    marginirostral
inframarginal    marginalia

**\*Mater, matr**is: mother.

maternal          maternology          matrilineal          pia mater

**\*Matrix, matric**is: a breeding animal; womb; the groundwork in which anything is cast, or develops.

matrical          matrix          matrixitis          sarcomatrix
matrices

**\*Matura**re, **maturat**um: to make ripe. **Matur**us: ripe.

immature          maturant          maturation          premature

**\*Maxill**a: jaw, upper jawbone.

bimaxillary          maxilliped          maxillula          pharyngomaxillary
inframaxillary          maxillodental          nasomaxillary          submaxillary
maxilla          maxillomandibulary

**\*Mea**re: to go, pass. **Meat**us: passage.

hyperpermeable          meatometer          permeate          suprameatal
impermeable          meatus          postmeatal

**\*Medi**us: middle.

admedial          inferomedian          mediate          supermedial
dorsomedian          mediad          mediators
immediate          mediastinum          mediopectoral

**Medull**a: marrow, marrow-like, pith.

extramedullary          medulliadrenal          medulloculture
medullation          medullispinal          medullosuprarenoma

**Mel, mell**is: honey.

diabetes mellitus          melliferous          mellite          mellivora

**Membran**a: membrane.

intramembranous          membrane          membranula

**\*Mens, ment**is: mind.

commentary          mentalia          mentality          mentism
dementia

**Mens**a: table.

commensalism          mensal

**\*Mens**is: month. **Menstru**us: monthly.

bimensal          menses          menstrual          postmenstrua

**\*Ment**um: chin.

hyomental          mentigerous          occipitomental          supramental
labiomental          mentoanterior          submental

**Micturi**re, **micturit**um (**mict**um): to urinate.

emictory          miction          micturition

**Mili**um: millet-seed; white nodula resembling millet seed.

miliaria          miliary

**\*Misce**re, **mixt**um: to mix.

commixtus          immiscible          miscegenation          promiscuous

**\*Mitte**re, **miss**um: to let go, send.

| | | |
|---|---|---|
| dorsicommissure | intromittent | remittent |
| emissary | postcommissure | transmissible |

**Mol**a: millstone. **Molar**is: adapted for grinding.

| | | |
|---|---|---|
| molar | molariform | premolar |

**Mole**s: mass.

| | | |
|---|---|---|
| bimolecular | mole | molecule |

**\*Moll**is: soft. **Molli**re, **mollit**um: to soften. **Molluscu**s: soft.

| | | |
|---|---|---|
| emollient | mollipilose | molluscous |
| mollescent | mollities | Mollusca |

**Monstr**um: a divine portent, omen; malformed fetus.

| | | |
|---|---|---|
| monoaxial monster | monstrucide | monstrum deficiens |
| monstriparity | monstrum abundans | |

**\*Morb**us: disease.

| | | |
|---|---|---|
| morbidity | morbigenous | premorbid |
| morbific | morbilli | |

**\*Mors, mort**is: death. **Mori, mortu**um: to die.

| | | | |
|---|---|---|---|
| abmortal | mortal | mortification | postmortal |
| moribund | mortician | mortinatality | premortal |

**\*Move**re, **mot**um: to move.

| | | | |
|---|---|---|---|
| emotion | motile | motorium | ultromotivity |
| locomotion | motoceptor | oculomotor | vasomotor |

**Mucro, mucron**is: sharp point.

| | | | |
|---|---|---|---|
| mucrones | mucronulate | mucronule | unimucronate |

**\*Muc**us: mucus.

| | | |
|---|---|---|
| mucific | mucocellulose | mucus |
| mucilage | mucopurulent | seromucus |

**\*Mult**us: many.

| | | | |
|---|---|---|---|
| multidentate | multilocular | multiped | multocular |
| multifid | multipara | multituberculate | multungulate |

**\*Mus, mur**is: mouse. **Muscul**us: little mouse; muscle.

| | | |
|---|---|---|
| intermuscular | murine | muscule |
| muridae | musculature | musculocutaneous |

**Musc**a: fly.

| | | |
|---|---|---|
| muscacide | muscicapa | muscivora |
| muscae volitantes | muscid | muscula |

**\*Muta**re, **mutat**um: to change.

| | | | |
|---|---|---|---|
| biomutation | dismutation | mutation | transmutation |
| commutator | mutarotation | permutate | |

# N

**Naev**us: birthmark, mole.

| | | |
|---|---|---|
| nevoid | nevose | nevus depigmentosus |

**\*Nar**is: nostril.

| | | |
|---|---|---|
| internarial | narial | postnarial |
| nares | naricorn | |

**\*(G)nasc**i, **(g)nat**um: to be born.

| | | |
|---|---|---|
| adnate | denatality | natimortality |
| antenatal | innate | postnatal |
| connatal | nascent | pregnant |

**\*Nas**us: nose.

| | | | |
|---|---|---|---|
| nasion | nasorostral | pernasal | subnasal |
| nasolacrimal | nasosinuitis | pharyngonasal | supranasal |

**Necte**re, **nex**um: to bind, join.

| | | |
|---|---|---|
| annectens | connective | nexus |

**\*Nerv**us: sinew; nerve.

| | | |
|---|---|---|
| digitinervate | enervate | laterinerved |
| enervose | innervation | nerve |

**\*Nid**us: nest; the point of origin or development.

| | | |
|---|---|---|
| denidation | nidation | nidifugous |
| innidiation | nidicolous | nidulus |
| intranidal | nidificate | pilonidal |

**\*Niger, nigr**i: black.

| | | |
|---|---|---|
| denigrate | nigripes | nigritude |
| nigrescent | nigrities | seminiger |

**\*Noce**re, **nocit**um: to harm, hurt. **Noxi**us; **Nocu**us: hurtful.

| | | |
|---|---|---|
| innocent | nociassociation | nocuity |
| innocuous | nociceptive | noxious |

**Nod**us: knot

| | | |
|---|---|---|
| internodia | nodulation | nodulose |
| node | noduliferous | trinodal |

**\*Nomen, nomin**is: name, means of knowing.

| | | | |
|---|---|---|---|
| binomial | innominate | multinomial | nomenclature |

**Norm**a: a measure, standard or pattern; regular or normal.

| | | |
|---|---|---|
| abnormal | normolineal | normotonic |
| normal | normosexual | seminormal |
| normoblast | normotensive | subnormal |

**\*Nox, noct**is: night.

| | | |
|---|---|---|
| equinoctial | noctiluca | nocturia |
| noctambulation | noctilucent | |

**\*Nud**us: naked, uncovered.

| | | |
|---|---|---|
| denudate | nudicaudate | nudiflorous |
| nudibranchiate | nudicaul | seminude |

**\*Nutri**re, **nutrit**um: to nourish, feed.

| | | |
|---|---|---|
| excitonutrient | nutriment | subnutrition |
| malnutrition | nutritorium | supernutrition |

**\*Nux, nuc**is: nut. **Nucle**us: little nut, kernel, core.

| | | |
|---|---|---|
| binucleate | nucellus | nucleofugal |
| circumnuclear | nuciferous | nucleolar |
| enucleation | nucivorous | polynucleate |

## O

**\*Ocul**us: eye; bud.

| | | | |
|---|---|---|---|
| binocular | intraocular | ocellated | sinistrocular |
| circumocular | monocule | ocellus | |
| inoculation | multocular | ocular | |

**\*Ole**re: to emit a smell. **Odor**: a smell.

| | | |
|---|---|---|
| malodorous | olfactie | olfactory |
| odoriferous | olfactometer | redolent |

**Ole**um: oil (as suffix, **-ol**).

| | | |
|---|---|---|
| ichthyol | olein | phenol |
| oleaginous | oleotherapy | rhigolene |

**\*Omn**is: all, every.

| | | |
|---|---|---|
| omni hora | omnipotence | omnivorous |

**Opercul**um: cover, lid.

| | | |
|---|---|---|
| operculate | operculigenous | suboperculum |
| operculiform | operculum | |

**\*Orb**is: circle, wheel. **Orbit**a: path, track.

| | | | |
|---|---|---|---|
| antorbital | orbicular | orbitomalar | suborbital |
| circumorbital | orbit | semiorbicular | supraorbital |

**\*Ordo, ordin**is: order, arrangement.

| | | |
|---|---|---|
| incoordination | ordinate | superorder |
| order | ordinatopunctuate | |

**\*Ori**re, **ort**um: to rise, be born. **Origo, origin**is: beginning.

| | | | |
|---|---|---|---|
| aboriginal | abortient | disorientation | origin |
| aborticide | abortion | orientation | |

**\*Os, or**is: mouth, opening. **Orifici**um: making an opening, orifice.

| | | |
|---|---|---|
| aborad | oral | osculum |
| circumoral | orificialist | peroral |
| interosculate | oscitation | preoral |

**\*Os, oss**is: bone.

| | | | |
|---|---|---|---|
| coossify | interosseous | ossicle | ossifluence |
| deossification | osseous | ossification | ossiphone |

**Osti**um: door, small opening.

| | | | |
|---|---|---|---|
| ostiate | ostiolar | ostiole | ostium |

**\*Ov**um: egg, female reproductive cell. **Ovari**um: place for the ova.

| | | |
|---|---|---|
| ovariotomy | oviposit | superovulation |
| ovary | ovisac | synovia |
| oviparous | ovoviviparous | uniovular |

# P

**\*Palat**um: roof of the mouth, palate.

| | | |
|---|---|---|
| maxillopalatal | palatonasal | transpalatine |
| palate | salpingopalatine | vomeropalatine |

**Palli**um: covering, mantle. **Palliat**us: covered, cloaked; eased, mitigated.

| | | | |
|---|---|---|---|
| archipallium | neopallium | palliopeda | sinupalliate |
| integripalliate | palliate | pallium | |

**Palm**a: palm of the hand.

| | | |
|---|---|---|
| palm | palmatifid | palmula |
| palmar | palmatilobate | totipalmate |

**\*Palpar**e, **palpat**um: to stroke, touch. **Palp**us: soft palm of the hand; feeler.

| | | |
|---|---|---|
| impalpable | palpatorium | palpimacula |
| palpacle | palpi | palpocil |
| palpate | palpiger | pedipalp |

**Palpebr**a: eyelid.

| | | | |
|---|---|---|---|
| interpalpebral | palpebra | palpebral | palpebration |

**Palpita**re, **palpitat**um: to quiver, throb.

| | |
|---|---|
| palpitant | palpitation |

**Papul**a: pimple, small elevation. **Papill**a: nipple.

| | | | |
|---|---|---|---|
| epapillate | papilla | papilliform | papulae |
| maculopapular | papillary | papillomacular | papuliferous |

**\*Parer**e, **part**um: to bring forth, give birth to. **Parturi**re, **parturit**um: to be in labor of giving birth to.

| | | | |
|---|---|---|---|
| antepartum | gemmiparous | parturifacient | primapara |
| biparous | muciparous | parturition | puerperium |
| fissiparity | nonparous | postpartum | |

**\*Paries, pariet**is: wall (of an organ or cavity).

| | | | |
|---|---|---|---|
| intraparietal | occipitoparietal | parietal | squamoparietal |
| mastoparietal | paries | parietotemporal | subparietal |

**\*Pars, part**is: part. **Parti**re, **partit**um: to divide.

| | | |
|---|---|---|
| part | partition | pluripartite |
| partite | pedatipartite | septempartite |

**Patell**a: a small pan; kneepan.

| | | | |
|---|---|---|---|
| infrapatellar | patelliform | prepatellar | retropatellar |
| patellar | | | |

**\*Pate**re: to spread open. **Patul**us: spreading widely.

| | | |
|---|---|---|
| patency | patulous | repatency |
| patulent | prepatent | semipatulous |

**Pecten, pectin**is: comb.

| | | |
|---|---|---|
| bipectinate | pectinate | pinnatopectinate |
| pecten | pectinellae | |

**\*Pect**us, **pector**is: breast, chest.

| | | |
|---|---|---|
| angina pectoris | mediopectoral | pectoriloquy |
| expectorate | pectoral | subpectoral |

**\*Pelle**re, **puls**um: to push, impel, strike, beat.

| | | | |
|---|---|---|---|
| compulsion | lateropulsion | pulse | repellent |
| interpellant | propulsion | pulsellum | retropulsion |

**\*Pell**is: skin.

| | | |
|---|---|---|
| appellous | pellibranchiate | pelliculate |
| pellagra | pellicle | |

**\*Pelv**is: basin, basin-shaped cavity.

| | | | |
|---|---|---|---|
| intrapelvic | pelvirectal | pelvis | pelvisection |

**\*Pende**re, **pens**um: to hang. **Appendix, appendic**is: something "hung to," appendage; appendix.

| | | |
|---|---|---|
| appendage | appendiculate | suspensory |
| appendicitis | pendulous | |

**Pen**is: tail; the male organ of copulation.

| | | |
|---|---|---|
| penial | penicillin | penis |
| penicillate | penicillus | |

**\*Penn**a: feather, plume, wing; fin. (see **Pinn**a).

| | | |
|---|---|---|
| brevipennate | longipennate | penniform |
| demipenniform | penniferous | semipennate |

**\*Pes, ped**is: foot. **Petiol**us: little foot; stalk, stem. **Pedicul**us: little foot; stem; louse.

| | | | |
|---|---|---|---|
| biped | pedicle | pedicure | pinnatiped |
| breviped | pedicular | peduncle | quadruped |
| carpopedal | pediculicide | petiolate | subpeduncular |
| interpediculate | pediculofrontal | petiole | subpetiolate |
| longipes | pediculosis | petiolule | talipes |
| pedatilobed | | | |

**\*Pete**re, **petit**um: to seek.

| | | |
|---|---|---|
| acropetal | basipetal | impetigo |
| appetite | centripetal | rectipetality |

**Pigment**um: paint, pigment. **Pinge**re, **pict**um: to paint.

| | | |
|---|---|---|
| depigmented | multipictus | pigmentatus |
| impictus | pigment | superpigmentation |

**Pil**a: ball.

| | | |
|---|---|---|
| pill | pilule | stenopilus |
| pilular | pilulifera | |

**Pile**us: cap.
    callipileum        pileolus            pileum
    pileated         pileorhiza

**\*Pil**us: hair.
    caterpillar        piliation         pilonidal
    depilate         pilifer           pilose
    horripilation     pilomotor       pilosebaceous

**\*Pinn**a: feather, wing; fin. (see **Penn**a).
    bipinnatisect   paripinnate   pinnatilobate   pinnula
    digitipinnate   pinnatifid     pinnatiped

**\*Pisc**is: fish.
    pisces         pisciform        pisculent
    pisciculture    piscivorous

**Pistill**um: small club; pestle; seed-bearing organ of a flower.
    pistil         pistillate      pistillidium

**Pituit**a: phlegm, mucus.
    dyspituitarism   pituitary      prepituitary
    hypopituitarism  pitutrin

**\*Plant**a: a sprout or cutting; sole of the foot.
    calcaneoplantar  extraplantar  laminiplantar  plantula
    digitoplantar   implantation  plantigrade  scutelliplantar

**\*Plan**us: flat, level.
    applanate    planicaudate  planocellular  planum
    peneplane    planirostrate  planula    uniplanar

**\*Plecte**re, **plex**um: to plait, interweave. (see **Amplex**us).
    amplectant   complex    plexiform    subplexal
    cerviciplex   plexeoblastus  plexus

**\*Plica**re, **plicat**um: to fold. **-ple**: fold.
    centuple    duplicodentate  plicidentin  replicatile
    complicant   plication   quadruplicate  sextuple

**\*Plum**a: feather.
    deplumation   plumage    plumiped    plumule
    filoplume    plumicome  plumose

**Plumb**um: lead.
    plumbiferous     plumbism     plumbotherapy

**Plus, plur**is: more.
    pluriaxial    plurilocular   pluripotent
    pluriceptor   plurineuclear

**Pollen, pollin**is: fine flour; the mass of microspores in seed plants.
    pollen       polliniferous   pollinosis
    pollinate    pollinium

**Pollex, pollic**is: thumb.
    pollex valgus   pollical    pollices    prepollex

**Pom**um: fruit, apple.

pome pomiculture pomifera

**\*Pone**re, **posit**um: to place, put.

anteposition decompose posture transposition
component ovipositor retroposed

**Pons, pont**is: bridge; a slip of tissue connecting two parts of an organ.

pons cerebelli ponticular pontimeter subpontine
pontibrachium ponticulus postpontile

**Poples, poplit**is: the hollow of the knee.

poples poplitaeus popliteal

**Port**a: gate, entrance.

portacaval porta hepatis portal portella

**\*Porta**re, **portat**um: to carry.

portable portagion portligature
portacid portcaustic transport

**\*Pota**re, **potat**um: to drink. **Potio, potion**is: drink, potion.

compotation potable potion
guttipotor potator

**\*Potens, potent**is: having power, potent.

equipotential pluripotent prepotency
impotence potentiation totipotent

**Prandi**um: luncheon, meal.

postprandial prandial preprandial

**\*Preme**re, **press**um: to press.

adpressed decompression repression
compress depressor suppression

**Prol**es: offspring.

proliferate prolific proligerous

**Pron**us: inclined, bending forward.

pronation pronator pronograde semipronation

**Propri**us: its own, proper.

proprietary proprioceptor propriodentium propriogenic

**Pruri**re, **prurit**um: to itch. **Prurigo, prurigin**is: an itching.

prurient pruriginous prurigo pruritic

**\*Pubes, puber**is: adult; pubic bone.

impuberism puberty pubofemoral suprapubic
postpuberal pubescence retropubic

**\*Pulmo, pulmon**is: lung.

extrapulmonary pulmobranchia pulmotor
intrapulmonary pulmonary renopulmonary
gastropulmonary pulmones subpulmonary

**Punge**re, **punct**um: to prick. **Punct**um: a point.

acupuncture  punctiform  pungent

punctate  punctum  renipuncture

\***Pup**a: doll, child; stage after larva of insects. **Pupill**a: pupil of the eye.

interpupillary  prepupa  pupate  pupillomotor

opticopupillary  puparium  pupillary  pupiparous

\***Pus, pur**is: pus.

mucopurulent  purulence  suppurate

presuppurative  seropurulent

**Pustul**a: blister, pimple.

papulopustular  pustulation  pustule  pustulocrustaceous

**Putre**re: to be rotten.

putrefactive  putrescent  putrid

# Q

**Quadra**re, **quadrat**um: to make four-cornered, to square.

palatoquadrate  quadrate  quadrature

quadrant  quadratojugal

**Quate**re, **quass**um: to shake, strike. (see **Cute**re).

concussion  percussion  quassation  succussation

# R

\***Rabe**re: to rage, be mad. **Rabid**us: mad, raging. **Rabi**es: rage, madness.

antirabic  rabid  rabific

rabicidal  rabies

**Racem**us: bunch, cluster (as of grapes).

racemation  racemiferous  racemule

raceme  racemose

\***Rade**re, **ras**um: to scrape, scratch. **Radul**a: scraper.

abradant  erasion  rasorial

abrasive  radula  rastellum

corrasion  radulate  rasura

\***Radi**us: rod, spoke, ray, beam; bone on outer side of forearm.

dorsoradial  octoradiate  radiology  radioulnar

equibiradiate  postradiation  radiomutation  radium

irradiation  radial  radiotherapy

\***Radix, radic**is: root.

eradicate  radiciflorous  radicula

radicel  radiciform  radiculitis

radices  radicivorous  radiculomedullary

**\*Ram**us: branch.

| biramous | ramification | ramisection | ramulose |
| postramus | ramiflorous | ramous | ramulus |
| ramicorn | ramiform | ramuliferous | |

**\*Rege**re, **rect**um: to keep straight. **Rect**us: right, straight. **Rect**um (**intestinum**): the distal part of the large intestine.

| arrector | intrarectal | rectipetality | rectum |
| corrigent | perirectal | rectitis | regimen |
| erectile | rectification | rectovesical | subrectal |
| inanorectal | rectilineal | | |

**\*Ren, ren**is: kidney.

| adrenalin | prerenal | reniportal | suprarenogenic |
| circumrenal | renal | renipuncture | |
| intrarenal | reniculus | renogastric | |

**\*Repe**re, **rept**um; **Repta**re, **reptat**um: to crawl, creep.

| repent | reptant | reptile | reptilia |

**Rete, ret**is: net, network. **Retin**a: the innermost coat of the posterior part of the eyeball.

| cilioretinal | reticulated | reticulum | subretinal |
| intraretinal | reticulocyte | retina | |
| retial | reticulose | retinerved | |

**Rigor**: stiffness; cold.

| rigidity | rigor mortis | rigor nervorum | rigorous |

**Rim**a: crack, chink, fissure.

| rima | rimicolous | rimulose |
| rimal | rimose | |

**\*Rode**re, **ros**um: to gnaw.

| corrosive | rodent | rosorial |
| erosion | rodenticide | |

**Ros**a: a rose; red skin eruption, rash.

| rosacea | rosellate | rosular |
| rosaceous | roseola | |

**\*Rostr**um: beak, snout.

| angustirostrate | hamirostrate | planirostrate | rostrum |
| fissirostral | latirostral | rostellum | subrostral |

**\*Rot**a: wheel. **Rota**re, **rotat**um: to cause to go around.

| birotulate | rotator | rotuliform |
| levorotation | rotifer | |

**\*Ruber, rubr**is: red. **Rubigo, rubigin**is: rust.

| bilirubin | rubefacient | rubiginous |
| erubescent | rubella | rubor |
| pseudorubella | rubeola | rubricauda |

**\*Rug**a: wrinkle, crease, fold.

| corrugator | rugae | rugulose |
| lacunosorugose | rugose | |

**Rumen, rumin**is: gullet, throat. **Ruminar**e: to chew the cud.

| rumen | ruminant | ruminatia | ruminator |

**\*Rumpe**re, **rupt**um: to break, burst.

| abruption | eruption | ruptile |
| erumpent | interruptive | rupture |

## S

**\*Sacc**us: bag, sac, pouch.

| ovisac | sacciform | sacculus |
| sacciferous | sacculation | |

**\*Sacer, sacr**i: sacred, holy; bone forming the back of the pelvis.

| lumbosacral | postsacral | sacroiliac | vertebrosacral |
| (os) sacrum | sacriplex | sacrospinal | |

**\*Saep**ire, **saept**um: to enclose, hedge off, separate.

| dissepiment | multiseptate | septulum | supraseptal |
| interseptal | septomarginal | septum | |

**Sagitt**a: arrow; suture between two bones of the skull.

| sagittal | sagittifolia | semisagittate |
| sagittarius | sagittocyst | |

**\*Sal, sal**is: salt.

| desalination | saliferous | saline |
| salia effervescentia | salifiable | salinometer |

**\*Sali**re, **salt**um (**sult**um): to leap, jump. **Salta**re, **saltat**um: to dance.

| dissilient | resilium | saltatorial |
| insultus hystericus | salientia | saltigrade |
| resilient | saltation | transilient |

**\*Saliv**a: saliva.

| insalivate | salivary | salivator | venomosalivary |

**Salus, salut**is: health, safety. **Salubr**is: healthful, wholesome.

| salubrious | salutarium | salutary | salutiferous |

**\*Sana**re, **sanat**um: to heal, cure. **San**us: sound, healthy, well.

| fucosan | sanative | sanicult | sanity |
| insanity | sanatorium | sanitation | |

**\*Sanguis, sanguin**is: blood.

| consanguinity | sanguification | sanguirenal |
| exsanguination | sanguinolent | sanguivorous |
| sanguicolous | sanguinopurulent | serosanguineous |

**Sani**es: bloody matter, serum and blood.

| sanies | saniopurulent | sanious | sanioserous |

**Sapo, sapon**is: soap.

| | | |
|---|---|---|
| sapolanolin | saponaceous | saponification |

**\*Sax**um: rock, stone.

| | | | |
|---|---|---|---|
| saxatile | saxicavous | saxicolous | saxifrage |

**Scabi**es: roughness, scurf, itch. **Scaber**: rough.

| | | |
|---|---|---|
| scabicide | scabiophobia | scabrities |
| scabies | scabrate | scabrous |

**Scalpr**um: knife.

| | | |
|---|---|---|
| scalpel | scalpriform | scalprum |

**Scande**re, **scans**um: to climb.

| | | | |
|---|---|---|---|
| ascendent | descendent | scandent | scansorial |

**\*Scapul**a: shoulder, shoulder-blade.

| | | | |
|---|---|---|---|
| cervicoscapular | infrascapular | scapulalgia | suprascapular |
| costoscapular | interscapilium | scapulectomy | |
| humeroscapular | scapula | scapuloclavicular | |

**\*Scinde**re, **sciss**um: to cut, split.

| | | | |
|---|---|---|---|
| abscission | discission | scissilabra | scissiparity |
| circumscissile | exscind | scission | scissura |

**\*Sci**re, **scit**um: to know.

| | | |
|---|---|---|
| coconsciousness | preconscious | subconsciousness |
| conscious | prescience | |

**Scop**a: twigs, broom of twigs; brush.

| | | |
|---|---|---|
| scopate | scopula | scopulite |
| scopiferous | scopuliform | |

**\*Scribe**re, **script**um: to write, draw.

| | | |
|---|---|---|
| circumscribe | scribomania | superscription |
| prescribe | subscription | |

**Scrob**is: ditch; furrowed or pitted.

| | | |
|---|---|---|
| scrobe | scrobicula | scrobiculate |

**Scrof**a: a breeding sow; tuberculosis of lymphatic glands.

| | | | |
|---|---|---|---|
| scrofula | scrofuloderma | scrofulophyma | scrofulotuberculous |

**Scrot**um: bag; pouch of skin containing male sex glands.

| | | |
|---|---|---|
| intrascrotal | scrotitis | scrotum |
| scrotal | scrotocele | |

**Scut**um: shield, plate; scale, flake.

| | | | |
|---|---|---|---|
| exscutellate | scutellation | scutellum | scutiped |
| scute | scutelliplantar | scutiform | scutum |

**\*Seb**um: grease, fatty secretion.

| | | |
|---|---|---|
| pilosebaceous | sebific | seborrhea |
| sebiferous | sebiparous | sebum |

**\*Seca**re, **sect**um: to cut. **Insect**um: insect. **Segment**um: part, segment.

| | | | |
|---|---|---|---|
| bipinnatisect | insecticide | ramisection | segmentation |
| bisect | insectivore | resection | transection |
| cosecant | intersegmentalia | secant | venesection |
| dissect | intrasegmental | sectile | vivisect |
| insectarium | prosector | | |

**\*Sede**re, **sess**um: to sit. **Sedar**e, **sedat**um: to settle, calm.

| | | |
|---|---|---|
| insessorial | sedative | sessile |
| insidious | sedentary | subsessile |
| obsession | sediment | supersedent |

**\*Semen, semin**is: seed.

| | | |
|---|---|---|
| disseminated | semen | seminivorous |
| inseminate | seminiferous | seminuria |

**Semper**: always.

| | | | |
|---|---|---|---|
| semperflorens | sempervirens | sempervivum | sempiternal |

**Senex, sen**is: old man.

| | | |
|---|---|---|
| presenescence | presenium | senescent | senile |

**\*Senti**re, **sens**um: to sense, feel, perceive.

| | | | |
|---|---|---|---|
| hypersensitive | sensilla | sensorium | supersensory |
| sensation | sensimeter | sentient | |
| sensigenous | sensomobile | sentisection | |

**Sepal**um: leaf of a calyx.

| | | |
|---|---|---|
| rubrisepalum | sepaline | trisepalous |
| sepal | stenosepalous | |

**Sequ**i, **secut**um: to follow.

| | | | |
|---|---|---|---|
| consequent | secutor | sequela | sequence |

**\*Sere**re, **sert**um: to join, connect. **Seri**es: row, orderly arrangement. **Seriat**um: arranged in regular order.

| | | |
|---|---|---|
| curviserial | serial | seriations |
| exserted | seriate | seriatopora |
| pluriserial | seriatim | series |

**\*Serpe**re: to creep. **Serpigo, serpigin**is: a creeping eruption.

| | | | |
|---|---|---|---|
| serpent | serpenticola | serpiginous | serpulite |
| serpentaria | serpentine | serpigo | |

**\*Serr**a: saw, saw-like notches.

| | | | |
|---|---|---|---|
| serranoid | serratifolius | serratirostral | serriped |
| serrated | serration | serratodenticulate | serrulate |

**\*Ser**um: watery fluid, blood serum.

| | | |
|---|---|---|
| antiserum | serolactescent | serosity |
| intraserous | seromucous | serum |
| seroculture | seropurulent | subserous |
| serofibrinous | serosanguineous | |

**Sesqui**: one-half more, one and one-half.
| | | |
|---|---|---|
| sesquibasic | sesquichloride | sesquipedal |
| sesquicarbonate | sesquihora | |

**\*Seta**: bristle.
| | | | |
|---|---|---|---|
| equisetum | setiferous | setirostral | ultrasetaceous |
| setaceous | setigerous | setula | |

**Sexus**: sex.
| | | | |
|---|---|---|---|
| ambisexual | bisexual | homosexuality | sexology |
| asexual | heterosexual | sex | unisexual |

**\*Siccus**: dry.
| | | |
|---|---|---|
| desiccate | exsiccative | siccoles |
| electrodesiccation | siccolabile | siccostabile |

**Signum**: mark, sign, indication. **Sigillum**: small mark; seal.
| | | |
|---|---|---|
| sigil | sign | signature |
| sigillate | signa (s. or sig.) | signiphora |

**\*Silex, silicis**: flint; dust containing silicon dioxide.
| | | | |
|---|---|---|---|
| silex | silicious | silicole | silicotic |
| siliciferous | silicoalkaline | silicosis | silicotuberculosis |

**Siliqua**: pod.
| | | |
|---|---|---|
| silicle | silique | siliquose |
| silicular | siliquiform | |

**Singultus**: hiccup.
| | | |
|---|---|---|
| singultation | singultous | singultus |

**\*Sinister, sinistri**: left, on the left.
| | | | |
|---|---|---|---|
| ambisinistrous | sinistraural | sinistrodextral | sinistrorse |
| sinistrad | sinistrocular | sinistromanual | |

**\*Sinus**: curve, bent surface; cavity or recess.
| | | | |
|---|---|---|---|
| sinospiral | sinuous | sinus | sinusotomy |
| sinoventricular | sinupalliate | sinusoid | |

**\*Sol, solis**: sun.
| | | | |
|---|---|---|---|
| insolation | solarium | solar plexus | solstice |
| solar | solarization | sol-lunar | |

**Solvere, solutum**: to loosen, dissolve.
| | | | |
|---|---|---|---|
| dissolvent | soluble | solution | solvent |

**\*Somnus**: sleep.
| | | | |
|---|---|---|---|
| insomnia | somnambulism | somnifacient | somnolence |
| semisomnus | somnarium | somniloquence | |

**\*Sonare, sonatum**: to make a sound. **Sonus**: sound.
| | | | |
|---|---|---|---|
| consonation | multisonous | sonometer | transonance |
| dissonant | resonance | sonorous | ultrasonics |
| magnisonant | soniferous | supersonic | |

**\*Sopor, soporis**: deep sleep.
| | | | |
|---|---|---|---|
| sopor | soporiferous | soporific | soporous |

**\*Sorbe**re, **sorpt**um: to suck in.

| absorbent | resorption | sorbefacient |
| adsorption | sanguisorba | sorbile |

**\*Sparge**re, **spars**um: to scatter.

| aspergilliosis | aspersorium | dispersity | interspersion |
| aspergillus | dispersion | inspersion | |

**Spati**um: space.

| interspace | spatial | spatiotemporal | spatium |

**\*Spece**re, **spect**um: to see, look at. **Specta**re: to look at.

| inspection | specillum | spectrum | transpicuous |
| introspect | specimen | spectroscope | |
| retrospection | spectacled | speculum | |

**\*Speci**es: sight, view, appearance; form, kind.

| interspecific | speciation | species | specific |
| specialist | | | |

**Spic**a: point, spike; ear of corn or wheat.

| interspicular | spicate | spicule | spiculiform |
| spica | spicose | spiculiferous | |

**\*Spin**a: thorn; spine.

| cerebrospinal | juxtaspinal | spiniferous | spinule |
| infraspinous | spina | spinifugal | tectospinal |
| intraspinal | spinescent | spinocortical | |

**\*Spira**re, **spirat**um: to breathe, blow. **Spiracul**um: breathing-hole. **Suspiri**um: deep breath, sigh.

| aspiration | irrespirable | spiracle | suspirious |
| expiration | perspiration | spiraculate | |
| inspiratory | respiratory | spirometer | |

**Sput**um: spit.

| consputa | sputamentum | sputum |

**\*Squam**a: scale, flake, thin plate.

| desquamation | squamella | squamosa |
| esquamate | squamocellular | squamula |
| squama | squamoparietal | squamulose |

**\*Stamen, stamin**is: thread, fiber; male part of flower.

| instaminate | stamen | staminigerous |
| multistaminate | staminiferous | staminodium |

**Stapes, staped**is: a stirrup; innermost ossicle of the ear.

| extrastapedial | mediostapedial | stapedius | stapes |

**\*Sta**re, **stat**um: to stand.

| aerostat | equidistant | interstice | substitution |
| anteprostate | frigostabile | obstetrics | transubstantiation |
| distal | instability | status | |

**Stell**a: star.
constellation      stellectomy      stellular
stellate      stelliform

**Stercus, stercor**is: fecal matter, dung.
stercoraceous      stercoremia      stercorolith
stercoral      stercoricolous

*****Sterne**re, **strat**um: to spread out, lay out.
humistratus    straticulate    stratigraphy    substratum
interstratify    stratification    stratocumulus
prostration    stratiform    stratum

**Sternuta**re: to sneeze.
sternutation      sternutator      sternutatory

*****Still**a: a drop.
auristillae    instillation    stillicidium    stilligout
distillation    stillatim    stilliform

**Stil**us: pointed instrument for writing; pricker.
Incorrectly **styl-** in stylate, stylet, stylifer; (see Greek **Styl**os).

*****Stimul**us: a goad, prick. **Stimula**re: to goad, excite.
contrastimulism    stimulose    vasostimulant
stimulation    stimulus

**Stipes, stipit**is: log, stem, branch; stalk.
exstipulate    stipe    stipitiform    stipule
labiostipes    stipellate    stipular

**Stirps, stirp**is: stock, stem; lineage
extirpate    inextirpable    stirpiculture    stirps

*****Stri**a: furrow, groove, streak.
corpus striatum    striae    striocellular    striopunctuate
corticostriate    striated    striola    striospinoneural

**Stride**re: to cry; to make a harsh sound.
strident    stridor dentium    stridulous
stridor    stridulate

**Strig**a: ridge, furrow; bristle.
striga      strigillose      strigose

*****Stringe**re, **strict**um: to draw tight, press together.
astriction    constrictor    perstriction    stricturoscope
astringent    infraconstrictor    stricture    subastringent

*****Strue**re, **struct**um: to arrange, construct, build up. **Strum**a: something
heaped up; tumor; goiter.
antistrumous    obstruction    struma    strumiprivous
constructive    obstrurent    strumiferous    strumulose
deobstruent    structure    strumiform    strumose
instrument

**Stupe**re: to be struck senseless, stupefied.

| | | | |
|---|---|---|---|
| stupefacient | stupemania | stupor | stuporous |

**Suber**: cork-oak, cork.

| | | |
|---|---|---|
| suber | suberin | suberose |
| suberiferous | suberization | |

*****Succ**us: juice, fluid.

| | | |
|---|---|---|
| gastrosuccorrhea | succagogue | succulent |
| insuccation | succiferous | succus |

*****Suda**re: to sweat. **Sudor, sudor**is: sweat.

| | | |
|---|---|---|
| antisudoral | sudamina | sudor | sudoriparous |
| exudation | sudatorium | sudorific | transudate |

*****Sulc**us: furrow, groove.

| | | | |
|---|---|---|---|
| costal sulci | semisulcus | sulcate | sulculus |
| multisulcate | subsulcus | sulciform | sulcus |

*****Supin**us: bending backwards, supine, lying on back.

| | | |
|---|---|---|
| resupinate | supination | supine |
| semisupination | supinator | |

*****Sutur**a: a sewing, suture, seam.

| | | |
|---|---|---|
| resuture | sutural | suture |
| sutura dentata | suturation | suturiform |

## T

*****Tabes**: a wasting away.

| | | | |
|---|---|---|---|
| antitabetic | tabes | tabetic | tabid |
| contabescence | tabescent | tabetiform | tabification |

*****Tal**us: ankle, ankle-bone.

| | | | |
|---|---|---|---|
| taligrade | talipomanus | talocrural | talotibial |
| talipes | talocalcanean | talofibular | talus |

*****Tange**re (**tag**-) **tact**um: to touch.

| | | |
|---|---|---|
| contact | tactor | tactual |
| contagious | tactile | tangent |
| contiguous | tactometer | tangoreceptor |

*****Tard**us: slow.

| | | | |
|---|---|---|---|
| retardation | tardigrade | tardive | tardivola |

*****Tege**re, **tect**um: to cover.

| | | |
|---|---|---|
| detection | protegulum | tectospinal | tegula |
| integument | subintegumental | tectum | tegument |
| protection | tectorium | tegmen | |

**Tellus, tellur**is: the earth.

| | | | |
|---|---|---|---|
| tellurian | tellurism | tellurite | tellurium |

**Tempera**re, **temperat**um: to mix, moderate.

| | | |
|---|---|---|
| distemper | temperament | temperature |
| intemperant | temperantia | |

**\*Tempor**a: the temples.

| | | | |
|---|---|---|---|
| bitemporal | occipitotemporal | temporal | transtemporal |
| infratemporal | subtemporal | temporofacial | |
| meditemporal | supertemporal | temporomalar | |

**\*Tempus, tempor**is: time.

| | | |
|---|---|---|
| contemporaneous | temporal | tempostabile |
| tempolabile | temporary | |

**\*Tende**re, **tent**um, **tens**um: to stretch.

| | | | |
|---|---|---|---|
| extensor | subtentorial | tendon | tension |
| hypertension | superdistension | tensibile | tensor |
| hypotensive | tendinosuture | tensiometer | tentorium |
| semitendinosus | tendinous | | |

**\*Tene**re, **tent**um: to hold, keep. **Tenacul**um: a means of holding.

| | | | |
|---|---|---|---|
| abstention | retention | sustentacular | tenacity |
| incontinence | retinaculum | tenacious | tenaculum |

**\*Tenta**re, **tentat**um: to try, test; feel, touch.

| | | |
|---|---|---|
| intertentacular | tentacle | tentative |
| multitentaculate | tentation | |

**Tenu**is: stretched out, slender, thin; weak.

| | | |
|---|---|---|
| attenuate | extenuator | tenuispina |
| attenuation | tenuirostral | |

**\*Tere**re, **trit**um: to rub (off), chafe; cleanse.

| | | | |
|---|---|---|---|
| attrition | detritus | lithotrity | triturate |
| detrition | electrolithotrity | tritor | |

**\*Terg**um: the back.

| | | | |
|---|---|---|---|
| tergal | tergite | tergolateral | tergum |
| tergiferous | tergiversate | tergopleural | |

**Termin**us: boundary, end, limit.

| | | |
|---|---|---|
| abterminal | coterminous | exterminate |
| atterminal | determinant | |

**\*Terr**a: earth.

| | | |
|---|---|---|
| fluvioterrestrial | terra alba | terraqueous |
| subterranean | terrane | terricolous |

**Test**is: witness; testicle.

| | | | |
|---|---|---|---|
| ovotestis | testicle | testiculate | testis |
| testibrachial | testicond | testimonial | |

**\*Tibi**a: pipe, flute; the shinbone, the inner and larger bone of the lower leg.

| | | | |
|---|---|---|---|
| femorotibial | pretibial | tibiotarsal | talotibial |
| posttibial | tibia | tibiocalcanean | |

**Tonsill**a: tonsil.

| | | | |
|---|---|---|---|
| infratonsillar | supratonsillar | tonsillitis | tonsillopathy |
| peritonsillar | tonsil | tonsillolith | tonsilloprive |

**Torpe**re: to be stiff, numb.

| torpent | torpidity | torporific |
|---|---|---|
| torpid | torpor | |

**\*Torque**re, **tort**um, **tors**um: to twist, turn.

| abtorsion | extorsion | torsion | torticollis |
|---|---|---|---|
| acutorsion | intorsion | torsive | torticone |
| contorsions | sinistrotorsion | torsiversion | tortuous |
| detorsion | torquate | torsoclusion | tubatorsion |
| distortion | torque | | |

**Tor**us: swelling; protuberance.

| torose | torulose | torus (palatinus) |
|---|---|---|

**Tot**us: all, entire.

| totiety | totipalmate | totipotent |
|---|---|---|

**Trabs, trab**is: beam, timber; band, bar.

| intertrabecula | trabeated | trabecula |
|---|---|---|

**\*Trahe**re, **tract**um: to draw.

| abstraction | contracture | protractor | tractellum |
|---|---|---|---|
| attrahent | extract | retractor | traction |
| contractile | retrahens | tract | |

**\*Treme**re: to tremble, shake, quiver.

| delirium tremens | tremolabile | tremulor |
|---|---|---|
| tremograph | tremor | tremulous |

**\*Trude**re, **trus**um: to thrust, push.

| contrude | extrudoclusion | protrusible | trusion |
|---|---|---|---|
| detrusor | intrusion | retrusion | |

**\*Tub**a; **Tub**us; tube, pipe.

| extubation | pertubation | tubiform | tubuliflorous |
|---|---|---|---|
| intubate | tuba | tubovaginal | tubulosaccular |
| intubator | tubatorsion | tubule | |

**\*Tuber, tuber**is: hump, knob, swelling; projection.

| multituberculy | tuber | tuberculum |
|---|---|---|
| protuberance | tuberculate | tuberiferous |
| subtuberal | tuberculocide | tuberosity |

**\*Tume**re: to swell.

| detumescence | tumefacient | tumid |
|---|---|---|
| intumescence | tumentia | tumor |

**\*Tunde**re, **tus**um: to beat, strike.

| contusion | obtuse | obtusipennate | retuse |
|---|---|---|---|
| obtundent | obtusilingual | pertusate | |

**Tunic**a: blouse, tunic; covering.

| tunic | tunicate | tunicle |
|---|---|---|

**\*Turba**re, **turbat**um: to stir, disturb. **Turbid**us: muddy. **Turbo, turbin**is: whirlwind, whirling; top-like (bone of the nose); spiral.

| | | | |
|---|---|---|---|
| maxilloturbinal | turbid | turbidity | turbine |
| nasoturbinal | turbidimetry | turbinate | turbinectomy |

**\*Turge**re: to swell out.

| | | |
|---|---|---|
| turgescent | turgidity | turgometer |
| turgid | turgidization | turgor |

**Turr**is: tower.

| | | |
|---|---|---|
| turreted | turriculate | turritopsis |
| turricephaly | turriform | |

**\*Tuss**is: cough.

| | | | |
|---|---|---|---|
| antitussive | pertussis | tussicula | tussive |
| contratussin | posttussis | tussis | |

# U

**\*Ulcus, ulcer**is: open sore, ulcer.

| | | |
|---|---|---|
| ulcer | ulcerocancer | ulcerous |
| ulcerate | ulceromembranous | |

**Uln**a: elbow, the inner and larger bone of the forearm.

| | | |
|---|---|---|
| radioulnar | ulna | ulnar | ulnocarpal |

**Umbilic**us: the navel.

| | | |
|---|---|---|
| hepatoumbilical | umbilication | umbiliferous |
| periumbilical | umbilicus | umbiliform |

**Umbr**a: shade, shadow.

| | | |
|---|---|---|
| penumbral | umbelligerous | umbriferous |
| umbel | umbraculum | |

**\*Unc**us: hook, barb.

| | | | |
|---|---|---|---|
| aduncate | unciform | uncinulus | uncirostrum |
| unciferous | uncinate | uncipressure | uncus |

**\*Und**a: wave. **Undula**re, **undulat**um: to have a wavy motion, fluctuate.

| | | |
|---|---|---|
| inundate | undose | undulatory |
| redundant | undulation | |

**\*Ungue**re, **unct**um: to anoint, smear on. **Unguent**um: ointment, salve.

| | | |
|---|---|---|
| inunction | unctuous | unguentum |
| unction | unguentin | |

**\*Ungu**is: nail, claw, hoof.

| | | | |
|---|---|---|---|
| multungulate | subungual | unguiculus | unguis |
| polyunguia | unguiculata | unguinal | ungula |

**\*Urin**a: urine.

| | | | |
|---|---|---|---|
| genito-urinary | urinalysis | urination | uriniparous |
| urinaccelerator | urinary | urine | urinogenous |

**Uter, utr**is: a bag (of skin or hide).

| | | |
|---|---|---|
| utricle | utriculosaccular | utriform |
| utricular | utriculitis | |

**\*Uter**us: womb.

| | | |
|---|---|---|
| intrauterine | vesicouterovaginal | uterogestation |
| postuterine | uteralgia | uterotubal |
| rectouterine | uterocervical | uterus |

**Uv**a: grape. **Uvul**a: small lobe hanging from palate.

| | | | |
|---|---|---|---|
| uvea | uveitis | uvula | uvulotomy |
| uveal | uviform | uvulitis | |

# V

**\*Vaccin**us: relating to a cow (**vacc**a).

| | | | |
|---|---|---|---|
| postvaccinal | vaccination | vaccinia | variolovaccine |
| serovaccination | vaccinator | vacciniculturist | |
| vaccigenous | vaccine | vaccinifer | |

**\*Vacu**us: empty.

| | | | |
|---|---|---|---|
| abevacuation | evacuator | vacuole | vacuum |
| evacuant | vacuolar | vacuome | |

**\*Vagin**a: sheath, sheath-like structure; vagina.

| | | | |
|---|---|---|---|
| evagination | invaginator | vagina | vaginovesical |
| intravaginal | subvaginal | vaginismus | vaginula |
| invaginate | supravaginal | vaginofixation | |

**Vag**us: wandering.

| | | |
|---|---|---|
| electrovagogram | vagotonia | vagrant |
| vagotomy | vagotropic | vagus (nerve) |

**\*Vale**re: to be strong, be well.

| | | | |
|---|---|---|---|
| ambivalent | invalid | prevalence | valetudinarianism |
| convalescence | multivalent | univalent | |
| equivalent | nonvalent | valence | |

**Valg**us: bent outward, twisted.

| | | |
|---|---|---|
| calcaneovalgocavus | genu valgum | talipes valgus |
| coxa valga | planovalgus | valgipes |

**Vall**is: valley, depression.

| | | | |
|---|---|---|---|
| vallecula | vallecular | valleculate | vallis |

**\*Vall**um: wall, rampart. **Valla**re: to surround with a wall or rim.

| | | |
|---|---|---|
| circumvallate | convallariaceous | vallum (unguis) |
| contravallation | vallate | |

**\*Valv**a: leaf of a door; valve.

| | | |
|---|---|---|
| bivalve | spirivalve | valviform |
| inequivalve | univalve | valvula |
| pseudovalves | valvar | valvulitis |

**\*Vari**us: changing, variegated, spotted.

| | | | |
|---|---|---|---|
| convariation | varicellation | variolate | variolovaccine |
| intervarietal | varietism | varioliform | |
| varicella | variola | varioloid | |

**\*Varix, varic**is: enlarged and tortuous vein.

| | | | |
|---|---|---|---|
| varicellate | variciform | varicose | varicosity |
| varices | varicocele | varicosis | varicula |

**Var**us: crooked, bent inward.

| | | |
|---|---|---|
| coxa vara | equinovarus | pollex varus |
| divarication | genu varum | talipes varus |

**\*Vas**: vessel.

| | | | |
|---|---|---|---|
| cerebrovascular | gastrovascular | vasodepressor | vascular |
| circumvascular | vasiform | vasodilation | vasculiferous |
| extravasate | vasoconstriction | vasomotor | vasculum |

**\*Vehe**re, **vect**um: to carry.

| | | | |
|---|---|---|---|
| advehent | convex | vection | vehicle |
| convection | evectional | vector | |

**Vela**re, **velat**um: to cover, veil. **Vel**um: veil, covering.

| | | | |
|---|---|---|---|
| velamentum | velarium | veliform | velum |
| velar | velate | veliger | |

**\*Velle**re, **vuls**um: to tear, puck. **Vellica**re, **vellicat**um: to twitch.

| | | | |
|---|---|---|---|
| avulsion | divulsion | postconvulsive | revellent |
| convulsion | evulsion | preconvulsant | vellication |

**\*Ven**a: vein.

| | | | |
|---|---|---|---|
| intravenous | vein | venesuture | venopressor |
| paravenous | venation | venipuncture | venose |
| supervenosity | venesection | venofibrosis | venule |

**\*Venen**um: poison,

| | | | |
|---|---|---|---|
| antivenin | veneniferous | venenosalivary | venom |
| venenation | venenific | venenum | |

**\*Ven**ire, **vent**um: to come.

| | | |
|---|---|---|
| adventitious | intervention | preventorium |
| circumvent | prevention | supervene |

**\*Venter, ventr**is: belly, abdomen, cavity.

| | | | |
|---|---|---|---|
| dorsiventral | venter | ventricose | ventrolateral |
| eventration | ventral | ventriculopuncture | |
| interventricular | ventricle | ventriflexion | |

**Venus, Vener**is: Venus, the goddess of love.

| | | |
|---|---|---|
| antivenereal | venereology | venery |
| venereal | venerophobia | |

**\*Verge**re: to bend, turn.

| | | |
|---|---|---|
| convergent | deorsumvergence | sursumvergence |
| diverge | supravergence | vergence |

**\*Verm**is: worm.

| | | |
|---|---|---|
| invermination | vermicular | vermifugal |
| vermicide | vermiform | vermination |

**Verruc**a: a wart.

| | | |
|---|---|---|
| verruca | verruciform | verrucosis |
| verruca tuberculosa | verrucose | |

**\*Verte**re, **vers**um; (**vorte**re, **vors**um): to turn. **Vertex, vertic**is: summit, top; crown of head. **Vortex, vortic**is: a whirl, spiral arrangement. **Vertebr**a: a joint (of the spine).

| | | | |
|---|---|---|---|
| ambiversion | extrovert | sinistrorse | vertex |
| anteversion | introversion | subvertebral | vertical |
| costotransverse | inversion | transverse | verticil |
| dextrorsal | invertebrate | versicolored | vertiginous |
| diverticulum | pervert | version | vertigo |
| eversion | retroversion | vertebra | vortex |

**\*Vesic**a: bladder, blister.

| | | | |
|---|---|---|---|
| cervicovesical | vesica | vesicle | vesicular |
| urethrovesical | vesical | vesicofixation | vesiculiform |
| vaginovesical | vesicate | vesicospinal | |

**\*Vi**a: way, path, passage.

| | | | |
|---|---|---|---|
| bivium | deviometer | quadrivial | retrodeviation |
| deviation | impervius | pervius | viable |

**Vibra**re, **vibrat**um: to shake, vibrate.

| | | | |
|---|---|---|---|
| vibraculum | vibrator | vibrio | vibromasseur |
| vibratile | vibration | vibrissae | vibrometer |

**\*Vide**re, **vis**um: to see.

| | | | |
|---|---|---|---|
| bivisum | visibility | vision | visuosensory |
| television | visile | visuometer | |

**Vill**us: tuft of hair, shaggy hair.

| | | |
|---|---|---|
| intervillous | villiferous | villose |
| villi | villiform | villositis |

**\*Vir**: man. **Virtus, virtut**is: manliness, virtue, strength.

| | | | |
|---|---|---|---|
| eviration | virile | virilism | virtual |
| subvirile | virilescence | viripotent | |

**Virg**a: twig, branch.

| | | | |
|---|---|---|---|
| virgal | virgate | virgula | virgultosa |

**\*Virid**is: green.

| | | |
|---|---|---|
| sempervirens | viridescent | viridity |
| virescent | viridiflora | |

**\*Vir**us: a potent juice, poison.

| | | | |
|---|---|---|---|
| ultravirus | virulent | viruliferous | virose |
| virucidal | virulicidal | virology | virus |

**\*Visc**um: birdlime of mistletoe; a sticky substance

| | | |
|---|---|---|
| viscid | viscoidal | viscose |
| viscin | viscometer | viscosity |

**\*Viscus, viscer**is: internal organ, especially one in a cavity of the body; bowels.

| | | | |
|---|---|---|---|
| devisceration | parietovisceral | viscera | viscerosensory |
| evisceration | retrovisceral | viscerad | viscus |

**\*Vit**a (French, **Vie**): life.

| | | | |
|---|---|---|---|
| advitant | nonviable | viable | vitals |
| avitaminosis | previable | vital | vitamin |
| devitalize | subvitaminosis | vitalism | vitaminogenic |

**Vitell**us: yolk of the egg.

| | | | |
|---|---|---|---|
| vitellarium | vitellin | vitellorubin | vitellus |
| vitelligenous | vitelline | vitellose | |

**\*Vitr**um: glass.

| | | |
|---|---|---|
| devitrification | vitreous | vitrina |
| vitrella | vitrescent | vitriol |
| vitreodentin | vitriform | vitropression |

**\*Viv**us: living. **Vive**re, **vict**um: to live.

| | | | |
|---|---|---|---|
| ovoviviparous | victual | vivification | vivisection |
| revivify | vivescent | viviperception | vivosphere |

**\*Vola**re: to fly.

| | | | |
|---|---|---|---|
| nonvolatile | volant | volatile | volatilization |

**\*Volve**re, **volut**um: to roll, roll up.

| | | | |
|---|---|---|---|
| circumvolve | evolution | obvolute | volvulus |
| convolution | involucrum | subinvolution | vulva |
| devolution | involution | volute | vulviform |

**Vomer**: plowshare; a bone in the septum of the nose.

| | | |
|---|---|---|
| ethmovomerine | vomer | vomerabasilar |
| prevomer | vomerine | vomeronasal |

**Vome**re, **vomit**um: to throw up, vomit.

| | | | |
|---|---|---|---|
| vomitive | vomitory | vomiturition | vomitus |

**\*Vora**re: to eat, devour.

| | | |
|---|---|---|
| baccivorous | herbivorous | nucivorous |
| carnivorous | insectivorous | sanguinovorous |
| frugivorous | lactivorous | voracious |

**Vox, voc**is: voice. **Voca**re, **vocat**um: to call.

| | | |
|---|---|---|
| evocator | provocative | vocal | vox cholerica |

## GREEK PREFIXES

Prefixes were extensively used by the ancient Greeks in the building of their vocabulary and the pattern of their original use has been continued in word construction ever since. In the use of Greek prefixes the following observations should be noted:

A. Most Greek prefixes were prepositions and adverbs which in the original language had independent existence as separate words, for example, PERI as in περὶ τὴν κεφαλήν (*around* the head), and EXO as in ἔξω τὴν χεῖρα ἔχειν (to keep the hand *on the outside*). The term "prefix," therefore, should not be applied to a noun, adjective, or verb stem which is used as a first component of a compound word; ADENO-, for example, in "adenocarcinoma" is not a prefix.

A few prefixes were inseparable particles which in the Greek language were not used as separate words but which appeared frequently as elements of compound words; for example:

> **a-, an-**: "not, without," as in ἀνώνυμος (*without* a name).
> **archi-**: "chief, superior," as in ἀρχιτέχτων (*master*-builder).
> **di-**: "two, double," as in διχέραιος (*two*-horned).
> **dys-**: "bad, ill," as in δύσπνοια (*difficulty* of breathing).
> **hemi-**: "half," as in ἡμίχυχλον (*semi*circle).

B. A Greek prefix may impart to the word to which it is attached either its literal physical meaning or a metaphorical one; or it may convey in varying degrees an intensive or perfective force; for example:

> **ana**batic: a going *up* ............. (literal).
> **ana**dipsia: *intense* thirst ............. (metaphorical).
> **an**eurysm: a widening "*up*" ............. (perfective).
>
> **cata**dromous: a running *down.*
> **cat**holicon: an "*entire*" whole.
>
> **ec**topia: *out of* place.
> **ec**lampsia: a shining "*out.*"
>
> **epi**demic: *upon* the people.
> **ep**hidrosis: *excessive* perspiration.
>
> **para**nephric: *near* the kidney.
> **para**logia: *disordered* state of reason.

C. More than one prefix may be attached to a single stem. In compound terms of Greek origin, therefore, the appearance of a prefix within a word is very common.

asynchronism (**a-, syn-**)         neur*anag*enesis
antiantidote (**anti-, anti-**)       bar*ag*nosis
hemiasynergia (**hemi-, a-, syn-**)   hemo*dia*pedesis
parepithymia (**para-, epi-**)        hyper*eso*phoria
hyperhypophysis (**hyper-, hypo-**)

D. When the following prefixes ending in a vowel are attached to a word beginning with a vowel or h, elision (loss of the final vowel of the prefix) usually occurs:

**Ana-:** *an*eurysm (EURYS, wide), *an*ion (ION, going).

**Anti-:** (irregular: in older words the final -*i* is elided; in neologisms it generally does not elide. It is usually hyphenated before another *i*.) *ant*arthritic (ARTHRON, joint), *ant*ergia (ERGON, work), *ant*helminthic (HELMINS, worm), *ant*helion (HELIOS, sun), *anti*oxidant (OXYS, sharp), *anti*-icteric (IKTEROS, jaundice).

**Apo-:** *ap*eidosis (EIDOS, form), *ap*helion (HELIOS, sun).

**Cata-:** *cat*ion (ION, going), *cat*optrics (OP-, to see), *cat*holicon (HOLOS, whole), *cat*hemoglobin (HAIMA, blood; GLOBUS, ball).

**Dia-:** *di*opter (OP- to see), *di*uretic (OURON, urine).

**Ecto-:** (also often hyphenated) *ect*ostosis (OSTEON, bone), *ecto*-enzyme (EN-, in, ZYME, ferment).

**Endo-:** (also often hyphenated) *end*odontitis (ODONT-, tooth), *end*osmosis (OSMOS, thrusting), *endo*-angiitis (ANGEION, vessel).

**Ento-:** *ent*amebiasis (AMOIBE, change), *ent*optic (OP-, to see), *ent*otic (OT-, ear).

**Epi-:** (occasionally does not elide before *o*) *ep*arterial (ARTERION, vessel), *ep*axial (AXIS, axis), *Ep*hedra (HEDRA, seat), *ep*hidrosis (HIDROS, sweat), *epi*otic (OT-, ear), *ep*onym (ONYMA, name).

**Eso-:** (also often hyphenated) *es*odic (HODOS, road), *eso*-ethmoid (ETHMOS, sieve).

**Exo-:** (also often hyphenated) *ex*odic (HODOS, road), *exo*-antigen (ANTI-, against; GEN-, produce).

**Hypo-:** (also often hyphenated) *hyp*ergasia (ERGON, work), *hyp*esthesia (AISTHESIS, feeling), *hyp*hemia (HAIMA, blood), *hyp*hidrosis (HIDROS, sweat), *hypo*-adenia (ADEN, gland).

**Meta-**: *met*encephalon (ENKEPHALON, brain), *met*hemoglobin (HAIMA, blood; GLOBUS, ball), *met*hod (HODOS, road), *met*onymy (ONYMA, name).

**Opistho-**: *opisth*encephalon (ENKEPHALON, brain), *opisth*otic OT-, ear).

**Para-**: (also often hyphenated) *para*cusis (AKOU-, to hear), *par*odontia (ODONT-, tooth), *para*-analgesia (AN-, not; ALGOS, pain).

E. The final vowel of the following prefixes does not elide before another vowel or h:

**Amphi-**: *amphi*arthrosis (ARTHRON, joint), *amphi*aster (ASTER, star), *amphi*erotic (EROS, love), *Amphi*oxus (OXYS, sharp).

**Hemi-**: *hemi*algia (ALGOS, pain), *hemi*epilepsy (EPI-, on; LEPSIS, seizure), *hemi*hypertonia (HYPER-, excessive; TONOS, tension), *hemi*opia (OP-, to see).

**Peri-**: *peri*axial (AXIS, axis), *peri*enteric (ENTERON, intestine), *peri*odontal (ODONT-, tooth), *peri*ungual (UNGUIS, nail).

**Pro-**: *pro*agglutinoid (AGGLUTIN-, to fasten to), *pro*enzyme (EN-, in; ZYME, ferment), *pro*otic (OT-, ear).

F. The alternate forms of **anth-** for **anti-**; **aph-** for **apo**; **cath-** for **cata-**; **eph-** for **epi-**; **hyph-** for **hypo-**; and **meth-** for **meta-** are explained by the above rules of elision and by the principles of consonant change explained on page 54. For example:

ἀντί (against) plus ἑλμινθικός (pertaining to worms) = ἀνθελμινθικός (the -ι of ἀντί elides before the vowel ε; the smooth mute τ then becomes aspirated before the rough breathing, changing to θ, which is the rough mute of the same class. The rough breathing mark disappears).

κατά (down) plus ὅλικον (entire) = καθόλικον (the final -α of κατά elides before o. The τ is then changed to θ for the same reason as given in the previous example).

ἐπί (upon) plus ἴδρωσις (perspiration) = ἐφίδρωσις (the final -ι of ἐπί elides before ι. The π is aspirated to φ before the rough breathing).

ὑπό (under) plus αἷμα (blood) = ὑφαῖμα (the final -o of ὑπό elides; the π before rough breathing becomes φ).

G. For explanation of the variant forms of **en-** and **syn-** see page 54.

\* \* \* \* \* \* \* \* \* \* \*

1. **A-, an-** (called "the Alpha-privative"): not, without, lack of.

acephalous (KEPHALE, head)   asepsis (SEPSIS, decay)
analgesic (ALGOS, pain)   asthenia (STHENOS, strength)
abiogenesis          anesthesia          atom
achromatic         anhidrosis         cardiasthenia
anemia

2. **Amphi-, ampho-, amphotero-**: around about, both, in two ways.

amphibious (BIOS, life)      amphogenic (GEN-, to produce)
amphiarthrosis        amphodiplopia      amphoterodiplopia
amphimixis          amphoteric (amphoterous)

3. **Ana-, ano-**: up, back, anew, again, throughout, (intensive).

anabatic (BA-, to go)      aneuryism (EURYS, wide)
analysis (LY-, to loosen)   anode (HODOS, road)
anabiosis           anamnesis         anion
anabolism          anaplasty         anoopsia
anadipsia

4. **Anti- (anth-)**: against, opposed to, resisting.

antiblastic (BLASTOS, sprout)  antarthritic (ARTHRON, joint)
antipyretic (PYR, fire; fever)  anthelion (HELIOS, sun)
antergia           anticatalyst       antiseptic
anthelix            anticlinal         antithrombin
anthelminthic      antidote          antitoxin
anthypnotic        antioxidant

5. **Apo- (aph-)**: from, separation, lack.

apeidosis (EIDOS, form)     apochromatic (CHROMA, color)
aphelion (HELIOS, sun)      apostasis (STA-, to stand)
apanthropia         apophylaxis     apophysis
aponoia

6. **Arche-, archi-**: first, chief, primitive.

archegonium (GONOS, offspring) archiblast (BLASTOS, bud)
archetype (TYPOS, type)     archigaster (GASTER, belly)
archecentric        archinephros      archiplasm
archicoel

7. **Cata- (cath-)** or **kata-**: down, lower, under, complete, (intensive).

catabatic (BA-, to go)      cathode (HODOS, road)
catadromous (DROMOS, a    kataphylaxis (PHYLAXIS,
  running)               protection)

catabolism            catatonia             cation
catalepsy             catharsis             catoptrics
cataphrenia           catheresis            katakinetomeric
catarrh               catholicon            kataphraxis

8. **Di**-: twice, twofold, double.

dicephalous (KEPHALE, head)    diptera (PTERON, wing)
catadicrotism         dimorphic             diphonia
diatomic

9. **Dia**-: through, across, apart, thoroughly.

diameter (METRON, measure)   diagnosis (GNOSIS, knowledge)
diabetes              diarrhea              diuretic
diapyesis             diathermy

10. **Dicha**-: in two, double, asunder.

dichocarpous (KARPOS, fruit)   dichotomy (TOME, cut)
dichogamy             dichogeny

11. **Dys**-: bad, difficult, hard, disordered, painful.

dysentery (ENTERON, intestine)  dysphrasia (PHRASIS, speech)
dysgenic (GEN-, birth,          dysstasia (STASIS, standing)
        production)
dysacousia            dysgalactia           dystopia
dysarthrosis          dyspepsia             dystrophy
dyschromatopsia       dyssystole

12. **Ek**-, **ex**-: out from, outside.

eccentric (KENTRON, center)    exanthema (ANTHE-, flower)
ectopia (TOPOS, place)         exodontia (ODONT-, tooth)
ecdemomania           ecmnesia              exenteration
ecdysis               ectopotomy            exophthalmus
eclampsia

13. **Ekto**-: on the outside, without.

ectocardia (KARDIA, heart)     ectomere (MEROS, part)
ectoderm (DERMA, skin)         ectostosis (OSTEON, bone)
ectoblast             ectophylaxination     ectozoon
ectocranial

14. **En**- (**em**- before b, m, p): in, within, among, (intensive).

encephalon (KEPHALE, head)     endemic (DEMOS, people)
encysted (KYSTIS, bag)         emphraxis (PHRAG-, block up)
embolism              endermic              enzyme
endeictic

15. **Endo**-: within.

endameba (AMOIBE, ameba) endothecium (THEKE, sheath)
endospora (SPORA, seed) endothermic (THERMOS, warm)
endobiotic endocranial endodontitis
endoblast endocrine endosmosis
endocarp endoderm

16. **Ento**-: within.

entocele (KELE, hernia) entotic (OT-, ear)
entosarc (SARX, flesh) entozoa (ZOON, animal)
entamebiasis entophyte entoptic
entodermal entoplasm

17. **Epi**- (**eph**-): upon, on.

ephemeral (HEMERA, day) epipetaly (PETALON, petal)
epiblepharon (BLEPHARON, eponym (ONYMA, name)
   eyelid)
eparterial ephidrosis epidermis
epaxial epicranium epigastrocele
ephebogenesis epidemic epiglottis

18. **Eso**-: inward, within.

esophoria (PHOROS, carrying) esotropic (TROPE, turning)
esophylaxis esotoxin

19. **Eu**-: well, good, normal, easy.

eupeptic (PEPT-, digest) euthanasia (THANATOS, death)
euosmia (OSME, smell) euthenic (THE-, place, put)
euergasia eunoia eusthenia
eugenics

20. **Exo**-: outside, outward, outer.

exocolitis (KOLON, colon) exophylaxis (PHYLAXIS, protect-
        ion)
exogamy (GAMOS, marriage) exoplasm (PLASMA, moulded)
exodic exopathy exotropia
exogenic exosepsis

21. **Hemi**-: half, partly.

hemialgia (ALGOS, pain) hemiplegia (PLEGE, blow, stroke)
hemimorphic (MORPHE, shape) hemiptera (PTERON, wing)
hemianacusia hemiatropny hemihydrate
hemianesthesia

22. **Hyper-**: above, over, excessive.

hyperemic (HAIMA, blood)       hypernoia (NOOS, mind)
hyperhidrosis (HIDROS, sweat)  hypertonic (TONOS, stretching)
hyperalgesic       hyperkinesia       hypertrophy

23. **Hypo-**: under, below, deficient in.

hypesthesia (AISTHESIS,        hypobranchial (BRANCHION,
    feeling)                       gill)
hyphemia (HAIMA, blood)        hypodermic (DERMA, skin)
hypergasia         hypodactylia       hypoglycemia
hyphidrosis        hypoglottis

24. **Meta-** (**meth-**): after, among, beyond, behind; change, transformation.

metacarpal (KARPOS, wrist)     metencephalon (ENCEPHALON,
                                   brain)
metathesis (THE-; place, put)  metheme (HAIMA, blood)
ametabolic         methemoglobin      metodontiasis
metabolism         metamorphosis      metonymy
metachromasia      metapyretic

25. **Opistho-**: behind.

opisthobranchia (BRANCHION,    opisthognathism (GNATHOS,
    gill)                          jaw)
opisthencephalon   opisthotic         opisthotonos

26. **Pali(n)-**: back, again, once more, backwards.

palikinesia (KINE-, move)      palinmnesia (MNE-, remember)
palilalia          palinesthesia      palingenesis
palindromous

27. **Para-**: by the side of, near, accessory; abnormal, perverted.

paranephric (NEPHROS, kidney) parenteral (ENTERON, intestine)
paranoia (NOOS, mind)          parodontal (ODONT-, tooth)
paracusis          parakinesis        paramastoid
paraectasia        paralogia          paraphyte

28. **Peri-**: around.

periosteum (OSTEON, bone)      peristome (STOMA, opening)
periphery (PHER-, carry)       perithecium (THEKE, case, sheath)
periaxial          perinephrium       peristalsis
pericardium        periodontium       peritoneum

29. **Pro**-: before, in front of, forward, forepart.

prodromata (DROMOS,      prophase (PHA-, appear)
       running)
prognosis (GNOSIS, knowledge)    proptosis (PTO-, fall)
proenzyme       prognathism       prophylactic
proglossis

30. **Pros**-: to, in addition, near.

prosthesis (THE-, place, put)     prosencephalon (ENCEPHALON,
                                 brain)
prosenchyma       prosocele

31. **Proso**-, **prostho**-: forward, before, in front.

prosodemic (DEMOS, people)    prosthodontia (ODONT-, tooth)
emprosthotonus      prosoplasia        prosopyle
prosogaster

32. **Syn**- (**sym**- before b or p; **sy**- before s if followed by a mute; assimilated before m, l, and s): with, together.

symbiosis (BIOS, life)      sy(s)somus (SOMA, body)
syndactylism (DAKTYLOS,    systylous (STYLOS, pillar)
       finger)         syndesis (DE-, bind, tie)
asynchronism     syndrome       synergism
symblepharon      synema         sy(s)sarcosis
symphysis

## GREEK SUFFIXES

In the growth of the Greek language, many words were formed by the addition of suffixes to existing roots and stems. These suffixes imparted more specific meanings to the words and also assisted in characterizing them as nouns, adjectives, verbs, etc. Greek suffixes are very numerous, and only those which are most important in scientific terms are given here. They are arranged under: (A) Verbal Suffix, (B) Substantival (Noun) Suffixes, and (C) Adjectival Suffixes. Suffixes closely related in meaning are listed together under a group number.

# A. VERBAL SUFFIX

| Suffix | Meaning | Stem or base to which attached | Examples |
|--------|---------|-------------------------------|----------|
| 1. **-ize** | to do, do as, imitate. | Noun or Adjective | cauterize (KAUTER, burner), sterilize (STERILIS, bare, unfruitful), pasteurize, anesthetize, paralyze, analyze (via French, analyse). |

# B. SUBSTANTIVAL (NOUN) SUFFIXES

| | | | |
|--------|---------|-------------------------------|----------|
| 1. **-tes** (-της) **-ter** (-τηρ) **-tor** (-τωρ) **-ist** (-ιστης, which is the agent suffix **-tes** added to the stem **-is** from **-izo** verbs.) | the agent; he who; that which. | Verb<br><br>Verb or Noun | diabetes (DIA-, through; BE-, to go), Dermatoryctes (DERMAT-, skin; ORYK-, to dig), cauter (KAU-, to burn), chiropractor (CHEIR, hand; PRAK-, to do), orthodontist (ORTHOS, straight; ODONT-, tooth), sphincter, catheter, ureter, anesthetist, psychiatrist, antagonist, geologist, anatomist. |
| 2. **-sis** (-σις) | Action, Process, Condition. | Verb | analysis (ANA-, up; LY-, to loosen), sepsis (SEP-, to rot), basis, prognosis, ectasis, hematopoiesis, paralysis, osmosis, symbiosis. |
| **-osis** (-ωσις) (the **o** is part of the verbal stem) | Condition (usually morbid). | Noun or Adjective | stenosis (STENOS, narrow), narcosis (NARKE, numbness), neurosis, sclerosis, arthrosis, necrosis, thrombosis. |
| **-iasis** (-ιασις) (the **-ia** is a verbal stem meaning "to heal") | Condition (needing healing); disease; infection by micro-organisms, or infestation. | Noun | lithiasis (LITHOS, stone), helminthiasis (HELMINTH-worm), amebiasis, psoriasis, acariasis, elephantiasis. |

| Suffix | Meaning | Stem or base to which attached | Examples |
|---|---|---|---|
| 3. **-sia** (-σια) | Action, Process, Condition. | Verb | dyspepsia (DYS-, bad; PEPT-, to make soft), asphyxia (A-, not; SPHYX-, to throb), anesthesia, androlepsia. |
| **-ia** (-ια) | Action, Process, Condition. | Verb | mania (MAIN-, to be frenzied), hemiplegia (HEMI-, half; PLEG-, to hit), hypsiphobia, monobulia. |
| **-ia** (-ια) | Quality, Condition. | Noun or Adjective | malacia (MALAKOS, soft), asthenia (A-, not; STHENOS, strength), hyperemia, leukopenia, ophthalmia. |

Many words having the suffix **-ia** entered English through the French; these, and others on the basis of analogy to them, end in -*y*; for example: agony, anatomy, appendectomy, cheiloplasty, dysentery, histology.

| | | | |
|---|---|---|---|
| 4. **-ma** (-μα) | Result of action. | Verb | phyma (PHY-, to grow), stigma (STIG-, to brand), aroma, asthma, eczema, edema, miasma, mitoma, trauma. |

In English words the final -*a* is often omitted; for example: chasm, diaphragm, gram, miasm, plasm, phlegm, system.

| | | | |
|---|---|---|---|
| **-oma** (-ωμα) (the **o** is part of the verbal stem) | Swelling or tumor (result of morbid action.) | Noun or Adjective | glaucoma (GLAUKOS, grey-green) lipoma (LIPOS, fat), carcinoma, hemangioma, sarcoma, trachoma, xyloma. |
| **-mos** (-μος) | Result of action. | Verb | sphygmos (SPHYG-, to throb), thermos (THER-, to be hot, warm), marasmos, desmos, rhythmos, spasmos. |

In English this suffix is usually reduced to -*m*; for example: c(o)elom, rhythm, spasm, therm.

| Suffix | Meaning | Stem or base to which attached | Examples |
|--------|---------|-------------------------------|----------|
| **-ismos** (-ισμος) (this is the verbal suffix **-is** to which has been added the suffix **-mos**). | Result of action; Condition; Doctrine; Sect. | Various | embolism (EN, in; BOL-, throw), isodactylism (ISOS, equal; DAKTYLOS, finger), hypnotism, melanism, laryngismus, parametrismus, strabismus, mesmerism, Darwinism. |

In English words the final -*os* of the Greek suffix is usually dropped or changed to -*us*, the corresponding masculine suffix of Latin.

| | | | |
|--------|---------|-------------------------------|----------|
| 5. **-ion** (-ιον) **-idion** (-ιδιον) **-arion** (-αριον) **-iscos** (-ισκος) | Small; Diminutive. | Noun | bacterium (BAKTRON, staff), mastigion (MASTIX, whip), antheridium (ANTH-OS, flower), coccidium (KOKKOS, grain), conidium (KONIS, dust), sporidium (SPORA, sowing), anthroparion (ANTHROP-OS, man), Hipparion [antelopinum] (HIPPOS, horse), asterisk[os] (ASTER, star), Basiliscus (BASILEUS, king) meniscus (MEN, month). |

English derived terms usually, but not always, change the terminations -*os* (masculine) and -*on* (neuter) of the Greek words to the corresponding -*us* and -*um* of Latin words.

| | | | |
|--------|---------|-------------------------------|----------|
| 6. **-ides** (-ιδης) (**-idae,** **-ida**) | Descended from; Related to; (patronymic). | Noun | Aerides (AER, air), Arachnida (ARACHNE, spider), Muscidae (MUSCA, fly), Nymphalidae (NYMPHE, bride, nymph), Potamides (POTAMOS, river). |

These suffixes are used extensively on names in zoology and botany as terminal indices of rank and classification.

## C. ADJECTIVAL SUFFIXES

In scientific terminology words with Greek adjectival suffixes are widely used as nouns as well as adjectives.

| Suffix | Meaning | Stem or base to which attached | Examples |
|---|---|---|---|
| 1. **-ticos** (-τικος) | Capability, Fitness, Pertaining to. | Verb | acoustic (AKOUS-, to hear), spastic (SPAS-, to draw, pull), aesthetic, analytic, cathartic, emetic, narcotic, prophylactic, septic, static, styptic, synthetic, zygomatic. |
| **-icos** (-ικος) **-acos** (-ακος) | Relation, Fitness, Ability. | Noun | hypodermic (HYPO-, under; DERMA, skin), cardiac (KARDIA, heart), anthropomorphic, arsenic, celiac, clinic, graphic, sporadic, thoracic, tonic, toxic. |

Note that the English derivatives usually drop the Greek -os inflectional suffix (acousticos, cardiacos, etc.). In Latin form, the endings would of course be in -us, -a, -um (e.g., acousticus, -a, -um).

In the Greek language many adjectives formed with the suffixes **-ticos, -icos,** and **-acos** virtually became nouns. The Romans, therefore, when they borrowed these Greek words and wished to make them adjectives, added to them their equivalent suffix **-alis** ("pertaining to"). This practice continued thereafter, although not consistently, and accounts for the fact that many Latin and English words have both the Greek and Latin suffixes, for example: prac-**tic-al,** phys-**ic-al,** cri-**tic-al,** log-**ic-al,** method-**ic-al.** No consistent differentiation of meaning can be made between those words which use one and those which use both suffixes, although usage does make a differentiation between some pairs. For example: MEDIC and MEDICAL; PHYSIC and PHYSICAL; GEOGRAPHIC and GEOGRAPHICAL; HISTORIC and HISTORICAL; GYMNASTIC and GYMNASTICAL; METHODIC and METHODICAL; PHARMACEUTIC and PHARMACEUTICAL; ACOUSTIC and ACOUSTICAL; ECONOMIC and ECONOMICAL. For some words there is only one acceptable form. For example: CARDIAC, CEPHALIC, DRAMATIC, DYNAMIC, MATHEMATICAL, SPHERICAL. In hybrid words the Latin suffix is usually used if the last component is a Latin stem and the Greek suffix if the last component is Greek; for example: LIENOGASTR**IC,** GASTROLIE-N**AL.**

There is a tendency in modern times to use these suffixes substantively by the addition of the letter -**s** to designate specialized branches of knowledge or science; for example: PHYSICS, GENETICS, ORTHODONTICS, PEDIATRICS, ATHLETICS, TACTICS, MATHEMATICS, DYNAMICS, POLITICS, DRAMATICS. Occasionally, however, the -**s** is not used as, for example, in LOGIC.

These adjectival suffixes from Greek, as well as the corresponding Latin adjectival suffixes -**alis** and -**aris,** have been found especially convenient in the construction of English words. Since the English language has no suffix by which it converts a noun into an adjective, the noun itself has been used adjectivally; for example: "ankle bone"; "eye disease." The Greek and Latin adjectival suffixes have therefore been of great practical usefulness and convenience, especially in compound terms where multiple relationships have to be expressed as, for example: "cervicofac*ial* nerve"; "atrioventricul*ar* valve"; "prosthe*tic* dentistry"; "cytogen*ic* reproduction."

| Suffix | Meaning | Stem or base to which attached | Examples |
|---|---|---|---|
| 2. -**ion**<br>(-ιον) | Belonging or related to; "the part which." | Noun | epigastrium (EPI-, upon; GASTR-, stomach), perineurium (PERI-, around; NEURON, nerve), acromium, epimysium, myocardium, parametrium, pericardium. |

Again, note in the derivatives the preference for the Latin termination -*um* over the Greek -*on.*

| | | | |
|---|---|---|---|
| 3. -**ite(s)**<br>(-ιτης;<br>-ιτες) | Belonging to; of the nature of. | Noun | dendrite (DENDRON, tree), saurites (SAUROS, lizard), chlorite, dynamite, phyllites, somite. |

In pathology a word using this suffix may modify the omitted, but understood, noun ὕδρωψ (dropsy), for example: ascites, tympanites.

| Suffix | Meaning | Stem or base to which attached | Examples |
|--------|---------|-------------------------------|----------|
| 4. **-itis** (-ιτις) | Condition, usually an inflammation. | Noun | arthritis (ARTHRON, joint), nephritis (NEPHROS, kidney), bronchitis, bursitis, enteritis, laryngitis, rhinitis, sinusitis. |

Many words using this suffix may originally have modified the feminine noun νόσος (disease); the noun was then gradually omitted in common usage and the adjective became a substantive.

| | | | |
|--------|---------|-------------------------------|----------|
| 5. **-oid** (**-oides**; **-odes**) | Like; in the shape of. | Noun | colloid (KOLLA, glue), xiphoid (XIPHOS, sword), adenoid, Eriocampoides, Lucodes, pterygoid, sigmoid, thyroid. |

**-oid** is not strictly a suffix; it developed from the noun εἶδος (shape, form).

## GREEK NUMERALS

Only the CARDINAL numbers are listed here. Of the Greek ORDINALS, only the first four are often used in compound words and those are included in the General Greek Vocabulary list; the four are: **prot**os (first), **deuter**os (second), **trit**os (third), and **tetart**os (fourth).

**Hen**: one.
    henogenesis        henosis
**Dyo**: two.
    dyad        dyaster        hendyadys        pentdyopent
**Treis, tria**: three. **Tricha**: three-fold.
    catatricrotic        triactinal        trichotomism
    isotrimorphism        triandrous        triskaidekaphobia
    somatotridymus        tricephalus

**Tettara (tetra-)**: four.

| | | |
|---|---|---|
| tetracarpellary | tetrad | tetratomic |
| tetracerous | tetrameric | |

**Pente**: five.

| | | | |
|---|---|---|---|
| pentacapsular | pentadactyl | pentamerous | pentapterous |
| pentachromic | pentagon | pentapetalous | |

**Hex**: six.

| | | | |
|---|---|---|---|
| discohexaster | hexacyclic | hexahydrate | hexastichous |
| hexacanth | hexahedron | hexapod | |

**Hepta**: seven.

| | | |
|---|---|---|
| heptachromic | heptagon | heptandrous |
| heptad | heptagynous | |

**Okto**: eight.

| | | |
|---|---|---|
| octamerous | octopetala | octostichous |
| octogynous | octopus | trisoctahedron |

**Ennea**: nine.

| | | |
|---|---|---|
| ennead | enneaphylla | enneatic |

**Deka**: ten.

| | | |
|---|---|---|
| decapod | dekastigma | triskaidekaphobia |

**Hendeka**: eleven.

| | |
|---|---|
| hendecagon | (h)endecatomus |

**Dodeka**: twelve.

| | | |
|---|---|---|
| dodecamerous | dodekadactylon | dodekahedron |
| dodecandrous | dodekagynus | |

**Hekaton (hecto-)**: one hundred.

| | | | |
|---|---|---|---|
| hectogram | hecatomeric | hecatoncephalus | hecatophyllous |

**Chilioi (kilo-)**: one thousand.

| | | |
|---|---|---|
| chilianthus | kilerg | kilodyne |

**Myrioi**: ten thousand; innumerable.

| | | |
|---|---|---|
| myriad | myriapod | myriophyllum |

## GENERAL GREEK VOCABULARY

Many Greek words have been adopted into English without any change; many others have undergone only slight changes by adjusting their terminations to those used in Latin, French, or English. The following words are some examples:

## Greek Words Adopted without Change

| | | | |
|---|---|---|---|
| ἀνάλυσις: | analysis | κόρυζα: | coryza |
| ἄσβεστος: | asbestos | κῶμα: | coma |
| αὐτόματον: | automaton | κρατήρ: | crater |
| βάσις: | basis | μακρόν: | macron |
| γένεσις: | genesis | ὄνυξ: | onyx |
| δυσπεψία: | dyspepsia | παράλυσις: | paralysis |
| ἕλιξ: | helix | σκελετόν: | skeleton |
| ζώνη: | zone | στίγμα: | stigma |
| θώραξ: | thorax | συνκοπή: | syncope |
| ἰσοσκελής: | isosceles | τροπή: | trope |
| κάλυξ: | calyx | χαρακτήρ: | character |
| κλίμαξ: | climax | χολέρα: | cholera |
| κόσμος: | cosmos | | |

## Greek Words Adopted with Latin Terminations

| | | | |
|---|---|---|---|
| ἄκανθος: | acanthus | βῶλος: | bolus |
| ἄντρον: | antrum | ναυσία: | nausea |

## Greek Words Adopted with French or English Terminations

| | | | |
|---|---|---|---|
| ἀνθηρός: | anther | πλανήτης: | planet |
| δίαιτα: | diet | πληγή: | plague |
| δόσις: | dose | στυπτικός: | styptic |
| ἐπιληψία: | epilepsy | σύριγξ: | syringe |
| φερμός: | therm | χορδή: | chord |

Because the base of a Greek NOUN belonging to Declension I or Declension II is apparent from the nominative singular, that form only is given on the entry line of the word list below. For most nouns belonging to Declension III, both the nominative and the genitive singular forms are given because their bases are not often evident from the nominative form.

When the base of a Greek ADJECTIVE is apparent from the nominative masculine form, only that form is given; when it is apparent only from the spelling of the genitive case or from the form of the feminine gender, those forms also are given.

For Greek VERBS (except for some irregulars), the present infinitive (uncontracted) is used as the regular entry form. In those instances where the true stem or variants which are used in derivatives differ from the present stem, those forms also are given on the entry line.

The list contains approximately 885 Greek word entries. If a reduction from this number is desired, the more useful words (about 470) have been marked with asterisks.

\* \* \* \* \* \* \* \* \* \*

## A

**Achille**us: a Greek legendary hero vulnerable only in his heel; heel-tendon; yarrow (a plant).

| | | |
|---|---|---|
| achilleaefolia | achillodynia | achillotenotomy |
| achillobursitis | achillorrhaphy | achillotomy |

**Adelph**os: brother, twin, twin fetal monster.

| | | | |
|---|---|---|---|
| adelphogamy | deradelphus | endadelphos | ischiadelphus |
| adelphotaxy | diadelphous | heteradelphia | monadelphous |

**\*Aden, aden**os: gland.

| | | |
|---|---|---|
| adenalgia | adenolipomatosis | blennadenitis |
| adenitis | adenoma | blepharoadenitis |
| adenocarcinoma | adenomyoma | dacryadenalgia |
| adenochondrosarcoma | adenopathy | maschaladenitis |
| adenodynia | adenophyllous | polyadenous |
| adenoid | adenopodous | sialadenitis |
| adenoidectomy | anadenia | splenadenoma |

**\*Aer**: air; gas.

| | | | |
|---|---|---|---|
| aeration | aerogenous | aerostat | anaerophyte |
| aerendocardia | aerohydrotherapy | aerotaxis | anaerosis |
| aerobion | aeropathy | aerotherapeutics | helioaerotherapy |
| aeroembolism | aerophore | aerotropism | hemataerometer |
| aerogastria | aerosporin | anaerobe | microaerobion |

**\*Agog**os: leading; promoting the flow, expelling.

| | | |
|---|---|---|
| anagogic | chromagogue | hypnagogic |
| anagotoxic | dacryagogatresia | lithagogic |
| cholagogue | galactagogue | sialagogue |

**Agoni**a: anguish, struggle, intense suffering, the struggle preceding death.

| | | |
|---|---|---|
| agonist | antagonist | preagonal |
| agony | coagonize | proagonic |

**Agor**a: a bringing together; assembly. **Paregorik**os: consoling, soothing.

| | | |
|---|---|---|
| agoraphobia | category | paregoric |

**\*Agr**a: a taking, catching; painful seizure.

| agremia | cardiagra | gonatagra |
| anconagra | cheiragra | melagra |
| arthragra | cleidagra | podagra |

**\*Aisthes**is: feeling, sensation, perception. **Aisthet**os: perceptible.

| acanthesthesia | anesthesia | cryesthesia | paresthesia |
| acroparesthesia | anesthetic | hemianesthesia | postanesthetic |
| akinesthesia | baresthesia | hyperesthesia | preanesthetic |
| allesthesia | caumesthesia | oxyesthesia | synesthesia |

**Aither**: the upper air; ether.

| ether | etheriform | etheromania | subteretherial |
| etherification | etherion | etherometer | |

**\*Aiti**a: cause.

| aetiogenous | etiopathology | nosetiology | somatetiological |
| etiology | etiotropic | pyretoetiology | |

**Akanth**a: thorn, spine, prickle.

| acanthesthesia | acanthocladous | acantholysis | homacanth |
| acanthocarpous | acanthopodious | acanthosis | paracanthosis |

**\*Ak**e; **akm**e: point, tip; highest point of.

| aciphyllous | acmesthesia | epacmastic |
| acmastic | acospore | heteracme |
| acme | diacmic | paracmastic |

**Akos, ake**os: relief, remedy, cure. **Akest**os: healed.

| aceology | acestoma | panacea |
| acesodyne | acognosia | |

**\*Akou**ein: to hear.

| acouesthesia | acousmatagnosis | bradyacusia | paracusis |
| acoulalion | acoustic | diplacusis | presbyacusia |
| acouophone | anacousia | hemianacusia | |

**\*Akr**os: at the end, summit; extremities.

| acragnosis | acrocyanosis | acromion | acrosome |
| acroasphyxia | acrodermatitis | acroparesthesia | acrospore |
| acroblast | acrodrome | acropetal | megalakria |
| acrocephalosyndactylia | | acrophobia | pachyacria |
| acrocephaly | acroedema | | |

**\*Akt**is, **aktin**os: ray; light rays for chemical effects; raylike or radiating structure.

| abactinal | actinocymography | actinomorphic | adiactinic |
| actinic | actinodermatitis | actinomyces | desmactinic |
| actinocarpous | actinogen | actinotherapy | diactinic |
| actinocladothrix | | | |

**Alex**ein: to ward off, defend.

| | | |
|---|---|---|
| alexeteric | alexipharmac | alexocyte |
| alexin | alexipyretic | toxalexin |

*****Algos, alge**os: pain. **Alges**is: sense of pain.

| | | |
|---|---|---|
| adenalgia | causalgia | hyperalgesia |
| algedonic | cephalalgia | neuralgia |
| algeoscopy | chirobrachialgia | otalgia |
| algesichronometer | coccygalgia | paranalgesic |
| algesthesia | erythromelalgia | prosopalgia |
| algophobia | genyantralgia | sphincteralgia |
| analgen | gonalgia | splenalgia |
| antodontalgic | haphalgesia | sternalgia |
| arthralgia | hemihypalgesia | telalgia |
| brachialgia | | |

**Allas, allant**os: sausage. **Allanto**is: an embryonic organ of reptiles, birds, mammals.

| | | |
|---|---|---|
| allantiasis | allantoic | allantois |
| allantochorion | allantoidoangiopagus | allantotoxicon |
| allantogenesis | allantoinuria | mesallantoid |

*****All**os: other, different, external, foreign. **Allel**on: of each other. **Allotri**os: strange. **Allach**ou: elsewhere.

| | | | |
|---|---|---|---|
| allachesthesia | allocentric | alloplast | allotropic |
| allelomorph | allochiria | allotriodontia | chondralloplasia |
| allergy | allogamy | allotriophagy | parallelism |
| allobiosis | allopathy | allotriosmia | parallelometer |

**Alopeki**a: fox-mange; loss of hair, baldness.

| | | |
|---|---|---|
| alopecia | alopecic | alopecist |

**Amauros**is: darkness, condition of dimness; blindness.

| | | |
|---|---|---|
| amaurosis | hemiamaurosis | molybdamaurosis |
| amaurotic | meramaurosis | |

*****Ambly**s: dulled, blunt.

| | | | |
|---|---|---|---|
| amblyacousia | amblygeustia | amblyopiatrics | hemiamblyopia |
| amblychromasia | amblygon | amblypod | |

*****Amni**on: the innermost membrane enclosing the fetus.

| | | | |
|---|---|---|---|
| amnioclepsis | amnionitis | amniotome | oligohydramnion |
| amniogenesis | amniorhexis | anamniotic | proamnion |
| amnioma | amniorrhea | hypamnion | |

*****Amoib**e: change.

| | | | |
|---|---|---|---|
| amebicidal | amebiosis | ameboid | Dimastigamoeba |
| amebiasis | amebocytogenous | amoebae | mesameboid |

*****Amygdal**e: almond; tonsil.

| | | | |
|---|---|---|---|
| amygdala | amygdalitis | amygdalolith | periamygdalitis |
| amygdalectomy | amygdaloglossus | amygdalopathy | |

**\*Amyl**on: starch.

| | | | |
|---|---|---|---|
| amylaceous | amylogenic | amylolysis | amylorrhea |
| amylemia | amyloid | amylophagia | amylosuria |
| amylobacter | amyloidosis | amyloplast | |

**Anem**os: wind.

| | | |
|---|---|---|
| anemograph | anemone | anemotaxis |
| anemometer | anemophile | anemotropism |

**\*Aner, andr**os: a man, male; stamen of flower.

| | | | |
|---|---|---|---|
| anandria | androecium | andropathy | dodecandrous |
| andranatomy | androgen | androphile | ergatandrous |
| andrase | androgynous | androphonomania | gynander |
| andreioma | android | apandria | gynandromorphism |
| andriatrics | andrology | clinandrium | misandria |
| androcyte | andromimetic | | |

**\*Angei**on: vessel (for blood, lymph, bile, etc.); a case.

| | | |
|---|---|---|
| allantoidoangiopagus | angioscotoma | gasterangiemphraxis |
| anagioplastic | cholangiitis | hemangioma |
| angiitis | cholangiogastrotomy | lithangiuria |
| angioblast | cholangiogram | sporangium |
| angiocarditis | chylangioma | telangiitis |
| angiohypertonia | euangiotic | telangioma |
| angioma | | |

**Ank**on: something bent; the elbow. **Ankylos**is: state of being crooked or hooked; claws; adhesion of parts.

| | | | |
|---|---|---|---|
| anconagra | anconitis | ankyloglossia | ankylotomy |
| anconal | ankylochilia | ankyloses | panankyloblepharon |
| anconeus | ankylodactylia | ankylostomatic | pseudankylosis |

**\*Anth**ein: to blossom; to break out, erupt. **Anthos, anthe**os: flower; rash.

| | | | |
|---|---|---|---|
| anthema | anthotaxis | erythranthema | proteranthous |
| anther | anthoxanthine | exanthemata | spiranthy |
| antheridium | exanthematous | gymanthous | teleianthous |
| anthocarpous | | | |

**Anthrax, anthrak**os: coal; carbuncle.

| | | | |
|---|---|---|---|
| acacanthrax | anthracoid | anthracosis | cacanthrax |
| anthracia | anthraconecrossi | anthracotic | glossanthrax |

**\*Anthrop**os: man, a human being.

| | | | |
|---|---|---|---|
| anthropoid | anthropophilic | exanthrope | zoanthropy |
| anthropology | apanthropia | hippanthropia | |
| anthropometry | enanthrope | philanthropy | |

**\*Antr**on: cave; cavity, sinus.

| | | | |
|---|---|---|---|
| antrocele | antroscope | genyantralgia | prosopantritis |
| antrodynia | antrostomy | hypantrum | |
| antropyloric | antrum | metopantralgia | |

**Aphrodite**: Greek goddess of love; Venus. **Aphrodisiak**os: sexual.

| | | |
|---|---|---|
| antaphrodisiac | hermaphrodite | hyperaphrodisia |
| aphrodisia | hypaphrodisia | |

**Arachn**e: spider or spider's web; a brain membrane.

| | | | |
|---|---|---|---|
| arachnephobia | arachnids | arachnogastria | subarachnoid |
| arachnidism | arachnodactyly | pi(a)arachnoid | |

*****Archai**os: ancient. **Arch**e: beginning, origin, primitive. (Cf. **Arche-** in Prefixes).

| | | |
|---|---|---|
| archaeornis | archebiosis | archeocyte |
| archaezoid | archenteron | menarche |

**Arch**os: the anus.

| | | |
|---|---|---|
| archocele | archorrhagia | archostenosis |
| archoptosis | archorrhea | archosyrinx |

*****Argyr**os: silver.

| | | | |
|---|---|---|---|
| argyric | argyrochlamys | argyrophyllous | hydrargyria |
| argyrite | argyrophil | argyrosis | |

*****Arteri**a: "windpipe"; vessel; artery.

| | | |
|---|---|---|
| arteriole | dysarteriotony | periarteritis |
| arteriosclerosis | endarteritis | stetharteritis |
| arteriostrepsis | intraarterial | |

*****Arthr**on: joint, juncture of bones; sound in speech.

| | | | |
|---|---|---|---|
| arthragra | arthrocentesis | arthroplastic | hemarthrosis |
| arthralgia | arthroclasia | arthropterous | holarthritis |
| arthrempyesis | arthroclisis | arthroxerosis | hydrarthrosis |
| arthritic | arthrodesis | chirarthritis | osteoarthritis |
| arthritis | arthroncus | dysarthria | synarthrosis |
| arthrocace | arthropathy | enarthrosis | |

**Arytain**a: pitcher, cup, ladle; a cartilage of the larynx.

| | | | |
|---|---|---|---|
| arytenoid | arytenoidectomy | interarytenoid | thyroarytenoid |

**Askaris, askarid**os: thread; worm, intestinal worm.

| | | | |
|---|---|---|---|
| ascaricide | ascarid | ascar(id)iasis | ascariosis |

*****Ask**os: a leather bag; bladder; spore envelope.

| | | | |
|---|---|---|---|
| ascidium | ascites | ascocarp | ascogonium |
| ascigerous | ascitogenous | ascococcus | ascospore |

**Aspis, aspid**os: shield; asp.

| | | |
|---|---|---|
| aspidobranchiata | aspisoma | pychnaspide |
| aspidosperma | porphyraspis | rhinaspis |

*****Aster**; **astr**on: star. -*aster*: pertaining to structure or origin.

| | | | |
|---|---|---|---|
| amphiaster | asterospondylous | astroglia | spiraster |
| aster | astroblastoma | astroid | tetraster |
| asterion | astrocyte | oxyaster | |

**Asthma, asthmat**os: panting, short breath, gasping.

| | | |
|---|---|---|
| antiasthmatic | asthmatic | pseudoasthma |
| asthma | asthmogenic | |

**\*Astragal**os: anklebone, ball of the ankle joint.

| | | |
|---|---|---|
| astragalectomy | astragaloscaphoid | astragalus |
| astragalocalcanean | astragalotibial | |

**Ather**e: porridge, cereal, mush; degeneration.

| | | |
|---|---|---|
| atheroma | atheronecrosis | atherosclerosis |

**\*Atlas, atlant**os: a mythological demigod who supported the world on his shoulders; the first neck vertebra.

| | | |
|---|---|---|
| antlantad | atlantoaxial | atlantomastoid |
| atlantal | atlantodidymus | atlanto-odontoid |

**Atm**os: air, breath, vapor, steam.

| | | |
|---|---|---|
| atmiatry | atmograph | atmosphere |
| atmocausis | atmolysis | atmotherapy |

**\*Aut**os: self, by itself.

| | | | |
|---|---|---|---|
| autacoid | autogenous | autolytic | autopsy |
| autism | autohypnosis | automatic | autosynthesis |
| autochthonous | autolysis | autophyllogeny | |

**\*Aux**ein: to increase. **Auxan**ein: to grow.

| | | | |
|---|---|---|---|
| auxanography | auxilytic | bradyauxesis | splenauxe |
| auxanology | auximone | epauxesiectomy | tachyauxesis |
| auxesis | auxocardia | hepatauxe | trichauxe |
| auxetic | auxometer | | |

# B

**\*Ba-, (be-)**: to go, walk. **Bas**is: a walking; that on which one steps or stands, foundation, base.

| | | | |
|---|---|---|---|
| abasia | basilar | basophobia | diabetogenic |
| ananabasia | basion | brachybasia | dysbasia |
| basicranial | basipetal | catabatic | hypnobatia |
| basidium | basophil | diabetic | neuroprobasia |
| basidorsal | | | |

**\*Bakteri**on: a little staff, rod; bacteria.

| | | | |
|---|---|---|---|
| abacterial | bacteremia | bacteriostasis | megabacterium |
| amylobacter | bacteria | gymnobacteria | streptobacteria |
| antibacterial | bacteriology | haplobacteria | |

**Balan**os: acorn, barnacle; balanus, the glans penis.

| | | | |
|---|---|---|---|
| balanite | balanocele | balanophora | balanoplasty |
| balanitis | balanochlamyditis | | Chrysobalanus |

**\*Ball**ein: to throw, toss, put. **Bol**e; **bol**os: a throw. **Metabol**e: change.

| | | | |
|---|---|---|---|
| aeroembolism | ballistics | dysbolism | metabolism |
| ametabolic | ballistocardiograph | glycometabolism | sporobola |
| anabolism | balopticon | hemiballism | strephosymbolia |
| ballism | catabolism | hypermetabolism | xenembole |

**\*Baros, bare**os: weight, pressure. **Bary**s: heavy.

| | | | |
|---|---|---|---|
| abarognosis | barotrauma | baryphonia | isobaric |
| baragnosis | baryglossia | hemabarometer | |
| barometer | barylalia | hypobaropathy | |

**\*Bathy**s: deep, inner. **Bathos, bathe**os: depth.

| | | | |
|---|---|---|---|
| bathycardia | bathyesthesis | bathyseism | eurybathic |
| bathycentesis | bathygastria | bathysphere | polybathic |

**Benthos, benthe**os: depth (of the sea).

| | | |
|---|---|---|
| archibenthos | epibenthic | holobenthic |
| benthosaurus | eurybenthic | phytobenthon |

**\*Bi**os: life. **Bios**is: a living, way of living.

| | | | |
|---|---|---|---|
| abiogenesis | abiotrophy | antibiotic | microbe |
| abiology | aerobion | biocytoneurology | psychobiology |
| abionarce | amphibious | biology | symbiont |
| abionergy | anabiosis | eubiotics | symbiosis |
| abiophysiology | anaerobe | hematobium | |

**\*Blast**os: bud, shoot, sprout, embryonic cell.

| | | | |
|---|---|---|---|
| ablastemic | blastolysis | hemocytoblast | nesidioblast |
| acroblast | blastophore | holoblastic | neuroblast |
| angioblast | blastula | lipoblastoma | spermatoblastic |
| archiblast | chondroblast | lymphoblast | teloblast |
| astroblastoma | erythroblastosis | meroblastic | trophoblast |
| blastoderm | | | |

**Blenn**os: mucus.

| | | |
|---|---|---|
| blennadenitis | blennostasis | gastroblennorrhea |
| blennemesis | blennuria | otoblennorrhea |
| blennorrhea | dacryoblennorrhea | polyblennia |

**\*Blep**ein: to see. **Blephar**on: eyelid.

| | | | |
|---|---|---|---|
| ablepharous | atretoblepharia | blepharoplasty | monoblepsia |
| ablepsia | blepharochalasis | blepharoptosis | oxyblepsia |
| achloroblepsia | blepharochromidrosis | hemiablepsia | pachyblepharosis |
| acyanoblepsia | blepharoclonus | hydroblepharon | pseudoblepsis |
| ankyloblepharon | blepharoncus | macroblepharia | |

**Bol**os: rounded mass, lump, clod.

| | | | |
|---|---|---|---|
| bolus | pilobolus | sphygmobologram | sphygmobolometer |

**Bothr**os: trench, pit, trough. **Bothri**on: a little trench; socket. A sucking
  groove of Cestoids.

| | | |
|---|---|---|
| bothrenchyma | Chrysobothris | odontobothrion |
| bothrium | dibothriocephaliasis | Stenobothrus |

**Botry**s: cluster of grapes.

| botrycymose | botryomycosis | botryotherapy |
| botryoid | botryosporium | Botrytis |

**Boubon, boubon**os: groin; bubo, a swelling of a lymph gland.

| antibubonic | bubonic | bubonulus |
| bubonalgia | bubonocele | hysterobubonocele |

*****Boul**e: will, wish.

| abulia | dysbulia | hypobulia | parabulic |
| bulesis | hyperbulia | monobulia | |

**Bous, bo**os: ox.

| bucardia | boophilus | buphthalmus |
| bulimia | boopia | |

*****Brachi**on: arm, upper arm; armlike process.

| abrachiocephalia | brachiocephalic | chirobrachialgia |
| brachia | brachiofaciolingual | intercostobrachial |
| brachialgia | brachiotomy | macrobrachia |

*****Brachy**s: short.

| brachybasia | brachyknemic | brachyuran |
| brachycephalic | brachypellic | brachyuranic |
| brachycheilia | brachyphalangia | symbrachydactylia |

*****Brady**s: slow.

| bradyacusia | bradydiastole | bradylogia | bradystalsis |
| bradyauxesis | bradykinetic | bradypnea | bradytrophic |
| bradycardia | bradylexia | bradypragia | myobradyia |
| bradycrotic | | | |

*****Branchi**a: gills

| abranchiate | branchicolous | branchiopod | inferobranchiate |
| branchia | branchiomere | dibranchiate | nudribranchiate |

**Bregma, bregmat**os: the front part of the skull at junction of coronal and sagittal sutures.

| bregma | Eurybregma | trachelobregmatic |
| bregmatodymia | stenobregmatic | |

**Bro-**: to eat. **Broma, bromat**os: food.

| abrosia | bromatotoxism | gastrobrosis |
| bromatology | diabrotic | osteanabrosis |
| bromatotherapy | enterobrosis | theobromine |

**Brom**os: stench.

| antibromic | bromidrosiphobia | bromism | bromopnea |
| bromide | bromidrosis | bromoderma | hydrobromide |

*****Bronch**os: windpipe, trachea.

| bronchadenitis | bronchophony | intrabronchial |
| bronchiolitis | bronchopneumonia | peribronchiolar |
| bronchitis | bronchorrhaphy | tracheobronchoscope |
| bronchography | bronchostenosis | transbronchial |
| broncholith | bronchostomy | |

**\*Bry**ein: to be full, swell.

acrobryous | bryony | embryogeny | polyembryony
bryocytic | embryo | embryology

**Bry**on: moss.

bryanthus | bryoma | bryophyte
bryology | bryophyllum | bryozoon

## C

**\*Chait**e: hair.

achetinous | chaetoplankton | oligochaete | spirochaete
chaetophorus | chaetotaxy | polychaetous

**Chala**ein: to slacken, loosen, relax. **Chalastik**os: laxative.

achalasia | chalastic | chalone
blepharochalasis | chalastodermia | dermatochalasis

**Chalk**os: cooper, bronze; yellow.

chalcography | chalcopyrite | chalcosoma
chalcone | chalcosis | chalkitis

**Chamai**: on the ground. **Chamel**os: creeping.

chamaecranial | chamaesaura | chamelognathous
chamaephytes | chameleon | platychamaecephalous

**Charakter** (**charass**ein: to sharpen, engrave): a graving tool; an engraved or impressed mark.

biocharacter | characteristic | microcharacter
character | characterology | polycharacteristic

**\*Chasma, chasmat**os: cleft, opening. **Chas**is: separation, division.

chasma | chasmogamy | pleiochasium
chasmantherous | chasmophyte | uraniscochasma
chasmatoplasson | hygrochasy | xerochastic

**\*Cheil**os: lip.

acheilary | cheilognathoschisis | macrocheilia
acheilia | cheiloplasty | pachychilia
ankylochilia | cheilosis | synchilia
brachycheilia | genychiloplasty | xerocheilia
cheilitis

**\*Cheir, cheir**os: hand.

acephalochiria | chirarthritis | encheiresis
acheiria | chirobrachialgia | heterochiral
cheiragra | chiropodist | surgery
cheiromegaly | chiropractor | synchiria
cheiropterygium

**Chel**e: claw.

| | | | |
|---|---|---|---|
| Achelata | chelicerae | cheloid | chelophores |
| chela | cheliferous | cheloma | |

**\*Chiasma**; **chiast**os: crossed, decussation.

| | | |
|---|---|---|
| chiasm | chiasmotype | chiastoneural |
| chiasmatic | chiastometer | postchiasmatic |

**Chlamys, chlamyd**os: cloak, mantle.

| | | |
|---|---|---|
| achlamydeous | chlamydate | Chlamydozoa |
| balanochlamyditis | chlamydospore | haplochlamydeous |

**\*Chlor**os: green, yellowish green, yellow.

| | | |
|---|---|---|
| achloroblepsia | chloranthy | dechlorination |
| achloropsia | chlorine | erythrochloropia |
| anachlorhydria | chloromycetin | hyperchlorhydria |
| chloasma | chlorosis | |

**\*Chol**e: bile, gall; bitter anger.

| | | |
|---|---|---|
| acholuria | choledochectomy | cholic |
| cholagogue | cholelith | cholochrome |
| cholangiitis | cholelithiasis | choloplania |
| cholangiogastrotomy | cholera | hypercholesterolemia |
| cholangiogram | choleric | melancholia |
| cholecystitis | cholesterin | paracholia |
| cholecystogram | cholesterol | pericholecystic |

**\*Chondr**os: granule; cartilage.

| | | |
|---|---|---|
| adenochondrosarcoma | chondromalacia | hypochondriac |
| chondrification | chondromucoid | hypochondrium |
| chondriosome | chondrosis | mitochondria |
| chondroblast | dyschondroplasia | perichondrium |
| chondrocranium | endrochondral | synchondrosis |
| chondroma | | |

**\*Chord**e: gut-string, sinew, cord.

| | | | |
|---|---|---|---|
| acrochordon | chorditis | c(h)ordopexy | notochord |
| chordectomy | chordoma | chordotonal | pygochord |

**\*Chorei**a: dancing; St. Vitus' dance.

| | | |
|---|---|---|
| chorea | choreo-athetosis | monochorea |
| choreic | hemichorea | pseudochorea |
| choreiform | | |

**\*Chori**on: skin; the outermost membrane enveloping the fetus; tunic of the eyeball.

| | | |
|---|---|---|
| allantochorion | choroiditis | ectochoroidea |
| choriocele | choroidoiritis | endochorion |
| chorion | cyclochoroiditis | mesochoroidea |
| chorionic | | |

**\*Chro**a; **chroma, chromat**os: surface of the body, skin; color of the skin; color.

| | | |
|---|---|---|
| achroacytosis | chromatin | dichromic |
| achroiocythemia | chromatodysopia | hemochromatosis |
| achromaturia | chromatolysis | heterochromia |
| amblychromasia | chromatophil | hypochromic |
| ametachromophil | chromatophore | leptochroa |
| amphichroic | chromidrosis | metachrosis |
| anisochromia | chromium | polychromatophilia |
| anti-achromotrichia | chromosome | xanthochroia |
| chromagogue | cyanochroia | |

**\*Chron**os: time.

| | | |
|---|---|---|
| algesichronometer | chronicity | heterochronia |
| asynchronism | chronobiology | isochronous |
| chronaxia | gastrochronorrhea | synchronia |
| chronic | | |

**\*Chrys**os: gold; yellow.

| | | |
|---|---|---|
| chryselephantine | chrysoderma | chrysophyll |
| chrysiasis | chrysolite | chrysotherapy |
| chrysocarpous | | |

**Chthon, chthon**os: earth, ground.

| | | |
|---|---|---|
| autochthonous | chthonosology | nosochthonography |
| chthonophagy | heterochthonous | |

**\*Chy-**; **che**ein: to pour. **Chym**os; **chyl**os: something poured, juice, fluid. **Choan**e: funnel.

| | | | |
|---|---|---|---|
| achylanemia | chylangioma | dyschylia | metachysis |
| achymia | chylocaulous | ecchymosis | oligochymia |
| cheoplastic | chylocyst | eleomyenchysis | parenchymatous |
| chlorenchyma | chylosis | enchylema | pyecchysis |
| choana | chyluria | enchyma | spaerenchyma |
| choanocyte | chylomicron | euchylia | synchysis |
| choanoid | collenchyma | karyochylema | urecchysis |
| choanosome | dermenchysis | | |

# D

**Daimon, daimon**os: a divine power, demon.

| | | |
|---|---|---|
| demoniac | demonomania | demonophobia |
| demonology | demonopathy | |

**\*Dakry**on: tear.

| | | |
|---|---|---|
| chromodacryorrhea | dacryocyst | dacryopyosis |
| dacryadenalgia | dacryocystoptosis | dacryorrhea |
| dacryagogue | dacryocystorhinostomy | rhinodacryolith |
| dacryoblennorrhea | dacryolith | |

**\*Daktyl**os: finger, toe.

ankylodactylia
apodactylic
arachnodactyly
brachydactylia
camptodactyly

dactylopterous
dactylosymphysis
didactyledema
discodactylous

dodecadactylitis
isodactylism
streptomicrodactyly
syndactylism

**Dasy**s: thick-haired, shaggy, bushy.

dasycladous
dasypaedes

dasyphyllous
Dasypus

dasypygal
dasystoma

**\*De**ein: to tie. **Desm**os: band, bond, ligament.

arthrodesis
desmactinic
desmectasia
desmocyte
desmognathous
desmoid

epiphysiodesis
heterodesmotic
ophthalmodesmitis
opisthodetic
osteodesmosis

peridesmium
sclerodesmia
spondylosyndesis
syndesmology
syndesmosis

**\*Delt**a: a Greek letter, of triangular shape.

acromiodeltoid
clavodeltoid

deltoid
deltoiditis

pseudodeltidium
subdeltoid

**\*Dem**os: country, land; people of a country.

demography
ecdemic

endemic
epidemic

epidemiology
pandemic

prosodemic

**\*Dendr**on: tree; branched structure.

dendroid
dendrophagocytosis
klasmatodendrosis

neurodendron
oligodendroglia

peridendritic
telodendron

**Der**e: neck.

chlamydodera
deradelphus

deradenitis
deradenoncus

derencephalocele
derodidymus

**\*Derma, dermat**os: that stripped off; skin, hide.

acrodermatitis
actinodermatitis
atrophoderma
blastoderm
bromoderma
chalastodermia
dermatitis
dermatolysis
dermatomyositis
dermatophyte
dermatopsy
dermatoses

dermatosome
echinoderm
ectoderm
endermic
entoderm
erythroderma
hypodermic
hypodermoclysis
intradermic
keratodermatitis
leiodermia

leukoderma
melanoderma
mesoderm
myxodermia
pachydermia
pyoderma
scleroderma
streptodermatitis
toxicoderma
xanthoderm
xeroderma

**Deuter**os (**deuto-**): second, next.

deuteranopia   deuteropathy   deuterotoxin   deutoplasm
deuterium   deuterostoma   deutipara

**Dexi**os: right (as opposed to "left").

dexiocardia   dexiotropic

*****Diait**a: life, way of living.

diet   dietetics   dietotherapy
dietary   dietitian   dietotoxicity

*****Didym**os: twofold, twin; one of the two testes. *-didymus* (*-dymus*): twin fetal monster.

anadidymus   epididymitis   opodidymus
atlodymus   gastrodidymus   perididymus
catadidymus   hetero(di)dymus   somatodidymus
craniodidymus   ischiodidymus   xiphodidymus
didymalgia

**Dikty**on: net.

dictyodendron   Dictyonema   dictyotic   sarcodictyum
dictyodromous   Dictyophora   Hydrodictyon
dictyogen   dictyostelic   paradictyum

**Diphther**a: tanned skin, leather; diphtheria.

antidiphtheritic   diphtherolysin   postdiphtheric
diphtherial   diphtherotoxin   pseudodiphtheria

*****Diplo**os: see **-plo**os.

*****Dips**a: thirst.

adipsia   dipsesis   hydrodipsomania
anadipsia   dipsotherapy   polydipsia

*****Disk**os: disc.

discal   discoblastula   discohexaster
disciflorous   discodactylous   discoidal

**Doch**e: receptacle, receiver. **Dochei**on: holder.

adiadochokinesis   choledochostomy   sialodochoplasty
choledochectomy   diadochocinesia   urodochium
choledocholithiasis

*****Dolich**os: long.

acrodolichomelia   dolichohieric   dolichoprosopic
dolichocephalic   dolichopellic   dolichuranic

*****Dos**is: a giving; dose. **Dote**os: to be given.

antidote   dose   dosimeter   dosiology

**Drepan**e: sickle, scythe.

drepaniform   drepanocladous   drepanocythemia
drepanium   drepanocyte   drepanoptera

**\*Drom**os: a running, course.

| | | |
|---|---|---|
| acrodrome | dromophobia | palindromic |
| anadromous | hemodromometer | photodromy |
| antidromic | heterodromous | prodrome |
| diadromous | katadromous | syndrome |
| dictyodromous | metadromic | |

**Dy**ein: to enter, put on, move. **Ependym**a: something put on over; membrane lining brain and spinal cord column.

| | | | |
|---|---|---|---|
| ekdysis | ependyma | ependymocyte | somatodymia |
| endysis | ependymitis | subependymal | |

**\*Dynam**is: power, active force.

| | | |
|---|---|---|
| ataxiadynamia | gnathodynamics | neuradynamia |
| cardiodynamics | hydrodynamics | pharmacodynamics |
| dynamogenesis | hyperdynamic | photodynamics |
| dynamometer | ideodynamism | thermodynamics |
| ergodynamograph | isodynamic | trophodynamics |

## E

**Ech**ein: to sound, peal. **Echo**: a sound, a returned sound.

| | | | |
|---|---|---|---|
| autoecholalia | echolalia | echopathy | metrechoscopy |
| echokinesis | echomimia | echopraxis | |

**\*Ech**ein (**sch-, isch-**): to have, hold; hold fast, keep back, suppress. (see **hex**is).

| | | |
|---|---|---|
| asynechia | ichemia | spermatoschesis |
| blepharosynechia | ischesis | synechenterotomy |
| chlorhistechia | ischidrosis | synechia |
| galactischia | ischochymia | synechiotomy |
| galactoschesis | sialoschesis | uroschesis |
| hematischesis | | |

**Echin**os: hedgehog; spiny appearance.

| | | | |
|---|---|---|---|
| echinate | echinococcus | echinoderm | echinostomata |
| echinochrome | echinoconus | echinosis | echinulate |

**\*Eidos, eide**os (**id-**: to see): that seen, form, shape. -*oid*: like, in shape of. **Ide**a: appearance; mental impression, thought.

| | | | |
|---|---|---|---|
| ameboid | eiloid | icteroid | ideomotor |
| apeidosis | ethmoidal | ideation | ideophrenic |
| eidetic | gynecoid | ideodynamism | ideoplastia |
| eidoptometry | haloid | ideoglandular | monoideaism |

**Eikon, eikon**os: image, likeness.

| | | |
|---|---|---|
| eikonogen | iconomania | isoiconia |
| iconantidyptic | iconomatography | |

**Eil-**: to roll, twist, roll up, cover. **Eile**os: twisted (bowel); colic.
blepharelosis    eiloid    ileac    ileus

**Elai**on: olive oil; oil.
elaeococca    eleoma    eleomyenchysis
elaeoplankton    eleometer    eleosaccharum
elaiopathy

**\*Elektr**on: amber; electricity.
electrocardiograph    electrocholecystocausis    electrotonus
electrocautery    electroencephalogram    parelectronomy

**Elephas, elephant**os: elephant.
elephantiasis    elephantopus    oschelephantiasis    Phytelephas

**Eleuther**os: free.
eleutherodactyl    eleutherophyllous    eleutherosepalous
eleutheropetalous

**\*Elytr**on: cover, sheath; the vagina; insects' anterior wings.
elytriform    elytrocleisis    elytrorrhaphy
elytritis    elytroplasty    elytrum
elytrocele    elytroptosis    hemelytra

**\*Eme**ein: to vomit. **Emet**os: vomiting.
blennemesis    emetine    hyperemesis
copremesis    emetotrophia    melanemesis
emesis    hematemesis    tyremesis
emetic    hemosialemesis

**\*Enema**: see **He**nai.

**\*Enter**on: that within, the intestine.
antidysenteric    enterogenous    gastroenterologist
archenteron    enterolith    myenteron
dysentery    enterolysis    orthoenteric
enteritis    enteroplexy    synechenterotomy
enterocele    enteroptosis    typhlenteritis
enteroclysis    exenteration

**Eo**s: the morning red, dawn; a rosy color; an early age.
eocene    Eogaea    eosinopenia    eosophobia
eocladous    eosin    eosinophil    hypereosinophilia

**Epheb**os: youth; puberty.
anephebic    ephebogenesis    phylephebic
ephebic    ephebology    Schizepheboceras

**Erethism**os: irritation, stirring up.
cysterethism    erethism    erethitic
dyserethisia    erethisophrenia    thelerethism

**\*Erg**on; **ergasi**a: work, functioning.

| | | |
|---|---|---|
| adrenergic | energy | hepatargia |
| allergen | erg | micrurgy |
| allergy | ergasia | orthergasia |
| cacergasia | ergasthenia | parergasia |
| deallergization | ergatandrous | synergic |
| dysergasia | ergatogynous | zymurgy |
| dyssynergia | hemiasynergy | |

**\*Eros, erot**os: love, lust.

| | | |
|---|---|---|
| autoerotism | erotic | erotopsychic |
| erogenic | erotopath | heteroerotism |

**\*Erythr**os: red. **Erythema, erythemat**os: a redness (of the skin). **Erysipelas**: disease with red patches.

| | | |
|---|---|---|
| cholerythrin | erythroclastic | erythropoiesis |
| erysipelas | erythrocyte | erythropsia |
| erythema | erythrocythemia | nephroerysipelas |
| erythremia | erythroderma | phycoerythrin |
| erythroblast | erythromelalgia | pneumoerysipelas |
| erythroblastosis | erythrophobia | ulerythema |

**Eschar**a: hearth, fireplace, pan of coals; scab from burn, scab, scar.

| | | |
|---|---|---|
| escaripora | Eschara | scar |
| eschar | escharotic | |

**\*Ethm**os: sieve, strainer.

| | | |
|---|---|---|
| ectethmoids | ethmoidal | ethmopalatal |
| esoethmoiditis | ethmonasal | ethmosphenoid |

**\*Ethnos, ethne**os: race, nation.

| | | |
|---|---|---|
| ethnic | ethnology | ethnozoology | paleoethnology |
| ethnography | ethnopsychic | holethnos | |

**\*Eury**s: wide, broad.

| | | |
|---|---|---|
| aneurism | eurycephalic | eurypterid | hystereurynter |
| colpeurysis | eurygnathic | hypereuryopia | procteurysis |

# G

**\*Gala, galakt**os: milk.

| | | |
|---|---|---|
| agalactia | galactagogue | galactopoietic |
| agalactosuria | galactic | galactorrhea |
| agalorrhea | galactischia | galactose |
| androgalactozemia | galactocele | oligogalactia |
| galactacrasia | galactoplania | pneumogalactocele |

**\*Gam**os: marriage, wedlock. **Gamet**es; **gamet**e: husband, wife; germ or reproductive cell.

| | | |
|---|---|---|
| agamogenesis | exogamy | isogame |
| allogamy | gamete | misogamy |

**\*Gam**os  (*contd.*)

| | | |
|---|---|---|
| autogamy | gametogenic | phanerogam |
| cryptogam | gametogonium | progamous |
| digametic | gamobium | syngamy |
| endogamy | gamopetalous | xenogamy |

**\*Gangli**on: a mass of nerve cells; a small hard cyst or swelling.

| | | |
|---|---|---|
| diplogangliate | ganglion | otoganglion |
| gangliasthenia | ganglioneure | polyganglionic |
| gangliectomy | heteroganglionic | |

**\*Gaster, gastr**os: belly, stomach; the bulging fleshy part of a muscle.

| | | |
|---|---|---|
| acephalogaster | epigastrium | gastropod |
| aerogastria | extragastric | gastrorrhagia |
| agastroneuria | gastritides | gastrostaxis |
| arachnogastria | gastritis | gastrostomy |
| archigaster | gastrocele | gastrula |
| bathygastria | gastroenterologist | hypogastric |
| cholangiogastrotomy | gastroenterostomy | megalogastria |
| digastric | gastrohepatic | mesogastrium |

**\*Ge**: earth.

| | | |
|---|---|---|
| apogeotropic | geode | geotropism |
| biogeography | geography | hypogeous |
| epigeal | geonyctonastic | isogeotherm |
| geanticline | geopathology | phytogeography |
| geocarpic | geophagia | zoogeography |

**\*Gen-**: to become, be produced, be born. **Genes**is: being produced, coming into being, origination. **Genos, gen**eos: breed, race, kind. **Gene**a: stock, descent.

| | | |
|---|---|---|
| abiogenetic | exogenous | myelogenous |
| acrogenous | gamogenesis | palingenesis |
| actinogen | gene | parthenogenesis |
| aerogenous | geneology | pathogenesis |
| agamogenetic | genesis | psychogenic |
| agenosomia | genetics | pyogenic |
| agenesis | genoblast | pyrogen |
| agnogenic | genotype | rachitogenic |
| anagenesis | glycogen | rhodogenesis |
| autogenous | glyconeogenesis | spermatogenesis |
| cacogenesis | halogen | sporogenesis |
| carcinogenic | hematogenous | stromatogenous |
| crinogenic | heterogeneous | symphyogenesis |
| cryptogenic | hydrogen | syngenesioplasty |
| dysgenic | iatrogenic | xenogenesis |
| enterogenous | idiogenesis | zymogen |
| eugenics | | |

**\*Geny**s: jaw; cheek. **Genei**on: chin.

| genial | genioplasty | genyoschiza |
| genioglossus | genyantralgia | microgenia |
| genion | genychiloplasty | platygenia |

**\*Geron, geront**os: old man, old person. **Geras, gera**os: old age.

| acrogeria | geroderma | gerontophilia |
| agerasia | geromorphism | gerontotherapy |
| geratic | gerontology | progeria |
| geriatrics | | |

**\*Geus**is: taste.

| ageusia | dysgeusia | oxygeusia |
| amblygeustia | hemiageusia | parageusia |

**Gigas, gigant**os: giant.

acromegalogigantism   gigantism   gigantocyte   gigantosoma

**Ginglym**os: hinge; a hinge joint.

| ginglymo-arthrodial | ginglymoid | ginglymus |
| ginglymocladus | ginglymostoma | |

**\*Glauk**os: gleaming; sea-green, greenish-blue, gray.

| aglaukopsia | glaucoma | glaucosuria |
| glaucescent | glaucomatous | phacoglaucoma |
| glaucogonidium | glauconite | |

**Glen**e: cavity, socket of the eye, eyeball.

| Aglenus | glenoid | postglenoid |
| glenohumeral | glenospora | supraglenoidal |

**\*Gli**a: glue.

| astroglia | gliacyte | gliosarcoma | mesoglioma |
| ectoglia | glioma | gliosis | neuroglia |
| glia | gliomyoma | macroglia | |

**\*Gloss**a; **glott**a: tongue.

| aglossia | glossopharyngeal | proglossis |
| aglossostomia | glossotheca | proglottis |
| amygdaloglossus | hyoglossus | schistoglossia |
| ankyloglossia | hypoglossal | styloglossus |
| baryglossia | macroglossate | supraglottic |
| genioglossus | macroglossia | trachyglossate |
| glossanthrax | melanoglossia | uloglossitis |
| glossodynia | | |

**Glout**os: buttock.

| ectogluteus | gluteofemoral | glutitis |
| gluteal | gluteus | glutoid |

**\*Glyky**s; **glyker**os: sweet; sugar.

aglycemia glycerin glycopenia
aglycone glycerol glycosuria
glucogenic glycogen hyperglycemia
glucose glycogenosis hyperglycistia
    glyconeogenesis orthoglycemic

**Glyph**ein: to carve, engrave. **Glypt**os: carved.

Cicada hieroglyphica glyptography petroglyph
glyptodont Ophioglypha syphonoglyph

**\*Gnath**os: jaw.

agnathostomatous gnathodynamics micrognathia
campylognathia gnathoschisis pachygnathous
eurygnathic gnathotheca prognathism
gnathion hemignathia saurognathous

**\*Gno**nai: to know, judge. **Gnos**is: a knowing, knowledge. **Gnomon**:
one who knows, judge; index.

abarognosis anagnosasthenia dysanagnosia
aceognosia anosognosia lalognosis
acousmatagnosis astereognosis pathognomy
acragnosis baragnosis physiognomy
acrognosis chromodiagnosis pragmatagnosia
agnogenic cyesiognosis prognosis
agnosia diagnosis stereognostic

**\*Gon**e: generation, semen, seed; offspring.

amphigony gonidangium oogonium
aposporogony gonidiophore perigonium
endogonidium gonocyte protogonocyte
gonad gonorrhea spermatogonium
gonadopathy hypogonadism zoogony

**\*Goni**a: corner, angle.

intergonial polygonal stethogoniometer
goniocraniometry trigonum
goniometer

**\*Gon**y, **gonat**os: knee, joint.

gonalgia gonitis gonyoncus
gonarthrocace gonycampsis polygonaceous
gonatagra gonyectyposis

**\*Graph**ein: to draw, write, inscribe. **Gramma, grammat**os: something
drawn or written, mark, record.

agrammaticism electrocardiograph kymograph
agraphia engram palingraphia
bronchography grapho-analysis paragrammatism
cholangiogram

**\*Gymn**os: naked.

| | | |
|---|---|---|
| archigymnosperms | gymnocyte | gymnospore |
| gymnanthous | gymnoplast | hemigymnocarpous |
| gymnobacteria | | |

**\*Gyne, gynaik**os: woman; pistil of flower.

| | | |
|---|---|---|
| androgynous | gynandromorphism | gyn(o)ecium |
| dodecagynous | gynecoid | gynopathy |
| ergatogynous | gynecology | macrogynospore |
| gynander | gynecomastia | spanogyny |

**\*Gyr**os: circle, ring, turn.

| | | | |
|---|---|---|---|
| gyrate | gyrospasm | macrogyria | pachygyria |
| gyrencephalic | gyrus | oculogyric | polygyria |

# H

**\*Haima, haimat**os: blood.

| | | |
|---|---|---|
| acardiohemia | hematocrit | hemolysis |
| achroiocythemia | hematogenous | hemophilia |
| anematosis | hematology | hemostatic |
| anemia | hematoma | hemothorax |
| anhydremia | hematomyelia | hyperemia |
| antianemic | hematopexis | hyperglycemia |
| bactaremia | hematopoietic | hypoglycemia |
| copremia | hematoporphyrin | ischemia |
| drepanocythemia | hematorachis | leukanemia |
| encephalemia | hemic | leukemia |
| erythremia | hemocelom | lipemia |
| haematobium | hemochromatosis | septicopyemia |
| hemangioma | hemocytoblast | spanemia |
| hemarthrosis | hemoglobin | typhemia |
| hematemesis | hemokonia | uremia |
| hematocatharsis | | |

**\*Hair**ein: to take, grasp. **Kathaires**is: destruction.

| | | |
|---|---|---|
| catheresis | cytodiaeresis | hemocatheresis |
| catheretic | dieresis | neurexairesis |
| cholaneresis | exeresis | phlebexairesis |

**\*Hals, hal**os: salt.

| | | | |
|---|---|---|---|
| halobios | haloid | halophyte | stenohaline |
| halogen | halophile | hyperalonemia | |

**Hamart**ia: error, sin.

| | | |
|---|---|---|
| hamartia | hamartoblastoma | hamartoplasia |
| hamartite | hamartophobia | |

**\*Haplo**os: see **-plo**os.

**\*Hapt**ein: to fasten, fasten upon, attach; to grasp, seize, touch. **(H)aps**is: joining, juncture. **Haph**e: the sense of touch.

| | | | |
|---|---|---|---|
| chirapsia | haphephobia | hyperaphic | synaptic |
| dysaphia | haptics | karyapsis | telosynapsis |
| haphalgesia | haptometer | paraphia | |

**Heb**e: youth, puberty; pubic bone.

| | | |
|---|---|---|
| hebeanthous | hebetic | hebosteotomy |
| hebephrenia | heboid | ischiohebotomy |

**\*Hed-; hid- (his-, hiz-)**: to sit, to cause to sit, to place. **Hedr**a: sitting place, anus, base or side.

| | | |
|---|---|---|
| akathilia | hedrocele | scalenohedron |
| ephedrine | kathisophobia | subtrihedral |
| hedratresia | polyhedral | synizesis |

**Hedon**e: pleasure.

| | | | |
|---|---|---|---|
| algedonic | hedonism | hyperhedonia | parhedonia |
| hedonia | hedonophobia | hyphedonia | |

**\*Heli**os: sun.

| | | |
|---|---|---|
| helioaerotherapy | heliosis | heliotropism |
| helioencephalitis | heliotaxis | helium |
| heliopathia | heliotherapy | |

**\*Helix, helik**os: something spiral-shaped, a coil; a snail.

| | | |
|---|---|---|
| ant(i)helix | helicocarp | helicopod |
| helices | helicoid | helicotrema |
| helicobacterium | helicopepsin | |

**\*Helk**os: sore, ulcer.

| | | |
|---|---|---|
| carcinomelcosis | helcoid | stomatelcia |
| dacryelcosis | helcology | thymelcosis |
| gastrohelcosis | omphalelcosis | |

**\*Helmins, helminth**os: worm.

| | | |
|---|---|---|
| anthelminthic | helminthiasis | nemathelminth |
| helminth | helminthology | platyhelminth |
| helminthagogue | helminthophobia | pseudelminth |

**Hel**os: nail, nail-head; callus, corn.

| | | | |
|---|---|---|---|
| anthelotic | helobacterium | helosis | myceleconidium |
| ephelis | heloma | helotomy | protomycelium |

**\*Hemer**a: day.

| | | |
|---|---|---|
| ephemeral | hemeralopia | monohemerous |
| ephemerid | hemeranthous | nyctohemeral |

**\*He**nai: to send going, send, let go. **Enema, Enemat**os: a sending in. **Pares**is: a letting go; paralysis. **Katheter**: that sent or let down; a tube for passage of fluids.

| | | |
|---|---|---|
| angioparesis | enemator | paresis |
| catheter | enteroparesis | paretic |

**\*He**nai (*contd.*)

catheterization
catheterostat
enema
enemata

gastroparesis
hemiparesis
monoparesis

pneumonoparesis
polyparesis
salpingocatheterism

**\*Hepar, hepat**os: liver.

gastrohepatic
heparin
hepatargia
hepaticostomy
hepatization

hepatocirrhosis
hepatoduodenal
hepatomegaly
hepatopathy
hepatotropic

hydrohepatosis
icterohepatitis
intrahepatic
perihepatitis

**\*Herpes, herpet**os: a creeping; spreading blisters. **Herpet**on: a creeping animal, especially snake or reptile.

antherpetic
cephalerpeton

herpangina
herpes

herpetic
herpetology

**\*Heter**os: other, different from.

dermatoheteroplasty
heteradelphia
heterandrous
heterochromia
heterochthonous

heterocladic
heteroecious
heterogeneous
heterologous
heteronomous

heteroploid
heterotaxia
heterotopic
myeleterosis

**Hex**is: a having, holding; habit (of body), bodily condition, permanent condition.

cachéctic
cachexia

hexiology
osteocachexia

pleonexia

**\*Hidros, hidrot**os: sweat, perspiration.

acrohyperhidrosis
anhidrotic
blepharochromidrosis
bromidrosis

chromidrosis
cyanephidrosis
hidradenitis
hidrosis

hyphidrosis
maschalephidrosis
paridrosis

**Hier**on: sacred place, temple; the sacrum (bone).

dolichohieric
hieralgia

hieromania
hierophobia

hierotherapy
platyhieric

**Hippocrates**: Greek physician of 5th century B. C., founder of modern medicine.

hippocratic
hippocratism
neo-hippocratism

**Hipp**os: horse. **Hippokamp**os: a sea horse; an elongated ridge in cavity of brain.

ephippium
hippanthropia

hippiatric
hippocampal

hippuric
posthippocampal

**\*Hist**os; **histi**on: tissue, web.

chlorhistechia
cytohistogenesis

histiocyte
histionic

histomorphology
histozoic

**\*Hist**os  (*contd.*)

| hemohistoblast | histoclastic | hyperglycistia |
| histamine | histodialysis | neurohistology |
| histic | histology | |

**\*Hod**os: road, way, path.

| centrode | exodic | kinesodic |
| diodangium | hodology | odometer |
| eisodic | kathodic | pneumatode |

**\*Hol**os: whole, entire, all.

| hemiologamous | holoblastic | holomastigote |
| holarthritis | holocrine | holorachischisis |
| | | holotrichous |

**\*Homal**os: even, level, flat; regular.

| anomalotrophy | deuteranomalopia | homalocephalus |
| anomaly | geomalism | homalocladous |

**\*Hom**os; **homoi**os: like, the same as, equal.

| homeopathy | homodesmotic | homonomous | homothermal |
| homeozoic | homodromous | homosexuality | |

**\*Hormon, hormon**os: setting in motion, arousing, exciting.

| auxohormone | exormia | hormone | neurohormone |
| dyshormonism | hormonagogue | hormonopoietic | parahormone |

**\*Hyal**os: glass.

| cytohyaloplasm | hyalitis | hyalomere |
| hematohyaloid | hyaloid | hyalomucoid |
| hyaline | hyaloma | hyalopterous |

**Hydatis, hydatid**os: a drop of water; a watery cyst or vesicle.

| hydatid | hydatidocele | hydatigenous |
| hydatidism | hydatiform | hydatoma |

**\*Hydor, hydat**os: water, fluid.

| achlorhydria | hydriatic | hydrophobia |
| aerohydrotherapy | hydroa | hydropic |
| anhydremia | hydrocele | hydrorrhea |
| dehydrated | hydrocenosis | hydroscapha |
| hemohydraulics | hydrocephalus | hydrostatic |
| hydrangiology | hydrogen | hydrotherapy |
| hydrargyrum | hydromegatherm | oligohydramnion |
| hydrarthrosis | hydropericardium | oscheohydrocele |

**\*Hydrops, hydrop**os: dropsy.

| anthydropic | hydropic | hydropotherapy |
| hydrops | hydropigenous | |

**\*Hygiei**a: health, soundness of mind or body.

| antihygienic | hygieist | hygiogenesis |
| hygiastics | hygiene | |

**\*Hygr**os: wet, moist, fluid.

hygroblepharic    hygrometer    hygrophobia    hygrostomia
hygroma    hygrophilous    hygroscopic    mesohygromorphic

**\*Hyl**e: wood; matter.

hyle    hyloma    hylotropic
hylephobia    hylophagous    hylozoism
hylogenesis    hylotomous    mesohyloma

**\*Hymen, hymen**os: skin, membrane of vagina.

hydrohymenitis    hymenophore    hymenotomy
hymen    Hymenoptera    neohymen

**\*Hyoeid**es: like the upsilon, i.e., U-shaped. Bone at base of tongue.

epihyoid    hyothyroid    stylohyoideus
hyoglossus    infrahyoid    subhyoid
hyoid    sternohyoid    tympanohyal

**\*Hypn**os: sleep. **Agrypn**os (**agre-**: to hunt for; **hypn**os): sleepless, wakeful.

agrypnia    autohypnosis    hypnobatia    neurohypnology
agrypnocoma    hypnagogic    hypnosis    parahypnosis
ahypnia    hypnapagogic    hypnotic

**\*Hypsi**: on high, aloft. **Hypsos, hypse**os: height.

hypsibrachycephalic    hypsokinesis    hypsophyll
hypsiphobia    hypsometer    hypsotherapy
hypsodont    hypsonosus

**\*Hyster**a: womb, uterus.

acrohysterosalpingectomy    hysterectomy    hysterotomy
celiohysterotomy    hysteria    hysterotrachelotomy
colpohysterectomy    hysteropexy    laparohysterotomy
dihysteria

# I

**\*Ia**esthai: to heal. **Iatr**os: one who heals, physician. **Iatrei**a: healing, treatment.

amblyopiatrics    hydriatric    pediatrics
cyniatrics    iatrarchy    podiatry
geriatrics    iatrogenic    presbyatrics
gyniatrics    iatrotechnics    psychiatry
hippiater    orthopsychiatry

**\*Ichthys**: fish.

acanthichthyosis    icthyolite    ichthyosaur
ichthyismus    ichthyology    ichthyosis
ichthyol    ichthyopterygia    panichthyophagous

**\*Ide**a: see **Eidos**.

**\*Idi**os: one's own, peculiar.

| idiochromidia | idiomuscular | idiosyncrasy | nucleoidioplasm |
| idiogenesis | idiopathic | idiothermous | |
| idiolalia | idioplasm | idiotropic | |

**\*Ikter**os: jaundice.

| anticteric | icteroid | preicteric |
| icterohemoglobinuria | metaicteric | splenicterus |
| icterohepatitis | pedicterus | subicteric |

**\*Iris, irid**os: the rainbow; colored membrane of the eye.

| aniridia | irides | iridoplegia |
| choroidoiritis | iridic | keratoiridoscope |
| iridauxesis | iridocyclitis | mesiris |
| iridencleisis | iridodialysis | |

**\*Is, in**os: strength; muscle, fiber, tissue.

| hyperinosis | inoma | inosteatoma |
| inemia | inosclerosis | inotropic |
| inochondritis | inositis | onkinocele |

**\*Ischi**on: hip-joint, hip.

| galactischia | ischiopodite | pubioischiatic |
| ischiadelphus | ischiorectal | sacrosciatic |
| ischiococcygeal | ischium | sciatic |
| ischiofemoral | | |

**\*Is**os: equal.

| anisocarpous | isochronous | isomastigote | isomicrogamete |
| anisochromia | isodactylism | isomerous | isopetalous |
| anisocytosis | isodontic | isometropia | isotonia |
| anisognathous | isogamy | | |

**\*Isthm**os: a narrow neck or passage.

| isthmectomy | isthmitis | isthmoplegia | isthmus |
| isthmian | isthmocholosis | isthmospasm | paristhmion |

## K

**\*Kain**os: new. **Kainot**es: newness, novelty.

| caenomorphism | cenogenesis | misocainia |
| caenotophobia | cenopsychic | synkainogenesis |
| caenozoic | | |

**\*Kak**os: bad, disordered, abnormal.

| acacanthrax | cachexia | cacomelia | kakidrosis |
| arthrocace | cacodontia | cacosmia | osteocachectic |
| cacergasia | cacogenesis | gonarthrocace | stomatocace |
| cacesthesia | | | |

**\*Kal(l)os:** beautiful.

| | | |
|---|---|---|
| calisthenics | callodendron | kallikak |
| calligraphy | callomania | kalopsia |

**\*Kalyx, kalykos:** covering, shell; circle of sepals of a flower.

| | | |
|---|---|---|
| calycanthus floridus | calyciform | calyx |
| calyciflorous | calycle | Gymnocalycium |

**\*Kamptos; kampylos:** bent

| | | |
|---|---|---|
| acampsia | campylognathia | osteocampsia |
| camptocormia | dactylocampsodynia | rachiocampsis |
| camptodactyly | gonycampsis | |

**Kanthos:** corner of the eye.

| | | | |
|---|---|---|---|
| acantha | canthoplasty | canthotomy | epicanthus |
| canthal | canthorrhaphy | canthus | kantholysis |

**Kar-** (keirein): to cut. **Akares:** too short to cut; tiny; a mite. **Kormos:** result of cutting; trunk (of tree or body).

| | | | |
|---|---|---|---|
| acarian | acarinosis | corm | cormophylogeny |
| acariasis | acormus | cormel | cormophyte |
| acaricide | camptocormia | cormidium | epicormic |
| acarid | | | |

**\*Kardia:** heart.

| | | |
|---|---|---|
| acardiohemia | cardiology | pericardiocentesis |
| acephalocardia | cardioplasty | pericardiostomy |
| acleistocardia | electrocardiograph | pericardium |
| aerendocardia | endocardium | pneumopericardium |
| angiocarditis | epicardium | subepicardial |
| bradycardia | hydropericardium | tachycardia |
| cardiac | myocarditis | telecardiophone |

**\*Karkinos:** crab; cancer.

| | | |
|---|---|---|
| adenocarcinoma | carcinomata | carcinosis |
| carcinogenic | carcinomatosis | chondrocarcinoma |
| carcinogenicity | carcinomelcosis | phlebocarcinoma |

**\*Karpos:** the wrist.

| | | |
|---|---|---|
| carpal | carpometacarpal | cubitocarpal |
| carpectomy | carpoptosis | metacarpophalangeal |

**\*Karpos:** fruit, seed.

| | | |
|---|---|---|
| acanthocarpous | carpophore | pyrenocarp |
| acrocarpus | carposporangium | sarcocarp |
| ascocarp | dichocarp | schizocarp |
| carpels | geocarpic | syncarp |
| carpogonium | gymnocarpous | xanthocarpous |
| carpophagus | intercarpellary | xylocarp |

**\*Kary**on: nut, kernel, nucleus.

| | | |
|---|---|---|
| acaryote | karyogamy | karyotheca |
| amphikaryon | karyokinesis | megakaryocyte |
| caryopsis | karyoklasis | parikaryon |
| diplokaryon | karyolysis | protokaryon |
| karyochromatophil | karyo(r)rhexis | |

**\*Kathars**is: a cleansing, emptying.

| | | |
|---|---|---|
| acatharsia | cathartic | hematocatharsis |
| anacatharsis | cephalocathartic | hypercatharsis |

**\*Kaus**os; **kaum**a: burning heat. **Kaust**os; **kaut**os: burnt. **Kauter**ion: searing-iron.

| | | |
|---|---|---|
| atmocausis | caustic | electrocautery |
| caumesthesia | cauterize | thermocautery |
| causalgia | catacausis | thoracocautery |

**\*Kel**e: tumor, hernia.

| | | |
|---|---|---|
| celology | encephalocele | kelectome |
| celosomia | enterocele | meningocele |
| colpocele | galactocele | omphalocele |
| cystocele | gastrocele | splenocele |
| derencephalocele | hydrocele | thyrocele |
| ectokelostomy | | |

**Kelis, kelid**os: stain; scar.

| | | |
|---|---|---|
| celotomia | keloid | keloplasty |
| kelis | keloidosis | |

**\*Ken**os: empty. **Kenos**is: an emptying.

| | | |
|---|---|---|
| cenangium | gastralgokenosis | kenotoxic |
| cenapophytes | hydrocenosis | lithocenosis |
| cenophobia | | |

**\*Kente**ein: to goad, prick. **Kentr**on: sharp point, center. *-centesis*: perforation, surgical puncturing.

| | | |
|---|---|---|
| archicentra | dorsocentral | paracentesis |
| arthrocentesis | eccentropiesis | pericardiocentesis |
| centocinesia | keratocentesis | pleurocentesis |
| centrotaxis | laryngocentesis | rachiocentesis |

**\*Kephal**e: head. **Enkephal**on: that within the head; the brain.

| | | |
|---|---|---|
| acephalobrachia | clinocephaly | hydrocephalus |
| acephaly | diencephalon | leptocephalus |
| acrocephalosyndactylia | diplocephalus | opisthencephalon |
| acrocephaly | dolichocephalic | oxycephalous |
| anencephaly | electroencephalogram | pneumoencephalogram |
| brachiocephalic | encephalemia | polioencephalitis |
| brachycephalic | encephalitis | porencephaly |
| cephalad | encephalocele | postencephalitic |
| cephalalgia | encephalomalacia | prosencephalon |

**\*Kephal**e (*contd.*)

| | | |
|---|---|---|
| cephalic | encephalomeningitis | scaphocephalic |
| cephalopod | encephalomyelitis | stenocephalous |
| cephalotheca | eurycephalic | telencephalon |

**\*Keras, kerat**os: horn, horny tissue; cornea.

| | | |
|---|---|---|
| aceratosis | keratectasia | keratomalacia |
| brachycerous | keratocentesis | keratosis |
| ceratonosus | keratoconus | kerectasis |
| cyclokeratitis | keratodermatitis | monocerous |
| keracele | keratoma | splenceratosis |

**Kerk**os: tail.

| | | | |
|---|---|---|---|
| cercaria | cercocystis | cysticercoid | procercoid |
| cercaricidal | cercus | heterocercal | |

**Ker**os: wax.

| | | |
|---|---|---|
| Ceriomyces | cerotic | Ceroxylon |
| ceroplastic | cerotype | myokerosis |

**Kest**os: stitched, embroidered; girdle; tapeworm.

| | | |
|---|---|---|
| Cestocrinus | cestodiasis | metacestode |
| Cestoda | cestoid | |

**\*Kine**ein: to move.

| | | |
|---|---|---|
| acrocinesis | cinemascopia | kinesthetic |
| adiadochokinesis | capodyskinesia | kinetoblast |
| akinesis | echokinesia | ookinesis |
| akinesthesia | hyperkinesia | palikinesia |
| anakinetomere | karyokinesis | photokinetic |
| autokinetic | kinesiology | synkinesis |
| bradykinetic | | |

**\*Kirrh**os: tawny, orange, yellow.

| | | |
|---|---|---|
| cirrhonosus | cirrhotic | nephrocirrhosis |
| cirrhosis | hepatocirrhosis | pneumonocirrhosis |

**Kirs**os: a varix; dilated vein.

| | | |
|---|---|---|
| cirsectomy | cirsodesis | hydrocirsocele |
| cirsenchysis | cirsoid | |

**\*Kla**ein: to break, destroy. **Klad**os; **klasma, klasmat**os; **kl**on: that which is broken off, a piece; branch or twig, a sprout.

| | | |
|---|---|---|
| acanthocladous | clasmatosis | karyoklasis |
| aclasia | colloidoclasia | lithoclast |
| actinocladothrix | cranioclast | odontoclasts |
| arthroclasia | diaclasia | onychoclasis |
| cardioclasis | eocladous | osteoclast |
| chondroclast | erythroclastic | periodontoclasia |
| cladocarpous | heterocladic | phyllocladium |
| cladode | histoclastic | thromboclasis |
| cladoptosis | | |

**\*Klei**ein: to sheathe, close. **Kleist**os: closed. **Kleis, kleid**os: a means of closing, a bar, a key; the clavicle. **Kleitoris**: the clitoris.

| | | |
|---|---|---|
| acleistocardia | cleistogamy | enteroapocleisis |
| arthroclisis | cleistothecium | iridencleisis |
| cleidagra | clitoridoauxe | neurosarcokleisis |
| cleidocostal | clitoridotomy | otocleisis |
| cleidocranial | colpocleisis | splenocleisis |
| cleidotomy | corenclisis | sternocleidomastoid |
| cleistocarp | | |

**Klept**ein: to steal, hide. **Klept**es: thief.

| | | |
|---|---|---|
| clepsydra | kleptomania | mycokleptic |
| kleptobiosis | kleptophobia | |

**Klimax, klimak**os: ladder. **Klimakt**er: rung of a ladder; critical stage.

climacorhizal    climacteric    clymacophobia    clymacterium

**\*Klin**ein: to bend, turn, slope; make recline, lean; lie down. **Klis**is: inclination. **Klinik**os: pertaining to bed; clinic.

| | | |
|---|---|---|
| anaclinotropism | clinoscope | oxyklinocephalic |
| anaclitic | clinostatic | patroclinous |
| clinandrium | cliseometer | subclinical |
| clinic | enclitic | thermocline |
| clinomania | | |

**\*Klon**os: confused motion, turmoil; muscular spasm.

| | | | |
|---|---|---|---|
| blepharoclonus | clonograph | myoclonia | synclonus |
| clonic | clonospasm | paramyoclonus | |
| clonicotonic | clonus | pseudoclonus | |

**\*Klyz**ein (**klyd-, klys-**): to wash, wash out.

| | | |
|---|---|---|
| bronchoclysis | coloclyster | metroclyst |
| clysis | enteroclysis | phleboclysis |
| clyster | hypodermoclysis | proctoclysis |
| clysterium | lithoclysmia | |

**Knem**e: the lower leg; tibia, shin. **Knemis, knemid**os: greave, legging.

| | | | |
|---|---|---|---|
| acnemia | brachyknemic | gastrocnemius | psilocnemis |
| ancylocnemis | cnemis | macrocnemia | |
| anisocnemic | entocnemial | paracnemis | |

**Knid**e: a nettle. **Knidos**is; **knism**os: itching.

| | | |
|---|---|---|
| cnidoblast | cnidophore | cnidosis | knismogenic |
| cnidocil | cnidopod | eucnide | |

**Kochli**as: snail with a spiral shell; spiral cavity of the inner ear.

| | | |
|---|---|---|
| cochlea | Cochliomyia | ecochleation |
| cochleariform | cochliovestibular | gyrocochlea |
| cochlearthrosis | | |

**\*Koili**a: cavity. **Koil**os: hollow. **Koilom**a: a hollow cavity, body cavity.

| | | |
|---|---|---|
| acoelomate | celomic | koilonychia |
| amphicelous | Coelenterata | myocelialgia |
| atriocoelomic | coelosperm | splanchnocoel |
| celiac | cystidoceliotomy | syringocoele |
| celiectasia | encephalocoele | thoracoceloschisis |
| celiotomy | hemocelom | |

**\*Koin**os: common.

| | | |
|---|---|---|
| biocoenosis | coenogamy | koinonia |
| cenotype | coenosteum | koinoniphobia |
| c(o)enesthesia | epicene | koinotropic |
| c(o)enobium | hypercenesthesia | paracenesthesia |
| coenoecium | | |

**\*Kokk**os: berry, grain, seed; berry-shaped bacteria.

| | | |
|---|---|---|
| cocci | coccogone | megacoccus |
| coccidiosis | coccolith | meningococcemia |
| Coccidoides | coccomelasma | pneumococcus |
| coccogenous | diplococcus | staphylococcemia |

**\*Kokkyx, kokkyg**os: cuckoo; a bone at end of spinal column said to resemble a cuckoo's bill.

| | | |
|---|---|---|
| coccygalgia | coccygotomy | ischiococcygeal |
| coccygeus | coccyx | rectococcypexy |
| coccygodynia | intercoccygeal | sacrococcygeal |

**\*Kole**os: sheath; the vagina.

| | | | |
|---|---|---|---|
| coleitis | coleocystitis | coleopterous | coleorhiza |
| coleocele | coleopod | coleoptosis | coleotomy |

**\*Koll**a: glue.

| | | | |
|---|---|---|---|
| collagen | colleter | colloidoclasia | kollophore |
| collenchyma | collodion | colloidopexy | pseudocolloid |
| collencyte | colloid | isocolloid | |

**\*Kol**on: lower part of the bowels, the colon.

| | | |
|---|---|---|
| aerocolia | colodyspepsia | megacolon |
| colauxe | colopexy | mesocolon |
| colic | ectocolostomy | nephrocolic |
| colicystopyelitis | gastrocoloptosis | retrocolic |
| colitis | laparocolostomy | typhlocolitis |
| coloclysis | | |

**\*Kolp**os: swollen out; bosom; vagina.

| | | |
|---|---|---|
| celiocolpotomy | colpohysterectomy | myocolpitis |
| colpectasia | colpoperineoplasty | pachycolpismus |
| colpocele | colpopexy | pyocolpocele |
| colpocleisis | | |

**Koly**ein: to check, hinder.

| colyone | kolyphrenia | kolytic |
| kolypeptic | kolyseptic | |

**\*Koma, komat**os: deep sleep, coma.

| agrypnocoma | comatose | psychocoma | semicomatose |

**\*Kom**e: hair.

| albicomous | comosum | opisthocomus | prokomion |
| Callicoma | floricome | plectocomia | |
| comatulid | melanocomous | plumicome | |

**\*Konch**e: mussel, shell.

| concha | conchitis | conchoscope | protoconch |
| conchiform | conchology | conchotomy | pseudoconch |

**\*Kondyl**os: knuckle, joint.

| ampicondylous | diacondylar | epicondyle | supracondylar |
| condyle | entepicondylar | ectocondyle | |
| condyloma | epicondylalgia | intercondylar | |

**\*Konis, koni**os: dust.

| conidiophore | coniophage | konometer |
| conidiospore | conioses | otoconia |
| conidium | coniotoxicosis | pneumonoconiosis |
| coniofibrosis | dermatoconiosis | pycnoconidium |
| coniology | hemokonia | |

**\*Kon**os: pine cone, cone.

| conenchyma | conophorophyta | hypocone | metacone |
| coniferous | deuterocone | keratoconus | phragmoconic |

**\*Kopr**os: dung.

| acoprosis | coprolalomania | coprophilic | oligocopria |
| copremesis | coprolite | coproporphyrin | ornithocopros |
| copremia | coprophagous | coprostasis | |

**Kopt**ein (**kop-**): to strike, smite, cut off; to tire, weary. **Kop**os: a beating; fatigue.

| apocoptic | copopsia | ophthalmocopia |
| copodyskinesia | copos | syncope |

**Korax, korak**os: raven, crow. **Korakoeid**es: like a raven's (beak); a hooklike (curved) process over the shoulder joint.

| acrocoracoid | coracoid | procoracoid |
| acromiocoracoid | hypocoracoid | sternocoracoideus |

**\*Kor**e: maiden, doll; pupil (of the eye).

| anisocoria | coreplasty | dyscoria | microcoria |
| corectopia | dicoria | isocoria | stenocoriasis |
| corelysis | diplocoria | korenclisis | |

**Koron**e: crow, crown; apophysis.

| | | | |
|---|---|---|---|
| corona | coronion | coronoid | stenocoronine |

**Koryn**e: club.

| | | | |
|---|---|---|---|
| corynebacterium | corynidia | corynocarpous | leptocorynus |

**Kosm**os: order, world.

| | | | |
|---|---|---|---|
| cosmaesthesia | cosmos | macrocosm | paleocosmology |

*****Kotyl**e: something hollow; socket; cup; a first leaf of a sporophyte.

| | | |
|---|---|---|
| acotyledon | cotyloid | polycotyledonous |
| cotyledon | cotylophorous | syncotyledous |

*****Kranion**: cranium, skull.

| | | | |
|---|---|---|---|
| acrania | craniate | cranioschisis | intracranial |
| basicranial | cranioclast | dolichocranial | migraine |
| chondrocranium | craniometry | epicranium | pericranium |
| cleidocranial | craniopagus | | |

*****Kras**is: a mixing, mixture; temperament.

| | | |
|---|---|---|
| crasis | galactacrasia | malcrasis |
| dyscrasia | idiosyncrasy | metacrasis |

*****Kreas, kreat**os: flesh; muscle tissue.

| | | |
|---|---|---|
| apancrea | creophilae | kreatinuria |
| creatine | dyspancreatism | pancreatic |
| creatophagous | gastropancreatitis | |

**Krik**os: a ring. **Krikoeid**es: like a ring; a cartilage of the larynx.

| | | | |
|---|---|---|---|
| cricoderma | cricoid | cricotracheotomy | keratocricoid |

*****Krin**ein: to separate; distinguish, decide; emit, secrete. **Kris**is: point of decision.

| | | |
|---|---|---|
| allocrine | dyscrinism | exocrine |
| angiocrinosis | dysendocrisiasis | hematocrit |
| chromocrinia | eccrinology | heterocrisis |
| crinogenic | endocrine | holocrine |
| crisis | epicritic | hypocrinism |
| critical | | |

*****Krot**os: a striking, beat; pulse-beat. **Krotes**is: a knocking, clapping.

| | | |
|---|---|---|
| acrotism | anatricrotic | dicrotic |
| anacrotism | bradycrotic | gonycrotesis |
| anadicrotism | catadicrotism | polycrotic |

*****Kryos; krym**os: ice-cold, frost. **Krystall**os: clear ice; crystal.

| | | |
|---|---|---|
| cryanesthesia | cryogen | crystalluria |
| cryesthesia | cryophylactic | hematocryal |
| crymodynia | cryoplankton | hemocryoscopy |
| crymophilia | crystal | isocrymal |
| crymophyte | crystalloiditis | urinocryoscopy |
| crymotherapy | | |

**\*Krypt**os: hidden.

cryptocarp
cryptogam
cryptogenic
cryptolith

cryptoradiometer
cryptozoic
crypts
electrocryptectomy

kryptomnesic
onychocryptosis
syncryptic

**Kteis, kten**os: comb.

ctene
ctenidiobranch

ctenidium
ctenoid

ctenophora
ctenostichous

**\*Kyan**os: dark blue.

acrocyanosis
acyanoblepsia
acyanopsia
chrysocyanosis

cyanemia
cyanephidrosis
cyanochroia

cyanophilous
cyanophyll
cyanosis

hematocyanin
pyocyanic
urocyanosis

**\*Ky**ein: to swell; be pregnant. **Kyma, kymat**os: a swell, wave. **Kystis, kystid**os; **kyst**e: sac. **Kyt**os: a hollow receptacle; cell.

acephalocyst
achroacytosis
achroiocythemia
actinokymography
amebocytogenous
anisocytosis
cholecystogram
chylocyst
cyesiognosis
cyesiology
cyesis
cyme
cysticotomy
cystidoceliotomy
cystidolaparotomy
cystitis
cystocele
cystolithectomy
cystoma

cystotrachelotomy
cytaster
cythemolytic
cytobiology
cytogamy
cytometer
cytotropism
cytula
dacryocyst
desmocyte
drepanocythemia
eccyesis
encyopyelitis
ependymocyte
erythrocyte
excystation
gigantocyte
gliacyte
hemocytoblast

histocyte
hypercyesis
kymograph
kymotrichous
leukocytopoiesis
lochiocyte
lymphocyte
macrocytic
metacyesis
mykokymia
oocyte
pericholecystic
perikymata
pseudocyesis
psychokym
pyelocystitis
spermatocystitis
thrombocytolysis
thymocyte

**\*Kykl**os: circle, ring, wheel.

cyclarthrosis
cyclic
cyclochorioiditis
cyclophoria

cyclostome
cyclothymic
iridocyclitis
isocyclic

pericycle
polycyclic
pseudocyclosis

**\*Kym**a: see **Ky**ein.

**Kyon, kyn**os: dog.

cynanche
cynanthropy

cyniatrics
cynocephalic

cynodont
cynopodous

kynophobia

**Kyphos**is: curvature with dorsal convexity; humpbacked.

| | | |
|---|---|---|
| kypholordosis | kyphotic | rhinokyphosis |
| kyphoscoliorrhachitic | kyphotone | trachelokyphosis |
| kyphoscoliosis | rachiocyphosis | |

***Kyst**e: see **Ky**ein.

***Kyt**os: see **Ky**ein.

# L

***Lab**ein (**Lep-**): to take, grasp, seize. **Lab**e: handle. **Leps**is: seizure.

| | | | |
|---|---|---|---|
| acataleptic | Cercolabes | litholabe | pyknolepsy |
| amphilepsis | epilepsy | narkolepsy | tricholabion |
| analeptic | kataleptoid | photolepsy | trilabe |
| astrolabe | | | |

***Labyrinth**os: a maze or system of intercommunicating passages; the internal ear.

| | | |
|---|---|---|
| labyrinth | labyrinthitis | perilabyrinth |
| labyrinthectomy | neurolabyrinthitis | pyolabyrinthitis |

***Lal**ein: to talk, chat, speak.

| | | | |
|---|---|---|---|
| acoualion | dyslalia | laliatry | palilalia |
| alalia | echolalia | lalopathy | rhinolalia |
| barylalia | embololalia | laloplegia | tachylalia |
| bradylalia | idiolalia | mogilalia | |

***Lamp**ein: to shine forth, flash. **Lampr**os: clear, bright.

| | | | |
|---|---|---|---|
| eclampsia | lamp | lamprosoma | psycheclampsia |
| eclamptogenic | lamprophonia | preeclampsia | |

**Lapar**a: the loins, flank; abdomen.

| | | |
|---|---|---|
| cystadolaparotomy | laparocolostomy | laparotomy |
| elytrolaparatomy | laparohepatomy | thoracolaparatomy |
| hysterolaparotomy | | |

***Larynx, laryng**os: the organ of voice at the upper part of the trachea.

| | | |
|---|---|---|
| endolaryngeal | laryngitis | laryngotracheitis |
| laryngeal | laryngocentesis | laryngoxerosis |
| laryngemphraxis | laryngoplegia | otorhinolaryngology |
| laryngismus | | |

**Lekith**os: yolk of egg.

| | | |
|---|---|---|
| alecithal | eutelolecithal | oligolecithal |
| centrolecithal | lecithalbumin | toxolecithin |
| ectolecithal | lecithin | tropholecithus |

**Leichen, leichen**os: tree-moss; eruptive skin disease.

| | | |
|---|---|---|
| lichen | lichenism | lichenoid |
| licheniasis | lichenography | lichenology |

**\*Lei**os: smooth.

| | | | |
|---|---|---|---|
| leiodermia | leiomyosarcoma | leiothric | liorhizae |
| leiofibroma | Leiophyllum | lienteric | liostethus |
| leiomyoma | leiosperma | | |

**\*Leip**ein (**lip-**): to leave, abandon; fail, neglect.

| | | |
|---|---|---|
| ellipsis | lipophrenia | lipsis |
| leiphemia | lipothymia | lipsotrichia |
| lipogastry | lipoxemy | paralipophobia |

**Lemm**a: something peeled off; a husk, peel; sheath.

| | | |
|---|---|---|
| alemmal | lemmoblast | oolemma |
| aneurilemmic | lemmocyte | sarcolemma |
| axilemma | neurilemma | telolemma |

**Leon, leont**os: lion.

| | | | |
|---|---|---|---|
| leontiasis | Leontodon | Leontopodium | leopard |

**\*Lep-**: see **Lab**ein.

**\*Lepis, lepid**os: scale, rind, flake.

| | | | |
|---|---|---|---|
| haplolepideous | lepidoma | lepidosis | mesolepidoma |
| lepidodendron | lepidophyton | lepidotrichia | neolepidoptera |

**\*Lepr**os: scaly. **Lepr**a; **lepros**is: leprosy.

| | | |
|---|---|---|
| leper | lepraphobia | leprosy |
| lepra | leproma | paraleprosis |
| Leprantha | leprosarium | phymolepra |

**\*Leptyn**ein: to make thin. **Lep**ein: to peel. **Lept**os: peeled, thin, delicate.

| | | |
|---|---|---|
| iridoleptinsis | leptochroa | leptophyllous |
| keratoleptynsis | leptodontous | leptorhine |
| leptocephalus | leptonema | perileptomatic |
| leptocercal | leptophonia | |

**\*Leth**e: oblivion, forgetfulness. **Letharg**os: drowsiness.

| | | |
|---|---|---|
| alethia | lethe | letheomania |
| antilethargic | lethargogenic | lethologica |
| | lethargy | Lethonymous |

**\*Leuk**os: white.

| | | |
|---|---|---|
| aleukemia | leucoplasts | leukomyelopathy |
| aleukocytosis | leukemia | leukonychia |
| leucite | leukoderma | leukopenia |
| leucocarpous | leukoencephalitis | leukotrichia |
| leucocytosis | | |

**\*Lex**is (**leg**ein, to speak): speech, word, phrase, diction, reading.

| | | |
|---|---|---|
| alexia | dyslexic | typhlolexia |
| bradylexia | paralexia | |

**Lim**os: hunger, famine.

| | | |
|---|---|---|
| bulimia | limosis | limitrophic |
| limophthisis | limotherapy | |

***Lip**os: fat. **Liparos**: oily, fat.

| | | |
|---|---|---|
| adenolipomatosis | liparocele | lipoma |
| alipogenetic | liparodyspnea | lipomatosis |
| cardiomyoliposis | liparomphalus | liposarcoma |
| chromolipoid | lipemia | osteolipochondroma |
| hypoliposis | | |

***Lith**os: stone.

| | | |
|---|---|---|
| antilithic | enterolith | microlith |
| broncholith | lithagogic | otolith |
| bursolith | lithiasis | phlebolite |
| choledocholithiasis | lithoclast | rhinolith |
| cholelith | lithonephritis | sialolithotomy |
| coprolith | lithophagous | splanchnolith |
| cryptolith | lithophyll | typhlolithiasis |
| dacryolith | lithotomy | zoolith |
| cystolithectomy | lithotrips | |

***Lob**os: a pod, lobe.

| | | | |
|---|---|---|---|
| intralobular | lobopodia | lobostomy | multilobate |
| lobar | lobose | lobotomy | pinnatilobate |

**Lochi**a: pertaining to childbirth, especially the vaginal discharge after childbirth.

| | | |
|---|---|---|
| dyslochia | lochiocolpos | lochiopyra |
| lochial | lochiocyte | lochiorrhea |

***Log**os: word, speech; thought; reason; discourse, treatise; ratio, proportion. -*logy*: body of knowledge, science of. (Cf. **Lex**is).

| | | | |
|---|---|---|---|
| andrology | epidemiology | heterologous | neologism |
| anthropology | gerontology | logagnosia | phycology |
| biology | gynecology | logoplegia | polylogia |
| bradylogia | hematology | logorrhea | typhlology |
| dyslogia | | | |

***Loph**os: ridge, crest.

| | | |
|---|---|---|
| ectoloph | lophodont | monolophous |
| lophius | lophosteon | protoloph |
| lophobranchiate | Lophotrichia | trilophous |
| lophocercal | metaloph | |

**Lord**os: bent backward.

| | | | |
|---|---|---|---|
| kypholordosis | lordoscoliosis | lordosis | lordotic |

**Lox**os: oblique, slanting.

| | | |
|---|---|---|
| loxarthron | loxophthalmus | loxotomy | odontoloxia |
| loxia | loxotic | metroloxia | |

*Lyein: to loosen, break up. Paralysis: loss of motion or sensory function.

| | | |
|---|---|---|
| amylolysis | histodialysis | neuroparalysis |
| analysis | karyolysis | odynolysis |
| antistaphylohemolysis | katolysis | photolytic |
| autolysis | lyophil | psychoanalysis |
| autolytic | lyophobe | spasmolysant |
| blastolysis | lysemia | steatolysis |
| chromatolysis | lysin | stromatolysis |
| corelysis | lysis | thermolysis |
| dermatolysis | lysogen | urinalysis |
| enterolysis | lytic | zymolysis |
| hemolysis | | |

*Lympha (Latin version of nymphe): a body containing white cells, lymph.

| | | |
|---|---|---|
| hematolymphangioma | lymphedema | lymphosarcoleukemia |
| karyolymph | lymphoblast | macrolymphocyte |
| lymphadenopathy | lymphodermia | splenolymph |
| lymphatic | lymphogenic | thrombolymphangitis |

## M

*Makros: long, large.

| | | | |
|---|---|---|---|
| acromacria | macrocytic | macrophage | macrospore |
| amacrine | macroglossia | macropsia | macrostomia |
| macradenous | macrogyria | macroscopic | macrural |
| macrocheilia | | | |

*Malakos: soft. Malaxis: a softening.

| | | |
|---|---|---|
| chondromalacia | malacopterous | myelomalacia |
| dermalaxia | malacosarcosis | neuromalacia |
| encephalomalaxis | malacosteon | stomatomalacia |
| keratomalacia | malacotic | tarsomalacia |
| malacology | | |

*Mania: madness, frenzy, enthusiasm.

| | | | |
|---|---|---|---|
| acromania | hypomania | magalomania | sitomania |
| dipsomania | kleptomania | narcomania | |
| egomania | maniac | pyromania | |

*Manos: thin, rare; tension, pressure, density.

| | | |
|---|---|---|
| hematomanometer | manometer | manoxylic |
| manocyst | manoscopy | sphygmomanometer |

Marasmos; Marantikos: a wasting away.

| | | | |
|---|---|---|---|
| geromarasmus | marantic | marasmoid | marasmus |

Maschale: armpit, axilla.

| | | |
|---|---|---|
| maschaladenitis | maschaliatry | tragomaschalia |
| maschalephidrosis | maschaloncus | |

**\*Mass**ein: to knead; massage. **Mases**is: chewing. **Masset**er: chewer.

| | | | |
|---|---|---|---|
| amasesis | massage | masseur | massotherapy |
| dysmasesia | masseter | massodent | thermomassage |

**\*Mastix, mastig**os: whip, flagellum.

| | | |
|---|---|---|
| Dimastigamoeba | isomastigote | phytomastigopod |
| heteromastigote | mastigium | polymastigia |
| holomastigote | mastigobranchia | |

**\*Mast**os; **maz**os: breast. **Mastoeid**es: like a breast; process of the temporal bone.

| | | |
|---|---|---|
| acromastitis | mastitis | petromastoid |
| amazia | mastodynia | polymastism |
| eccyclomastoma | mastoid | sternocleidomastoid |
| gynecomastia | mastoideocentesis | stylomastoid |
| mastectomy | mazopexy | trachelomastoid |
| masthelcosis | | |

**Maz**a: barley-cake; the placenta.

| | | | |
|---|---|---|---|
| maza | mazocacothesis | mazolysis | mazopathy |

**\*Megas, megal**ou: large.

| | | |
|---|---|---|
| acromegalogigantism | megacolon | megalops |
| acromegaly | megakaryocyte | megazoospore |
| cardiohepatomegaly | megalogastria | nephromegaly |
| cheiromegaly | megalogonidium | somatomegaly |
| hepatomegaly | megalomania | splanchnomegaly |
| hydromegatherm | megalopthalmus | splenomegaly |

**\*Meion**: less, smaller.

| | | | |
|---|---|---|---|
| meiobar | meiotic | miopragia | osteomiosis |
| meiophylly | miocardia | miosis | pathomeiosis |
| meiotaxy | miohippus | miosphygmia | rhinomiosis |
| meiotherm | | | |

**Mekon, mekon**os: poppy; opium. **Mekoni**on: juice of the poppy; discharge from bowels of new-born infants.

| | | | |
|---|---|---|---|
| hydromeconic | meconidium | meconism | meconophagism |
| meconidine | meconiorrhea | meconium | |

**Mekos, meke**os: length.

| | | | |
|---|---|---|---|
| mecism | mecodont | Mecoptera | Somomecus |
| mecocephalic | mecometer | paramecium | |

**Mel**a: the cheeks.

| | | | |
|---|---|---|---|
| melitis | meloncus | meloplasty | melotia |

**\*Melas, melan**os: black, dark.

| | | |
|---|---|---|
| cardiomelanosis | melanephidrosis | melanonychia |
| coccomelasma | melanin | melanophore |
| hepatomelanosis | melanocyte | melanospermous |
| melancholia | melanoderma | pneumomelanosis |

**Meli, melit**os: honey. **Meliss**a: bee.

| | | | |
|---|---|---|---|
| melichera | melissophobia | meiltagra | melitoptyalism |
| Meliphaga | melissotherapy | melitemia | melituria |

**\*Melos, mele**os: limb.

| | | |
|---|---|---|
| acrodolichomelia | hemimelus | melosalgia |
| acromelalgia | macromelia | mesomelic |
| amelia | melagra | monomelic |
| cacomelia | melomelus | nanomelia |
| dolichostenomelia | melorheostosis | symmelia |
| erythromelalgia | | |

**\*Men, men**os: month. **Menisk**os: semi-lunar, crescent.

| | | | |
|---|---|---|---|
| algomenorrhea | dysmenorrhea | meniscitis | menopause |
| amenorrhea | emmenology | meniscocyte | menophania |
| catamenia | menarche | meniscus | monomeniscous |

**\*Meninx, mening**os: membrane; one of three membranes enveloping the brain and spinal cord.

| | | |
|---|---|---|
| encephalomeningitis | meningeal | meningocele |
| hydromeningitis | meninges | myelomeningocele |
| leptomeninges | meningitis | |

**\*Meros, mere**os: part, segment. **Merism**os: a partition. **Merist**es, a divider.

| | | |
|---|---|---|
| adenomere | isomer | meromorphism |
| amerism | merismatic | merotomy |
| anakinetomere | meristematic | metamere |
| blastomere | meristic | monomeric |
| dodecamerous | meristogenic | polymeria |
| dysmerogenesis | meroblastic | |

**Mer**os: thigh.

| | | |
|---|---|---|
| merocele | meroparesthesia | platymeria |
| merocoxalgia | merosthenic | tetrameric |

**\*Mes**os: middle, intermediate.

| | | | |
|---|---|---|---|
| diamesogamy | mesion | mesoderm | mesonephros |
| mesenteron | mesobranchial | mesogastrium | mesoprosopic |
| mesiad | mesocolon | mesoglioma | mesorachischisis |
| mesially | | | |

**\*Metr**a: womb, uterus.

| | | |
|---|---|---|
| ametrohemia | metrectasia | metroptosis |
| dimetria | metrectopy | myometrium |
| endometritis | metreurynter | parametritis |
| gastrometrotomy | metrocele | pyometra |
| mesometrium | | |

**\*Metr**on: measure, measuring instrument.

| | | |
|---|---|---|
| ametropia | dynamometer | micrometer |
| barometer | dysmetria | ophthalmometer |
| cliseometer | emmetropia | optometry |
| cytometer | hypermetrope | symmetry |
| dermametropathism | metronania | tachymeter |

**\*Mikr**os: small.

| | | |
|---|---|---|
| acromicria | microbe | microscope |
| amicroscopic | micrognathia | microtome |
| amphimicrobian | micrometer | splanchnomicria |
| chylomicron | microorganism | streptomicrodactyly |
| micracoustic | microphakia | |

**\*Mimes**is; **mimi**a: imitation.

| | | |
|---|---|---|
| amimetic | macromimia | pantomimetic |
| echomimia | mimesis | paramimia |
| hypermimia | necromimesis | pathomimesis |

**Mis**os: hate.

| | | |
|---|---|---|
| misandria | misogyny | misoneism |
| misocainia | misologia | misopedia |

**\*Mit**os: thread.

| | | |
|---|---|---|
| amitosis | gamomites | mitochondria | mitosis |
| chondromitome | karyomitotic | mitoschisis | telomitosis |

**Mitr**a: belt, girdle, headband.

| | | | |
|---|---|---|---|
| Gyromitra | mitral | mitrephorous | mitriform |

**\*Mna**esthai: to remember. **Mnem**e: memory. **Mnemonik**os: for remembering, memory.

| | | | |
|---|---|---|---|
| amnesia | ecmnesia | logamnesia | paramnesia |
| anamnesis | hypermnesia | mnemonics | pseudomnesia |
| catamnesis | kryptomnesic | palinmnesis | telemnemonike |
| dysmnesia | | | |

**Mogis**: with toil and difficulty, barely.

| | | |
|---|---|---|
| mogiarthria | mogilalia | mogitocia |
| mogigraphia | mogiphonia | |

**\*Mon**os: alone, single.

| | | |
|---|---|---|
| gynomonoecious | monatomic | monomorphic |
| monandrous | monoblepsia | monophobia |
| monarthritis | monoganglial | monoplegia |

**\*Mor**os: dull, sluggish, stupid.

| | | |
|---|---|---|
| monomoria | morology | morosaurus |
| moria | moron | morosis |

**\*Morph**e: form, shape, figure.

| | | |
|---|---|---|
| amorphous | histomorphology | monomorphic |
| anamorphosis | isomorphism | morphology |
| coremorphosis | meromorphous | morpholysis |
| geromorphism | metamorphopsia | pleomorphic |
| gynandromorphism | metamorphosis | rhizomorph |

**\*My**ein: to close, shut.

| | | |
|---|---|---|
| myope | myosis | pseudomyopia |
| myopia | myotic | |

**\*Myel**os: marrow; bone marrow; spinal cord.

| | | |
|---|---|---|
| amyelencephalia | macromyelon | myelophthisic |
| amyelotrophy | myelocyte | myeloplast |
| diastematomyelia | myelogenous | poliomyelitis |
| encephalomyelitis | myeloma | syringomyelia |
| hematomyelia | myelomalacia | syringomyelocele |
| leukomyelopathy | myelomeningocele | |

**Myi**a: a fly.

| | | |
|---|---|---|
| cochlimyia | Micromyiophilae | myiodesopsia |
| dermatomyiasis | myiasis | ophthalmomyiasis |
| enteromyiasis | | |

**\*Mykes, myket**os: mushroom; fungus, mold.

| | | |
|---|---|---|
| acromycosis | mycetoma | onychomycosis |
| actinomycetic | mycetophagous | saccharomycetes |
| aureomycin | mycogastritis | staphylomycosis |
| chloromycetin | mycology | Strobilomyces |
| mycetogenetic | mycorrhiza | trichomycosis |

**Myl**e: mill; grinders, molars.

| | | | |
|---|---|---|---|
| lithomyl | myloglossus | mylohyoid | stylomyloid |

**\*Myrinx, myring**os: a membrane, especially the ear-drum membrane

| | | |
|---|---|---|
| mycomyringitis | myringitis | myringotome |
| myringa | myringomycosis | myringotomy |

**\*Myrmex, myrmec**os: ant.

| | | | |
|---|---|---|---|
| myrmecoid | myrmecophagous | myrmecophyte | typhlomyrmex |
| myrmecology | myrmecophile | myrmecoxenous | |

**\*Mys, my**os: mouse; muscle.

| | | |
|---|---|---|
| acromyotonia | geomys | myoma |
| adenosarcorhabdomyoma | hydromys | myometrium |
| amyostasia | leiomyoma | myonymy |
| amyosthenia | monomyoplegia | myorrhaphy |
| amyotaxy | myalgia | paramyoclonus |
| amyotrophy | myenteron | perimysium |
| dermatomyositis | myocarditis | rhabdomyochondroma |

**\*Mys** (*contd.*)

| | | |
|---|---|---|
| dysmyotonia | myocardium | stethomyitis |
| electromyogram | myodynamic | thoracomyodynia |
| endomysium | myoischemia | trachelomyitis |
| epimysium | myokymia | |

**\*Myx**a: slime; mucus.

| | | |
|---|---|---|
| amyxia | myxasthenia | myxoid |
| amyxorrhea | myxedema | myxoma |
| gastromyxorrhea | myxodermia | myxopodium |
| hypomyxia | myxoflagellate | |

# N

**Nan**os (**nann**os): dwarf.

| | | |
|---|---|---|
| hypernanosoma | nan(n)oplankton | nanomelia |
| metronania | Nannorhynchia | nanophyll |
| nanism | nanocephalia | |

**Narcissus**: In Greek mythology, a beautiful youth who fell in love with his own image; self-love.

| | |
|---|---|
| narcissi | narcissism |

**\*Nark**e: numbness, stupor.

| | | |
|---|---|---|
| abionarce | encephalonarcosis | narcotic |
| acronarcotic | narcoanesthesia | narkolepsy |
| anarcotin | narcomania | osmonarcotic |
| electronarcosis | narcosis | |

**Nast**os: pressed close.

| | | | |
|---|---|---|---|
| epinasty | geonyctonastic | hyponasty | photonastical |

**\*Naus**: ship. **Naut**es: sailor. **Nausi**a: seasickness.

| | | |
|---|---|---|
| aeronautic | naupathia | nausea |
| Cyphonautes | nauseate | |

**\*Nekr**os: dead body; dead.

| | | |
|---|---|---|
| diaspironecrosis | necropsy | otonecrectomy |
| necrectomy | necrosis | rhinonecrosis |
| necrobiotic | necrotic | steatonecrosis |
| necrology | | |

**Nekt**os: swimming. **Nech**ein: to swim.

| | | | |
|---|---|---|---|
| Callinectes | nectocalyx | nectophore | nectosome |
| Eunectes | nectocyst | nectopod | nekton |

**\*Nema, nemat**os: thread.

| | | | |
|---|---|---|---|
| diplonema | nematode | nematophore | Treponema |
| leptonema | nematogone | nematospermia | |
| nemathelminth | nematology | spironeme | |

**\*Ne**os: new, young.

erythroneocytosis    neologism    neophilism
glyconeogenesis    neomorph    neoteny
misoneism    neonatal    pseudoneoplasm

**\*Nephel**e; **neph**os: cloud, mist.

nepheligenous    nephelometry    nephelopsychosis
nepheloid    nephelopia    nephology

**\*Nephr**os: kidney.

archinephron    nephremphraxis    nephrotoxic
cystonephrosis    nephritis    protonephron
epinephroma    nephropathic    pyelonephritis
hepatonephromegaly    nephropexy    pyonephrosis
mesonephros    nephroptosis    ureteronephrectomy

**Nes**os: island. **Nesidi**on: islet; (islands of Langerhans of the pancreas).

nesidiectomy    nesidioblastoma    nesophylax
nesidioblast    nesomys

**\*Neur**on: sinew, tendon; nerve.

acroneurosis    neuralgia    neurotropism
acrotrophoneurosis    neurasthenia    perineurium
agastroneuria    neurilemma    polyneuritis
biocytoneurology    neuroblast    protoneuron
dysneuria    neuroglia    psychoneurosis
endoneurium    neuropathology    teleneuron
epineurium    neuropterous    toponeurosis
gastrohyponeuria    neurosis    trophoneurosis
mononeuritis    neurotomy    zygoneure

**\*Nom**os: law, ordering.

aitionomy    heteronomous    organonomy    phytonomy
autonomic    nomotopic    pathonomy    taxonomy
economy    nosonomy    physionomy

**\*No**os (**nous**): mind. **Noema, noemat**os: thought.

anoesia    eunoia    noematachometer    noopsyche
anoia    hypernoia    noematic    nousic
aponoia    mononoea    noometry    paranoia
dianoetic

**\*Nos**os: sickness, disease.

anosognosia    hematonosis    pedonosology
anthracnose    neuronosis    trichonosis
ceratonosus    nosetiology    trophonosis
cirrhonosus    nosochthonography    zoonosis
dermonosology    nosogenic

**Not**on: the back; a ridge.

| | | |
|---|---|---|
| notalgia | notocirrus | notopodium |
| notencephalocele | notomelus | nototrematous |
| notochord | notomyelitis | nototribe |

**Nymph**e: bride, female; labium minus; pupa or chrysalis of moths.

| | | |
|---|---|---|
| nymphae | nympholepsia | nymphoncus |
| nymphohymeneal | nymphomania | nymphotomy |
| nymphoidal | | |

**Nystagm**os: nodding, slumbering; drowsiness; movement of the eyeball.

| | | |
|---|---|---|
| nystagmiform | nystagmus | pseudonystagmus |
| nystagmograph | nystagmus-myoclonus | |

**\*Nyx, Nykt**os: night.

| | | | |
|---|---|---|---|
| autonyctonastic | nyctalopia | nyctitropism | nyctophobia |
| nyctaphonia | nyctigamous | nyctohemeral | nycturia |


# O

**\*Odous, odont**os: tooth.

| | | |
|---|---|---|
| acrodont | leptodontous | orthodontia |
| anisodont | monophyodont | pedodontics |
| anodontia | odontalgia | periodontium |
| cacodontia | odontogeny | periodontoclasia |
| erythrodontia | odontoptosis | rhynchodont |
| exodontology | odontorrhagia | scolecodont |
| glyptodont | odontostomatous | xanthodontous |
| haplodont | odontotripsis | |

**\*Odyn**e: pain.

| | | | |
|---|---|---|---|
| acrophotodynia | glossodynia | odynophobia | tenontodynia |
| anodyne | mastodynia | omodynia | trachelodynia |
| antrodynia | odynacusis | pleurodynia | xiphodynia |
| enterodynia | odynolysis | | |

**\*Oidema, oidemat**os: a swelling. **Oide**ein: to swell.

| | | | |
|---|---|---|---|
| acroedema | lymphedema | myxedematous | pneumonedema |
| cephaledema | melanedema | (o)edema | staphyledema |
| dactyledema | myoedema | phleboedesis | trophedema |
| edematous | | | |

**\*Oik**os: house, dwelling.

| | | | |
|---|---|---|---|
| androecium | ecomania | metoecious | ooecium |
| coenoecium | economy | monogynoecial | synoecious |
| dioecious | gyn(o)ecium | oikophobia | |
| ecology | heterecious | oikoplast | |

**\*Oistr**os: gadfly; sexual desire, breeding period.

| anoestrum | estrus | oestromania |
| estrogenic | metoestrous | (o)estruation |

**\*Oisophag**os: esophagus, the gullet.

| esophagalgia | esophagomycosis | periesophageal |
| esophagectasis | esophagostenosis | pharyngoesophageal |

**Olekran**on: elbow.

| olecranarthritis | olecranoid | olekranarthrocace |
| olecranarthropathy | olecranon | |

**\*Olig**os: few, small, scanty.

| oligocarpous | oligogalactia | oligotokous |
| oligochylia | oligohydramnion | oligotrichia |
| oligocythemia | oligoptyalism | oliguria |
| oligodontous | oligospermous | |

**Omma, ommat**os: eye.

| Anommatophora | monomma | ommatophore |
| erythromma | ommatidium | rhinommectomy |

**\*Om**os: shoulder.

| acromiocoracoid | acromion | omagra | omodynia |
| acromiothoracic | brachyome | omitis | omohyoid |

**\*Omphal**os: the navel.

| acromphalus | omphalelcosis | omphalotomy |
| cirsomphalos | omphalocele | paromphalocelic |
| exomphalos | omphalomesenteric | periomphalic |
| hematomphalocele | omphaloncus | sarcomphalocele |
| hepatomphalos | | |

**\*Onk**os: bulk, mass, tumor.

| arthroncus | glossoncus | oncocyte | onkinocele |
| blepharoncus | gonyoncus | oncogenous | staphyloncus |
| cheiloncus | mastoncus | oncology | uloncus |
| deradenoncus | melonchus | oncolysis | |

**\*Onoma, onomat**os (**onyma, onymat**os): name.

| anonomia (anomia) | myonymy | onomatomania |
| anonymous | neuronymy | onomatopoiesis |
| eponymic | | |

**\*Onyx, onych**os: nail of a finger or toe; claw; hoof.

| acronyx | koilonychia | onychauxis | onychorrhexis |
| anonychia | leukonychia | onychia | pachyonychia |
| epiparonychia | melanonychia | onychoclasis | paronychia |
| eponychium | mononychous | onychomycosis | platyonychia |
| hyponychial | onychalgia | onychophagous | schizonychia |

**\*O**on: egg, ovum.  **Oophor**on: the ovary.

| | | |
|---|---|---|
| epoophoron | ookinesis | oophyte |
| oocyesis | oolemma | oosperm |
| oocyte | oophorectomy | ootheca |
| ooecium | oophorocystosis | perioophoritis |
| oogonium | | |

**\*Op-**: to see.  **Ops**is: the look or appearance, aspect; view.  **Ops, op**os: eye; face, countenance.  **Prosop**on: face.  **Metop**on: forehead. (See **optik**os).

| | | |
|---|---|---|
| achloropsia | emmetropia | necropsy |
| amblyopia | erythropsia | nyctalopia |
| amblyopiatrics | hyperope | opalgia |
| ametropia | leptoprosope | opodidymus |
| amphodiplopia | macropsia | photopsia |
| anisopia | megaprosopus | presbyopia |
| anomalopia | metopantralgia | prosopalgia |
| anorthopia | metopic | prosopantritis |
| asthenopia | metopion | prosoposchisis |
| ateloprosopia | metopodynia | stereopsis |
| autopsy | metopoplasty | thanatopsia |
| copopsia | myopic | xanthopsia |
| diprosopus | | |

**Ophis; ophidi**on: snake.

| | | | |
|---|---|---|---|
| Ophidia | ophidiophobia | ophiotoxemia | toxicophidia |
| ophidiophilia | ophioderma | thanatophidia | |

**\*Ophthalm**os: eye.

| | | |
|---|---|---|
| Acrophthalma | ophthalmiatrics | ophthalmotropometer |
| endophthalmitis | ophthalmomycosis | photophthalmia |
| enophthalmos | ophthalmoplegia | xerophthalmia |
| megalophthalmus | ophthalmoscope | |

**Opi**on: poppy juice, opium.

| | | |
|---|---|---|
| cryptopia | opiate | opiophagy |
| opiase | opiomaniac | |

**\*Opisth**en: behind, at the back, backward.  **Opisthi**os: hinder, hinder part.

| | | |
|---|---|---|
| opisthencephalon | opisthocomus | opisthognathism |
| opisthiobasial | opisthodont | opisthotic |
| opisthion | opisthoglossal | opisthotonos |
| opisthocoelous | | |

**Opse**: late.

| | | |
|---|---|---|
| opsigamy | opsigony | opsomenorrhea |
| opsigenes | opsimathy | |

**Ops**on: food, dainties. **Opsoni**on: what is bought for food; a substance in the blood which makes microorganisms more suitable for phagocytosis.

| | | |
|---|---|---|
| bacteriopsonic | opsonin | opsonotherapy |
| hemopsonin | opsonocytophagic | opsophagy |
| opsiuria | opsonophilia | tuberculoopsonic |

**\*Optik**os: pertaining to vision or the eye. **Opt**os: seen, visible. (See **Op-**).

| | | |
|---|---|---|
| cataoptrics | opticociliary | optomyometer |
| optesthesia | opticopupillary | optotype |
| optical | optometry | orthoptic |

**\*Orchis, orchid**os: testis, testicle; a plant.

| | | | |
|---|---|---|---|
| cryptorchism | mesorchium | orchidectomy | orchitis |
| enorchia | orchid | orchiodynia | periorchium |
| leptorchis | orchidaceous | orchiopexy | synorchism |

**\*Orex**is: a reaching after; desire; appetite.

| | | | |
|---|---|---|---|
| anorexia | hyperorexia | orexia | parorexia |
| dysorexia | orectic | orexigenic | |

**\*Organ**on (**erg**on): something that does work; instrument, tool; organ of the body.

| | | | |
|---|---|---|---|
| microorganism | organography | organophyly | teleorganic |
| organogenic | organonomy | organotrophic | |

**\*Ornis, ornith**os: bird.

| | | | |
|---|---|---|---|
| ichthyornis | ornithophilous | ornithopterus | Teratornis |
| ornithology | ornithopod | ornithosis | |

**Orrh**os: whey; serum.

| | | |
|---|---|---|
| orrhodiagnosis | orrhomeningitis | orrhotherapy |
| orrhology | **orrhorrhea** | polyorrhymenitis |

**\*Orth**os: straight; correct, normal.

| | | | |
|---|---|---|---|
| anorthopia | orthodontics | orthophony | orthosis |
| metrorthosis | orthogamy | orthopnea | orthostichous |
| orthergasia | orthoglycemic | orthopterous | orthotonus |
| orthobiosis | orthopedics | | |

**Osche**on: the scrotum.

| | | |
|---|---|---|
| hematoscheocele | oscheohydrocele | oscheoma |
| hyposcheotomy | oscheolith | synoscheos |
| oschelephantiasis | | |

**\*Osm**e; **osphres**is: smell, sense of smell. **Oze**: bad smell, stench.

| | | |
|---|---|---|
| anosmatic | hyposmia | osphresis |
| cacosmia | microsmatic | oxyosphresia |
| disozonise | osmesis | ozena |
| dysosmia | osmesthesia | ozocrotia |
| euosmia | osmidrosis | ozone |
| hemianosmia | osphresiology | ozostomia |
| hyperosmia | osphresiophilia | parosmia |

**\*Osm**os: thrusting, pushing.

| | | | |
|---|---|---|---|
| aposmotaxis | exosmosis | osmology | osmotherapy |
| endosmometer | isosmotic | osmosis | zoosmosis |

**\*Oste**on: bone.

| | | |
|---|---|---|
| acrostealgia | osteoclast | osteoporosis |
| coenosteum | osteomalacia | osteosclerotic |
| craniostosis | osteomyelitis | osteosis |
| dyschondrosteosis | osteopetrosis | osteostixis |
| exostosis | osteophyte | osteosynthesis |
| osteoanagenesis | osteoplasty | periosteum |
| osteoarthritis | osteopoikilosis | synosteosis |

**Ostrak**on: shell.

| | | |
|---|---|---|
| arthrostracous | leptostraca | periostracum |
| hypostracum | ostracodermous | proostracum |

**\*Oul**e: scar.

| | | | |
|---|---|---|---|
| phyllula | ulectomy | ulodermatitis | ulotomy |
| synulotic | ulerythema | uloid | |

**\*Oul**on: the gum.

| | | |
|---|---|---|
| epulis | ulalgia | ulitis |
| parulis | ulatrophy | uloglossitis |
| ula | ulemorrhagia | uloncus |

**\*Our**a: tail.

| | | | |
|---|---|---|---|
| anthurus | mastigure | uromelus | urosteon |
| brachyurous | saururus | urosome | urosthenic |

**\*Ouran**os: sky, heaven; the palate. **Ouranisk**os: the palate, roof of the mouth.

| | | |
|---|---|---|
| brachyuranic | uraniscochasma | uranoplasty |
| cheilognathouranoschisis | uranosconitis | uranoplegia |
| dolichuranic | uraniscorrhaphy | uranostomatoscope |
| mesuranic | uraniscus | |

**\*Our**on: urine. **Ouret**er: one of ducts carrying urine from kidneys to bladder. **Ourethr**a: duct from bladder to surface.

| | | |
|---|---|---|
| acholuria | glaucosuria | uremia |
| achromaturia | glycosuria | ureter |
| aconuresis | hypouresis | ureterocele |
| agalactosuria | nephroureterectomy | ureterostenosis |
| allantoinuria | nycturia | urethra |
| amylosuria | oliguria | urethreurynter |
| blennuria | periurethritis | urinalysis |
| chyluria | polyuria | urologist |
| cystourethrogram | stranguria | uropenia |
| diuretic | urelcosis | uroporphyrin |
| enuresis | | |

**\*Ous, ot**os: ear.

| | | |
|---|---|---|
| anotia | otalgia | pachyotia |
| hydroparotitis | otic | parotiditis |
| hydrotis | otolith | polyotia |
| macrotia | otorhinolaryngology | tetraotus |
| opisthotic | otorrhea | |

**\*Oxy**s: sharp, swift, quick; sour, acid. (*ox*- and *oxy*- very often refer to oxygen).

| | | | |
|---|---|---|---|
| anoxemia | megoxycyte | oxygnathous | oxyphonia |
| anoxia | oxyaster | oxylalia | oxyrhine |
| dioxide | oxyblepsia | oximetry | oxytocic |
| gastroxynsis | oxycephalous | oxyosmia | oxytropism |
| hemoxometer | oxyesthesia | oxyphilic | paroxysm |
| hyperoxemia | | | |

# P

**\*Pachy**s; **pachyl**os: thick. **Pachyns**is: thickening.

| | | |
|---|---|---|
| acropachy | pachydermia | pachyonychia |
| blepharopachynsis | pachygnathous | pachyotia |
| myopachynsis | pachylosis | pachyphyllous |
| pachychilia | pachymeningitis | |

**\*Pais, paid**os: child.

| | | |
|---|---|---|
| lithopedion | paidonosology | pedobaromacrometer |
| logopedia | pedarthrocace | pedodontics |
| misopedia | pediatrics | pedogamy |
| orthopedics | | |

**\*Palai**os: old, ancient.

| | | |
|---|---|---|
| ornithopaleontologist | paleontology | paleophrenia |
| paleogenetic | paleopathology | paleozoology |

**\*Palin**: again, back.

| | | |
|---|---|---|
| osteopalinclasis | palindromic | palinmnesis |
| palikinesia | palingenesis | palinphrasia |
| palilalia | palingraphia | palirrhea |

**\*Pares**is: see **He**nai.

**Parthen**os: virgin.

| | | |
|---|---|---|
| hemiparthenosperm | parthenocarpic | parthenospore |
| heteroparthogenesis | parthenogonidia | parthenoxylon |

**\*Pas, pantos**; **pan**: all, entire.

| | | |
|---|---|---|
| pamplegia | pandemic | pantophobia |
| panacea | panotitis | pantopterous |
| pancreatic | pantatrophy | |

**\*Pathe**in: to be affected, experience, suffer. **Pathos, pathe**os: feeling, suffering, disease. *-pathy*: suffering, disease; system of treating a disease.

acropathy
aeropathy
allopathy
andropathy
apathetic
cholepathia
echopathy
empathy
etiopathology
gynopathy

heliopathia
homeopathy
hyperpathia
hypobaropathy
idiopathic
lalopathy
lymphadenopathy
myopathy
neuropathology
osteopathy

parasympathetic
pathocrinia
pathodontia
pathogenesis
pathognomonic
pathology
pathomimesis
psychopathology
sympathy
telepathy

**Peda**ein: to leap, spring; throb. **Pedes**is: a leaping.

diapedesis
hemodiapedesis

leukopedes
metapedesis

pedetic

**\*Peg-**; **pag-**: to make fast, fix, fasten. *-pexis, -pexy*: fixation. **Pag**os: something firm-set, united. *-pagus*: a fetal monster.

chloropexia
chromopexic
colopexostomy
colopexy
craniopagus

gastrothoracopagus
hematopexis
hysteropexy
ischiopagia
nephropexy

pneumopexy
pygopagus
somatopagus
sympexis

**Peira**ein: to attempt, try, test.

anapeiratic
anempeiria

empiric

metempirics

**\*Pell**a; **pelyx, pelyk**os: bowl; pelvis.

acanthopelyx
brachypellic
dolichopellic

leptopellic
pelycalgia
pelycology

pelycoscopy
platypellic

**\*Peni**a: poverty, need, deficiency. **Pein**a: hunger.

chloropenia
glycopenia
leukopenia

panhematopenia
peinotherapy
sideropenic

thrombocytopenia
uropenia

**\*Pept**ein: to make soft, cook, digest.

bradypeptic
colodyspepsia
dyspepsia

eupeptic
pepsin
peptogaster

peptone
proteopepsis

**Perine**on: the region of the body between the anus and the scrotum.

colpoperineoplasy
ischioperineal

perinauxis
perineal

perineorrhaphy
urethroperineoscrotal

**Perone**: for piercing; something pointed, brooch, fibula; the outer bone of the lower leg.

| | | |
|---|---|---|
| antiperonosporin | peronarthrosis | peroneotibial |
| ilioperoneal | peroneal | peronospora |

**Peros**: maimed.

| | | |
|---|---|---|
| perocephalus | perognathus | peropus |
| perochirus | peromelus | perosomus |
| perodactylism | | |

**\*Petalon**: leaf.

| | | |
|---|---|---|
| acropetaly | petal | polypetalous |
| eleutheropetalous | petalobacteria | stenopetalous |
| homopetaly | platypetalous | |

**\*Petra**: rock, crag. **Petros**: stone.

| | | |
|---|---|---|
| endopetrion | petroccipital | petrosphere |
| osteopetrosis | petromastoid | squamopetrosal |
| petrifaction | petrositis | |

**\*Phagein**: to eat, devour.

| | | |
|---|---|---|
| aphagia | karyophagy | phagology |
| (bacterio)phage | macrophage | polyphagia |
| chthonophagy | neurophags | sarcophagous |
| dysphagia | onychophagist | scolecophagous |
| geophagist | phagocyte | tachyphagia |
| isophagy | | |

**\*Phainein (phan-, pha-)**: to bring to light, show; appear, be seen; shine. **Phaneros**: evident. **Phasis**: appearance, aspect, stage of development. **Phasma**: apparition, ghost. **Phantasma**: vision, illusion (as in delirium).

| | | |
|---|---|---|
| aphantobiont | meophania | phanerosis |
| chromophane | ophthalmodiaphanoscope | phantasm |
| dermatodysphasia | phaenantherous | phantasmoscopia |
| diaphanoscope | phaenocarpous | phasmaphobia |
| diphasic | phaenoecology | prophase |
| epiphenomenon | ph(a)enomenon | sporophase |
| fantasy | phanerogam | tonophant |
| gastrodiaphany | phanerogenetic | |

**Phakos**: a lentil; lens.

| | | |
|---|---|---|
| aphakia | phacocele | phacomalacia |
| microphakia | phacoglaucoma | phacopalingenesis |
| periphacitis | phacoma | phacoscope |

**\*Phalanx, phalangos**: line of soldiers; bone between joints of fingers and toes.

| | | |
|---|---|---|
| brachyphalangia | metacarpophalangeal | phalangigrade |
| hemiphalangectomy | phalangectomy | symphalangism |
| hyperphalangism | phalanges | tarsophalangeal |

**Phall**os: phallus, the penis.

| | | |
|---|---|---|
| diphallia | phallic | phalloncus |
| phallanastrophe | phallodynia | schistophallus |

\***Pha**nai: to speak; *-phasis*: speech. **Phem**e: voice. **Phon**e: voice, sound.

| | | |
|---|---|---|
| acataphasia | baryphonea | phonasthenia |
| acouophone | bronchophony | phoniatrician |
| allophasis | dactylophasia | spasmophemia |
| aphasia | diphonia | stethophone |
| aphemesthesia | dysphonia | tachyphemia |
| aphemia | heterophonia | trachyphonia |
| aphonia | nyctaphonia | xenophonia |
| ataxophemia | orthophony | |

\***Pharmak**on: drug, medicine, remedy; poison.

| | | |
|---|---|---|
| alexipharmac | pharmacopeia | photopharmacology |
| pharmacodynamics | pharmacophobia | phytopharmacology |
| pharmacology | pharmacotherapeutics | zoopharmacology |

\***Pharynx, pharyng**os: throat, pharynx.

| | | |
|---|---|---|
| cricopharyngeal | nasopharynx | retropharyngeal |
| epipharyngeal | pharyngemphraxis | rhinopharyngocele |
| glossopharyngeal | pharyngitis | stylopharyngeus |
| hypopharynx | pharyngobranchial | |

\***Pher**ein: to bear, carry. **Phor**os: bearing, carrying, bringing.

| | | |
|---|---|---|
| aerophore | dysphoria | perioophoritis |
| anaphoria | euphoria | periphery |
| ascophoric | exocataphoria | phoranthium |
| chaetophorous | idiopher | phosphorescent |
| chromatophore | melanophore | phosphorous |
| diaphoresis | oophorectomy | sporophore |
| diphorophyll | pathophoresis | telpher |

\***Phil**ein: to love. **Phili**a: love, affinity for.

| | | |
|---|---|---|
| anthropophilic | gerontophilia | philanthropy |
| argyrophil | halophile | philiater |
| basophil | hemophilia | photophilic |
| chromatophil | hygrophila | psychrophilic |
| coprophilic | karyochromatophil | spasmophilia |
| crymophilia | Micromyiophilae | symphily |
| eosinophil | neophilism | xerophilous |
| erythrophil | oxyphilic | |

\***Phleg**ein: to burn, become hot. **Phlegma, phlegmat**os: flame, heat; phlegm. **Phlegmasi**a: heat, inflammation (of fever). **Phlox, phlog**os: flame. **Phlogos**is: inflammation.

| | | |
|---|---|---|
| antiphlogistic | phlegmonous | Phlox |
| leukophlegmasia | phlogistic | ureterophlegma |

metrophlogosis        phlogocyte          uterophlegmasia
phlegmatic            phlogogen
phlegmatopyra         phlogosis
phlegmon

**\*Phleps, phleb**os: vein.

celophlebitis         phlebemphraxis      phlebopiezometry
endophlebitis         phlebitis           pylephlebitis
phanerophlebia        phlebostrepsis      spermophlebectasia
phlebectopia          phlebotomy          thrombophlebitis

**Phlyktain**a: blister.

phlyctena             phlyctenosis        phlyctenule
phlyctenophthalmy     phlyctenotherapy    phlyktioplankton

**\*Phob**os: fear, flight.

acrophobia            erythrophobia       monophobia
agoraphobia           halophobe           oikophobia
algophobia            hydrophobia         photophobic
anemophobe            kathisophobia       triskaidekaphobia
arachnephobia

**\*Phon**e: see **Pha**nai.

**\*Phor**os: see **Pher**ein.

**\*Phos, phot**os: light.

acrophotodynia        photesthesis        photophobic
chromophototherapy    photobiology        photophthalmia
isophotophyll         photodynamics       photopsia
phosgenic             photolytic          photosynthesis
phosphorescent        photonastic         phototaxy
phosphorus            photophilous        spirophototropous

**\*Phras**is: speech, expression.

aphrasia              dysphrasia          paraphrasia
bradyphrasia          palinphrasia        pychnophrasia

**\*Phrass**ein (**phrag-**; **phrak-**; **phrax-**): to fence in, block up.
    **Diaphragma**: a blocking across; partition.

arthrophragm          ethmophract         pharyngemphraxis
diaphragmatocele      gasterangiemphraxis phlebemphraxis
diaphragmodynia       hemidiaphragm       phragma
diphragmida           kataphraxis         splenemphraxis
emphractic            nephremphraxis      urethrophraxis
endophragm

**\*Phron**eein: to think, understand. **Phron**esis: good sense. **Phren,**
    **phren**os: diaphragm; mind; phrenic nerve.

aphronesia            hyperphrenia        phrenohepatic
aphronia              idiophrenic         phrenoptosis

**\*Phrone**ein *(contd.)*

bradyphrenia
dysphrenia
epiphrenic
frenetic
hebephrenia

oligophrenia
phrenasthenia
phreniclasis
phrenicotomy
phrenicotripsy

phronesis
presbyophrenia
schizophrenia
tachyphrenia

**\*Phthi**ein; **phthin**ein: to decline, waste away, decay. **Phthis**is: a wasting away, decay.

antiphthisic
cystophthisis
gastrophthisis
hemophthisis
laryngophthisis

limophthisis
megakaryophthisis
myelophthisic
neurophthisis
phthinoid

phthisiogenesis
phthisiotherapy
phthisis
pneumonophthisis

**\*Phy**ein: to be by nature, grow, arise. **Phys**is: growth, nature. **Phyt**on; **phyma**: a growth, plant; tumor.

abiophysiology
anaerophyte
anapophysis
apophysis
chromophytosis
cytophysiology
dermatophyte
ekphyma
encephalophyma
entophyte
epiphyte
hepatophyma
hypophysis
metaphysics

microphyte
monophyodont
oophyte
osteophyma
osteophyte
paraphyte
pericardiosymphysis
phyma
phymatology
physical
physiognomy
physiotherapy
phytobiology

phytogeography
phytopathogenic
phytophagous
philophyton
pteridophyta
rhinophyma
saprophyte
splanchnapophysis
sporophyte
symphyogenesis
symphysis
symphysodactylia
xerophyte

**Phyk**os: seaweed, algae.

Cyanophyceae
melanophyceae

phycochrome
phycoerythrin

phycology
phycoxanthin

**\*Phylass**ein (**phylak-, phylax-**): to guard, protect, make immune.

ananaphylaxis
anaphylactic
anaphylactotoxin
apophylaxis

cryophylactic
ectophylaxination
kataphylaxis
phylaxin

phylaxiology
prophylactic
stomatophylaxis
tachyphylaxis

**\*Phyll**on: leaf.

adenophyllous
blastophyllum
chlorophyll
leiophyllum
leukophyll

mesophyll
phyllochlorin
phyllode
phyllophagous
phylloptosis

phyllotaxis
sclerophylly
xanthophyll
xiphophyllous

***Phyl**on: race, tribe; a primary division of the animal or vegetable kingdom.

| | | |
|---|---|---|
| anaphylotoxin | monophyletic | phylogerontic |
| blastophyly | phylephebic | phylum |
| cytophyletic | phylogeny | polyphyletic |
| homophylic | | |

**Phys**a: air, wind; bellows. **Physema**: inflation.

| | | |
|---|---|---|
| Diplophysa | physocele | physohydrometra |
| gastrophysema | physohematometra | physopyosalpinx |
| physema | | |

***Piez**ein: to press. **Pies**is: a pressing, pressure.

| | | |
|---|---|---|
| aeropiesotherapy | hematopiesis | piesesthesia |
| anisopiesis | hyperpiesis | piezometer |
| eccentropiesis | phlebopiezometry | piezotropism |

**Pikr**os: sharp, bitter.

| | | |
|---|---|---|
| picric | picrodendron | picrorrhiza | picrotoxin |

***Plagi**os: oblique, aslant.

| | | |
|---|---|---|
| geoplagiotropism | plagiocephalic | plagiodromous |
| plagianthus | plagiodont | plagioheliotropism |

***Plan**os; **plankt**os: wandering.

| | | |
|---|---|---|
| choloplania | leukocytoplania | plankton |
| coproplanesis | meroplankton | planoblast |
| elaeoplankton | mesoplankton | planocyte |
| galactoplania | nanoplankton | planogamete |
| hypoplanktic | phacoplanesis | |

***Plass**ein: to form, mold. **Plast**os: formed, molded; *-plast*: primitive living cell. **Plasm**a: something formed; fluid portion of blood.

| | | |
|---|---|---|
| achondroplasty | dysembryoplasia | plasmolysis |
| amyloplast | elytroplasty | plasmoschisis |
| anaplasty | epiploplasty | plastodynamia |
| aplasia | genioplasty | protoplasm |
| arthroplastic | genychiloplasty | sialodochoplasty |
| blepharoplasty | ideoplastia | somatoplasm |
| cardioplasty | neoplasm | trophoplast |
| cheiloplasty | osteoplasty | uranoplasty |
| colpoperineoplasty | plasma | zooplasty |
| coreplasty | plasmacyte | |

***Platy**s: broad, flat. **Plax, plak**os: flat or broad plate; a patch of eruption.

| | | |
|---|---|---|
| amphiplatyan | plate | platyhelminth |
| hyperrhinoplaty | platelet | platyonychia |
| leukoplakia | platycephalic | platypodia |
| malacoplakia | platycoria | platyrrhine |
| placobranchia | platydactyl | platyspondylia |

**\*Pleg-:** see **Pless**ein.

**Pleion; pleon:** more, increased.

| | | |
|---|---|---|
| pleiochromia | pleiophyllous | pleomorphism |
| pleiocyclic | pleocytosis | pleonexy |

**Plek**ein: to plait, twist, weave. **Plex**is: weaving.

| | | |
|---|---|---|
| enteroplexy | plectocomia | plekolepidous |
| metaplexus | plectospondyly | plekoptera |
| paraplectenchyma | | |

**\*Pless**ein (**pleg-, plek-, plex-**): to strike, hit, smite. **Pleg**e: stroke, blow.

| | | | |
|---|---|---|---|
| antapoplectic | hemiplegic | paraplegia | psychoplege |
| apoplectic | laryngoplegia | plegaphonia | quadriplegia |
| cataplexia | panplegia | plessor | thermoplegia |

**\*Pleur**a: rib, side.

| | | |
|---|---|---|
| anisopleural | pleurocarpous | pleurohepatitis |
| bronchopleuropneumonia | pleurocele | pneumopluritis |
| pleurapophysis | pleurocentesis | somatopleure |
| pleurisy | pleurodont | |
| pleurobranchiae | pleurodynia | |

**\*-plo**os: folded. **Diplo**os: twofold, double. **Haplo**os: single, simple.

| | | |
|---|---|---|
| diplacusis | diploteratology | haplopia |
| diplobacterium | epiplomerocele | heteroploid |
| diplocephalus | epiploon | monodiplopia |
| diplococcemia | epiloplasty | polyploid |
| diplocoria | haplochlamydeous | tetraploid |
| diploic | haplodermatitis | triplopia |
| diplopore | haplodont | |

**\*Pne**ein (**pneu-**): to blow, breathe. **Pnoi**a; **pno**e: breath, breathing.
**Pneuma, pneumat**os: a blowing; wind, air, gas.

| | | |
|---|---|---|
| adiapneustia | eupnea | pneumatophore |
| anapnoic | hepatopneumonic | pneumoencephalogram |
| anapnometer | liparodyspnea | pneumopericardium |
| anapnotherapy | orthopnea | polypnea |
| apneustic | pneodynamics | spanopnea |
| bradypnea | pneumarthrosis | tachypnea |
| dyspnea | pneumatocardia | trepopnea |
| electropneumograph | pneumatocele | |

**\*Pneum**on: lung.

| | | |
|---|---|---|
| bronchopneumonia | pneumococcus | pneumonophthisis |
| mesopneumon | pneumoconiosis | pneumopexy |
| metapneumonic | pneumonia | pneumothorax |
| pneumocentesis | | |

**\*Pod-:** see **Pous.**

**\*Poie**ein: to make, produce.

| | | |
|---|---|---|
| cholanopoiesis | hematopoietic | pharmacopeia |
| erythropoiesis | onomatopoiesis | sarcopoietic |
| galactopoietic | | thrombopoiesis |

**Poikil**os: spotted, mottled; changeful, diversified.

| | | |
|---|---|---|
| osteopoikilosis | poikilocyte | poikilonymy |
| pecilocyte | poikilodentosis | poikilothermal |
| Platypoecilus maculatus | poikiloderma | poikilothymia |

**Pogon, pogon**os: beard.

| | | |
|---|---|---|
| calopogon | Pogonia | pogonorhynchus |
| ophiopogon | pogoniasis | pogonotrophy |

**\*Poli**os: gray.

| | | |
|---|---|---|
| polioencephalitis | polioplasm | poliothrix |
| poliomyelitis | poliosis | trichopoliosis |
| polioneuromere | | |

**\*Pol**os: pivot, hinge, axis.

| | | |
|---|---|---|
| apolar | parapolar | tetrapolar |
| myopolar | polotropism | |

**\*Poly**s: much, many; more than usual. **Pollakis**: often. (See also **Pleion**)

| | | |
|---|---|---|
| gymnopolyspermous | polycythemia | polyphyodont |
| hydropoly | polydipsia | polypnea |
| pollakicoprosis | polygonal | polyposis |
| pollakiuria | polyhedral | polypus |
| polycarpellary | polyneuritis | polyuria |
| polychromatophilia | polyphagia | thermopolypnea |

**\*Por**os: passage; pore.

| | | |
|---|---|---|
| chondroporosis | neuropore | porencephaly |
| coelomopore | osteoporosis | porotomy |
| micropore | poradenitis | pseudopore |

**\*Porphyr**a: purple, red.

| | | |
|---|---|---|
| coproporphyrin | porphyraspis | porphyroleucus |
| hematoporphyrin | porphyrin | uroporphyrin |

**\*Pous, pod**os: foot; stalk.

| | | | |
|---|---|---|---|
| acephalopodia | phinopolypus | pododerm | strephenopodia |
| chiropodist | platypodia | podotheca | sympus |
| gastropod | podagra | polyposis | tripus |
| macropodia | podiatry | polypus | xanthopous |
| nectopod | podobromidrosis | pseudopod | |

**\*Pragma, pragmat**os (**Pratte**in, **prag-,** to do): a thing done, deed; fact. **Praxis**: a doing. **Praktik**os: fit for doing, practical.

| | | | |
|---|---|---|---|
| actinopraxis | dyspragia | hyperpraxia | pragmatism |
| apraxia | echopraxia | parapraxia | praxiology |
| bradypragia | eupraxia | pragmatagnosia | tachypragia |
| chiropractor | hemiapraxia | | |

**\*Presby**s; **presbyt**es: an old person.

hyperpresbyopia presbyophrenia presbytiatrics
presbyacusia presbyotic

**\*Prokt**os: the anus.

coloproctostomy proctencleisis proctorrhaphy
hemoproctia proctoclysis proctoscope
periproctitis proctologist ureteroproctostomy
proctalgia

**Prosop**on: see **Op-.**

**Proteus**: a god who could assume many shapes; changeable.

proteacae proteosoma proteus (bacteria)
protean

**\*Prot**os: first; primitive; simple. **Protei**os: first, primary; protein.
**Proter**os: earlier.

chromoprotein proteranthous protonephron
hyperproteinemia proteroglyph protoplasm
protandry protoblast protozoan
protein protogyny protozoology
proteolysis proton xanthoprotein
proteopepsis

**Psamm**os: sand.

psammoma psammophyte psammotherapy
psammophilous psammosarcoma uropsammous

**\*Pseudes, pseude**os: false, imaginary.

chromatopseudopsis pseudoanorexia pseudocyst
pseudanthic pseudoblepsis pseudomnesia
pseudholoptic pseudocyesis pseudopod

**\*Psil**os: bare, smooth, thin.

Meropsilus psilodermata psilosis
psilocnemis psilophyton psilosomata

**Psittak**os: parrot.

lophopsittacus psittacomorphous psittacosis
psittacism

**Pso**a: loin; loin muscle.

iliopsoatic psoas psodymus psoitis

**\*Psor**a: itch, scab, mange.

parapsoriasis psoric psorophthalmia
psorenteritis Psorophora psorosperms
psoriatic

**\*Psych**e: breath of life; spirit, soul; mind. **Psychos**is: mental activity;
disorder of mental activity.

algopsychalia parapsychology psychoneurosis
apsychia physiopsychic psychopathology

**Psych**e (*contd.*)
    bradypsychia       psychasthenia      psychoses
    histopsychology    psychiatry         psychosomatic
    micropsychia       psychic            psychotherapy
    neuropsychiatrist   psychoanalysis     psychotic
    noothymopsychic    psychobiology     technopsychology
    orthopsychiatry    psychogenic

**\*Psychr**os: cold.
    isopsychric        psychrophilic      psychrotherapy
    psychrokliny      psychrophobia     thermopsychrophorous
    psychrometer     psychrophytes

**Pteris, pterid**os: feathery leaves; fern.
    aminopterin       pteridifolia       pteridophyte
    Cystopteris       pteridology      pteroid

**\*Pter**on: feather, wing. **Pteryx, pteryg**os: wing. **Pterygi**on: fin.
    anisopterous     neuropterous     pterygiophore
    apterous         Pteridophyta     pterygium
    arthropterous    pteropaedes      pterygoid
    hyalopterous     pterosaur        pterygopalatine
    malacopterous    pterostigma      xanthopterin

**\*Ptos**is: a falling. **Ptom**a, **ptomat**os: a fall; fallen body; corpse.
    blepharoptosis    monosymptom    ptosis
    cardioptosis      nephroptosis     splanchnoptosis
    carpoptosis       omphaloproptosis  symptom
    cladoptosis       proptosis       tarsoptosis
    enteroptosis      ptomaine        thyreoptosis

**\*Pty**ein: to spit.
    aptyalia     hypoptyalism    ptyalagogue    ptyalism
    emptysis    melitoptyalon    ptyalectasis   ptyalorrhea
    glycoptyalism  oligoptyalism   ptyalin       pyoptysis
    hemoptysis

**\*Pyel**os: basin, trough; the pelvis.
    colicystopyelitis   encyopyelitis    pyelogram
    cystopyelonephritis pyelitis        pyelonephritis
    diastematopyelia  pyelocystitis    ureteropyelitis

**\*Pyg**e: rump, buttocks.
    dipygus    pygalgia    pygomelus    steatopygous
    psilopyga  pygidium   pygopagus    suprapygeal
    pygal      pygochord  pygostyle

**\*Pykn**os: close, frequent, thick, dense.
    apyknomorphous  pycnidium    pyknolepsy
    clinopycnidium   pyknemia     pyknosis
    desmopyknosis    pyknic       pyknosphygmia
    pycnidiophore

**\*Pyl**e: gate, entrance. **Pylor**os: gatekeeper; the distal aperture of the stomach.

| | | |
|---|---|---|
| antropyloric | micropyle | pylethrombosis |
| cardiopyloric | prepyloric | pylocyte |
| eurypylous | pylemphraxis | pyloristenosis |
| gastropylorectomy | pylephlebitis | pylorospasm |
| hemipylorectomy | | |

**\*Py**on: pus.

| | | | |
|---|---|---|---|
| antipyogenic | empyema | pyarthrosis | pyuria |
| arthrempyesis | nephropyosis | pyorrhea | septicopyemia |
| dacryopyosis | ostempyesis | pyosalpinx | spondylopyosis |
| diapyesis | otopyorrhea | pyosis | tracheopyosis |

**\*Pyr, pyr**os; **pyret**os: fire, heat, fever. **Pyrex**is: ill of fever.

| | | | |
|---|---|---|---|
| alexipyretic | galactopyra | metapyretic | pyromania |
| antipyretic | hyperpyrexia | pyretotherapy | rheumapyra |
| apyrexial | lochiopyra | pyrogen | traumatopyra |
| electropyrexia | | | |

**Pyren, pyren**os: fruit-stone, pit.

| | | |
|---|---|---|
| dipyrena | pyrenematous | pyrenochaeta |
| pyrene | pyrenocarp | tetrapyrenous |

# R

**Rhabd**os: rod, wand.

| | | |
|---|---|---|
| adenosarcorhabdomyoma | rhabdolith | rhabdopod |
| heterorhabdic | rhabdomyochondroma | rhabdus |
| Rhabditis | rhabdomyoma | statorhab |
| rhabdoid | rhabdophobia | |

**\*Rhach**is: the spine; a ridge.

| | | |
|---|---|---|
| acephalorachia | koilorrhachic | rachiodont |
| craniorachischisis | pneumorachis | rachiostichous |
| encephalorachidian | rachiocampsis | rachitogenic |
| hematorachis | rachiocentesis | rhacimorphous |

**\*Rhag-**: to break, burst. **-rrhagia**: bleeding. **-(r)rexis**: a bursting, rupture. **Rhagas, rhagad**os: cleft; crack, fissure.

| | | |
|---|---|---|
| amniorhexis | karyorrhexis | rhagadiose |
| anarrhexis | odontorrhagia | rhagidiform |
| desmorrhexis | onychorrhexis | tracheorrhagia |
| gastrorrhagia | rhagades | |

**Rhamph**os: beak, neb, bill.

| | | | |
|---|---|---|---|
| anisorhamphus | brachyrhamphus | leukorhamphus | rhamphotheca |

**\*Rhapt**ein (**rhaph-**): to sew, stitch. **Raph**e: seam, suture. **Rhaphis, rhaphid**os: needle.

achillorrhaphy
aneurysmorrhaphy
branchorrhaphy
celiorrhaphy
herniorrhaphy

myorrhaphy
perineorrhaphy
proctorrhaphy
raphides
raphidiferous

staphylorrhaphy
tarsorrhaphy
uranorrhaphy

**\*Rhe**ein: to flow. **Rhe**os; **rheuma, rheumat**os: flow, stream, current.

anarrhea
catarrh
dacryoblennorrhea
dacryorrhea
diarrhea
galactorrhea
gonorrhea

hydrorrhea
logorrhea
melorheostosis
otorrhea
ptyalorrhea
pyorrhea

rheology
rheotaxis
rheotropic
rheum
rheumapyra
rheumatism

**\*Rhis, rhin**os: nose.

chromorhinorrhea
dacryocystorhinostomy
laringorhinology
leptorhine
macrorhiny
otorhinolaryngology

oxyrhine
platyrrhine
rhinenchysis
rhinitis
rhinocleisis
rhinokyphosis

rhinolith
rhinoscleroma
rhinoscopy
rhinotheca
siphorhinal

**\*Rhiz**a: root; nerve root.

Glycyrrhiza
notorhizal
pararhizoclasia
rhizanasthesia

rhizanthous
rhizobium
rhizocarp
rhizodontropy

rhizoidal
rhizoneure
rhizophagous
rhizotomy

**\*Rhod**on: rose; red, purple.

Rhodococcus
rhodocyte

rhodogenesis
rhodophylactic

rhodophyll
rhodopsin

rhodorhiza

**Rhomb**os: spinning top, magic wheel, rhomb.

pseudorhombohedral
rhombencephalon

rhomboatloideus
rhombocoele

rhombogen
rhomboid

**\*Rhynch**os: beak, snout.

ecchinorhynchus
Harpyrhynchus

Microrhyncus
rhynchodont

rhynchophorous
rhynchostome

**\*Rhythm**os: rhythm, measure.

anisorhythmia
arrhythmia
bradyrhythmia

dysrhythmia
eurhythmia
pararrhythmia

rhythmophone
rhythmotherapy

# S

**\*Sakchar**on: sugar.

eleosaccharum saccharine Saccharomyces
monosaccharide saccharogalactorrhea saccharuria
saccharimeter saccharometabolism

**\*Salpinx, salping**os: trumpet; tube; Fallopian or Eustachian tube.

acrohysterosalpingectomy mesosalpinx salpingitis
endosalpingoma oophorosalpingitis salpingo-oophorectomy
hematosalpinx pyosalpinx salpingopalatine
hydroparasalpinx rhinosalpingitis salpyngemphraxis

**\*Sapr**os: see **Seps**is.

**\*Sarx, sark**os: flesh.

adenochondrosarcoma liposarcoma sarcoma
adenosarcorhabomyoma polysarcia sarcophagous
anasarca sarcocarp sarcosperm
hydrosarcocele sarcogenic xanthosarcoma
leukosarcoma sarcoid

**\*Saur**os: lizard.

dinosaur ophiosaurus sauriasis Saurophthalmus
ichthyosaur pterosaur sauriderma sauropod
megalosaur saurian saurognathous saururus

**\*Schiz**ein: to split, cleave. **Schist**os: cleft.

holoschisis schizocarp schizostele
onychoschizia schizogenesis schizothymic
prosoposchisis schizogony spondyloschisis
rhachischisis schizoid staphyloschisis
schistocyte schizophrenia stomatoschisis
schistoglossia schistosomiasis thoracoschisis

**\*Sei**ein (**seis-**): to shake. **Seism**os: earthquake.

bathyseism myoseism seismogram
isoseismal odontoseisis seismotherapy
mesoseismal seisesthesia

**\*Sema, semat**os; **semei**on: mark, sign, token.

allosematic asemasia urosemiology
aposemitically mesosemia

**\*Sepal**on (from **skep**e, covering): a segment of the calyx; sepal.

episepalous sepal stenosepalous
gamosepalous sepalody synsepalous
macrosepalous sepaloid trisepalous

**\*Seps**is: rotting, putrefaction. **Septik**os: putrid. **Sapr**os: decayed, rotten.

antiseptic sapremia saprozoic septicopyemia
asepsis saprophyte semisaprophyte stomatosepsis
pyosepticemia sapropyra septicemia typhosepsis

**\*Sial**on: saliva.

| | | |
|---|---|---|
| antisialagogue | hemosialemesis | sialodochoplasty |
| asialia | hypersialosis | sialolithotomy |
| glycosialia | polysialia | sialoschesis |
| | sialadenitis | sialosis |

**\*Sider**os: iron.

| | | |
|---|---|---|
| hemosiderin | sideroscope | siderosis |
| sideropenic | siderosilicosis | sideroxylon |
| siderophilous | | |

**Sigma**: the Greek letter S, sometimes written C.

| | | |
|---|---|---|
| colosigmoidostomy | mesosigmoid | sigmaspire |
| dolichosigmoid | perisigmoiditis | sigmoid |
| macrosigma | proctosigmoidectomy | sigmoidotomy |

**\*Siphon, siphon**os: tube, pipe.

| | | |
|---|---|---|
| siphon | siphonostele | siphuncle |
| siphonogamous | siphonostomatous | thermosiphon |
| siphonoglyph | siphorhinal | |

**\*Sit**os; **sit**ion: grain; food, bread.

| | | | |
|---|---|---|---|
| autosite | enterosite | parasite | sitotherapy |
| ectoparasites | eusitia | sitomania | sitotropism |
| endoparasite | necroparasite | sitophobia | xenoparasite |

**Skalen**os: uneven, triangle with unequal sides.

| | | |
|---|---|---|
| mediscalenus | scalene | scalenohedron |
| m. scalenus | scalenectomy | |

**Skaph**e: something hollowed out, bowl, boat; one of the carpal or tarsal bones.

| | | |
|---|---|---|
| Hydroscapha | scaphognathite | scaphoplankton |
| scapha | scaphohydrocephaly | taloscaphoid |
| scaphobrya | scaphoid | |
| scaphocephalic | scapholunar | |

**\*Skelet**os: dried, dried body, skeleton.

| | | |
|---|---|---|
| dermoskeleton | exoskeleton | skeletogenous |
| endoskeleton | skeletal | skeletography |
| episkeletal | | |

**\*Skel**os: leg.

| | | | |
|---|---|---|---|
| macroscelia | microscelous | scelalgia | tetrascelus |
| mesoskelic | polyscelia | skelasthenia | |

**\*Ski**a: shadow.

| | | |
|---|---|---|
| Ascia | hyperstereoskiagraphy | skiagraph |
| chromatoskiameter | orthoskiagraphy | skiascope |
| dentiaskiascope | | |

**\*Skirrh**os: hard coat or covering; hard tumor.

| | | |
|---|---|---|
| cystoscirrhus | mastoscirrhus | scirrhoblepharoncus |
| dacryadenoscirrhus | melanoscirrhus | scirrhosarca |

**\*Skler**os: hard.

| | | |
|---|---|---|
| acroscleroderma | osteosclerotic | sclerophylly |
| arteriosclerosis | phacosclerosis | sclerostenosis |
| cystosclerosis | rhinoscleroma | sclerotium |
| isosclerosis | scleroblastema | sclerotomy |
| nephrosclerosis | scleroderma | |

**Skolex, skolek**os: worm.

| | | | |
|---|---|---|---|
| deutoskolex | scoleciform | scolecoiditis | scolectomy |
| proskolex | scolecite | scolecophagous | scolite |
| scoleciasis | scolecodont | scolecosporum | |

**Skoli**os: curved, twisted, crooked.

| | | |
|---|---|---|
| kyphoscoliorrhachitic | rachioscoliosis | scoliosiometry |
| kyphoscoliosis | scoliodontic | scoliotic |
| lordoscoliosis | | |

**\*Skope**ein: to look at, view.

| | | | |
|---|---|---|---|
| bronchoscope | hygroscope | proctoscope | stereoscopic |
| conchoscope | macroscopical | rhinoscopy | stethendoscope |
| cystoscopic | microscope | scopophobia | stethoscope |
| diaphanoscope | ophthalmoscope | | |

**Skor, skat**os: dung.

| | | |
|---|---|---|
| scatemia | scatophilia | scoracratia |
| skatophagy | scatoscopy | |

**Skot**os, **skot**eos: darkness.

| | | |
|---|---|---|
| angioscotoma | scotography | scotophilia |
| hemiscotosis | scotoma | scototropism |
| kinetoscotoscope | | |

**Skyph**os: cup.

| | | |
|---|---|---|
| scyphiferous | scyphistoma | scyphozoan |
| scyphiform | scyphose | scyphule |

**\*Soma, somat**os: body.

| | | | |
|---|---|---|---|
| acrosome | disomus | psilosomata | somasthenia |
| agenosomia | eksomatics | psychosomatic | somatomegaly |
| celosomia | leptosomic | schistosomiasis | somatoplasm |
| chondriosome | nanosoma | | |

**\*Spa**ein (**spas-**): to draw, rend, wrench. **Spasm**os; **spasma**: a wrenching, drawing, convulsion.

| | | | |
|---|---|---|---|
| blepharospasm | epispastic | myospasmia | spasmophemia |
| chirospasm | gyrospasm | pylorospasm | spasmophilia |
| clonospasm | hemospasia | spasmolysant | spastic |

**Span**os; **spani**os: scarce, rare.

| | | |
|---|---|---|
| spanandry | spanemia | spanomenorrhea |
| spananthus | spanogyny | spanopnea |

**Spathe**: a flat blade; **spat(h)ula** (LAT.): instrument with flat blade.

spathe                spathiflorous        spathiphyllum        spatulate
spathella             spathion             spatula

*__Speira__: a coil, twist, winding.

sigmaspire            spiricles            spirobacteria        spironeme
spiradenitis          spiriferous          spirochete           spirophototropous
spiraster             spirillum            spirochetemia

*__Sperma, spermatos__: that which is sown, seed; germ, semen, sperm.
    __Speirein__: to scatter, sow.

cystospermatis        spermatangium        spermatocystitis
diaspironecrobiosis   spermatheca          spermatogenesis
oligospermous         spermatic            spermatozoon
pyospermia            spermatoblastic      spermetemphraxis

*__Sphaira__: sphere, ball, globe.

ectosphere            sphaeridia           spheroid
microspherocytosis    spheraster           spherometer
pterosphere           spherobacteria       spherula
sphaerenchyma         spherocyte

*__Sphen, sphenos__: wedge; wedge-shaped bone at base of skull.

acanthosphenote       esosphenoiditis      sphenoparietal
acrosphenosyndactylia sphenofrontal        sphenotripsy
basisphenoid          sphenoid             sphenozygomatic
diplosphene

**Sphinkter**: that which binds; a ringlike muscle that closes a natural
    orifice.

sphincter             sphincteroplasty     sphincterotomy
sphincteralgia        sphincteroscope      sphinctriform

*__Sphyzein__ (**sphyx-**): to throb, beat. **Sphygmos**: a throbbing; pulse.

acroasphyxia          chronosphygmograph   sphygmomanometer
anisosphygmia         hypersphixia         sphygmotonometer
asphygmia             microsphygmia        sphygmus
bradysphygmia         sphygmograph

*__Splanchnon__: a viscus, entrail.

eusplanchnia          splanchnicotomy      splanchnopleure
microsplanchnia       splanchnocoel        splanchnoptosis
splanchnectopia       splanchnomegaly

*__Splen, splenos__: the spleen.

eusplenia             microsplenia         splenelcosis
exosplenopexy         nephrosplenopexy     splenic
gastrosplenic         perisplenitis        splenomegaly
hepatosplenitis       splenectomy          splenophrenic
laparosplenectomy     splenectopia

**\*Spondyl**os: a vertebra.

| | | |
|---|---|---|
| diplospondylic | spondylexarthrosis | spondylolysis |
| hypospondylotomy | spondylitis | spondylopyosis |
| platyspondylia | spondylodesis | spondyloschisis |
| spondyl | spondylodynia | stereospondylous |

**Spong**os; **spongi**a: sponge.

| | | |
|---|---|---|
| proterospongia | spongin | spongiose |
| spongicolous | spongioplasm | spongoblast |

**\*Spor**a (**speir**ein): a sowing; seed; offspring; spore. **Sporas, sporad**os: scattered.

| | | | |
|---|---|---|---|
| ambisporangiate | gymnospore | microsporosis | sporidiole |
| ascospore | Haemosporidia | sporadic | sporidium |
| chlamydospore | megazoospore | sporangiferous | sporogenesis |
| conidiospore | microsporaphyll | sporangium | sporophyte |

**\*Sta-**; **ste-**: to cause to stand, set, fix. **Stas**is: a standing, stoppage, arresting. **Apostas**is: a deep-seated abscess; end or crisis. **Diastas**is: separation. **Diastema**: space, fissure.

| | | |
|---|---|---|
| acatastasia | diastematomyelia | nephrapostasis |
| ananastasia | ecstasy | orthostatic |
| apostasis | hemostatic | prostatectomy |
| bacteriostasis | hydrostatic | splanchnodiastasis |
| cholestasia | hypostasis | stasidynic |
| diastasis | metastasis | statolith |
| diastema | | |

**\*Stal-, stol-** (**stell**ein): to send; bring together; contract.

| | | |
|---|---|---|
| anastalsis | diastole | peristaltiphone |
| anastole | dyssystole | peristole |
| asystole | hyperperistalsis | thermosystaltic |
| bradydiastole | peristaltic | |

**\*Staphyl**e: bunch of grapes; uvula.

| | | |
|---|---|---|
| antistaphylococcic | salpingostaphyline | staphylorrhaphy |
| hypsistaphylia | staphyledema | staphyloschisis |
| leptostaphyline | staphyloma | stylostaphyline |
| peristaphylitis | staphyloplasty | |

**\*Stax**is: a falling drop by drop, dripping; oozing.

| | | |
|---|---|---|
| cystistaxis | gastrostaxis | urethrostaxis |
| epistaxis | splanchnostaxis | |

**\*Stear, steat**os: fat, tallow.

| | | | |
|---|---|---|---|
| hyposteatolysis | parasteatosis | stearin | steatoma |
| inosteatoma | steapsin | stearodermia | steatorrhea |
| neurostearic | stearic | steatocele | urostealith |

**Stel**e: pillar, post; cylinder of tissue in stem and roots of vascular plants.

| | | |
|---|---|---|
| dictyostelic | schizostele | stele |
| meristele | siphonostele | Stelorrhinus |
| protostele | stelar (system) | |

**\*Sten**os: narrow.

| | | |
|---|---|---|
| bronchostenosis | stenion | stenothermal |
| dolichostenomelia | stenocephalous | stenotic |
| gastrostenosis | stenopetalous | tracheostenosis |
| laryngostenosis | stenosis | typhlostenosis |
| sclerostenosis | | |

**\*Stere**os: solid.

| | | |
|---|---|---|
| actinostereoscopy | stereophoroscope | stereoscopic |
| astereognosis | stereoplasm | stereospondylous |
| cholesterol | stereopsis | stereotropism |
| hypercholesterolemia | | |

**\*Stern**on: chest, breast; breastbone.

| | | |
|---|---|---|
| entosternum | sternalgia | sternotribe |
| episternum | sternocleidomastoid | sternotrypesis |
| mesosternum | sternomastoid | xiphisternum |
| schistasternia | | |

**\*Steth**os: chest, breast.

| | | |
|---|---|---|
| endostethoscope | stethendoscope | stethomyitis |
| liostethus | stethometer | stethoscope |

**\*Sthen**os: strength.

| | | |
|---|---|---|
| adenasthenia | asthenopia | psychasthenia |
| amyosthenia | calisthenics | sthenometer |
| anagnosasthenia | microsthenic | sthenopyra |
| anisosthenic | myosthenometer | thrombasthenia |
| asthenia | neurasthenia | urosthenic |

**\*Stich**os: row, file, arrangement.

| | | |
|---|---|---|
| heptastichous | polystichous | stichidium |
| orthostichy | rachiostichous | tetrastichous |
| parastichy | | |

**\*Stiz**ein (**stig-, stix-**): to prick, puncture; to brand. **Stikt**os: punctured. **Stigma, stigmat**os: effect of pricking; dot, mark, spot or impression; portion of pistil on which pollen falls.

| | | |
|---|---|---|
| anastigmatic | stictopetalous | stigmatodermia |
| astigmatism | stigma | stigmatospore |
| hemostix | stigmatiferous | Stizolobium |
| osteostixis | | |

**\*Stoma, stomat**os: mouth; an outlet, opening (often surgically effected).

| | | |
|---|---|---|
| acephalostomia | dacryocystorhinostomy | scyphistoma |
| amphistomatic | enteroenterostomy | stomacace |

**\*Stoma** *(contd.)*

anastomosis
ancylostomatic
atretostomia
bronchostomy
cholecystogastrostomy
colocolostomy

gastroenterostomy
gastrostomy
laparocolostomy
macrostomia
pericardiostomy

stomata
stomatitis
stomatoschisis
stomions
xerostomia

**Strabism**os: a squinting.

strabismometer

strabismus

strabotomy

**\*Streph**ein: to turn, twist. **Streps**is; **stroph**e: a turning. **Strept**os: turned, twisted, bent.

arteriostrepsis
cardianastrophy
exstrophy
phlebostrepsis
strephenopodia

strephosymbolia
streptobacteria
Streptococcus
streptocarpous

streptosepticemia
streptostylic
Streptothrix
strophocephaly

**Strobil**os: something twisted; cone.

strobilaceous
strobilanthes
strobiliferous

Strobilocephalus
strobiloid

strobilomyces
strobilus

**Stroma, stromat**os: something spread over; a cover; framework of connective tissue.

blastostroma
chaetostroma

stroma
stromatogenous

stromatolysis
xylostromatoid

**\*Styl**os: pillar, peg; slender projection from temporal bone; stem supporting the stigma.

axostyle
dolichostylous
heterostyled
macrostylous
polystylar

pygostyle
sarcostyle
streptostylic
styloglossus
stylohyoideus

stylomastoid
stylopharyngeus
systylous
tylostyle
zygostyle

**\*Styps**is: a drawing together; astringency.

hemostyptic
hyostyptic

hypostypsis
stypsis

styptic

**\*Syrinx, syring**os: a shepherd's pipe; pipe, tube; fistula; syringe. **Syringm**os: whistle, ringing.

dacryocystosyringotomy
hydrosyringomyelia
microsyringe
sialosyrinx

syringitis
syringmophonia
syringmus
syringobulbia

syringomyelia
syringomyelocele
syringotomy

# T

**\*Tachy**s: swift, quick, rapid. **Tach**os, **tache**os: swiftness, speed.
- cardiotachometer
- hematotachometer
- noematachograph
- pneumotachograph
- tachyauxesis
- tachycardia
- tachydromous
- tachypnea
- tachypsychia

**\*Tars**os: frame of wicker-work; flat of the foot; framework of tissue for eyelid.
- mediotarsal
- metatarsus
- tarsadenitis
- tarsectopia
- tarsocheiloplasty
- tarsomalacia
- tarsophalangeal
- tarsoptosis
- tarsorrhaphy
- tarsus

**Tauto**: the same.
- tautogeneity
- tautomenial
- tautomeral
- tautomorphous

**\*Tax**is: arrangement. **Tass**ein (**tag-**): to arrange in order. **Tagma, tagmat**os: an arranged body; order.
- aerotaxis
- ataxia
- ataxiaphasia
- cardiataxia
- diataxis
- dystaxia
- heliotaxis
- heterotaxia
- inotagmata
- neurotagma
- paratagma
- phototaxis
- rhizotaxis
- syntactic
- tagma
- taxonomy
- thermotaxis

**\*Techn**e: art, skill, craft.
- architectonic
- iatrotechnics
- odontotechny
- technic
- technique
- technopsychology
- tonotechnic
- zymotechnic

**\*Tein**ein, (**tan-, ten-**): to stretch, strain. **Ektas**is: stretching out, dilation; extraction. **Tetan**os: stretched; spasm. **Taini**a: band, ribbon, tape; tapeworm. **Teinesm**os: straining at stool. (cf. **Ton**os).
- bronchotetany
- cardiectasis
- cholangiectasis
- cystotaenia
- dacryocystectasia
- desmectasia
- diplotene
- gastrectasis
- hemitetany
- neoteinia
- nephrectasis
- lithectasy
- ptyalectasis
- splenectasis
- taeniacide
- taeniopteris
- tenesmus
- teniasis
- tetanigenous
- tetanilla
- tetanus
- typhlectasis

**\*Tele**: far off, at a distance.
- bradyteleocinesia
- telalgia
- telecardiophone
- telekinesis
- telencephalon
- telepathy
- telestethoscope
- television

**\*Telos, tele**os: fulfillment, completion; end; an end part; purpose.
**Telei**os: complete.

| | | | |
|---|---|---|---|
| atelectasis | atelopodia | myelatelia | teleneuron |
| atelocardia | dysteliology | telangiitis | teleological |
| ateloglossia | entelechy | teleianthous | telosynapsis |

**\*Tenon, tenont**os (**tein**ein, to stretch): sinew, tendon.

| | | |
|---|---|---|
| achillotenotomy | tenomyotomy | tenontophyma |
| syntenosis | tenonectomy | tenontothecitis |
| tenodesis | tenontagra | |

**\*Teras, terat**os: a marvel; a monster; fetal monster.

| | | |
|---|---|---|
| diploteratology | teratogenic | teratophyllum |
| hemiterata | teratoid | Teratornis |
| teramorphous | teratology | teratosaurus |
| teratism | | |

**Tetart**os: fourth, quarter.

| | | | |
|---|---|---|---|
| tetartanopia | tetartocone | tetartohedral | tetartophyia |

**\*Thalam**os: inner room, chamber; anterior portion of the brain stem.

| | | |
|---|---|---|
| epithalamus | sporothalamia | thalamophora |
| paleothalamus | thalamencephalic | thalamus |
| polythalamous | thalamocoele | |

**\*Thall**os: young shoot.

| | | |
|---|---|---|
| heterothallic | prothallium | thallospore |
| hypothallus | thallium | thalliotoxicosis |
| merithallos | thalliophyte | thallus |

**\*Thanat**os: death.

| | | |
|---|---|---|
| apothanasia | thanatobiologic | thanatopsia |
| electrothanasia | thanatognomonic | thanatosis |
| euthanasia | thanatoid | |

**Thei**on: sulphur.

| | | |
|---|---|---|
| hydrothionemia | thiemia | thiogenic |
| monothionic | thiodotherapy | thiopexy |

**\*Thek**e: sheath, cover, case.

| | | |
|---|---|---|
| cleistothecium | perioothecitis | tenontothecitis |
| endothecium | perithecium | theca |
| karyotheca | spermatheca | thecitis |
| neurothecitis | sporotheka | thecodont |
| ootheca | | |

**\*Thel**e: nipple; a nipple-like protuberance, a papilla.

| | | |
|---|---|---|
| athelia | epithelium | thelerethism |
| chordo-epithelioma | mesothelium | thelitis |
| desmepithelium | perithelium | thelorrhagia |
| endothelium | polythelia | |

**Thely**s: female.

| | | |
|---|---|---|
| thelyblast | Thelygonum | thelyplasm |
| thelygenic | thelyotopy | thelytocia |

*****The**nai: to put, place, set down. **Thes**is: a putting, a setting down; a
  proposition.

| | | |
|---|---|---|
| athetoid | diathesis | prosthesis |
| cacothesis | enthesis | synthesis |
| choreoathetosis | metathesis | synthetic |
| cytothesis | osteosynthesis | thesis |
| dermepenthesis | | |

**Thenar**: palm of hand; sole of foot.

| | | |
|---|---|---|
| hypothenar | opisthenar | thenar |
| mesothenar | thenad | |

**Ther**; **theri**on: wild beast, beast; lower animals.

| | | |
|---|---|---|
| theriatrics | theriotherapy | theroid |
| theriomimicry | theriotomy | theromorph |

*****Therapeu**ein: to be a servant to, to take care of; to heal, treat medically.
  **Therapei**a: treatment (by therapy).

| | | |
|---|---|---|
| actinotherapy | limotherapy | physiotherapy |
| bromatotherapy | massotherapy | pyretotherapy |
| crymotherapy | pharmacotherapeutics | teletherapy |
| dipsotherapy | phototherapy | therapeutics |
| gerontotherapy | phthisiotherapy | therapy |
| helioaerotherapy | psychotherapy | thermotherapy |
| heliotherapy | psychrotherapy | trophotherapy |
| hydrotherapy | | |

*****Therm**os: hot, warm. **Therm**e: heat; heat of fever.

| | | |
|---|---|---|
| acrohypothermy | hyperthermalgesia | thermolysis |
| diathermy | hypothermy | thermometer |
| dysthermosia | stenothermal | thermopolypnea |
| homothermal | synthermal | thermotaxis |
| hydromegatherm | thermodynamics | thermotropism |

*****Thorax, thorak**os: breastplate; chest.

| | | |
|---|---|---|
| acephalothoracia | hemothorax | suprathoracic |
| acromiothoracic | iliothoracopagus | thoracentesis |
| chylothorax | laparothoracoscopy | thoracic |
| gastrothoracopagus | pneumohydrothorax | |

*****Thrix, trich**os: hair.

| | | |
|---|---|---|
| achromotrichia | eutrichosis | poliothrix |
| actinocladothrix | heterotrichosis | schizotrichia |
| amphitrichous | holotrichous | sclerotrichia |
| atrichia | hypertrichosis | trichatrophia |
| clastothrix | leiothric | trichauxe |

**\*Thrix** (*contd.*)

| | | |
|---|---|---|
| districhiasis | Leptotrichia | trichinosis |
| epitrichium | pachytrichous | trichomycosis |

**\*Thromb**os: a thickening; clot.

| | | |
|---|---|---|
| antithrombin | osteothrombosis | thromboclasis |
| athrombia | phlebothrombosis | thrombocyte |
| hematothrombin | pylethrombophlebitis | thrombophlebitis |
| histothrombin | thrombasthenia | thrombosis |
| leukothrombin | | |

**\*Thym**os: breath, spirit, soul, mind; strong feeling, anger.

| | | |
|---|---|---|
| abepithymia | exothymopexy | parepithymia |
| amphithymia | hemothymia | poikilothymia |
| cyclothymosis | hyperthymergasia | schizothymic |
| dysthymia | lipothymia | thymopathy |
| euthymus | noothymopsychic | thymopsyche |

**Thym**os: a warty excrescence; a ductless gland in region of the neck.

| | | |
|---|---|---|
| acrothymion | exothymopexy | thymelcosis |
| cacothymia | megalothymus | thymocyte |
| cyclothymia | thymectomy | thymus |

**\*Thyre**os: a shield in the shape of a door (**Thyr**a); the thyroid gland.

| | | |
|---|---|---|
| athyroidemia | hemithyroidectomy | thyrocarditis |
| cardiothyrotoxicosis | hyperparathyroidism | thyrogenic |
| cricothyreotomy | parathyroid | thyroid |
| dysparathyroidism | sternothyroid | thyrophyma |
| exothyropexy | thyreoptosis | |

**\*Tok**os: a bringing forth, childbirth.

| | | | |
|---|---|---|---|
| atokous | eutocia | ootocous | thelytocia |
| bradytocia | hysterotokotomy | oxytocic | tocology |
| distocia | mogitocia | polytocous | tocophobia |
| embryotocia | oligotokous | | |

**\*Tom**os: cutting. **Tom**e: a cutting, a segment. **Temn**ein: to cut.

| | | |
|---|---|---|
| achillotomy | cholangiogastrotomy | micranatomy |
| adenoidectomy | choledochectomy | microtome |
| amygdalectomy | diatomic | phlebotomy |
| anatomicopathological | dichotomy | temnospondylous |
| anatomy | entomology | tomotocia |
| ankylotomy | hylotomous | xylotomous |
| atom | | |

**\*Ton**os: stretching, tension, tonicity, vigor. (cf. **Tein**ein).

| | | |
|---|---|---|
| antrotonia | myodystonia | thermotonometer |
| atony | opisthotonos | tonic |
| dystonic | peritoneum | tonometer |
| hypertonus | sphygmotonometer | |

**\*Top**os: place, region, spot.

| | | |
|---|---|---|
| anatopism | isotopes | syndesmectopy |
| atopy | myectopy | topalgia |
| dystopic | osteectopia | topography |
| ectopic | splanchnectopy | topology |
| heterotopic | splenectopia | toponeurosis |

**\*Tox**on: a bow, bow and arrows. **Toxik**on (**pharmakon**): poison.

| | | |
|---|---|---|
| actinotoxemia | detoxicate | toxicity |
| allantotoxicon | deuterotoxin | toxicology |
| anagotoxic | ectotoxemia | toxiphobia |
| anaphylactotoxin | intoxication | toxophores |
| anatoxic | nephrotoxic | tyrotoxism |
| antitoxin | phytotoxic | urotoxic |
| bromatotoxism | picrotoxin | zootoxin |
| cardiothyrotoxicosis | toxemia | |

**\*Trachel**os: neck, throat, cervix.

| | | |
|---|---|---|
| cystotrachelotomy | macrotrachelous | trachelocystitis |
| hysterotrachelotomy | schistotrachelus | trachelodynia |
| laparotrachelotomy | trachelectomy | |

**\*Trachy**s; **trachei**a: rough. **Trachoma, trachomat**os: roughness; granular conjuctivitis.

| | | |
|---|---|---|
| cricotracheotomy | thermotracheotomy | trachomatous |
| endotracheitis | trachea | trachyglossate |
| laryngotracheitis | tracheotomy | trachyphonia |
| sternotracheal | trachoma | |

**Trag**os: he-goat; a prominence in front of opening of external ear; tuft of hair.

| | | |
|---|---|---|
| antitragus | tragacanth | tragomaschalia |
| lophotragus | tragi | tragophonia |

**\*Trauma, traumat**os: wound, injury.

| | | |
|---|---|---|
| barotrauma | traumata | traumatopyra |
| microtrauma | traumatism | traumatotaxis |
| neurotrauma | traumatology | |

**\*Trema, tremat**os (**tre-,** to bore): bored, a hole. **Tres**is: perforation. **Tret**os: bored, perforated.

| | | |
|---|---|---|
| atresia | dacryagogatresia | sphenotresia |
| atretoblepharia | lithotresis | trematode |
| atretocystia | nephrotresis | trematopora |
| atretopsia | posttrematic | tresis |
| atretostomia | pretrematic | |

**\*Trep**ein: to turn, bend. **Trop**e: a turning, attraction, affinity for.

| | | |
|---|---|---|
| allotropic | hepatotropic | stereotropism |
| chromatotropism | hypertropia | thermotropism |

**\*Trep**ein (*contd.*)

| | | |
|---|---|---|
| diatropism | idiotropic | Treponema |
| ectropion | neurotropism | trepopnea |
| esotropia | paraheliotropism | trepostomata |
| etiotropic | semianatropous | tropophyte |
| geotropism | | |

**\*Treph**ein (**threps-**): to nourish. **Troph**e: nourishment.

| | | |
|---|---|---|
| abiotrophy | dystrophy | trophology |
| acardiotrophia | hypertrophy | trophoneurosis |
| acrotrophoneurosis | polytrophia | trophoplast |
| anomalotrophy | threpsology | trophotherapy |
| asyntrophy | threptic | trophotropism |
| athrepsia | threphocyte | ulatrophy |
| atrophy | trichatrophia | |
| bradytrophic | trophodynamics | |

**\*Trib**ein (**trips-**): to rub, crush. **Trips**is: rubbing, friction.

| | | |
|---|---|---|
| anatripsis | lithotripsy | phrenicotripsy |
| cleidotripsy | neurotripsy | sternotribe |
| entripsis | nototribe | tripsis |
| hemocytotripsis | odontotripsis | xerotripsis |
| hepaticolithotripsy | paratrimma | |

**\*Tricho-**: see **Thrix.**

**Trism**os: a screaming, grinding; spasm; lockjaw.

| | | | |
|---|---|---|---|
| antitrismus | hysterotrismus | trismoid | trismus |

**Trit**os: third.

| | | | |
|---|---|---|---|
| tritanopia | tritocerebron | tritocone | tritoxide |

**\*Troch**ein: to run. **Trochili**a: pulley, roller of a windlass; the articular surface of a joint. **Troch**os: wheel, disk. **Trochant**er: runner; two bony processes of the femur.

| | | |
|---|---|---|
| intertrochanteric | trochanter | trochocephalia |
| peritrochanteric | trochate | trochoid |
| podotrochilitis | trochlea | trochosphere |
| supratrochlear | trochocardia | trochus |

**\*Trop**e (see **Trep**ein).

**\*Troph**e: (see **Treph**ein).

**\*Try**ein: to rub down; digest. **Tryp**e: effect of rubbing, a piercing; a hole. **Trypan**on: a borer; auger.

| | | |
|---|---|---|
| chymotrypsin | odontotrypy | trypanostoma |
| craniotrypesis | rhizodontrypy | trypesis |
| dystrypsia | sternotrypesis | trypsin |
| endotrypsin | trypanolysis | tryptic |
| hemotrypsia | trypanosoma | |

**Tyl**os: knob.

| | | |
|---|---|---|
| Monotylus | tylosis | tylotoxea |
| tylhexactine | tylostyle | tylus |
| Tylopoda | | |

\***Tympan**on: a drum; ear-drum.

| | | |
|---|---|---|
| antrotympanic | hypotympanic | tympanitis |
| craniotympanic | mastoidotympanectomy | tympanosclerosis |
| entotympanic | supratympanic | tympanotomy |
| gastrotympanites | tympanites | |

\***Typh**ein: to raise smoke, to smoulder; to conceal. **Typh**os: smoke, stupor; typhoid bacilli.

| | | |
|---|---|---|
| laryngotyphoid | pyretotyphosis | typhoid |
| meningotyphoid | splenotyphoid | typhophor |
| nephrotyphus | typhemia | typhus |
| paratyphoid | typhogenic | |

\***Typhl**os: blind; the caecum.

| | | |
|---|---|---|
| epityphlon | perityphlitis | typhlology |
| holotyphlon | typhlectasis | typhlon |
| laparotyphlotomy | typhlitis | typhlostenosis |
| nyctotyphlosis | typhlolexia | |

\***Typt**ein: to beat, strike, hit. **Typ**os: a blow; impression, form; type.

| | | |
|---|---|---|
| archetype | ecotypical | somatotypy |
| atypical | genotype | typology |
| chiasmatypy | heterotypic | |

**Tyr**os: cheese.

| | | |
|---|---|---|
| tyremesis | tyrogenous | tyroma |
| tyreusis | tyroid | tyrotoxism |

# X

\***Xanth**os: yellow.

| | | |
|---|---|---|
| pseudoxanthoma | xanthocarpous | xanthodont |
| xanthemia | xanthochromia | xanthoma |
| xanthine | xanthocyanopsia | xanthophyll |

\***Xen**os: foreign; stranger, host, guest. **Xeni**a: hospitality.

| | | | |
|---|---|---|---|
| heteroxenous | metoxenous | xenia | xenoparasite |
| lipoxeny | monoxeny | xenogamy | |
| menoxenia | xenembole | xenogenesis | |

\***Xer**os: dry.

| | | | |
|---|---|---|---|
| arthroxerosis | laryngoxerosis | xeroderma | xerophyte |
| colpoxerosis | Phylloxera | xerophilous | xerosis |
| dermatoxerasia | xerocheilia | xerophthalmia | xerostomia |

**\*Xiph**os: sword.

| | | | |
|---|---|---|---|
| chondroxiphoid | xiphisternum | xiphodynia | xiphophyllous |
| retroxiphoid | xiphodidymus | xiphoid | |

**\*Xyl**on: wood.

| | | | |
|---|---|---|---|
| epixylous | parthenoxylon | xyloma | xylotherapy |
| leptoxylem | xylobalsamum | xylophagous | xylotomous |
| manoxylic | xylocarp | xylose | |

## Z

**\*Ze**ein: to boil, seethe, bubble up. **Ekzem**a: a boiling out; skin eruption.

| | | | |
|---|---|---|---|
| eczematoid | eczematous | urozema | zestocautery |

**\*Zon**e: girdle, belt; zone.

| | | | |
|---|---|---|---|
| algaezone | sclerozone | zonated | zonociliate |
| scapulozona | zona | zonesthesia | zonula |

**\*Zo**on: something living; an animal.

| | | | |
|---|---|---|---|
| celozoic | histozoic | spermatozoon | zoology |
| Chlamydozoa | homozoic | zoanthropy | zoonosis |
| coprozoa | megazoospore | zoiatrics | zooplasty |
| enzootic | microzoon | zooerythrin | zootoxin |
| epizootic | protozoon | zoolith | zootrophic |
| hemacytozoon | | | |

**\*Zyg**on: yoke, crossbar. **Zygoma, zygomat**os: a yoking, yoke. **Zygot**os: yoked, joined.

| | | |
|---|---|---|
| azygobranchiate | heterozygosis | syzygy |
| azygospore | homozygote | zygodactyly |
| azygous | monozygotic | zygoma |
| enzygotic | sphenozygomatic | zygosis |
| epizygal | syzygiology | zygote |

**\*Zym**e: that which causes a seething, a ferment; leaven. **Zymos**is: fermentation.

| | | |
|---|---|---|
| antizymic | hematozymosis | zymocyte |
| azymia | lysozyme | zymogen |
| enzyme | microzyme | zymology |
| enzymic | nephrozymosis | zymolysis |
| erythrozyme | zymase | |

## WORD-ELEMENTS FREQUENTLY CONFUSED

Errors in the analysis of compound words sometimes occur because certain constructive units are exactly or almost alike or because their position in a compound term makes them appear like another word-element. The number of such errors can be sharply reduced by giving special attention to some of those constructive elements which are most easily confused. A selected list of these, with compound terms using them, follows:

1. *aesthe-* (αἴσθεσις): feeling, sensation.
   *astheno-* (α-; σθένος): debility, weakness.
   anaesthetic, paresthesia, myasthenia, neurasthenia.

2. *-agra* (ἄγρα): seizure, severe pain. (Usually a suffix).
   *agro-* (*ager, agri*): field, land. (Rarely a suffix).
   *argyro-* (ἄργυρος): silver.
   arthragra, podagra, agromania, agronomy, argyrophil, hydrargyrism.

3. *alg(e)o-* (ἄλγος): pain.
   *algi-* (*alga*): seaweed.
   *algo-* (*algor*): coldness.
   algophobia, analgesic, hemialgia, algicide, algoid, algology, algefacient, algogenic.

4. *ante-* (*ante*): before.
   *anti-* (ἀντί): against.
   antebrachium, antevert, antisudoral, antidote.

5. *anth-* (ἀντί as ἀνθ-): against.
   *anth(e)o-* (ἄνθος): flower.
   *anthropo-* (ἄνθρωπος): man.
   anthelminthic, anthoecology, anthodium, anthophore, exanthema, anthroopometry, apanthropia.

6. *arci-* (*arcus*): bow.
   *arche-, archi-* (ἀρχε-, ἀρχι-): first, chief.
   *archo-* (ἀρχός): anus, rectum.
   arciform, subarcuate, archegonium, archigaster, archoptoma, archosyrinx.

7. *auri-* (*aurum*): gold.
   *auri-* (*auris*): ear.
   *aura-* (*aura*): air; mental sensation.
   auriasis, aurotherapy, aurilave, sinistraural, aura, aural.

8. *bi-* (*bis*): twice, paired.
   *bio-* (βίος): life.
   biauricular, bicipital, biocatalyst, symbiont.

9. *brachio-* (βραχίων): upper arm.
   *brachy-* (βραχύς): short.
   *branchio-* (βράγχιον): gill.
   *broncho-* (βρόγχος): trachea.
   brachialgia, brachiocephalic, brachyuran, brachycephalic, branchiopod, nudibranchiate, bronchorrhagia, transbronchial.

10. *caeno-, ceno-, -cene* (καινός): new, recent.
    *caeno-, ceno-* (κοινός): common.
    *ceno-* (κενός): empty.
    c(a)enogenesis, cenopsychic, Eocene, c(o)enotype, c(o)enoecium, cenophobia, cenangium.

11. *carpo-* (καρπός): fruit.
    *carpo-* (καρπός): wrist.
    schizocarp, macrocarpous, carpalia, metacarpus, carpophangeal.

12. *celo-, kelo-, -cele* (κήλη): tumor, hernia.
    *celo-, -cele, celio-* (κοῖλος; κοιλία): hollow, cavity, belly.
    *celo-, kelo-* (κηλίς, κηλῖδος): spot, scar.
    celosomia, hematocele, kelotomy, blastocele, celozoic, celioparacentesis, keloid, celotomy, keloplasty.

13. *ceri-, kero-* (κηρός; *cera*): wax.
    *cera-, kero-, kerato-* (κέρας, κέρατος): horn; cornea.
    ceroplasty, keritherapy, keroid, kerectomy, keracele, ceratonosus.

14. *chordo-* (χορδή): cord (vocal, or other).
    *cordo-* (cord): cord (vocal, or other).
    *cordi-* (*cor, cordis*): heart.
    *choro-* or *choreo-* (χορός; χορεία): dance.
    *chorio-* (χόριον): skin, enveloping membrane.
    *cori-* (*corium*): skin, leather, skin layer beneath epidermis.
    *core-* (κόρη): doll; pupil of the eye.
    chorditis, chordectomy, corditis, cordopexy, cordiform, obcordate, choromania, choreiform, chorioma, chorimeningitis, coriaceous, excoriation, corectopy, coreometry.

15. *chromo-* (χρῶμα): color.
    *chrono-* (χρόνος): time.
    heliochrome, isochronic.

16. *cirro-* (*cirrus*): curl; ringlet.
    *cirrho-* (κιρρός): yellow, tawny.
    *cirso-* (κιρσός): varix, varicose vein.
    cirriped, cirrhonosus, cirsodesis.

17. *clavi-* (*clava*): club; thickened end.
    *clavi-* (*clavis*): key; collarbone.
    Claviceps, subclavate, interclavicular, subclavian.

18. -*cl(e)isis* (κλείειν): to shut, close.
    -*clysis* (κλύζειν): to wash out.
    arthroclisis, corenclisis, enteroclysis, phleboclysis.

19. *coni-* (κόνις): dust.
    *cono-, coni-* (κῶνος): cone.
    coniology, coniotoxicosis, conophorophyta, coniferous.

20. *dis-, di-* (*dis-*): apart from, asunder.
    *di-* (δίς): twice, double.
    *dia-, di-* (διά): through, thoroughly.
    discrete, dilaceration, digastric, dicrotic, diatherm, diuretic.

21. -*fer* (*ferre*): to bear, carry.
    *ferro-* (*ferrum*): iron.
    afferent, ferrotype, ferriferous.

22. *gen(i)-* (*gena*): cheek.
    *geni-* (γένειον): chin.
    *gen-* (γεν-): birth; descent; production.
    *genu-, genicul-* (*genu*): knee, joint.
    *geny-* (γένυς): jaw.
    genal, genioplasty, platygenia, gene, dysgenic, genuclast, genu-
    cubital, geniculata, genyplasty, genyantralgia.

23. *gluteo-* (γλουτός): buttock, rump.
    *glutini-* (*gluten, glutinis*): glue, gelatinous.
    *degluti-* (*deglutire*): to swallow.
    glutitis, gluteal, gluteofemoral, glutin, glutinous, glutoscope, deglu-
    tition, deglutible.

24. *gymno-* (γυμνός): naked.
    *gyno-* (γυνή): female.
    *gen-* (γεν-): be born.
    gymnogenous, gymnogynous, heterogynous, heterogenous.

25. *halo* (ἅλς, ἁλός): salt.
    *holo* (ὅλος): whole, entire.
    halophyte, holoblastic.

26. *hemo-* (αἷμα): blood.
    *hemi-* (ἡμι): half.
    hemoleucocyte, hemisotonic, hemialgia, hemihypertonia.

27. *hepato-* (ἧπαρ, ἥπατος): liver.
    *hepta-* (ἑπτά): seven.
    hepatatrophy, heptamerous.

28. *homeo-* (ὅμοιος): like, similar.
    *homo-* (ὁμός): the same, in common.
    *homi-, homin-* (*homo, hominis*): man.
    homeopathy, homochromatic, homomorphous, homunculus, homi-
    culture.

29. *hyo-* (ὑοειδής): U-shaped.
    *hyalo-* (ὕαλος): glass.
    hyoid, hyolithid, hyaloplasm, hyalomere.

30. *hypno-* (ὕπνος): sleep, stupor.
    *hypo-* (ὑπό): under.
    *hypsi-* (ὕψι): on high, height.
    hypnology, hyposphyxia, hypsicephalic.

31. *idio-* (ἴδιος): one's own; self-produced.
    *-idium* (-ιδιον): diminutive suffix.
    idioblast, idiopathic, antheridium, coccidium.

32. *ischio-* (ἰσχίον): hip, hip-joint.
    *ischo-*, *-ischia* (ἴσχειν): to hold back, suppress.
    ischioneuralgia, ischiodidymus, ischogalactic, hematischesis.

33. *-lepsis*, *-leptic*, *-lepsy* (λεπ-): to grasp, seize.
    *lepto-* (λεπτός): peeled, thin, delicate.
    *lepido-* (λεπίς, λεπίδος): scale, flake, husk.
    narcolepsy, analeptic, amphilepsis, leptophyllous, leptodontous, lepidolite, lepidotrichia.

34. *liga-* (*ligare*): to bind, tie.
    *ligni-* (*lignum*): wood.
    ligamentary, colligation, lignivorous, lignification.

35. *lipo-* (λείπειν): to leave, fail.
    *lipo-* (λίπος): fat.
    lipothymia, paralipophobia, lipodystrophy, liposarcoma.

36. *mal-* (*malus*): bad, faulty.
    *mal(o)-* (*mala*): cheek.
    *malaco-* (μαλακός): soft.
    malocclusion, malformation, maloplasty, frontomalar, malacology, malacosteon.

37. *mani-*, *manu-* (manus): hand.
    *mano-* (μανός): thin; pressure; tension.
    *mani-* (μανία): madness.
    maniluvium, manubrium, manometer, sphygmomanometer, pyromania, megalomania.

38. *megalo-* (μέγας, μεγάλου): large.
    *melano-* (μέλας, μέλανος): black.
    megalopsia, melanoderma.

39. *mel(o)-* (μέλος): limb.
    *melo-* (μῆλα): cheeks.
    *meli-*, *melito-* (μέλι, μέλιτος): honey.
    *melano-* (μέλας, μέλανος): black.
    melagra, acromelalgia, meloncus, meloplasty, melitemia, meliphaga, melanoderma, cardiomelanosis.

40. *mixi-* (μίξος): mixed.
    *myxo-* (μύξα): mucus, slime.
    mixochromosome, amphimixis, myxofibroma, myxospore.

41. *myo-* (μῦς): muscle.
    *my-* (μύειν): to close, shut.
    *myelo-* (μυελός): marrow.
    *myco-* (μύκης): fungus.
    *myxo-* (μύξα): mucus, slime.
    myasthenia, myocarditis, myopia, myelomeningocele, actinomycosis, mycohemia, myxasthenia, myxomycete.

42. *opsi-* (ὠψέ): late.
    *-opsia, -opsy* (ὄψις): appearance, view, vision.
    *opo-, -opia* (ὤψ, ὦπος): eye, face.
    *opso-, opsono-* (ὄψον; ὀψώνιον): food, provisions.
    opsigenes, opsigamy, erythropsia, autopsy, opalgia, presbyopia, opsophagy, opsonotherapy.

43. *-osis* (-ωσις): condition, physiological or pathological.
    *-osus* (*-osus*): full of, abounding in.
    arthrosis, stenosis, granulosus, rugose.

44. *osm-, -osmia* (ὀσμή): smell.
    *osmo-* (ὀσμός): thrust, push.
    osmosthesia, cacosmia, osmometer, isosmotic.

45. *ped-* (*pes, pedis*): foot.
    *ped-* (παῖς, παιδός): child.
    carpopedal, pedicure, pedometer, pediatrics, orthopedics, pedarthrocace.

46. *-phase, -phasic* (φάσις): appearance; stage of development.
    *-phasia, -phasis* (φα-): to speak.
    sporophase, diphasic, dysphasia, dactylophasia, allophasis.

47. *philo-, -phil* (φιλός): friendly, fond of, affinity for.
    *phylaco-* (φυλακ-): to guard, protect.
    *phyllo-, -phyll* (φύλλον): leaf.
    *phylo-* (φῦλον): race, class.
    philopterus, xerophilic, anaphylactic, kataphylaxis, phylloptosis, diphyllous, monophyletic, phylogeny.

48. *plagio-* (πλάγιος): slanting, sloping.
    *-plegia* (πληγή): blow, stroke.
    plagiocephalic, plagiodromous, panplegia, thermoplegia.

49. *-pore* (πόρος): passage, pore.
    *-spore* (σπορά): seeding, seed, cell.
    blastopore, micropore, archespore, gymnospore.

50. *pro-* (πρό): before, forepart.
 *pros-* (πρός): near.
 *proso-* (πρόσω): forwards, onwards.
 *prosopo-* (πρόσωπον): face.
 *prostho-* (πρόσθεν): before, in front of.
 *proto-* (πρῶτος): first.
   prognathous, prosethmoid, prosthesis, prosodemic, prosoplasia, prosopalgia, ateloprosopia, prosthodontia, emprosthotonus, protoblast, protonema.

51. *pur-* (*pus*, *puris*): pus.
 *pure* (*purus*): pure.
   puromucus, purulent, pure species, aqua pura.

52. *pyo-* (πύον): pus.
 *pyro-* (πῦρ, πυρός): fire; fever.
   pyosis, antipyogenic, pyrogen, antipyretic.

53. *radi-* (*radius*): rod, radius, ray.
 *radici-* (*radix*, *radicis*): root.
   irradiation, triradiate, eradicate, radicivorous.

54. *septi-*, *septem-* (*septem*): seven.
 *septico-* (σηπτικός): putrid, rotten.
 *sept-* (*saeptum*): separated off; dividing membrane.
   septan, septemfoliate, septipara, septicemia, septicopyemia, septal, multiseptate.

55. *spiro-* (*spirare*): to breathe.
 *spiro-* (σπείρειν): to scatter, sow.
 *spiro-* (σπεῖρα): coil, twisted.
   spirograph, inspiratory, diaspironecrobiosis, spirochete, spiriferous.

56. *stearo-*, *steato-* (στέαρ, στέατος): tallow, fat.
 *stereo-* (στερεός): solid.
   stearodermia, neurostearic, stereoplasm, actinostereoscopy.

57. *steno-* (στενός): narrow.
 *stheno-*, *-sthenia* (σθένος): strength.
   stenocardia, stenopetalous, sthenometer, myasthenia.

58. *tachy-* (ταχύς): swift.
 *tax-* (τάξις): arrangement.
 *trachy-*, *tracheo-* (τραχύς, τραχεῖα): rough; trachea.
   tachypnea, tachycardia, leucotaxis, taxonomy, trachycarpous, tracheostomy.

59. *thymo-* (θυμός): breath, spirit, strong feeling.
 *thymo-* (θύμος): a gland of the neck.
   euthymus, thymopsyche, megalothymus, thymocyte.

60. *-tomy* (τομός): cutting.
    *-stomy* (στόμα): mouth, opening.
    *-ost(e)osis* (ὀστέον): bone.
       phlebotomy, gastrotomy, cyclostomate, gastrostomy, exostosis, craniostosis, chondrosteoma.

61. *tricho-* (θρίξ, τριχός): hair.
    *tricho-* (τρίχα): three-fold.
       trichomycosis, trichophagy, trichotomism.

62. *trop-* (τροπή): turning.
    *troph-* (τροφή): nourishment.
       heliotropic, tropometer, autotrophic, trophotherapy, trophotropism.

63. *typ-* (τύπος): pattern, mold.
    *typho-* (τῦφος): smoke, stupor, typhoid.
       genotype, homeotypic, typhogenic, typhosepsis.

64. *ulo-* (οὐλή): scar.
    *ulo-* (οὖλον): the gum.
       ulectomy, ulodermatitis, ulalgia, uloglossitis.

The forewarned and practiced eye will not often err in analysis of words, even of those which use the elements listed above. But a few ambiguities and pitfalls will always remain; rare indeed is the person who does not stumble occasionally. Dissect the following words and formulate tentative definitions; then look them up in a medical dictionary:

| | | | |
|---|---|---|---|
| cyanemia | incostapedial | kathisophobia | microsmatic |
| hypergasia | inostosis | leiphemia | peropus |

CHAPTER V

# *Practical and Linguistic Factors*

## Compound Words: Gender, Stems and Bases, Combining Vowels

Many words in the ancient Greek and Latin languages were simple (i.e., uncompounded) terms using only a single stem. Many more of them, however, especially in Greek, were compound words formed by combining two or more stems into a single term. Through the use of a flexible system of synthesizing roots, stems, prefixes, and suffixes, the Greeks and Romans built up extensive vocabularies. Many of the Greek and Latin words thus formed, both simple and compound, have throughout the years been adopted without change as suitable for the vocabulary of science. The majority of the technical scientific terms in use today, however, have had to be coined to meet specific demands, and most of these are compound words formed by using Greek and Latin word-elements in manifold combinations. In the construction of these compound terms of science, an effort has been made to adhere to the original classical procedures in the use of prefixes, suffixes, stems, bases, and combining vowels.

The proportion of compound words to simple words is higher in ancient Greek than it is in ancient Latin. The somewhat greater flexibility of the Greek has always recommended its use in the construction of compound words and for this reason the more numerous and longer compound terms in modern scientific terminology are of Greek origin. Sometimes, therefore, a Latin or Latin-derived vocabulary may seem rather poor in multi-compound terms when it is compared to a Greek or Greek-derived vocabulary.

In every compound word constructed from two or more nominal (i. e., noun), adjectival, adverbial, or verbal elements, each one of its components stands in some syntactical relationship to the other components. When two or more words of equal rank are linked together, the resultant compound is called a *coordinate compound.* Such compounds are rarely made from English words, although "town-gown" and "farmer-labor," might be taken as examples.

In many more English compound words, the several components are not of equal rank but stand in varying syntactical relationships to each other. This might be illustrated by the English compounds "toothpick," "leg-plying," "strong-box," "onlooker," "hardheaded," and "downtown-building," in which it is evident that the first element of each word qualifies the second element. But the qualification is not the same in all the words: in the word "toothpick," made from two nouns and meaning "a pick for the teeth," the noun "tooth" has a limiting or referential (i.e., "in reference to the teeth") function in the compound; in "leg-plying," which uses a noun and a verbal adjective in its construction, the word "leg" is the direct object of "plying"; in "strong-box," an adjective functions as a direct modifier of a noun; in "on-looker," the first element functions as an adverbial modifier of a verbal noun; in "hard-headed," the qualifying function of the adjective "hard" is added to by the possessive idea introduced by the suffix -*ed* and therefore means "having a hard head"; in "downtown-building," a prepositional phrase ("down town") functions as an adjectival modifier of the second element.  In these examples, the second unit of each word furnishes the basic idea and the first unit, by introducing some qualification, is subordinate to the second. Such compounds are therefore called *subordinate compounds.*

In scientific words borrowed or derived from Greek and Latin, both coordinate and subordinate compounds are numerous. In subordinate compounds, the syntactical relationships between the several elements of the words are so diverse as to defy any attempt at complete analysis or classification. Nevertheless, a large number of compound scientific terms will be found to fall into one or another of the categories and subdivisions illustrated below.

1. *Coordinate Compounds*

> scapulohumeral: "pertaining to the scapula (*scapula*) and the humerus (*humerus*)."
> frontonasal: "pertaining to the frontal (*frons*) and nasal (*nasus*) bones."

dentilabial: "pertaining to the teeth (*dens*) and lips (*labium*)."
gastroenteritis: "inflammation of stomach (γαστήρ) and intestines (ἔντερον)."
pneumocardial: "pertaining to the lungs (πνεύμων) and heart (καρδία)."
gynandrous: "pistils (γυνή) and stamens (ἀνήρ) together."

2. *Subordinate Compounds*

    *a.* The first element is a descriptive adjective modifying the second element. Such compounds are very numerous.

        brachyuran: "short (βραχύς) tailed (οὐρά)."
        microspore: "small (μικρός) seed (σπόρος)."
        platyhelminthic: "broad (πλατύς) worm (ἕλμινς)."
        multifid: "much (*multus*) split (*findere*)."
        equivalence: "equal (*aequus*) worth (*valere*)."

    *b.* The first element is the direct object of the second, which is usually verbal.

        Anthophora: "bearing (φέρειν) flowers (ἄνθος)."
        halophilus: "liking (φιλεῖν) salt (ἅλς)."
        hematopoiesis: "formation (ποιεῖν) of blood (αἷμα)."
        lignivorous: "eating (*vorare*) wood (*lignum*)."

    *c.* The first element designates the place or thing in respect to which (where? what?) the meaning of the second element applies.

        omodynia: "pain (ὀδύνη) in the shoulder (ὦμος)."
        bronchostenosis: "narrowing or stricture (στενός) of the bronchus (βρόγχος)."
        somatomegaly: "largeness (μέγας) of body (σῶμα)."

    *d.* The first element stands in an "instrumental" or "means" (how?) relationship to the second.

        heliotherapy: "treatment (θεραπεία) by use of sun's (ἥλιος) rays."
        acupuncture: "pricking (*pungere*) with a needle (*acus*)."
        manufacture: "making (*facere*) by hand (*manus*)."
        dactylophasia: "speaking (φάσις) with the fingers (δάκτυλος)."

*e.* The first element qualifies the second in regard to "manner, or outstanding characteristic."

plantigrade: "walking (*gradi-*) on the entire sole (*planta*) of the foot."
phagocyte: "devouring (φάγειν) cell (κύτος)."
fissiparous: "producing (*parere*) by fission (*findere*)."

## A. GENDER OF COMPOUND WORDS (see also pp. 295-96; 306-07)

The gender of compound scientific names is generally governed by the following rules (most scientific names are Latin in form):

1. If the final component of a word is a noun, the gender of that noun in its original language determines the gender of the compound word. For example:

   a. "saccharomyces  is masculine because μύκης is masculine
   b. "dimorphotheca ' is feminine because θήκη is feminine
      "polygnathus" is feminine because γνάθος is feminine
   c. "ceratophyllum" is neuter because φύλλον is neuter
      "oxyrhynchus" is neuter because ῥύγχος is neuter
      "Trypanosoma" is neuter because σῶμα is neuter

If, however, the nominative suffix of the final element is changed, the gender of the word will accord with the grammatical gender of the terminal suffix. For example:

   a. "Hymenocarpus" (καρπός) is masculine, but "Polycarpaea" is feminine because the feminine terminal suffix -*aea* has been used instead of the masculine suffix -*us*.
   b. "Rhynchostoma" is neuter because στόμα is neuter, but "Bactrachostomus" is masculine because the nominative suffix -*us* has been attached. If the nominative suffix -*um* is attached, as in "Sclerostomum," the word is neuter.

2. If the final and the next to the final components of a compound are a noun and an adjective, respectively, the word is an adjective used in the regular manner. *But if such a compound is used as a substantive*—as often occurs in binomial nomenclature—the gender of the compound is determined by the gender of the noun. For example:

a. "Phylloxera" when used as a generic name is neuter because φύλλον is neuter, even though the -a ending would seem to identify the word as feminine gender.

b. "Cordyloides" is masculine because *Cordylus* is masculine; "Dasychiroides" is feminine because *Dasychira* is feminine; and "Centroptiloides" is neuter because *Centroptilum* is neuter. The suffix -*ides* may be any gender.

> [The Botanical Code, however, urges that all generic names ending in -*oides* or -*odes* shall be feminine (see p. 307)].

## B. STEMS AND BASES

A cardinal rule in the construction of scientific terms is to use as constructive units the true stems or bases of the Greek and Latin source words. This practice is supported both by classical usage and by recommendations in most of the *Codes* of scientific nomenclature. As has been explained (pp. 32-41; 47-52), the base of a Greek or Latin noun or adjective is best ascertained from the genitive singular form of the word, and the stems of a verb are seen in its present infinitive and perfect participle forms. Certain scientific terms furnish evidence that there has been some deviation from this recommended practice, however, and especially so in the case of compound words formed from the base of those nouns and adjectives which belong to Declension III and which increase by a syllable in the genitive case. The following words will illustrate how, in the constructing of scientific terms, not only the bases of some nouns have been used, but also the apparent nominative stems.

|      | Original Word | Apparent Nominative Stem | Base | Derivative Words |
|------|---------------|--------------------------|------|------------------|
| *Nom.* | φῶς, light | **phos-** | **phot-** | *phos*phorous |
| *Gen.* | φωτός |  |  | *phot*olytic |
| *Nom.* | δέρμα, skin | **derm-** | **dermat-** | *derm*oblast |
| *Gen.* | δέρματος |  |  | *dermat*ology |
| *Nom.* | γυνή, woman | **gyn-** | **gynaec-** | *gyn*androus |
| *Gen.* | γυναικός |  |  | *gyne*comorphous |
| *Nom.* | sanguis, blood | **sangui-** | **sanguin-** | *sangui*renal |
| *Gen.* | sanguinis |  |  | con*sanguin*eous |

The "short stems" from the nominative case of some nouns also appear frequently as terminal elements of compound words; for example: "poly*pus*" and "xantho*pous*" (πούς, ποδός, foot); "ecto*derm*" (δέρμα, δέρματος, skin); "gastro*stomy*" (στόμα, στόματος, opening); "acro*some*" (σῶμα, σώματος, body).

The use of the "short stem" in the construction of compound words, although for practical reasons usually avoided in the coinage of scientific terms, has some precedent in classical usage and on that basis occasionally finds advocacy in modern word construction. The following Greek and Latin words illustrate how compound words in those languages used both the "short" and the "long" stems of the words referred to above:

| *"Short" Stem* | *"Long" Stem* |
|---|---|
| φωσφόρος, bringing light | φωτοποιός, making light |
| δερμόπτερος, with membranous wings | δερματοφόρος, clothed in skins |
| γύνανδρος, of doubtful sex; womanish | γυναικοκρατία, dominion of women |
| *sangui*suga, blood sucker | *sanguin*arius, of blood |

The use of the "short stem" of Greek and Latin nouns and adjectives has therefore a measure of precedent in classical usage and may be interpreted, from a philological viewpoint, as a testimony of the strength and vitality of those languages. Nevertheless, the more usual practice in the Greek and Latin languages when forming compound words was to use the full stems rather than the "short stems."[1] Therefore, despite the fact that classical precedent can be found for the use of the "short stem" in the construction of compound words and despite the fact that the "short stem" may sometimes produce more easily pronounced terms, its general use in the construction of scientific words should be discouraged. Regular use of the "short stem" would be contrary to the best and most common

---

1. In an investigation of derivatives using stems from that large group of Greek neuter nouns ending in -μα with the genitive in -ματος, it was found that the "long stem" was used in most of the words; see Frederic E. Clements, "Greek and Latin in Biological Nomenclature," *University Studies of the University of Nebraska*, III (December, 1902), 31-32. See also, *International Bulletin of Bacteriological Nomenclature and Taxonomy*, II (April 30, 1952), 67-68.

precedent both ancient and modern, and its occasional and irregular use tends to cause uncertainty, indifference, and carelessness about determining the true stem. Indifference about the true stem, in turn, leads to many errors, malformations, and unnecessary synonyms. A quicker and surer recognition of constructive elements and their meaning, elimination of many unnecessary synonymous terms, and an avoidance of confusion arising out of an uncertainty and inconsistency of usage, are important nomenclatural advantages that accrue from regular use of the true stems and bases in the construction of scientific names and terms.

## C. COMBINING VOWELS

Combining vowels are a phonetic convenience for joining two constructive units of a compound word. If a base or stem used as a constructive unit begins with a consonant, a vowel is needed to attach that unit euphoniously to the previous unit of the compound; if the second unit begins with a vowel or diphthong, no additional vowel is needed (see pp. 5-6). Since the insertion of a combining vowel is mainly a matter or phonetic convenience, it might seem that any vowel could be used which would contribute to the euphony and the pronunciation of the compound word. Although that viewpoint might seem sound, it is nevertheless necessary to consider some linguistic and historical factors relating to the choice of combining vowels before a general policy is established.

As has already been pointed out (pp. 35; 39-40; 49), the true stems of many Greek and Latin words end in the vowels *a, e, i, o, u,* or *y*. Whenever one of these stems is used as a constructive unit of a compound word, there is a natural tendency to retain the terminal vowel of that stem as the connective medium between that unit and the one that follows. This has sometimes been advocated as the only reasonable and linguistically correct procedure and accounts in part for the fact that instances of the use of all the different vowels as connectives can be found among compound scientific terms constructed from Greek and Latin word-elements.

Classical Greek and Latin words show a preference for certain combining vowels. In classical Greek the usual combining vowel was o whether the stem of the noun or adjective ended in α, ο, ι, υ, or in a consonant. The final vowel of the stem was generally displaced by o or, if the stem ended in ι, υ, or a consonant, o was added. The following Greek words illustrate these usages:

γνώμη (stem, γνώμα-), maxim: γνωμολογία, speaking in maxims.
ἄνθρωπος (stem, ἄνθρωπο-), man: ἀνθρωποφάγος, man-eating.
φύσις (stem, φύσι-), nature, features: φυσιογνώμων, judging of man by his features.
ἰχθύς (stem, ἰχθύ-), fish: ἰχθυοφάγος, fish-eater.
παῖς (stem, παιδ-), child: παιδοτροφία, rearing of children.

The predominant use of o as combining vowel in classical Greek compound words may have been based partly on analogy with words belonging to Declension II, whose stems do end in o (see ἄνθρωπος, above).

There were some exceptions, however, to the use of o as the combining vowel in Greek words; other vowels also were used. For example:

ἀγορά (stem, ἀγορα-), market: ἀγορανόμος, clerk of the market.
θάλαμος (stem, θάλαμο-), chamber, room: θαλαμηπόλος, chambermaid.
λαμπάς (stem, λαμπαδ-), torch: λαμπαδηφόρος, torch-bearer.
φύσις (stem, φύσι-), nature: φυσίζοος, life-producing.

In classical Latin, i was by far the most prevalent combining vowel. The final stem-vowel of many Latin adjectives and nouns was a, o, or u, but these were usually displaced by i when those stems were used in compounds. This was due mainly to vowel gradation, by which the strong vowels a, o, or u were weakened to i (see p. 42). Sometimes the vowel was omitted altogether. If the stem ended in a consonant, the vowel i was added. The following Latin words illustrate these usages:

spica (stem, spica-), ear of grain: spicilegium, gleaning of ears.
caper (stem, capro-), goat: capricornus, horn of the goat.
ignis (stem, igni-), fire: ignicolorus, flame-colored.
cornu (stem, cornu-), horn: cornipes, horn-footed, hoofed.
dens (stem, dent-), tooth: dentifricium, tooth powder.
manus (stem, manu-), hand: manceps, purchaser, contractor.

In classical Latin, exceptions to the use of i as the combining vowel are rare. In late Latin, however, exceptions do occur and the use of other vowels, especially o, appears. For example:

*albus* (stem, *alba-*), white:   *albogilvus*, whitish yellow;
                                     *albogalerus*, white hat.
*caper* (stem, *capro-*), goat:   *capragenus*, flesh of the goat.

On grounds of classical prototype, therefore, sound precedent exists for the practice of using *o* as the predominant combining vowel in Greek-derived words and *i* in Latin-derived words.

Observance of this usage is enjoined or recommended by some scientific nomenclatural *Codes*[2] (see pp. 295; 306). Moreover, it may be said that most technical scientific terms do conform to the recommended usage in this respect. The following words are typical:

*bacca* (stem, *bacca-*), berry:     bacciform, baccivorous
*uncus* (stem, *unco-*), hook:     uncipressure, uncirostrum
*dorsum* (stem, *dorso-*), back:     dorsiflexion, dorsispinal
*caro* (stem, *carn-*), flesh:     carnification, carnivora
*fructus* (stem, *fructu-*), fruit:     fructiferous, fructiform
μορφή (stem, μορφα-), shape:     morphology, morphogenetic
ἄκρος (stem, ἄκρο-), point:     acroneurosis, acrophobia
νῆμα (stem, νήματ-), thread:     Nematocera, nematoblast
φύσις (stem, φύσι-), nature:     physiology, physiopsychic
ἰχθύς (stem, ἰχθύ-), fish:     ichthyophagy, ichthyotoxic

Some modern word coinages have followed the precedent set in late Latin and have used *o* instead of *i* for combining two Latin-derived elements. In hybrid terms the combining vowel is predominantly *o*. For example:

*scapula* (stem, *scapula-*), shoulder-blade: scapuloclavicular,
                                      scapulohumeral
*albus* (stem, *albo-*), white: albocerus, albocinereous
*serum* (stem, *sero-*), watery fluid: serofibrinous, seromucous
*apex* (stem, *apic-*), tip: apicolocator, Apicotermes
*alga* (stem, *alga-*), seaweed; φαγ-, eat: algophagus
*apex* (stem, *apic-*), tip; λύσις, destruction: apicolysis

Deviations from the most common classical usage in the matter of combining vowels are accounted for by (1) the power of analogy

---

2. Cf., *International Code of Botanical Nomenclature*, Recommendation 73G, (d); *International Bacteriological Code of Nomenclature* (1958 Ed.), Recommendation 27, i. p. 113.

with the Greek usage (the Greek language is rich in compound words and, as has been stated, the predominant combining vowel in words of that language is *o*) and (2) the fact that *o* is both the stem-vowel and the combining vowel for the many Latin nouns and adjectives of Declension II. The dominating *o* has even produced such malformations as "micr*o*custic" (for "micr*a*custic") and "ptyl*o*gogue" (for "ptyl*a*gogue") where it has usurped the place of the essential vowel *a* of the second constructive units. The effect of analogy is observed also in words which are not wholly of Greek or Latin origin. In the word "heartometer," for example, the combining vowel *o* is presumably used on the basis of analogy with "cardiometer"; for on the basis of the pattern set by other words of nonclassical origin (heartburn, heartwater, heartwood), "heartmeter" might have been expected.

Since the words of classical Greek and Latin do not reveal an absolutely unvarying pattern in the use of combining vowels, no single unassailable criterion for correctness in their use in modern coinages from Greek and Latin elements can be established on the basis of classical linguistic precedent. Variations of the kind mentioned above in classical usage, even though they are rare (especially in Latin), have occasionally furnished a basis for argument in defense of using combining vowels which deviate from the usual pattern.[3] Such variations may occasionally be justified, but rather on grounds of some gain in practical facility for a word than on grounds of linguistic precedent. In the terminology of biology and medicine, the soundest policy in regard to the use of combining vowels will be to conform with the recommendations of several *Codes* of scientific nomenclature and follow the characteristic classical precedent.

Uncertainty about classical and preferred modern usage in the matter of combining vowels has produced a considerable number of unnecessary variants in scientific terms. The numerous pairs of synonymous words (especially of Latin origin) in which one member of a pair differs from the other only in the combining vowel used have added bulk to dictionaries and sometimes cause confusion and uncertainty. The following examples are cited from medical terminology:

---

3. Cf., *International Bulletin Bacteriological Nomenclature and Taxonomy*, II (April 30, 1952), 65f.

oronasal and orinasal (*os, oris*, base *or-*)
sinoventricular and sinuventricular (*sinus*, base *sin-*)
arcicentrous and arcocentrous (*arcus*, base *arc-*)
venepuncture and venipuncture (*vena*, base *ven-*)
muscacide and muscicide (*musca*, base *musca-*)
tubatorsion and tubotorsion (*tuba*, base *tub-*)
ventrifixation and ventrofixation '*venter*, base *ventr-*)
ipsilateral and ipsolateral (*ipse*, base *ips-*)
septavalent and septivalent (*septem*)
nematocide and nematicide (νῆμα, base νήματ-)
gynephobia and gynophobia (γυνή, base γυναικ-)
staphylephoros and staphylophoros (σταφυλή, base σταφυλ-)

The variants apicectomy, apicoectomy, apiocectomy, apectomy, and apiceotomy (*apex*, base *apic-*), all synonyms and all given separate entries in Dorland's *Medical Dictionary*, reveal uncertainty not only about combining vowels but also about stems and elision.

Appertaining to the use of combining vowels are also those variations that occur in elision and hyphenation when two noun or adjective bases are combined. The usual practice in cases where the second member of a compound begins with a vowel is to allow that letter to serve as the combining vowel. For example:

*noct-* plus *ambulatio*: noctambulation
*terr-* plus *aqueus*: terraqueous
χειρ- plus ἄγρα: cheiragra
ὀρθ- plus ὀδόντ-: orthodontics

Some compounds, however, reveal an inserted combining vowel before the vowel of the second component. Sometimes such words are hyphenated compounds and sometimes not. For example:

radioulnar (*radi-o-ulnar*)
aestivoautumnal (*aestiv-o-autumnal*)
tempero-occipital (*temper-o-occipital*)
vesico-urethral (*vesic-o-urethral*)
microanatomy (μικρ-ο-ανατομή)
stethoendoscope (στῆθ-ο-ενδο-σκοπός).

If the usual procedure had been followed, the examples used above would have been spelled radiulnar, aestivautumnal, temperoccipital, vesicurethral, micranatomy, and stethendoscope. Whether the combining vowel *o* should be added or not in such instances, and whether the words should be hyphenated or not, are subtle questions involving consideration of clarity and euphony. But differing tastes and uncertainty in these matters have produced unnecessary duplications and indefensible forms. In Dorland's *Medical Dictionary* the following variants and irregularities occur:

> monarticular *and* mono-articular
> micranatomy *and* microanatomy
> micrangiopathy *and* microangiopathy
> pyarthrosis *and* pyoarthrosis
> micracustic (even microcustic!), *but not* microacustic
> micrencephaly and micro-encephaly, *but not* microencephaly
> baragnosis and baro-agnosis, *but not* baroagnosis
> meroacrania, *but not* meracrania
> gastrasthenia, *but not* gastro-asthenia
> gastroatonia, *but not* gastratonia

In most instances of the kind illustrated—and there are many in scientific dictionaries—it seems to be an altogether fortuitous matter whether elision should or should not occur, whether the compound should be hyphenated or not, and whether a single or double dictionary entry is necessary.

A further illustration of how uncertainty, or the power of analogy, can produce indefensible and confusing compounds may be seen in the words "endchondral," "endarterium," and "end-artery." The only plausible explanation for the omission of the *o* on *endo-* in "endchondral" is that on basis of analogy with words like "end-artery," "end-brain," "end-organ," and "end-plate," *end-* was thought to be a proper prefix. The definition of the word reveals that *endo-* ("within") is the prefix intended. In "endarterium" the loss of the *o* from *endo-* by elision is normal, and the compound is readily understood. In "end-artery" the prefix *end-* is not the same word as *end-* on "endarterium," and the two words have quite different meanings.

In the formation of compound words, adherence to the relatively simple recommended usages in the matter of combining vowels and elision will prevent many malformations and will avoid unnecessary duplication of terms.

## Pronunciation

The factors which influence the pronunciation of English words are so numerous and varied that it is not possible to give a few simple rules whereby correct pronunciation will always be assured. It is even difficult to insist that every word has an invariable "correct pronunciation." Instead, it is easier to maintain that every word has what may be called its "standard pronunciation," by which is meant the particular pronunciation which the majority of educated persons apply to the word at a given time and which dictionaries recognize as "correct." For most words this "correct" pronunciation remains stable, even though changes may occur from time to time or from place to place in any particular word.

The "rules" which apply to the pronunciation of technical words of science are on the whole the same as those which apply to English words generally.[4] In spite of the multiplicity and complexity of those "rules," a few which will be of assistance in pronouncing technical terms derived from the Greek and Latin can be stated as follows:

## A. ANGLICIZATION

Loan-words and derivatives from the Greek and Latin are anglicized and pronounced according to the standards for the pronunciation of English words. When the Greek word ψυχή (mind), for example, is taken into English as "psyche," it loses its Greek pronunciation and is pronounced sī'-kē; when anglicized, the Latin word *saeptum* loses some of its Latin phonetic value and is pronounced sep'-tum.

---

4. See the section on "Pronunciation" in any standard English dictionary.
The pronunciation of English words might well seem to be a matter of caprice when one observes the shifting syllabic quantities and accents on such words as the following:

a. Respirator is pronounced res'-pĭ-rā-ter; respiratory is pronounced re-spĭr'-a-tō-rĭ; respirometer is pronounced res-pĭ-rom'-e-ter.

b. Barbital, barbitalism, barbituism, and barbiturism are all accented on the first syllable; but barbiturate has the accent on the second syllable.

c. Webster's *Dictionary* recognizes three different pronunciations of salicylate, in order of preference as follows: sal'i-sil-at, sa-lis'i-lāt, sal'i-sil'āt. Dorland's *Medical Dictionary* gives only sal'i-sil''āt.

Although not all dictionaries of the English language or all scientific dictionaries are in agreement about the pronunciation of some words, the percentage of all English words over which there is disagreement about pronunciation is very small.

## B. SYLLABLES

A Greek or Latin word contains as many syllables as it has separate vowels and diphthongs; an English word, on the other hand, may have syllables which contain more than one vowel. For example:

> Greek: πράγματος, πρά-γμα-τος.
> Latin: *integumentum*, in-teg-u-men-tum.
> English: branchiostome, bran-chi-o-stome.

## C. VOWELS

1. Final *i* has the long sound, pronounced as "eye." For example: stimuli, radii.

2. Final *a* has the sound of "ah." For example: data, ameba.

3. Final *es* is pronounced like "ease." For example: bases, neuroses, phalanges.

## D. CONSONANTS

1. *c* and *g* are soft before e- and i- sounds (*e, i, y, ae, oe*) and otherwise hard. For example:

   *Soft*: cecum, cyanide, turcica; genus, gingiva, gyrus.
   *Hard*: carpal, costal, cutaneous; glottis, gonidium, guttural.

2. When preceded by an accented syllable, *c* or *t* before an *i* followed by another vowel has the sound of "sh." For example: so*ci*alis, spe*ci*es; calvi*ti*es, nigri*ti*es, scabri*ti*es, ra*ti*o. (Does not apply, for example, in a word like "cavities" because the -*ti* is not preceeded by an accented syllable).

3. Double *c* followed by *i* or *y* is pronounced as in "accident." For example: cocci, coccyx, flaccid, vaccine.

4. When *ps* represents an initial ψ of a Greek word it has the sound of "s"; otherwise it is pronounced as in "lips." For example: psychology, pseudopod, psilophyton, micropsychia, icopsychric; necropsy, opsigenes, sepsis, tripsis.

5. When *x* represents an initial ξ of a Greek word it is usually pronounced as "z"; it is always so pronounced when it is the first letter of an English word, and with only few exceptions also when

it is within a word. For example: xiphoid (ξίφος), xeroderma (ξηρός), xylophagus (ξύλον), pseudoxanthoma (ξάνθος), arthroxerosis (ξηρός). If the *x* represents a medial or final ξ of a Greek word, it is pronounced as in "ax." For example: oxygen (ὀξύς), taxonomy (τάξις), hexabasic (ἕξ).

6. *Ch* (the Greek double consonant χ) almost always has the hard pronunciation as in "chemical," "chondral," and "chromosome"; occasionally, via the French, it has the "sh" sound, as in "chancroid" (shang'-kroid).

## E. DIPHTHONGS

1. The Latin diphthongs *ae* and *oe* (which often represent original αι and οι of Greek words) are usually reduced to *e* in anglicization; but whether reduced or not, they are generally pronounced like "ee" in "heel"; for example: ameba (amoeba), cohere (cohaere), fetid (foetid), cenogenesis (caenogenesis). If the original diphthong is followed by two or more full consonants, there is a strong tendency to shorten the syllable (see F. below); for example: sĕptum (*saeptum*), cĕspitose (*caespes*).

2. *Ei* is usually reduced to *i*; but even when it remains *ei*, its pronunciation is as "i" in "file"; for example: cheiropodist, eiconometer.

3. *Au* is pronounced as in "fraught"; for example: caudal, glaucoma.

4. *Eu* is pronounced as in "neuter"; for example: neurology, pharmaceutical.

English pronunciation sometimes creates false diphthongs by running together two vowels which originally were parts of separate syllables. The words "aeriferous, aerophyte, and aerobe," for example, use the Greek stem **aer-**, which has two syllables **a-er** (ἀήρ); accordingly, the approved pronunciations are a-er-if'-er-us, a'-er-o-fit, and a'-er-ob. The **aer-** is often incorrectly pronounced "air" as if the letters "ae" represented an original Greek diphthong αι (as they do, for example, in a word like "aesthetic," from αἰσθητικός). In the words "ptomaine" and "cocaine" the *ai* appears to be the same diphthong as is used, for example, in "brain" and "train," and consequently is similarly pronounced. The *ai*, however, is not a true diphthong in "ptomaine" or in "cocaine," but is the result of adding the suffix **-ine** to the nominative forms of the words **ptoma** and **coca.** The "correct" pronunciations are therefore tō'-ma-in and kō'-ka-in, although the popular pronunciations ko-kān and to-mān are increasingly difficult to deny. Furthermore, because both of these words and their common pronunciations were widely known, **-cain(e)**, in spite of its unsound etymology, has been adopted as a common suffix on other words such as "novocain," "nupercain," "methycaine," and "procaine."

## F. QUANTITY

The quantity of a syllable is either long ( – ) or short ( ᴗ ). In Greek and Latin words a syllable is long if it contains: (a) a diphthong, or (b) a long vowel, or (c) a short vowel followed by two full consonants (except a mute plus *l* or *r*) or a double consonant (x; ζ, ξ, ψ). More often than not, the syllabic quantities of the original word are retained in derivative and loan-words. For example:

| Latin or Greek | English | Latin or Greek | English |
|---|---|---|---|
| *caecum* | cēcum | *nīdus* | nīdus |
| *cedere* | antecēdent | ἔντερον | enteritis |
| *haerere* | inhēre | παιδ- | pēdiatrics |
| *incīsus* | incīsor | πτῶμα | ptōmaine |
| *innocuus* | innocuous | σφαῖρα | sphēre |
| *sēta* | sētaceous | φήμη | aphēmia |

There is a marked tendency in English pronunciation, however, to disregard the original quantities of syllables, especially if a vowel or a diphthong is followed by two consonants. For example:

| Latin or Greek | English | Latin or Greek | English |
|---|---|---|---|
| *aedificium* | ĕdifice | *plēnus* | plĕnitude |
| *caeruleus* | cerūlean | *saeptum* | sĕptum |
| *caespes* | cĕspitose | αἰσθετικός | ĕsthetic |
| *formīca* | formĭcation | γλῶττα | epiglŏttis |
| *magnitudo* | măgnitude | οἶκος | ĕcology |
| *nātura* | nătural | | |

# G. ACCENTUATION

Technical words borrowed or derived from Greek and Latin, or words given Latin form, generally observe the rule that applies to the accentuation of Latin words. That rule is: "The last syllable (ultima) is never accented. If the next to the last syllable (penult) is long, it receives the accent; otherwise the accent falls on the preceding syllable (antepenult)." The crucial matter, therefore, is the quantity of the penult. The operation of the Latin rule regarding accentuation can be observed in the following words:

| | | |
|---|---|---|
| abdŏ́men | gingĭ́va | notálgia |
| amebĭ́asis | gymnocárpus | páresis |
| apparãtus | hiãtus | phenómĕnon |
| diagnŏ́sis | hypóthĕsis | sequéla |
| dilémma | isóchrŏnous | synópsis |
| forãmen | isóscĕles | sýnthĕsis |

The Latin rule of accent should of course be applied to the accentuation of all scientific words that are used as Latin, whether or not the classical Latin pronunciation is used in other respects. The rule is helpful also with English words whenever there is uncertainty about the accentuation of a word, but it can serve only as a general guide because other factors operate in English words to cause deviations from it. There is, for instance, a tendency in English pronunciation to shorten the vowel of an accented penult and to move the accent forward on the word. This tendency accounts for the pronunciation **ves**-ic-al instead ves-**ic**-al (*vesīca*), **cap**-il-la-ry instead of cap-**il**-la-ry (*capíllus*), meta-**morph**-o-sis instead of meta-morph-**o**-sis (μεταμόρφωσις). It also explains why many persons want to say **ab**-do-men instead of ab-**do**-men (*abdŏ́men*), **gin**-gi-va instead of gin-**gi**-va (*gingĭ́va*), and du-**od**-e-num instead of du-o-**de**-num (*duodḗnum*). The pronunciations of **sper**-ma-to-cele, **mel**-an-o-phore, **pter**-id-o-phyte, and **sal**-i-cyl-ate illustrate this same recessive tendency of the primary accent on polysyllabic compound words. But because this forward shift of the accent is only a tendency and not an established principle in the pronunciation of English, dictionaries are either not in complete agreement regarding the pronunciation of certain words or they recognize more than one acceptable pronunciation for the same word. If more than one pronunciation is recognized, the preferred version is usually that which has the sanction of most extensive use, even if that version should happen to be a pronunciation which violates the more commonly observed principles just mentioned (e.g., an-**gi**-na instead of **an**-gin-a [*ángĭna*], and ec-**ze**-ma instead of **ec**-ze-ma [ἔκζεμα]).

When pronouncing a compound word, there is a natural inclination to transfer to the compound word the syllabification and accentuation of its separate constituent elements, especially if attention is being centered on noting its structural parts. When this is done, the separate constructive units of the word may perhaps be made more easily discernible to the ear,[5] but it often leads to mispronouncing the term. A compound term should always be treated as a single and unified word, whose pronunciation is independent of the syllabification and accentuation of its constituent parts. The following words will furnish a few illustrations:

1. ambivalence (**ambi**-, both; **valere,** to be strong) is pronounced am-**biv**-a-lens, not am-bi-**val**-ens.
2. parenchymal (**para**-, beside; **en**-, in; **chymos,** juice) is pronounced pa-**reng**-ki-mal, not par-en-**ki**-mal.
3. rhynchospora (**rhynchos,** snout; **spora,** seed) is pronounced ring-**kos**-po-ra, not ring-ko-**spo**-ra.
4. anisognathous (**an**-, not; **isos,** equal; **gnathos,** jaw) is pronounced an-i-**sog**-na-thus, not an-i-so-**gna**-thus.
5. hypophysis (**hypo**-, under; **physis,** growth) is pronounced hi-**pof**-i-sis, not hi-po-**fis**-is.
6. catadromous (**kata**-, down; **dromos,** a running) is pronounced ka-**tad**-ro-mus, not ka-ta-**dro**-mus.
7. acropetal (**akron,** peak, summit; **petere,** to seek) is pronounced a-**krop**-e-tal, not ak-ro-**pet**-al.

Technical terms of science usually comply with the general principles of pronunciation stated above to a greater degree than ordinary English words do. Nevertheless, the preferred pronunciation of some scientific words may change from one edition of a dictionary to the

5. R. W. Brown (*Composition of Scientific Words*, p. 60) advocates a system of pronunciation which will reveal as clearly as possible the separate components of a word.

next. And occasionally, in order to increase uniformity and stability in nomenclature, a scientific society takes action through its publications or special committees to specify a standard pronunciation for certain widely used terms.

A few scientific terms are given below for practice in pronunciation:

| | | |
|---|---|---|
| androgyny | fungi | psoriasis |
| caecostomy | guttae | ramus |
| cheilosis | gyniatrics | scabies |
| coccygeal | hirsuties | strata |
| eidopometry | ischium | syntheses |
| expiratory | nuclei | traumata |
| facies | oedema | vertebral |
| fauces | ozaenae | xanthopsia |
| foci | phalanges | xyloma |

## Synonymy

In literary composition generally, the dextrous use of words which have identical or nearly identical meanings contributes much toward the attainment of good style. In scientific language, on the contrary, the use of synonymous terms is usually discouraged because, for the sake of attaining preciseness and uniformity in the communication of ideas, each entity ought to have only one name by which it is universally known. The use of synonymous terms in technical writing not only increases the risk of misinterpretation, but also needlessly increases the number of words in a terminology which is already burdensome because of its vastness. But although the use of synonyms in scientific language ought to be discouraged generally, it is an apparent fact that the language of biology and medicine reveals many instances where two or more names are in use for identifying the same thing (e.g., blister, vesicant, bulla, phlyctena; androspore, microspore; baldness, atrichia, alopecia, calvities; undulant fever, brucellosis, Malta fever). Synonymy in the nomenclature of the biological sciences is therefore a matter deserving some attention.[6]

6. The multiplication of synonyms was one of the main ills that beset anatomical terminology some sixty years ago and led to the reforms incorporated in the B. N. A. (see p. 289). Even in 1955, and against the unanimously accepted principle that "each structure shall be designated by one term only," the International Anatomical Nomenclature Committee in its proposed revision of the *Nomina Anatomica* was compelled to admit into the terminology of gross anatomy about forty pairs of synonyms (see p. 291).

Since investigations and discoveries in the biological sciences have continued for centuries and throughout extensive areas of the world, it is inevitable that different names, originating from many sources, at different times, and from many languages, will have been applied to the same scientific phenomena. For this reason, the subject of synonymy in the terminology of these sciences is one of such vast scope that only a brief treatment of it can be undertaken here.[7] In the discussion that follows, the illustrative terms are mainly single-word terms (but mostly compound words) having their origins in Greek and Latin and drawn largely from the terminology of medicine. Thus restricted, the discussion is arranged under the following heads: (a) Synonyms resulting from the use of Greek and Latin source words of equivalent meaning, (b) Synonyms resulting from the use of constructive elements derived from synonymous words of the same parent language, (c) Synonyms resulting from the use of constructive elements derived from nonequivalent Greek and Latin words, (d) Synonyms resulting from metathesis of the constructive units of a compound word, (e) Synonyms resulting from the use of variant bases of the same parent word, and (f) Synonyms resulting from miscellaneous orthographic variants.

A. *Synonyms resulting from the use of Greek and Latin source words of equivalent meaning.* One of the main reasons for the large number of synonymous words in the vocabulary of science is the fact that its terminology rests largely on the dual linguistic base of Greek and Latin. Since the elements used in the construction of scientific words have long been drawn from both of these languages, many twin sets of synonyms have been produced. This is apparent in the vocabulary of several scientific areas, but especially so in that of anatomy and pathology where corresponding Greek and Latin words for anatomical parts have been used in the construction of

---

7. Omitted from the present consideration is that aspect of the problem of synonymy which grows out of the use of epithets composed of several words, including eponyms, especially as it applies to the validity of the various published names of plants and animals in the binomial nomenclature of botany and zoology. For a helpful introductory treatment of this aspect of the problem, with illustrative cases, see Schenck and McMasters' *Procedure in Taxonomy*, 3rd Ed., pp. 17-23, and s. v. "synonymy" in the Index of Camp, Rickett, and Weatherby, *International Rules of Botanical Nomenclature*.

terms. Some of the most common of these Greek and Latin anatomical equivalents are the following:

| Greek | Latin | English |
|-------|-------|---------|
| aden | glandula | gland |
| cheilos | labium | lip |
| cheir | manus | hand |
| chole | bilis | bile |
| chondros | cartilago | cartilage |
| dakryon | lacrima | tear |
| dactylos | digitus | finger |
| derma | cutis | skin |
| didymus | testis | testicle |
| enkephalos | cerebrum | brain |
| enteron | intestinum | intestine |
| geneion | mentum | chin |
| glossa | lingua | tongue |
| gony | genu | knee |
| haima | sanguis | blood |
| histos | membrana | tissue |
| hystera | uterus | womb |
| is(inos) | fibra | fiber |
| kephalos | caput | head |
| kneme | tibia | shin |
| kolpos | vagina | vagina |
| kore | pupilla | pupil |
| kystis | vesica | bladder |
| lapara | lumbus | loin |
| mastos | mamma | breast |
| myelos | medulla | marrow |
| mys | musculus | muscle |
| myxa | mucus | mucus |
| nephros | ren | kidney |
| neuron | nervus | nerve |
| odous | dens | tooth |
| omos | humerus | shoulder |
| omphalos | umbilicus | navel |
| ophthalmos | oculus | eye |
| osteon | os (ossis) | bone |
| oulon | gingiva | gum |
| ouranos | palatum | palate |
| ous (otos) | auris | ear |
| phleps | vena | vein |
| pneumon | pulmo | lung |
| pous (podos) | pes (pedis) | foot |

| Greek | Latin | English |
|-------|-------|---------|
| prosopon | facies | face |
| pyelos | pelvis | pelvis |
| rhis (rhinos) | nasus | nose |
| splanchnon | viscus | bowels |
| splen | lien | spleen |
| spondyle | vertebra | vertebra |
| staphyle | uvula | uvula |
| stoma | os (oris) | mouth |
| thrix | capillus | hair |

Within the field of medicine, the area of descriptive anatomy has used the Latin words in the above list more than it has used the Greek words, whereas in the area of pathology and diagnosis the Greek words have been employed more generally than the Latin words.

Many synonymous terms are single-stem words derived with only slight modification from the Greek and the Latin words of corresponding meaning. For example:

| Greek | Latin | Meaning |
|-------|-------|---------|
| dermal (DERMA) | cutaneous (CUTIS) | pertaining to the *skin* |
| cystic (KYSTIS) | vesical (VESICA) | pertaining to the *bladder* |
| genesis (GENESIS) | origin (ORIGO) | *birth; origin* |
| neural (NEURON) | nervous (NERVA) | pertaining to the *nerves* |
| osteal (OSTEON) | osseous (OS, OSSIS) | pertaining to the *bones* |
| splanchnic (SPLANCH-NON) | visceral (VISCERA) | pertaining to the *bowels* |
| stoma (STOMA) | ostium (OSTIUM) | *mouth; opening* |

Numerous synonyms are compound terms whose component elements are derived from corresponding words in Greek and in Latin. For example:

| Derived from Greek | Derived from Latin |
|--------------------|--------------------|
| 1. exenteration (EX-, out; ENTERON, intestine) | 1. evisceration (E-, out; VISCERA, intestines) |
| 2. polyodontia (POLY-, many; ODONT-, tooth) | 2. multidentate (MULTI-, many; DENT-, tooth) |
| 3. diarthrosis (DIA-, through; ARTHRON, joint; -SIS, condition) | 3. perarticulation (PER-, through; ARTICULUS, joint; -IO, condition) |

SYNONYMY 253

4. encephalorachidian
(ENCEPHALOS, brain; RHACHIS, spine)

4. cerebrospinal
(CEREBRUM, brain; SPINA, spine)

5. dolichopus
(DOLICHOS, long; POUS, foot)

5. longipes
(LONGUS, long; PES, foot)

6. tetradactylous
(TETTARA, four; DAKTYLOS, finger)

6. quadridigitate
(QUADRI-, four; DIGITUS, finger)

7. dermatolysis
(DERMAT-, skin; LYSIS, loosening)

7. cutis laxa
(CUTIS, skin; LAXA, loose)

8. galactophorous
(GALACT-, milk; PHOR-, carry)

8. lactiferous
(LACTI-, milk; FER-, carry)

Many pairs of synonyms are compound words having one constructive element in common and another constructive element derived, in the one instance from a Greek word and in the other instance from the equivalent word in Latin. Many hybrid terms are thus produced. For example:

| Synonyms | Definition | Equivalent Source Words |
|---|---|---|
| 1. microdontism | abnormal smallness of the teeth | ODOUS (Gk.) |
| microdentism | | DENS (Lat.) |
| 2. ophthalmomycosis | any eye disease carried by a fungus | OPTHALMOS (Gk.) |
| oculomycosis | | OCULUS (Lat.) |
| 3. nephropathy | kidney disease | NEPHROS (Gk.) |
| renopathy | | REN (Lat.) |
| 4. meningo-encephalitis | inflammation of the meninges and the brain | ENKEPHALON (Gk.) |
| meningocerebritis | | CEREBRUM (Lat.) |
| 5. splenomalacia | abnormal softness of the spleen | SPLEN (Gk.) |
| lienomalacia | | LIEN (Lat.) |
| 6. coroscopy | test for determining refractive power of the eye | KORE (Gk.) |
| pupilloscopy | | PUPILLA (Lat.) |

| | | |
|---|---|---|
| 7. hepatopneumonic | pertaining to the liver | PNEUMON (Gk.) |
| hepatopulmonary | and the lungs | PULMO (Lat.) |
| 8. phleboclysis | injection of a fluid into | PHLEPS (Gk.) |
| venoclysis | a vein | VENA (Lat.) |
| 9. uloglossitis | inflammation of the | OULA (Gk.) |
| gingivoglossitis | gums and the tongue | GINGIVA (Lat.) |
| 10. polyonychia | occurrence of super- | ONYX (Gk.) |
| polyunguia | numerary nails | UNGUIS (Lat.) |
| 11. sternocleidal | pertaining to the sternum | KLEIS (Gk.) |
| sternoclavicular | and the clavicle | CLAVIS (Lat.) |
| 12. orthochromia | normal color of red | ORTHOS (Gk.) |
| normochromia | blood corpuscles | NORMA (Lat.) |
| 13. anoia | mental deficiency; | NOUS (Gk.) |
| amentia | idiocy | MENS (Lat.) |
| 14. chylopoiesis | the formation of chyle | POIESIS (Gk.) |
| chylofication | | FICATIO (Lat.) |
| 15. colocentesis | puncture of the colon | KENTESIS (Gk.) |
| colipuncture | | PUNCTURA (Lat.) |

Numerous synonyms of the same type as those listed above are produced by using the corresponding prefixes and suffixes of Greek and of Latin alternately on the same stem. For example: *hyper*motility and *super*motility; *peri*renal and *circum*renal; hem*ic* and hem*al*; *syn*genic and *con*genital; dendr*oid* and dendri*form*.

B. *Synonyms resulting from the use of constructive elements derived from synonymous words of the same parent language.* Many pairs of synonyms are the result of using synonymous or nearly synonymous words of the parent lagnuage as the source of one constructive unit in both terms. For example:

1. odontalgia (ALGOS, pain) and odontodynia (ODYNE, pain)
   "pain in a tooth; toothache"

2. helminthology (HELMINTH-, worm) and scolecology (SKOLEK-, worm)
   "the sum of knowledge concerning worms"

3. embololalia (LALIA, talk, chat) and embolophrasia (PHRASIS, speaking)
   "the interpolation of meaningless words into the speech"

4. macropus (MAKROS, long) and dolichopus (DOLICHOS, long)
   "long-footed"

5. niphotyphlosis (TYPHLOS, blind) and niphoablepsia (A-, not; BLEP-, see)
   "snow-blindness"

6. toxicophidia (TOXIKON, poison) and thanatophidia (THANATOS, death)
   "venomous snakes collectively"

7. acromegaly (MEGAL-, large) and pachyacria (PACHY-, thick)
   "enlargement of the bones, and soft parts of the hands, feet, and face"

8. anoia (A-, not) and aponoia (APO-, away from)
   "amentia; idiocy" (the use of synonymous Greek prefixes)

9. evisceration (E-, from) and devisceration (DE-, away from)
   "the removal of viscera" (the use of synonymous Latin prefixes)

10. alloplasia (ALLO-, other) and heteroplasia (HETERO-,other)
    "the replacement of normal by abnormal tissue"

11. gastroptosia (-IA, condition) and gastroptosis (-SIS, condition)
    "downward displacement of the stomach" (the use of synonymous suffixes of Greek or Latin)

12. bradycardia (KARDIA, heart), bradycrotic (KROTOS, a beating), bradyrhythmia (RHYTHMOS, rhythm), and bradysphygmia (SPHYGMOS, pulse)
    "abnormal slowness of the pulse"

13. colpoptosis (KOLPOS, vagina), coleoptosis (KOLEOS, sheath, vagina), elytroptosis (ELYTRON, case, vagina), kysthoptosis (KYSTHOS, genitals, vagina)
    "prolapse of the vagina"

As will be observed from the examples given above, the constructive units of each pair of synonyms are in most cases derived from words which in Greek and Latin had identical or nearly identical meanings (nos. 1, 2, 4, 8, 9, 10, 11). But it will also be noted that in some cases the constructive units are derived from words which in Greek and Latin did not have identical meanings but which have in modern usage acquired identical meanings (nos. 6, 7). This illustrates the fact that synonymous terms sometimes result from the modern practice of attaching limited or specialized meanings to word-elements which from the etymological viewpoint might very well have other significations: for example, the terminal elements -*adelphus* (**adelphos,** brother), -*didymus* (**didymos,** twin), and -*pagus* (**pagos,** fixation) might well convey clearly differentiated meanings, but modern medical usage has attached the same meaning to all three (e.g., ischiadelphus, ischiodidymus, and ischiopagus = "twin fetal monster united at the hips").

As has already been suggested, the specific meaning of a scientific term is that which has been assigned to it by officially approved definition or by widely accepted usage. Thus it happens that some pairs of words which from the etymological point of view might well be taken as synonyms are not actually synonymous.[8] For example:

1. adactylia (A-, not, without; DAKTYLOS, finger)
"congenital absence of fingers or toes"

   apodactylic (APO-, from, without)
"without the use of, or the touch of, the human fingers"

   (Compare these terms with the words in No. 8 above).

2. amentia (A-, not, lack of; MENT-, mind)
"congenital mental deficiency"

   dementia (DE-, away from, lack of)
"acquired mental deficiency"

3. androgynism (ANDRO-, male; GYN-, female)
"hermaphroditism in the female"

   gynandrism

   "hermaphroditism in the male"

---

8. The terms *phoria* and *phoresis*, for example, on the basis of their constituent parts might well have identical meanings. But in medical language *phoria*, used as an independent word or as a common terminal suffix (except in "dysphoria" and "euphoria"), has been given the meaning "any tendency to deviation of the visual axis of one of the eyes from the normal" (e.g., "anaphoria") while *phoresis*, when used alone, signifies "the transmission of chemical ions into the tissues by means of an electric current," and as a terminal suffix usually conveys the notion of "a carrying or transmission" in general (e.g., "diaphoresis," perspiration; "pathophoresis," the transmission of disease).

4. camera (CAMERA, chamber)     thalamus (THALAMOS, chamber)

"a chamber, compartment; chamber of the eye; pulp cavity of tooth"     "the anterior portion of the brain stem"

5. dentilabial (DENT-, tooth; LABI-, lip)     labiodental

"pertaining to teeth and lips"     "pertaining to the labial surface of a tooth"

6. diastasis (DIA-, through; STA-, stand)     diastema

"1. a dislocation in which there is a separation of two bones normally attached to each other without the existence of a true joint. 2. the rest period of the cardiac cycle."     "a space or cleft. In dentistry, a space between the teeth. In cytology, a narrow zone in the equatorial plane through which the cytosome divides in mitosis."

7. nephrocystosis (NEPHROS, kidney; KYSTIS, cyst)     cystonephrosis

"development of cysts in the kidney"     "cystiform dilation or enlargement of the kidney"

8. polytocous (POLY-, many; TOK-, give birth to)     multiparous (MULT-, many; PAR-, give birth to)

"giving birth to several offspring at one time"     "having given birth to many children"

C. *Synonyms resulting from the use of constructive elements derived from nonequivalent Greek and Latin words.* Numerous pairs of synonymous terms are derived from Greek and Latin words which are not of equivalent meaning or which are only remotely associated in meaning. For example:

1. paracnemis (PARA-, beside; KNEME, the leg between knee and ankle)     fibula (FIBULA, a brooch)

"the outer and smaller of the two bones of the leg"

2. ecphyadectomy (EKPHYAD-, outgrowth; EKTOM-, cut out)     appendectomy (AD-, to; PEND-, hang)

"surgical removal of the appendix vermiformis"

3. hysterotokotomy (HYSTERA, womb; TOKOS, birth; TOM-, cut)     cesarian section (CAES-, cut; SECT-, cut)

"delivery of the fetus by an incision through the abdominal and uterine walls"

4. dyschondroplasia (DYS-, bad; CHONDROS, cartilage; PLASS-, mould)

diaphyseal aclasis (DIA-, through; PHY-, grow; A-, not; KLA-, break)

"a condition of abnormal growth of cartilage at the diaphyseal end of long bones"

5. diaphoretic (DIA-, through; PHOR-, carry)

sudorific (SUDOR, sweat; FIC-, make)

"stimulating the secretion of sweat"

6. arachnodactylia (ARACHNE, spider; DAKTYLOS, finger, toe)

dolichostenomelia (DOLICHO-OS, long; STENOS, narrow; MELOS, limb)

"long and thin fingers or toes"

In this group of synonyms belongs the large number of eponyms (cf. pp. 280-86) for which there are equivalent descriptive words. For example:

1. Marie's disease    acromegaly (AKROS, extremity; MEGAL-, large)

2. brucellosis (Bruce)    undulant fever (UNDA, wave)

3. Mitchell's disease    erythromelalgia (ERYTHROS, red; MELOS, limb; ALGOS, pain)

4. Bauhin's valve    ileocecal valve (ILEUM, ileum; CAECUS, blind; caecum)

D. *Synonyms resulting from metathesis of the constructive units of a compound word.* Words of identical meaning are often produced by the transposition or rearrangement (metathesis) of the constituent elements of compound words. Since such synonymous terms are constructed of the same components, they ordinarily present little added burden to learning; they do, however, add considerable bulk to dictionaries. The following words are examples of synonyms resulting from metathesis:

1. mucoserous        and        seromucous
     "containing mucus and serum"

2. nasofrontal        and        frontonasal
     "pertaining to the nasal and frontal bones"

3. naso-oral        and        oronasal
     "pertaining to the nose and mouth"

4. scapulohumeral and humeroscapular
"pertaining to the scapula and humerus"

5. psychosomatic and somatopsychic
"pertaining to both body and mind"

6. androclinium and clinandrium
"bed of the anther in orchids"

7. osteomalacia and malacosteon
"softening of the bones"

8. natimortality and mortinatality
"the proportion of stillbirths to the general birth rate"

9. cardiophrenia and phrenocardia
"a psychic condition characterized by pain in the cardiac region"

10. megalodactylia and dactylomegaly
"abnormal largeness of fingers or toes"

11. ophthalmoxerosis and xerophthalmia
"conjunctivitis producing an abnormally dry and lusterless condition of the eyeball"

12. acromegaly and megalakria
"a chronic disease characterized by enlargement of bones and soft parts of the hands, feet, and face"

13. philoneism and neophilism
"morbid or abnormal love of novelty"

14. microsplanchnia and splanchnomicria
"abnormal smallness of the viscera"

In the pairs of synonymous words listed above there might seem to be little or no reason for preferring one to the other. In the case of coordinate adjectival compounds (nos. 1, 2, 3, 4, 5) the only basis for preference might be that in some instances one word is more euphonious or easier to pronounce than the other. If the synonymous words describe a condition or a state of being, however, an additional reason exists for preferring one of the terms. "Phrenocardia" (no. 9), for example, is defined by the medical dictionary as a psychic condition and not as a heart condition; the term "cardiophrenia," in which the suffix -ia (condition) is attached to the key base **phren-** (mind) is therefore more appropriate than "phrenocardia," in which the -ia suffix is attached to the subordinate and qualifying base **cardi-** (heart). Nevertheless, in the case of these two synonyms, Dorland's *Medical Dictionary* fully defines "phrenocardia" but accords "cardiophrenia" only a cross reference to "phrenocard-ia." Such an arrangement in the dictionary probably indicates that in spite of the considerations just mentioned, "phrenocardia" is the more widely used of the two terms. In the case of "acromegaly" versus "megalakria" (no. 12), the former is the recommended term since it describes a condition of "largeness" (**megal-**) qualified by the first component "at the extremities" (**akro-**); and in this instance Dorland's *Dictionary* gives the full definition under the theoretically preferred term and only a cross reference to it under the other term. It would be difficult to demonstrate on the basis of modern usage of scientific terms that any consistent principle operates to indicate which synonym in pairs of this sort is the preferred one.

And yet, as has been indicated, linguistically valid reasons exist for preferring one word to the other in the case of some pairs of synonymous words that result from the metathesis of constructive units.

When more than two basic constructive units are used in a compound term, varying arrangements of those units may produce synonymous words. For example:

1. acephalobrachia          and          abrachiocephalia
      (A-, not; KEPHALOS, head; BRACHION, arm)
2. dyschondroplasia          and          chondrodysplasia
      (DYS-, bad; CHONDROS, cartilage; PLASS-, mould)
3. hypertokotomy          and          hypertomotoky
      (HYPER-, excessive; TOKOS, birth; TOM-, cut)
4. sarcohydrocele          and          hydrosarcocele
      (SARC-, flesh; HYDR-, water; KELE, tumor)
5. symphysodactylia          and          dactylosymphysis
      (SYN-, together; PHYS-, growth; DAKTYLOS, finger)

"Symphysodactylia" and "dactylosymphysis" (no. 5) have a third synonym in the word "syndactylism." But "syndactylism" lacks one of the component elements (**phys-**) used by the other two words. This illustrates another nomenclatural procedure by which synonyms are multiplied, namely, by incorporating an additional constructive unit into a word which already may quite adequately describe a phenomenon.

Just as the transposition of the components of a compound word made up of two basic stems does not always result in synonymous terms, so rearrangement of the components of a compound word of three or more elements does not always result in synonyms. The word "endostethoscope," for example, is defined as "a stethoscope passed into the esophagus for ausculating the heart" (**endo-**, within; **stethos,** chest; **skop-**, see) but "stethendoscope" is defined as "a fluoroscope used in examination of the chest by roentgen rays." Such differences in the meanings of words composed of the same constructive units are of course due to usage or arbitrary decision and not to etymological considerations.

E. *Synonyms resulting from the use of variant bases of the same parent word.* Numerous pairs of words with identical meaning have been produced by using variant bases of the same Greek or Latin word, especially of words which belong to Declension III. The correct base of words belonging to Declension III is derived from their form in the genitive case, but not infrequently a "short" base or the nominative case form has been used as a constructive unit for derivatives. For example:

1. spermatheca and spermatotheca (Nom., **sperma,** Gen., **spermat**-os, seed; **theke,** sheath). The use of both the "short" and the "long" bases of Greek nouns belonging to Declension III, especially neuter nouns ending in -*ma*, has produced numerous pairs of synonyms. (For a discussion of these bases, see pp. 49-50; 235, and for examples, see derivatives under **derma, haima,** and **stoma** in the General Greek Vocabulary List; also under **geron, gyne, tenon**).

2. stipiform and stipitiform (Nom., **stipes,** Gen., **stipit**is, stem or stalk; **forma,** shape).

3. stercolith and stercorolith (Nom., **stercus,** Gen., **stercor**is, feces; **lithos,** stone).

4. aceology and acology (Nom., **akos,** Gen., **ake**os, cure; **logos,** word). The Greek word **akos** belongs to Declension III and its base, as can be observed from the genitive case form, is **ake**- But the base **ak**- has also been used in word composition, presumably because, on analogy with most Greek nouns ending in **-os,** the word was thought to belong to Declension II.

5. hidradenitis and hidrosadenitis (**hidros,** sweat; **aden**, gland). In this instance, as in others like it (e.g., gastrasthenia and gasterasthenia), the entire nominative case form of a word has been used as the combining form in a compound.

6. chylifaction and chylification (**chylos,** juice; **fac-** or **fic-**, make). In these derivatives alternate stems of the Latin verb **facere** have been used.

F. *Synonyms resulting from miscellaneous orthographic variants.* For example:

1. anidrosis and anhidrosis (**an-**, not; **hidros,** sweat). The former term has been used since Hippocrates' time, but modern practice is inconsistent in its inclusion or omission of the *h* in compounds which use an element derived from Greek words having rough breathing on the initial syllable (see pp. 59-61).

2. hyperglycemia and hyperglykemia (**hyper-**, excessive; **glyk-**, sweet; **haima,** blood). The more common transliteration of Greek ϰ is *c*, but *k* is sometimes preferred.

3. muscicide and muscacide (**musca,** fly; **cid-**, kill). The only difference between the two words is in the combining vowel which is used. Instances of this kind are numerous (see pp. 240-41).

4. pyarthrosis and pyoarthrosis (**py-**, pus; **arthron,** joint). The second term uses a combining vowel (*o*) in spite of the fact that the second element of the compound begins with a vowel (see pp. 241-42).

5. arhinia and arrhinia (**a-**, not; **rhin-**, nose). Such variants result from irregularity in modern practice regarding the use of a single or double *r* in transcribing a Greek word with initial ῥ (see p. 6).

6. symphalangism and synphalangism (**syn-**, together; **phalang-**, finger). The second word has failed to observe the usual partial assimilation of *n* before *p* (see p. 54).

7. spongoblast (**spongos,** sponge; **blastos,** bud, germ) and spongioblast (**spongia,** sponge). In this case, two Greek words of identical meaning but of slightly different spelling have been used in the construction of the derivatives.

8. hidradenitis and hydradenitis (**hidros,** sweat; **hydr-,** water; **aden,** gland; **-itis,** inflammation); xylonite and zylonite (**xylon,** wood); echophony and ecophony (**echo,** echo; **phone,** voice); myophone and miophone (**my-,** muscle; **phone,** voice). Variants such as these are caused by the similarity of sound in the pronunciation of the words and by errors in the transliteration of Greek letters.

9. caenotophobia, cainotophobia, and cenotophobia (**kainotes,** a strange thing; **phobos,** fear); ecophobia and oikophobia (**oikos,** home). These synonyms have been produced by variable transliteration of a Greek (or Latin) diphthong (see pp. 58-59).

10. alkalimeter and kalimeter (**alkali,** alkali; **metron,** measure); sternodidymus and sternodymus (**sternon,** sternum; **didymos,** twin); pachyemia and pachemia (**pachys,** thick; **haima,** blood); leucocytosis and leukosis (**leukos,** white; **kytos,** cell; **-osis,** condition); periclasia and periodontoclasia (**peri-,** around; **odont-,** tooth; **klasis,** breaking). The clipping of a stem or the abbreviation of a compound produces variant words of synonymous meaning (see pp. 264-65).

11. tenonitis, tenontitis, and tenositis (**tenon, tenont**os, tendon; **-itis,** inflammation); periectomy and peridectomy (**peri-,** around; **ek-,** out; **tome,** cutting). For reasons which generally are not clear, false letters are sometimes inserted into stems, as the *s* and the *d*, for example, have been inserted in "tenositis" and "peridectomy." Analogy with familiar words, or simplification of pronunciation, occasionally supply an explanation for some of the variants of this sort.

12. gomphiasis and agomphiasis (**gomphios,** a molar tooth; **agomphios,** without grinders). Both words are defined "looseness of teeth," and thereby is revealed a disregard of the basic significance of the constructive units used.

## Shortening, Malformations, Misnomers

## A. SHORTENING OF WORDS

The shortening of words is a familiar phenomenon in almost all languages. In the English language, which is especially fond of monosyllabic words, shortening occurs often: "car," for example, is used for "motorcar"; "bus" for "autobus"; "glasses" for "eyeglasses." The shortened versions may be taken from the first, the middle, or the terminal portion of the words; for example: "mike" for "microphone"; "flu" for "influenza"; and "phone" for "telephone."

The tendency to shorten words is stronger in ordinary language than it is in scientific language. Nevertheless, as "car," "bus," and "glasses" are abbreviations in ordinary language for longer original words or phrases, so also some of the more familiar scientific terms represent longer words or phrases; for example:

| Short Form | Long Form | Short Form | Long Form |
|---|---|---|---|
| leukopenia | leukocytopenia | alveolus | alveolus processus |
| leukosis | leukocytosis | defluvium | defluvium capillorum |
| polio | poliomyelitis | rectum | intestinum rectum |
| biceps | musculus biceps | jejunum | intestinum jejunum |
| pia | pia mater | trachea | arteria tracheia |
| arachnoidea | arachnoidea mater | thalamus | thalamus nervi optici |
| dura | dura mater | cornea | tela cornea |
| toxicon | toxicon pharmacon | | |

Frequently used word-elements are likely to be clipped when used in compounds; for example:

| Short Form | Long Form | Short Form | Long Form |
|---|---|---|---|
| atlodymus | atlantodidymus | sternodymus | sternodidymus |
| celiosite | celioparasite | typhloteritis | typhloenteritis |
| enterosite | enteroparasite | xanchromatic | xanthochromatic |

The telescoping of words may eliminate only one syllable or it may drastically shorten and alter the form of a word; for example:

| Short Form | Long Form | Short Form | Long Form |
|---|---|---|---|
| apilocator | apicolocator | torsoclusion | torso-occlusion |
| appestat | appetitestat | kalimeter | alkalimeter |
| polyp | polypus | hyther | hydrothermia |

If the last syllable of one component of a compound word is identical or similar to the first syllable of the next component, contraction of the word may occur. In Latin, for example, the words *semodius* and *nutrix* are contractions of *semimodius* (**semi-**, half; **modi**us, a peck-measure) and *nutritrix* (**nutrit-**, to nourish; **-trix,** she who). Such shortening is called "haplology," and is more likely to take place when a word is spoken than when it is written. The abbreviated written version usually develops from a recording of the sounds which are heard when the compound word is spoken rapidly. The following medical terms are examples of haplology:

| Short Form | Long Form | Short Form | Long Form |
|---|---|---|---|
| adenema | adenonema | nectarium | nectararium |
| appendectomy | appendicectomy | plasmeba | plasmameba |
| dermalaxia | dermamalaxia | pulmotor | pulmomotor |
| megastria | megagastria | thoracentesis | thoracocentesis |
| mesomula | mesosomula | urinalysis | urinanalysis |
| metopagus | metopopagus | | |

Although scientific terms do not yield to clipping and telescoping as easily and as frequently as ordinary terms do, they nevertheless share this characteristic with words generally. Some shortened words perform the several functions of good scientific terms very well and are therefore not objectionable; in some instances, especially in the case of very long words, the shortened forms are superior to the full forms (see pp. 16-17). As a rule, however, clipped terms suffer serious diminution in descriptive power and clarity of meaning because their etymology has been obscured by the loss of significant portions of their makeup. For this reason, it is a good policy to discourage the shortening of scientific terms.

## B. MALFORMATIONS

Some malformed terms can be found in the terminology of all scientific areas. Scientists' attitudes toward these malformed words are not uniform but, as indicated by statements in scientific publications and in international *Codes* of scientific nomenclature, the prevailing official viewpoint is that of a desire to refine the terminology by eliminating inappropriate and malformed names and to guard against further coinage of such terms. Not many scientific areas now insist on rigid adherence to the so-called "Law of Priority," which gives the term first applied to an entity, even if it is a poor one, permanent and sole claim to use as the official name of that entity. But even though it is possible to replace a poor term by one that is properly constructed or more appropriate, it is generally difficult to alter or remove the name which is first applied to a scientific phenomenon.

Malformed words in scientific terminology assume a variety of forms. Satisfactory explanations of how the malformations came about cannot always be given, but for some of the words there may be plausible explanations. Some examples of malformed words, mostly from medical terminology, are given below.

1. *Faulty Transliteration*

a. Greek υ transliterated as *i* or *u* instead of *y*:

   (1) Both "aneurism" and "aneuryism" (εὐρύς, wide) appear in the medical literature and dictionaries; only the latter is correct.

   (2) "Myobradia" and "miobradyia" (μῦς, μυός, muscle; βραδύς, slow) are both faulty.

   (3) "Pachulosis" and "pachylosis" (παχυλός, thickish) are both used; only the latter is correct.

b. Greek ι or ει transliterated as *y* instead of *i* or *ei*:

   (1) "Myosis" is sometimes used instead of the correct "miosis" (μείωσις, diminution).

   (2) "Barytosis" is not an acceptable variant of "baritosis" (*barite*, from βάρος, weight).

   (3) The incorrect version "olighydria" sometimes appears instead of the proper form "oligidria" (ὀλίγος, scanty; ἱδρώς, sweat).

c. Greek κ transliterated as *ch*; and χ as *c*.

   (1) "Oxyechoia" (ὀξυηκοία, a sharp, quick ear), defined as "a morbid acuteness of sense of hearing," ought to be "oxyecoia" or, even better, a nonexistent word, "oxyacousia" (ὀξύ, sharp, acute; ἀκουσ-, to hear).

(2) "Echophony" (ἠχώ, echo; φωνή, sound) should not be mis-spelled "ecophony."

d. Omission of initial *h* on a term derived from a Greek word with rough breathing:

"Elcosis" and "elkoplasty," for example, are not justifiable versions from Greek ἕλκος (ulcer); the initial *h* has been omitted. Although an argument might be made that an early form of the word was ἔλκος (smooth breathing), it is more likely that the malformations are due to the influence of the frequently occurring element -*elcosis* in such compounds as dacryelcosis, enterelcosis, cystelcosis, omphalelcosis, nephrelcosis, splenelcosis, thymelcosis. In these compounds, however, the *h* has properly been omitted because the Greek stem is not used as the first unit of the compounds. The loss of aspiration (i. e., initial *h*) from a Greek stem when it is prefixed has sound basis in original Greek practice (see p. 59). An *initial* syllable derived from an aspirated Greek stem, however, should always begin with an *h* in English.

2. *Incorrect or Irregular Bases and Stems*

a. Omission of vowels; for example:

In "megadont" (μέγα, large; ὀδούς, ὀδόντος, tooth) and "po-lydontia" (πολύ, many; ὀδούς, ὀδόντος, tooth) an important vowel (*o*) of the base **odont-** has been omitted. In the word "choroid" (χόριον, skin; εἶδος, shape; or χοριοειδής) an *i* has been omitted from the base **chori-**; the word should be spelled "chorioid." In "microcustic" (μικρός, small; ἀκουσ-, hear) and "amblykousis" (ἀμβλύ, dull; ἀκουσ-, hear) the initial *a* of the second element has been omitted. There may be several explanations for such omissions, but similarity or confusion of bases (as **odont-** and **dent-**; and **chori-** and **chor-** in the above illustrations) and uncertainty about elision and the proper use of combining vowels are likely causes for some of the errors.

b. Addition of vowels; for example:

In "copiopsia" (κόπος, fatigue; ὄψις, sight) and "geriopsychosis" (γῆρας, γήραος, old age; ψυχή, mind) a foreign *i* has been introduced into the stem of the first components. One suspects that in the latter word, false analogy with a familiar word like "geriatrics" (γῆρας, old age; ἰατρικός, healing) accounts for the insertion. In "metoxenous" (μετά, with; ξένος, stranger) the insertion of a false *o* obscures the makeup and meaning of the word.

c. Omission of an essential consonant of the base; for example:

**stear, steat**os (fat) has been used in the construction of many compound terms. In some of these terms the true base **steat-** has been used (e.g., *steat*ocele; ino*steat*oma) and in others the nominative form **stear-** (e.g., *stear*odermia; neuro*stear*ic). But to use **stea-**, as in "uro*stea*lith," is an unfortunate aberration.

d. Insertion of consonants; for example:

Rim*m*ose (**rim**a, crack; **-osus,** full of); glyco*s*emia (γλυκύς, sweet; αἷμα, blood); ly*s*emia (λύειν, to loosen; αἷμα, blood); abio*n*ergy (α-, not; βίος, life; ἔργον, work); peri*d*ectomy (περί, around; ἐκ, out; τομή, cut); teno*s*itis (τένων, τένοντος, tendon; -ιτις, inflammation); and synech*t*enterotomy (σύν, together; ἔχειν, to hold; ἔντερον, intestine; τομή, cut).

e. Occasional yielding to the temptation of using the entire nominative form of a word instead of its base as the constructive unit in a compound; for example:

"melosalgia" (μέλος, μέλεος, limb; ἄλγος, pain); "sinusotomy" (*sinus, sini*; sinus; τομή, cut); and "melasanthus" (μέλας, μέλανος, black; ἄνθος, flower).

f. Using as the constructive element of a compound the entire genitive singular form of a word instead of only its base; for example:

"Myositis," "dermatomyositis" (μῦς, μυός, muscle; -ιτις, inflammation; δέρματ-, skin) and other words ending in "-myositis"; "inositis" (ἴς, ἰνός, fiber; -ιτις, inflammation) and "hyperinosemia" (ὑπέρ, excessive; ἴς, ἰνός, fiber; αἷμα, blood). **Myos** and **inos** are complete genitive singular forms; the bases of μῦς and ἴς are **my-** and **in-**.

g. Confusion of similar stems; for example:

"Heptargia" (ἑπτά, seven; ἀργία, inactivity) and "hepatargia" (ἧπαρ, ἥπατος, liver; ἀργία, inactivity) as synonyms cannot be justified; the two stems are distinctly different, and to syncopate one, even if unwittingly done, is to inject another puzzle into scientific terms. In "aristocardia," defined as "deviation of the heart to the right side," the adjective ἄριστος (best) has been confused with ἀριστερός (right). Familiarity with a term like "aristogenesis" or other compounds which appropriately use **aristo-** as a constructive unit would prove an obstacle rather than a help in arriving at the meaning assigned to the term "aristocardia."

h. Creation of false stems; for example:

"Airbrasive," "triphibian," and "cyclotron." In the first term a false stem **bras-** has been created, presumably from an erroneous analogy with the word "abrasive" (**ab-**, from; **rad**ere, **ras**um, to scrape); the **b** is part of the prefix **ab-** and should not be used as part of the stem **ras-**. "Triphibian" has used the prefix **tri** on a fabricated stem **phib-**, which presumably was created on a supposed analogy with the word "amphibian" (ἀμφί, both; βίος, life); but the **phi** is part of the prefix **amphi-**, and the **b** is the first letter of the stem **bi-**. The **-tron** of "cyclotron" is not a true stem; it has been produced by false analogy with the word "electron," in which the -tr is part of the base **electr-**.

Compound scientific words which use a shorter stem derived from the nominative case form instead of the longer true stem derived from the genitive case form (e.g., "sanguivorous" instead of "sangui-nivorous" [**sanguis, sanguin**is, blood; **vora**re, to eat] and "gero-morphism" instead of "geróntomorphism" [γέρων, γέροντος, old man; μορφή, form]) need not, from a linguistic viewpoint invariably be regarded as malformations, because precedent for such usage can be found in both the Greek and the Latin vocabularies (see p. 236). From the viewpoint of a practical nomenclature, however, the use of such apparent nominative stems is not recommended, and in certain instances malformation may rightly be charged when use of such stems imparts to a word an ambiguity which might be avoided by the use of the true stem. If, for example, "kelidoplasty" (κηλίς, κηλῖδος, scar; πλάσσειν, to mold) had been used instead of "keloplasty," no ambiguity of meaning would have resulted through confusion with words such as "kelotomy" and others which use the proper base of the word κήλη (hernia). "Cervimeter" (**cervix, cervic**is, neck; μέτρον, measure), defined as "an apparatus for measuring the cervix uteri," might better have been spelled "cervicometer", lest someone suppose that the word has something to do with an instrument for measuring a deer (**cerv**us, deer). In the terms "tempostabile" and "tempolabile" (**tempus, tempor**is, time; **stabil**is, stable; **labil**is, unstable), the omission of the final consonant of the stem **tempor-** may have been deliberate in order to distinguish these words from the many anatomical terms which use the stem **tempor-** (the temples). A more likely explanation, however, is that these terms are malformations resulting from the erroneous assumption that the Latin noun **tempus** belongs to Declension II and that **tempo-** is therefore the true stem. Compounds arising from such erroneous assumptions regarding the declension and true stem of a parent word are malformations.

### 3. *Miscellaneous*

a. "Anosodiaphoria" (α-, not; νόσος, disease; διαφορά, difference) is defined as "indifference to the existence of disease" and "anosognosia" (α-, not; νόσος, disease; γνῶσις, knowledge) as "loss of ability in a person to recognize that he has a disease." A better arrangement of the components would be "nosadiaphoria" and "nosagnosia" since the adverbial prefix **a-** would more properly modify the verbal elements **diaphor-** and **gno-**, thereby conveying the meanings "indifference to" and "lack of knowledge of." A similar reason would recommend "xanthanopsia" (ξάνθος, yellow; α-, not; ὄψις, vision) over "axanthopsia" (yellow blindness); "baragnosis" (βάρος, weight; α-, not; γνῶσις, knowledge) over "abarognosis" (loss of weight sense); and "myoastasia" (μυ-, muscle; α-, not; στάσις, stand) over "amyostasia" (a tremor of the muscles).

b. The suffix **-ia** should not be used, as it is in "orthodontia" and "orthopedia," to designate a specialized area of study or practice. Properly employed, the suffix **-ia** means a condition, quality, or process.

c.  "Dyspermasia" (δυς-, bad; σπέρμα, seed) should be "dysspermasia"; the **s** of the prefix **dys-** is regularly retained, even before words beginning with **s** (e.g., dysstasia, dyssymmetry, dyssynergia).

## C. MISNOMERS.

A good name for a scientific phenomenon is one that "fits," that is, one which literally or metaphorically describes the phenomenon to which it is applied or which, by alluding to historical or legendary data, suggests a reason for the choice of that particular name. The reason for the choice of most scientific names is therefore not difficult to ascertain. But in almost all scientific areas there are a few terms, some old and familiar and others of recent coinage, which seem malappropriate or altogether inappropriate and which therefore come under criticism by commentators on scientific terminology. The criticisms are sometimes prompted by the desire of eliminating certain inappropriate terms from use in a profession; at other times, the critics realize the futility of any attempt to dislodge certain well-established terms even if they are inappropriate to the phenomena which they name, and hope rather that their criticisms may serve as warnings against further coinage of similar misnomers. Listed below are a few samples of what may be called scientific misnomers.

1. "Anemia" (α-, not, without; αἷμα, blood). Either of the synonymous terms "spanemia" (σπανός, scarce; αἷμα, blood) and "hypohemia" (ὑπό, deficient; αἷμα, blood) would be preferable because the condition is one of *deficiency* and not one of *absence* of blood. Likewise, "asphyxia" (α-, not, without; σφύξις, pulsation) is not in reality a condition of "without pulse." In "agomphiasis" (α-, not; γομφίος, molar tooth; -ιασις, diseased condition, infestation), however, the privative has lost its usual function altogether, for the word is defined as "looseness of the teeth" and is synonymous with "gomphiasis." Moreover "looseness" might have been explicitly expressed by using -*seisis* (σεῖσις, a shaking, or moving to and fro) or -*adesmia* (α-, without; δεσμός, fetter, binding), thus producing a term which would have preciseness and good orientation.

2. "Bradydactylia" and "bradyphalangia" (βραδύς, slow; δάκτυλος, finger; φάλαγξ, finger or toe bone) for "shortness" of

fingers or phalanges are incorrect. The adjective βραδύς (slow) has apparently been confused with the adjective βραχύς (short). When a psychiatric dictionary defines "brachycephalus" (βραχύς, short; κεφαλή, head) as "broad-headed" it has deviated from the standard meaning of that term as well as from the regular medical term for that particular condition, which is "eurycephalic" (εὐρύς, wide).

3. "Emptysis" (ἐν-, in, on; πτύσις, spitting), defined as "expectoration, especially blood; hemoptysis," has a small measure of support from classical usage (ἔμπτυσις), but "ekptysis" would have had stronger support from classical precedent (ἔκπτυσις) and would also have been more consistent with usual prefix usage as well as with the demands of the definition.

4. The etymology of "allochiral" (ἄλλος, other; χείρ, hand) gives a useful indication of the word's meaning, namely "reversed symmetry; having the relation of the right hand to the left." But the terms "allochiria" (pricking on one extremity being referred to the other), "dyschiria" (derangement of power to tell which side of body has been touched) and "synchiria" (same as "allochiria"), which might be thought from their makeup to mean "other-handed," "disordered hands," and "attached hands" seem to have little, if anything, to do with the hands.

5. For a term to describe "difficulty in drinking" "dysposis" (δυς-, impaired; πόσις, drinking) would be preferable to "dysdipsia" (δυς-, impaired; δίψα, thirst).

6. "Chalazodermia" would seem to have some connection with "a hail-like skin" (χάλαζα, a hailstone). The word's definition, "hypertrophy and looseness of skin; dermatolysis," however, shows that **chalasm-** (χαλασμός, loosened) is the stem that was intended.

7. "Nostology" (νόστος, a return; λόγος, word) is an unsatisfactory synonym for "gerontology" (γέρων, old man; λόγος, word).

8. There is nothing in the dictionary definition of "orthopedics" (ὀρθός, straight; παῖς, παιδός, child) which limits that branch of surgery to children.

9. What is there in the make-up of "hemodia" (αἷμα, blood; ὀδούς, tooth) that would indicate its meaning as "unusual sensitiveness of teeth"; or in "hemothymia" (αἷμα, blood; θυμός, soul, feeling) that would reveal its meaning as "an insane tendency to murder"?

10. The terminal element **-agogue** is repeatedly used in compound words to mean "increase or promote"; but in "chromagogue," defined as "tending to eliminate pigments," it has been made to mean "decrease."

11. To signify "a morbid desire to travel away from home," psychiatrists have devised the word "apodemialgia" (ἀπό, away from; δῆμος, country, home; ἄλγος, pain). This is a curious use of **-algia.**

12. "Ecchymosis" (ἐκ, out; χυμός, juice, chyme; -σις, condition) for "extravasation of blood" might better have been "exemosis" (ἐξ, out; αἷμα, blood).

13. "Pyorrhea," "hypnodontia," and "devitalization" are samples of the many terms which have recently been listed as objectionable for use by the dental profession.[9] "Pyorrhea" (πύον, pus; ῥε-, flow), it is claimed, designates neither the source nor the nature of the disease because often no "flow of pus" or suppuration is present; "hypnodontia" (ὕπνος, sleep, stupor; ὀδούς, ὀδόντος, tooth) suggests that the tooth is hypnotized, whereas it is the whole personality and not the tooth only that is affected by hypnosis; and "devitalization" (**de-** from; **vita,** life) of a tooth is inappropriate because a pulpless tooth continues to live, often with as much vitality as one with pulp.

14. "Stethoscope" (στῆθος, chest; σκόπειν, to view) ought to be "stethophone" (φωνή, sound) because use of the instrument involves hearing rather than viewing. "Stethophone" has formally been proposed as the superior word and has gained some recognition, but "stethoscope" will likely be the favorite term for a long time yet.

9. Cf., *Report of Second Nomenclature Conference* and *Report of Third Nomenclature Conference* (1953 and 1954), published by the Bureau of Library and Indexing Service, Amer. Dental Assn., Chicago.

15. "Autopsy" (αὐτός, self; ὄψις, view) is another term that will likely stand its ground for a long time in spite of its inappropriateness; "necropsy" (νέκρος, corpse) and "thanatopsy" (θάνατος, death) have been suggested as replacements.

16. "Lithotomy" (λίθος, stone; τόμη, cut) has been attacked because in the operation to which the term is applied it is the bladder that is cut and not the stone.

17. The etymology of "chiropodist" (χείρ, hand; πούς, ποδός, foot; -ιστης, one concerned with) clearly assigned equal importance to hands and feet. Nevertheless, since 1949 the approved meaning of the term designates one who treats affections of the feet only.

18. "Hysteria" (ὑστέρα, womb) is a form of neurosis which, strictly speaking, ought to apply to women only. But males suffer from the malady, too, and the same term is used to designate it. In 1886 Sanoaville de Lachèse proposed that the word "tarassis" (ταράσσειν, to agitate, disturb, trouble) be used to designate hysteria in the male, but in spite of its appropriateness the term has not received general acceptance. It is not always the superior scientific term that succeeds in winning approval.

## Hybrid Words

Viewpoints regarding the use of hybrid words in scientific terminology range from warm advocacy to most eloquent protests against any term constructed of elements drawn from two or more languages. The word "hybrid" is derived from the Greek word HYBRIS meaning "insolence or outrage," and persons who dislike the use of hybrid terms regard the construction and use of such terms as an insolent and outrageous defiance of sound linguistic practice.

Most official codes of scientific nomenclature take a moderate stand on the matter of hybrid terms; they generally discourage their coinage and use if equally satisfactory "purebred" terms are available, but they also recognize that there are occasions when hybrid terms are superior to purebred terms and that some hybrids have become so firmly entrenched in the terminology that it is futile to attempt to remove them.

A purebred term is generally preferable to a hybrid term for two reasons: (1) Elements taken from the same language usually combine into compound words more easily and euphoniously than do elements taken from different languages. (2) Past practice in the construction of scientific terms has produced many more purebred words than hybrid words, so that to construct a word from elements derived from more than one language is to deviate from the usual and the expected procedure.

Hybridization is both undesirable and unnecessary when it results in producing a word that is a synonym of a familiar and satisfactory purebred word. To designate the ankle bone, for example, both the Greek word ASTRAGALOS and the Latin word TALUS have supplied the desired constructive unit, the Latin word having been used somewhat more frequently than the Greek word. Since the purebred terms, "talocalcaneal," "talocrural," and "talotibial" are commonly used for designating relationship to the ankle bone and adjacent structures, there seems little need for the hybrid synonyms "astragalocalcanean," "astragalocrural," and "astragalo-tibial." In scientific writing, stylistic considerations would seldom be an important factor in choosing between the synonymous words. Scientific vocabulary, however, has numerous pairs of such synonyms (see pp. 253-54 for other examples.)

Even though preference should ordinarily be given to the use of purebred scientific terms, some situations exist where hybrid terms may be preferable to purebreds. The sanction of long and widespread use which is enjoyed by such common hybrid terms as "appendicitis" and "appendectomy," "tonsilitis" and "tonsilectomy," "uvulitis" and "uvulectomy," for example, will outweigh the advantage of linguistic purity which characterizes their synonyms "scolecoiditis" and "ecphyadectomy," "amygdalitis" and "amygdalectomy," and "staphylitis" and "staphylectomy." "Tuberculosis" has received universal sanction, and it is not likely in order to achieve linguistic purity in scientific terms that this word will be replaced by "phyma-tiasis" or "phymatiosis." The hybrid term "hypertension" is probably more commonly used than the purebred term "hyperpiesis," even though the latter term is superior to its synonym in most respects other than in familiarity and accepted use.

Not infrequently it becomes necessary to express in one word a relationship between two structures, each of which has only one standard name, but the names differing from each other in linguistic origin. In such a case a hybrid term cannot be avoided unless some new constructive unit based on an unfamiliar word is introduced to designate one of the structures. But to introduce an unfamiliar constructive element is undesirable because the new compound term would then lose the desirable qualities of orientation, functional facility, sanction, and perhaps also of specificity and economy, If, for example, a word should be needed to refer to some relationship between the anterior portion of the brain stem (*thalamus*) and the outer layer of the brain (*cortex cerebri*), the compound term "thalamocortical" would perform that function well. But the term is a hybrid. The Latin word for "chamber" which corresponds in meaning to the Greek word THALAMOS is *camera* (actually a Latin loan-word, but completely naturalized, from the Greek KAMARA) but that word ought not be used because *camera* in anatomical context regularly designates the eye-chamber (as *thalamus* specifically designates the brain-chamber). If, therefore, the desired word is to be quickly and easily undersood and if it is to possess the qualities of specificity and good orientation, hybridization is unavoidable. Moreover, it is also worth noting that by combining the Greek base *thalam-* with the Latin base *cortic-* the first component of the compound illumines and delimits the second to the extent that specificity is attained without use of the qualifying *cerebri* ("of the brain"). To find satisfactory substitute terms for the Greek-derived term "choroid" (the brown, vascular coat of the eye) and the Latin-derived term "retina" (the innermost tunic and perceptive structure of the eye) would not be easy. The two structures of the eye designated by "choroid" and "retina" are closely related, and if a term is needed to describe an inflammation of those parts, the hybrid word "choroidoretinitis" would be a logical choice. The word is well orientated and immediately meaningful. In like manner, the most logical and convenient word for making joint reference to the optic and the ciliary nerves is the hybrid adjective "opticociliary." The name "vagus" (Latin *vagus*, wandering) has been given to a special nerve of wide distribution in the pneumogastric region. But the aspects, relationships, conditions, and processes which are associated with the vagus and other nerves are in the terminology of anatomy, pathology, and physiology rather uniformly expressed by Greek-derived elements (e.g., vagotonia, electrovagogram, vagotropic). Under these and similar circumstances hybridization of terms is necessary and frequent.

In order to increase uniformity of usage in the terminology of hematology, a committee on the nomenclature of that field recommended that the Latin combining form *rubri-* (instead of the Greek *erythro-*) be used in terms referring to cells of the erythrocytic series even though the resultant words are hybrids. The committee stated that the nomenclatural advantages to be gained by consistent use of terms such as "rubriblast," "prorubricyte," "rubricyte," and "metarubricyte" would outweigh the criticism that the terms are hybrids.[10]

In dental terminology Latin prefixes and adjectives are extensively used to indicate variations or anomalies in position: *pro-*, *retro-*, *supra-*, *infra-*, *dextro-*, and *levo-*, for example, occur as constructive elements in compound descriptive terms so often that their meanings are immediately understood. But the names of some of the most common anatomical structures referred to in dentistry and with which the Latin prefixes and adjectives have to be used are derived from Greek and not from Latin (e.g., *cheil-*, lip; *odont-*, tooth; *gnath-*, jaw; *geni-*, chin; *stomat-*, mouth). This means that hybridization can hardly be avoided if the terminology of dentristry is to be logical and meaningful. Similar circumstances in other special areas of science make hybridization of terms almost inevitable.

In the fields of biology and chemistry specialized sets of suffixes have been adopted to designate taxonomic units and to indicate the basic nature of substances (e.g., *-ales*, *-ineae*, *-aceae*, *-oideae*, *-eae*, *-inae*; *-ase*, *-ine*, *-ose*). Since the words and word stems to which those suffixes must be attached vary widely in respect to their linguistic origin, it is not possible to avoid the use of hybrid terms in much of the technical language of biology and chemistry.

In coining compound terms, the scientist can avoid hybridization in most cases because, in selecting the constructive elements to be used, he has at his disposal stems of equivalent meaning from either Greek or Latin (e.g., *arthro-* from Greek or *articulo-* from Latin). In spite of this fact, however, there are certain stems, prefixes, and

<hr>

10. Cf., *Amer. Jour. Med. Tech.* XV (1949), 269.

suffixes in each of the two languages for which equivalents do not exist in the other; or, if equivalents do exist, scientific terminology has largely or altogether avoided using them. For such widely used Greek-derived elements as *pseudo-*, *para-*, *-mania*, and *-itis*, for example, no corresponding Latin-derived elements of equal favor are found; on the other hand, no Greek-derived word-elements have been able to compete, for example, with the highly favored Latin-derived terminal suffixes *-fugal* and *-petal* or the familiar combining forms *radio-* and *fibro-*. The result of this is hybridization such as occurs in the following words, for which there are no "purebred" equivalents:

> pseudoseptate: "apparently, but not morphologically, septate."
> parafunctional: "characterized by perverted or abnormal function."
> medicomania: "excessive fondness for physicians."
> appendicitis: "inflammation of the appendix vermiformis."
> basifugal: "growing away from the base."
> basipetal: "developing from the apex toward the base."
> radiotherapy: "the treatment of disease by roentgen rays, radium
>      rays, polonium rays, etc."
> fibrolipoma: "a fibrous tumor that is in part fatty."

Such words as these, even though they mingle Greek and Latin elements, are probably preferable to any strained or unfamiliar circumlocutions which might result from seeking strict linguistic purity.

It may therefore be concluded that in a terminology which must function in the complex and diversely interrelated phenomena of the medical and biological sciences, the desirable quality of linguistic purity in the construction of words must occasionally be sacrificed in order that the terms may possess other more important nomenclatural merits.

Numerous Greek words were adopted by the Romans into their language. Many of those Greek words became so thoroughly naturalized by extensive use in the Roman world that they were accepted as equals with native Latin words. When such words, although Greek in origin but Latin by adoption, are combined with Latin-derived elements in the construction of modern scientific terms, the question may be raised whether or not hybridization is involved at all. Such words as "brachiocubital," "brachiocrural," and "brachioradialis," which combine the form *brachio-* with word-elements derived from Latin are sometimes not regarded as hybrid terms because the Greek word BRACHION was adopted by the Romans and naturalized in the Latin language as *brachium*. "Centrifugal" should not offend the purist in language because *centrum* is a Latin word, fully naturalized from the Greek KENTRON. Other examples of such Greek loan-words in Latin are **axis, calyx, carpus, cera, gen-**, and **petra.** If this argument results in any yielding on the part of the purist, the opposition is then given the opportunity to press its view further. It will argue that throughout the centuries during which Latin was the language of science and learning, most of the Greek words now used in technical language were latinized. It will also point out that in those scientific fields which have officially latinized the technical names used in their nomenclature (as in gross anatomy, bacteriology, botany, and zoology), hybridization does not in fact occur at all because, according to agreement, all words are Latin whatever their origin may be. In spite of the attractiveness which this argument holds for some persons, most linguists and philologists maintain that there is a significant difference between a thoroughbred Latin word and one which is Latin by adoption. And contemporary latinization of technical terms usually signifies only that the terms use the Latin inflectional suffixes; the main structure of the words on which those Latin endings have been attached may be of any linguistic origin.

Hybridization does not refer only to the mixture of Greek and Latin elements in one word; elements from numerous languages may be involved. Such words as "enterocleaner," "fibrofatty," "heartometer," "lousicide," "microneedle," "macroteeth," and "ebonation" are hybrid terms combining English constructive elements with Greek or Latin elements; "hauptganglion" combines a German and a Greek element into one term. Words such as these are hybrids, but they border on the vernacular and are generally objectionable for that reason rather than because they are hybrids.

Hybrid terms are numerous in the vocabulary of ordinary English and they appear often also in the terminology of many specialized scientific areas. In spite of the fact that the official attitude in most scientific fields is a mild opposition to hybrids, a certain amount of miscegenation of linguistic elements in scientific compound terms continues to take place. "Antibody," for example, is a mixed term of relatively recent origin but one which is probably destined for a successful future because it is already very familiar both within and without scientific circles. In certain situations, therefore, hybrid terms are fully justified, but their free and thoughtless coinage and perpetuation in scientific terminology should be discouraged.

## Eponyms

An eponym is the name of a person, real or legendary, who is so prominently associated with something that his name has become a designation for the thing. In medical and biological nomenclature an eponym usually memorializes the discoverer of some significant scientific fact or honors a person who first fully described a scientific phenomenon. Occasionally, other less obvious reasons account for the use of a person's name in a scientific term; for example: "Achilles' tendon" was named after Achilles, a legendary hero of Homer's *Iliad* who was vulnerable only in the heel; intentional injury to one's own eyes was termed "oedipism" after Oedipus, an early king of Thebes who tore out his own eyes; and immunity against poison was called "mithridatism" after Mithridates, a king of Pontus in the last century B.C. who is said to have gained immunity against poisons by taking gradually increased doses.[11]

The use of eponyms in medical and biological terminology has long been a subject of controversy. More than a century ago Charles Darwin objected to eponymous names in biological nomenclature. He wrote to his friend J. D. Hooker as follows:

"I have lately been trying to get up an agitation (but I shall not succeed, and indeed doubt whether I have time and strength to go on with it) against the practice of Naturalists appending for perpetuity the name of the *first* describer to species. I look at this as a direct premium to hasty work, to *naming* instead of *describing*. A species ought to have a name so

11. Medical and biological terms derived from classical myths, legend, and history constitute an interesting division of eponyms. The following references (see Bibliography) are useful sources of information on this topic: (a) Yancey, *Origins From Mythology of Biological Names and Terms*; (b) Skinner, *The Origin of Medical Terms*; (c) Pepper, *Medical Etymology*; (d) Roberts, *Medical Terms, Their Origin and Construction*; (e) Field and Harrison, *Anatomical Terms: Their Origin and Derivation*; (f) "Mythology as Shown in Medical Words," *Jour. Iowa State Med. Soc.*, XXXII, 1942, 217-18; (g) "Historic Sidelights on Medical Terminology," *Jour. Mich. State Med. Soc.*, XXXV, 1936, 374-85; (h) "Classical Mythology in the *Systema Naturae* of Linnaeus," *Trans. Amer. Philological Assn.*, LXXVI, 1946, 333-57.

well known that the addition of the author's name would be superfluous, and a piece of empty vanity.[12]

In this connection Darwin's words to Hugh Strickland, who composed the first *Code of Rules for Zoological Nomenclature*, are interesting.

I have been led of late to reflect much on the subject of naming, and I have come to a fixed opinion that the plan of the first describer's name, being appended for perpetuity to a species, has been the greatest curse to Natural History ... I feel sure as long as species-mongers have their vanity tickled by seeing their own names appended to a species, because they miserably described it in two or three lines, we shall have the same *vast* amount of bad work as at present, and which is enough to dishearten any man who is willing to work out any branch with care and time. ... I think a very wrong spirit runs through all Natural History, as if some merit was due a man for merely naming and defining a species. ... I do not think more credit is due to a man for defining a species, than to a carpenter for making a box.[13]

Strickland's reply to Darwin defended the use of personal names in naming species; he wrote:

The object of appending the name of a man to the name of a species is not to gratify the vanity of the man, but to indicate more precisely the species.[14]

The extensive use of eponyms in the biological terminology of today, and the provisions made in the current *International Codes* of botanical and zoological nomenclature for use of personal names as a source of epithets for plants and animals attest to the fact that it is Strickland's rather than Darwin's viewpoint that has prevailed throughout the last century.

In the medical field one of the earliest protests against the use of eponyms came from Oliver Wendell Holmes, who expressed his distaste for them as follows:

If a doctor has the luck to find out a new malady, it is tied to his name, like a tin kettle to a dog's tail, and he goes clattering down the highway of fame to posterity with his aeolo attachment following at his heels.[15]

---

12. *The Life and Letters of Charles Darwin,* edited by Francis Darwin (D. Appleton and Co., 1887) Vol. I, p. 332.
13. *Ibid.*, pp. 334-35.
14. *Ibid.*, p. 338.
15. Cf., L. Benedict, "The Formative Periods of Medical Nomenclature," *The Medical and Surgical Reporter* LXX, 1894, 341.

In the year after Holmes' death, leading anatomists took action through the formulation of the B. N. A. (*Basle Nomina Anatomica*, see p. 289) to remove from the terminology of gross anatomy as many as possible of the excessive number of personal names that had come into use in that area of medicine. Many names were discarded, and although a few eponyms were retained for optional use, the general effect of the B. N. A. was to discourage the coinage and the use of eponymous terms in anatomical nomenclature. In spite of this, however, some eponymous terms continued to be used in anatomical terminology and gradually became very familiar; those and numerous subsequent coinages have had to be recognized as legitimate terms whenever they occur.[16] It was in the area of clinical medicine, however, as new diseases, bacteria, serums, etc., were discovered, that eponymous terms multiplied most rapidly. That eponyms are common in current medical terminology can easily be shown by making even a rapid examination of the entries in a medical dictionary under such words as bacillus, body, disease, duct, fever, fossa, gland, ligament, line, method, murmur, operation, reflex, serum, solution, suture, symptom, tract, tumor, ulcer, vaccine, and valve.[17]

The most common arguments against the use of eponyms in scientific nomenclature may be summarized as follows:

1. An eponym in itself is usually meaningless and therefore difficult to remember. A descriptive term, on the other hand, suggests relationships, topography, etiology, or other factors relevant to the context in which the term is used and is therefore a meaningful tool to the student and investigator. "Bright's disease," "Weil's disease," and "Hashimoto's disease," for example, give no clue to the nature or the etiology of the diseases, whereas the corresponding descriptive terms "nephritis," "leptospiral jaundice," and "chronic thyroiditis" are meaningful epithets. "Uterine tube," which is gradually becoming the preferred term, is more informative than "Fallopian tube";

16. Cf., Jessie Dobson, *Anatomical Eponyms*; and Louis R. Effler, *The Eponyms of Anatomy*. A sample of the present attitude toward medical eponyms is expressed by O. H. Perry Pepper in *Medical Etymology*, pp. 11-12.
17. One investigator has found that the eponyms in a medical dictionary, exclusive of the more familiar ones, would fill a total of 36 pages; see Jeanette Dean-Throckmorton in *Jour. Iowa State Med. Soc.* XXXII, 1942, 217.

"parotid gland duct" is clearer in meaning than "Stenson's duct." The case against eponyms is even stronger in the numerous instances where the eponymous terms are less familiar than those just cited. "Darling's disease," for example, would be better forgotten altogether in favor of "histoplasmosis" or even the somewhat cumbersome epithet "reticulo-endothelial cytomycosis."

2. Eponyms are often historically unjust. Leonardo Botallo, an Italian surgeon in Paris in the sixteenth century, has been "honored" by having the "ductus Botalli" named after him. But this duct was known centuries earlier by Galen, a Greek physician in Rome. Discoveries can seldom be credited completely to a single person. Facts necessary for making the crowning step of a discovery possible have generally been established through preliminary work of many persons. Sometimes the real discoverer is forgotten in favor of a later investigator. Moreover, the names of some of the greatest benefactors in science are omitted altogether from honorary eponymous terms, whereas many minor contributors have their names memorialized. The name of the great William Harvey, for example, does not appear in any list of medical eponyms.

3. Many eponyms, especially medical eponyms, carry with them a strong patriotic note, with the result that eponymic designations for an entity are multiplied to a point where they hamper and confuse the person who has to use them. The Swiss are likely to refer to the ileocecal valve as the valve of Bauhinus; the Dutch will call it the valve of Tulpius; and the Italians will honor their anatomist and surgeon, Costanzo Varolio, by referring to the same valve as the valve of Varolius. Although not described in published form until 1825, exophthalmic goiter was first clinically observed by the English physician Caleb Parry in 1786. Sir William Osler therefore referred to the goiter as "Parry's disease." But cases of the disease had been described in Italy as early as 1802 by Giuseppe Flajani, who was honored by his countrymen by having the malady called "Flajani's disease." In 1835 the Irish physician Robert James Graves described cases of the same disease in his country, and in his honor the French physician Armand Trousseau in 1860 introduced the eponym "Graves's disease." In Germany the name used is "Basedow's disease" in honor of Karl Adolph von Basedow, who described the disease in

1840. When several eponyms for the same entity have in this way been introduced and accepted into the scientific literature of a field, medical dictionaries must recognize all names as having claims to their attention. But they are generally of disservice to a nomenclature.

4. The prospect of having his name immortalized by an eponym sometimes causes a person to name a species before he has fully carried out his investigations. This usually results also in a poor and inadequate accompanying description of the species.

5. The honor bestowed upon a person by having his name used as an eponym may be a dubious one. The "honoree" may be cursed through the years by innumerable students who have to learn a meaningless term.

6. Eponyms contribute to an increase in the number of unnecessary synonymous terms in scientific language.

The most frequently used arguments in favor of employing eponyms in scientific nomenclature may be summarized as follows:

1. An eponym is at times a convenient means of labeling a combination of commonly associated factors. "Colles' fracture," for example, involves a set of factors and conditions which are usually alike in all instances and which would be very difficult to describe meaningfully in a single word. This is similarly true of a different set of conditions and details attendant upon a fracture known as "Pott's fracture." "Syme's amputation," for example, is an amputation of the foot at the ankle joint with removal of both malleoli; "Pirogoff's amputation," on the other hand, is one that is like Syme's except that a part of the os calcis remains in the flap at the lower end of the stump. "Throckmorton's reflex" is a variation of "Babinski's reflex," both involving several uniformly alike characteristics but each differing slightly from the other in certain respects. It is difficult to find terms which are not inordinately long and yet adequate for describing conditions which combine several coordinate or slightly deviating factors. Therefore, in phenomena or processes where the essential characteristics are usually alike in all occurrences, a single-term label such as an eponym provides a great convenience. An eponym, it may be said, can convey a paragraph of information.

2. The use of a personal name in generic and specific epithets assists in attaining precise and unmistakable identification because sometimes more than one person has described and given his name to the same entity, but only one of those names is valid. In a binomial or trinomial terminology, where the problem of classification is of special importance, personal names supply an easy source for a useful second or third word in an epithet.

3. Eponymous terms serve the very useful purpose of stimulating interest and investigation into the historical side of science. They are a doorway to rewarding acquaintanceships with many significant personages. Behind eponyms often lie many facts of human and cultural interest which will broaden and enrich scientific study at all levels.

4. Some eponyms are so well known that substitution of descriptive words for them would add to the burden of terminology rather than reduce it. Long-accepted use of many well-known eponyms, such as roentgen rays, for example, would make their abolishment not only difficult but undesirable. "Vincent's infection," for example, is a euphonious term familiar to dentists; to substitute for it the descriptive phrase "acute, necrotizing, ulcero-membranous gingivitis" would be of questionable wisdom.[18] Some eponyms meet well the objective of furnishing an exact and meaningful medium of communication in their field.

5. There are occasions when patients prefer to have the particular disease with which they are afflicted referred to by an eponymous term rather than by a descriptive or vernacular term; for example, "Weber's disease" rather than "nevoid amentia" or "amentia"; "neisserosis" (Albert Neisser) rather than "gonorrhea"; or "tysonitis" (Edward Tyson) rather than "inflammation of the odoriferous glands."

The prevailing attitude at present, especially in the medical sciences, is against the use of eponymous terms whenever satisfactory descriptive terms are available. If, however, a descriptive synonym for an eponymous term is not already available, official caution is expressed against coining a new word merely for the sake of getting a descriptive name.

---

18. Cf., *Jour. Dental Educ.* XIV, 1949, 42.

The *Bacteriological Code* recommends that genera be dedicated to persons only if unusual reasons justify it. The most recent edition (1952) of *Standard Nomenclature for Diseases and Operations* has avoided the use of eponymous names wherever adequate descriptive topographic-etiologic terms can be used. Unlike former editions, the 1952 edition does not list eponyms separately, but enters them in the regular alphabetical index and gives cross-references to the appropriate descriptive titles whenever they exist — a system very helpful to physician and investigator. One of the most recent and significant expressions against the use of eponyms is that made in 1955 by the International Anatomical Nomenclature Committee in its proposed revision of *Nomina Anatomica*. The unanimous wish of this committee is that the use of eponyms be excluded from the nomenclature of gross anatomy (for the exact recommendation see page 291). Most of the current scientific dictionaries supply full definitions for those eponyms which are well known and most familiar, but for the less familiar eponymous words they usually give cross-references to the appropriate descriptive terms, wherever these exist. In most areas of biology and medicine, therefore, preference is clearly indicated for descriptive terms over eponyms. If such preference is long continued and supported, it will have the effect of reducing the number of new eponymous terms which are introduced into scientific literature. To a certain extent it will also cause some of the eponyms in current use to die out from disuse. The treatment accorded eponyms by dictionaries, *Codes*, and nomenclatural indices can also be expected to encourage use of descriptive terms while perpetuating the use of the better-known and familiar eponyms. These effects will be only slowly noticeable, however. Meantime, because personal names are already very numerous and in daily use in the nomenclatural epithets of zoology, bacteriology, and botany, because the more familiar and well-established eponyms in the terminology of medical sciences will be perpetuated through their continued and accepted use by the profession, and because a few new eponymous terms will constantly be created, it may safely be assumed that, in spite of opposition to their use, eponyms will for a long time constitute an important element in the terminology of the medical and biological sciences.

# Codes and Rules of Scientific Nomenclature

When the word "nomenclature" is applied to the names used in a particular branch of knowledge, it implies that a systematic procedure is followed in the formation and the use of those names; the word also often implies some scheme of classification such as is used in botany and zoology. A good nomenclature is therefore expected to provide and preserve for its special field a sound basis for orderly and intelligent communication. In order that a nomenclature may satisfy these requirements, certain principles governing the choice of terms need to be agreed upon by those who create and use the terminology. Such agreement is not often easily attained and occasionally, because of the difficulties involved, is not even sought. If, however, no serious effort is shown in a scientific area to reach official agreement on basic nomenclatural procedures, it is doubtful that the terminology used in that area can properly be called a nomenclature. In most of the areas of the medical and biological sciences, sincere efforts are made to attain the advantages that accrue to investigation and communication from the use of a good nomenclature.

The several main divisions of the medical and biological sciences share considerable common ground in respect to the particular elements from the Greek and Latin languages which they employ in their nomenclature, as well as the general principles governing the use of those elements in the formation of their terms. This does not mean, however, that the several separate branches of science do not also have some nomenclatural problems and proprieties peculiar to themselves.

The nomenclatural proprieties established by certain scientific fields have been formulated into published codes, rules, principles, and recommendations, and where these have received international recognition they have been adopted as the official "International Code (or Rules)" of nomenclature in that scientific area. Some of the newer divisions or subdivisions of science (e.g., psychiatry, human genetics, dentistry) have not yet formutaled or adopted international codes, but through their professional societies are working toward that end. Within their national and international associations almost all the major branches of science have established perpetual committees or bodies whose responsibility it is to give constant attention to the nomenclatural problems of their fields. Even when international rules of nomenclature in a scientific area have been formulated and adopted, requirements imposed by new developments and more extensive knowledge subject those rules to periodic revision.

The manifold requirements in establishing a sound nomenclature for a scientific field demand that attention be given to considerations both theoretical and practical. The principles subscribed to in some of the official nomenclatural *Codes* as well as opinions expressed in other scientific publications reveal that most scientists have an enlightened awareness of both the theoretical and the practical factors which require attention in developing and maintaining a good nomenclature.[19] Of course many of the scientists' nomenclatural problems, especially those relating to specific needs in the newest branches of research, lie outside of those particular matters which are under primary consideration in this text. Nevertheless, several of the discussions and actions reported in official scientific publications and many of the factors referred to in the *Codes* are directly relevant to the subject-matter of this text. In order to illustrate this fact as briefly and as directly as possible, the next few pages will present short summaries of the nomenclatural history of a few selected scientific areas together with several extracts from some of the international *Codes* in those areas.

## *MEDICINE*

Modern medicine brings together numerous subjects, both theoretical and practical. Comprehended under medical studies are such areas of study and practice as chemistry, botany, anatomy, physiology, bacteriology, microscopy, pharmacology, parasitology, pathology, and psychology. Therefore, as the size of a standard medical dictionary will attest, a vast number of terms is required in order to convey the descriptions and the meanings of the numerous medical phenomena. Each of such clinical areas as surgery, pediatrics, neurology, gynecology, ophthalmology, dermatology, otolaryngology, psychiatry, and radiology must formulate, systematize, and develop

---

19. UNESCO has recognized the problem and is actively cooperating with many agencies for improvement of communication in science; see, e.g., the general catalog *UNESCO Publications*.

its own nomenclature. Articles and discussions in medical literature make it clear that terminology is one of the perennial problems with which investigators in these rapidly advancing branches have to deal and in almost every specialized field of medicine, action has been taken, usually through a special commission or committee, to systematize and improve the nomenclature of its particular area.[20] Selected as sample medical fields for review are the areas of Anatomy, Diseases and Operations, and Bacteriology.

## ANATOMY

One of the first attempts to systematize the terminology of the medical sciences was made over sixty years ago when the Anatomical Society in Germany appointed a committee to revise the entire nomenclature of gross (macroscopic) anatomy, and in particular to devise means of curbing or eliminating the rapidly growing trend toward using multiple designations for a single structure. After seven years of work this group of anatomists succeeded in devising a system of nomenclature for descriptive anatomy in which each structure had only one name, related structures had names that were similar, and all names were in Latin form[21] and grammatically correct. The number of terms used in gross anatomy was reduced from 50,000 to 5,000; approximately 45,000 names were eliminated as unnecessary synonyms. This system, adopted at the meeting of the Society in Basle, Switzerland, and first published in 1895 under the title of *Nomina Anatomica*, was approved and accepted by several countries including the United States, and since then has been internationally known as the B. N. A. (*Basle Nomina Anatomica*). Some of the difficulties in attaining a satisfactory nomenclature for a scientific area is well illustrated by the experiences of this early B. N. A. committee.[22] When compared with such medical fields as neurology, bacteriology, and psychiatry, where there are lively and continuing clinical investigations, the field of gross anatomy may reasonably be considered

---

20. See, for example, *Amer. Jour. Clin. Path.*, XVIII, 1948, 443-50, and XIX, 1949, 56-60; *Amer. Jour. Med. Tech.*, XIV, 1948, 324-36, and XV, 1949, 264-72.
21. The latinization was a latinization in form only because many words were of Greek origin.
22. A short account of the procedures used by the committee and a reprint of the B. N. A. may be found in A. C. Eycleshymer and D. B. Shoemaker, *Anatomical Names*, pp. 3-23.

one of relative stability; nevertheless, even in that relatively stable area it took continuous effort over several years to effect a fairly satisfactory nomenclature.

Even though the B. N. A. committee worked in an area in which the basic phenomena might be expected to remain relatively static, they realized that the terms they had selected would nevertheless be subjected to some revision. At different times minor modifications and refinements of the B. N. A. have been made by individual anatomical societies. The most significant effort at revision was that carried out at the Sixth International Congress of Anatomists held in Paris in July 1955.[23] The revised version of *Nomina Anatomica*[24] proposed at that Congress, although basically similar to the older B. N. A., is nevertheless significant because it reflects the consensus of scientists from many nations regarding the terms and the nomenclatural practices to be used in human anatomy. The following extracts from the *Introduction* to this latest proposed version of *Nomina Anatomica* have immediate relevance to several aspects of the present study:

Page vi: . . . it was unanimously agreed that the B. N. A. (1895) should be taken as the basis for an agreed International Anatomical Nomenclature, and that the number of changes effected in the B. N. A. (1895) should be restricted to the smallest number that proved practicable. . . . Having obtained unanimity on this important matter, the Committee felt that its first duty must be to consider the principles on which an International Anatomical Nomenclature should be based, and after a free and frank discussion extending over several sessions, the following principles were unanimously adopted:

---

23. In 1952 at a conference of the International Congress of Anatomists in London under the auspices of UNESCO, action was taken to bring the B. N. A. up-to-date by a conservative revision. Seven subcommittees, made up of anatomists representing ten countries, were appointed to prepare the necessary changes and to submit tentative lists of terms for each system of the organs of the human body. These revisions were presented at a London meeting in June 1954, and the final draft was submitted to the Congress held in Paris in 1955.

24. Published and distributed as a service to science by the Williams and Wilkins Co., Baltimore, 1956. The *Introduction* contains a good short summary of the history of the B. N. A. as well as of the nature of the nomenclatural problems with which the present committees had to deal. The main body of the publication lists 5,640 anatomical terms classified under eleven sections. Appendix II, which contains annotations about some of the terms in the list, is useful in indicating the viewpoints of the committees in arriving at certain decisions. Available also, with shorter introduction, in *Nomina Anatomica Parisiensia (1955) et B. N. A. (1895)*, edited by M. W. Woerdeman, (A. Oosthoek Publishing Co., Utrecht, 1957).

(a) "That, with a very limited number of exceptions, each structure shall be designated by one term only."

(b) "That every term in the official list shall be Latin, each country to be at liberty to translate the official Latin terms into its own vernacular for teaching purposes."

The Committee was very strongly of the opinion that in scientific publications, in anatomic and other medical journals, in abstracts and excerpta, the official Latin terms should always be employed—more especially in the titles of such publications. ...

(c) "That each term shall be, so far as possible, short and simple."

(d) "That the terms shall be primarily memory signs, but shall preferably have some informative or descriptive value."

(e) "That structures closely related topographically shall, as far as possible, have similar names" — e.g., Arteria femoralis, Vena femoralis, Nervus femoralis, etc.

(f) "That differentiating adjectives shall be, in general, arranged as opposites" — e.g., major and minor, superficialis and profundus, etc.

(g) "That eponyms shall not be used in the Official Nomenclature of Gross or Macroscopic Anatomy."

It should be stressed that these principles, which are almost identical with those enunciated sixty years ago by the B. N. A. (1895), received the full agreement of all the members of the Committee.

Page ix: Apart from the general principles which have already been set out [quoted just above], the problem becomes largely one of detail. Like the B. N. A. (1895) this nomenclature is set out in Latin, because Latin is still the most useful international language for scientific purposes.

In the B. N. A. (1895), eponyms were retained for optional use, but in this nomenclature they have been excluded by the unanimous wish of the I.A.N.C. [International Anatomical Nomenclature Committee]. Even the Wolffian and the Muellerian ducts appear only under informative names, and with no associated eponym (Ductus mesonephricus and Ductus paramesonephricus).

It was the original intention to avoid all use of alternative terms but, to obviate the possibility of confusion, the Committee was compelled to introduce alternatives in a number of cases — for example, the terms "mitral valve" and "mitral orifice" are retained as optional terms, to meet the strongly expressed wishes of clinicians and because the Committee felt that in such a case it was desirable that the student should be familiar with the old established term "mitral," as well as the more modern term "atrio-ventricular." In order to ensure wider agreement, some forty or more pairs of synonyms have been admitted.

## DISEASES AND OPERATIONS

To insure uniformity in the orthography and meaning of words used to designate human diseases and operations, the American Medical Association publishes a volume titled *Standard Nomenclature of Diseases and Operations*. This official guide aims to include the name of every disease that has been clinically recognized and to establish an acceptable and uniform terminology for all operative procedures. A dual system of classification is used whereby diseases are identified and coded according to (a) the portion of the body involved. (Topographic) and (b) the cause of the disease (Etiologic). The Topographic, in turn, is divided into twelve Systems (e.g., Musculoskeletal System; Respiratory System, etc.) and the Etiological into thirteen Categories (e.g., Diseases due to infections due to lower plant or animal parasite; Diseases due to disorder of metabolism, growth or nutrition, etc.). Operations are classified according to (a) Topography and (b) Procedure. The eleven Systems under Topography are the same as those used under Diseases, and there are nine basic Procedures (e.g., excision, destruction, suture, etc.). The editor states in the *Introduction* (p. x) that "English terms in good usage are employed wherever possible in preference to Latin and Greek terms." The statement apparently means that preference has been given to the anglicized forms of the words rather than to the Latin forms, for it is clear that the origins of most of the words are in the Greek and Latin languages. In the section devoted to the classification of operations, many technical words of Greek and Latin derivation are given together with their more common synonymous English equivalents.

Modifications and refinements in this nomenclature are continually being made by soliciting expressions of opinion from physicians and surgeons and by periodic revisions of the volume. The fourth edition, which appeared in 1952, is the version presently in use. This official guide to the terminology of diseases and operations is a good example of the extensive and thorough work done in one branch of the medical sciences to attain a well-founded and systematic nomenclature.

## BACTERIOLOGY

The invention of the microscope greatly accelerated progress in the field of bacteriology and increased the demand for new names. Bacteria were named according to the binomial system of Linnaeus, but it was soon found necessary to impose some restrictions on the naming procedures because of the excessive liberties that were being taken, especially in the naming of yeasts, molds and fungi. At the First International Microbiological Congress, held in Paris in 1930, the problem of bacterial nomenclature was put into the hands of a Nomenclature Committee, and in 1947 at its Fourth International Congress in Copenhagen the International Association of Micro-biologists adopted the *International Bacteriological Code of Nomenclature* which had been developed by their Judicial Committee (composed of twelve members of their Nomenclature Committee) and recommended by the Nomenclature Committee. This *Code* was published in the *Journal of Bacteriology* (LV, 1948, pp. 287-306). In 1950 at Rio de Janeiro, at the Fifth Congress, certain amendments were added to the *Code* and the Committee was instructed to study the problem of nomenclature further and to make recommendations for additional revisions to a plenary session at the Sixth Congress in Rome in September 1953. At that Congress in Rome the amended *Code* was adopted, and its official name changed to *The International Code of Nomenclature of Bacteria and Viruses* (as a short title *Bacteriological Code* is used).[25] The Nomenclature Committee continuously reviews matters dealing with the naming and classification of microorganisms and publishes the quarterly *International Bulletin of Bacteriological Nomenclature and Taxonomy* in which appear important discussions pertaining to the many phases of the nomenclature of bacteriology.

The nomenclature of bacteriology, which deals with bacteria, viruses and related organisms, is closely integrated with the system of naming used in botany and also to some extent with that used in zoology. As the recently published *Code* clearly reveals, determined effort is made to coordinate the *Codes* in those three fields. Micro-biologists had registered some complaints that although the botanical

---

25. *International Code of Nomenclature of Bacteria and Viruses* (Ames, Iowa, Iowa State College Press, 1958). The Foreword of this book has a good summary of the history of the *Code*, and the extensive "Annotations" throughout the text illumine many ambiguous points.

and zoological *Codes* recommend an orthography in names that would conform with the accepted usage of Latin and latinization, no outline of such usage had anywhere been provided. Accordingly, in an appendix of the latest *Bacteriological Code* a table is furnished outlining and illustrating the approved method of transliterating Greek words into Latin.[26]

Quoted below are some extracts from the *International Code of Nomenclature of Bacteria and Viruses* which have particular relevance to the subject of this text:

*Principle* 4: Scientific names of all taxonomic groups (taxa) are usually taken from Latin or Greek. When taken from any language other than Latin, or formed in an arbitrary manner, they are treated as if they were Latin. Latin terminations should be used so far as possible for new names.

*Annotations*: The meaning of the phrase "usually taken from Latin or Greek" is made clear by prevailing custom. The phrase does not mean that only those Latin and Greek words as found in the dictionaries and lexicons may be used, but that new words proposed as names or epithets may also be coined from the stems of these words singly or as compounds. It is assumed that the classic tradition for the forming of new names will be followed.

In general, it is clearly intended that a name taken from a language such as Greek should be transliterated in accordance with classic usage, and that the word be placed in the appropriate Latin declension with Latin endings.

*Rule* 1: The names of all taxonomic groups (taxa) above the rank of genus are substantives or adjectives used as substantives, of Greek or Latin origin, or Latinized words, in the plural number.

*Rule* 5 *a*: Names of genera and subgenera are substantives (or adjectives used as substantives) in the singular number and written with an initial capital. The names may be taken from any source whatever and may even be composed in an arbitrary manner. They are treated as Latin substantives.

*Recommendation* 5 *a*: Bacteriologists who are forming new generic or subgeneric names should attend to the following recommendations:

(1) Not to make names very long or difficult to pronounce.

(2) To make names that have an agreeable form readily adaptable to the Latin tongue.

26. Appendix A, pp. 137-40. The same useful table is published also in *International Bulletin of Bacteriological Nomenclature and Taxonomy* III (June 1, 1953), 63-69. For further helpful suggestions in this matter, see R. E. Buchanan, "How Bacteria are Named and Identified," in *Bergey's Manual of Determinative Bacteriology*, 7th Ed. (1957), pp. 15-28.

(3) Not to dedicate genera to persons quite unconnected with bacteriology or at least with natural science or to persons quite unknown.

(4) To avoid the use of adjectives as nouns.

(5) Not to make names by combining words from different languages (*nomina hybrida*).

(6) To give a feminine form to all personal generic names, whether they commemorate a man or a woman.

*Recommendation 6 b*: In forming specific epithets bacteriologists should attend to the following recommendations:

(1) To choose a specific epithet which, in general, gives some indication of the appearance, the characters, the origin, the history, or the properties of the species. If taken from the name of a person, it usually recalls the name of the one who discovered or described it or was in some way concerned with it.

(2) To avoid those which are very long and difficult to pronounce.

(7) To avoid compound specific epithets which include word stems from two or more languages (*epitheta hybrida*).

*Recommendation 12 f*: An author, when publishing a new generic or subgeneric name, should give its etymology and also that of a new epithet when the meaning is not obvious.

*Rule 27, Note 2*: The use of a wrong (or an alternative) connecting vowel or vowels (or the omission of a connecting vowel) in a generic or subgeneric name or in a specific or a subspecific epithet gives rise to an orthographic variant.

*Note 5*: The spelling of the name of a taxon or an epithet derived from the Greek but not transliterated by its author into Latin form in accordance with classic usage (Appendix A) may be corrected as an orthographic error by the Judicial Commission and placed in the list of preferred spellings (see Recommendation 27 a). ... Specific and other epithets and names of Greek origin differing merely by having Greek and Latin gender endings respectively are orthographic variants.

*Recommendation 27 i*: Names of taxa and specific epithets are often compound words, sometimes formed from Latin stems, more often from Greek stems, sometimes (less correctly) from stems from two different languages. Such compound words formed from the same stems may differ only in the connecting vowels.

(a) In the formation of compound names of taxa and of specific epithets from the Latin, the preferred connecting vowel is -*i*-. ...

(b) The combining vowel in Greek compounds in which the first component is a noun (substantive) or adjective is usually -*o*-. It may be omitted if the second component begins with a vowel or when the first component ends in *y*, e.g. *glycychylus*. Another combining vowel may be used if there is good Greek precedent, e.g., as in *Corynebacterium*. ...

(c) Compound words derived from two or more languages (*nomina hybrida*) are to be regarded as orthographic variants if they differ only in the combining vowel. ...

*Recommendation 27 j*: Authors should give the etymology of new generic names and also of new epithets when the meaning of these is not obvious.

*Recommendation 27 k*: When it is necessary to choose between words which have been validly published as names of taxa or as specific epithets and which differ in spelling only because of faulty or alternative spelling of Latin words, or because of faulty or alternative transliterations of Greek to Latin, or because of alternative transfer of endings denoting gender or the oblique cases, (particularly the genitive) from Greek to Latin, it is recommended that choices be governed by the provisions of Apendix B to this Code.

*Rule 28*: The gender of generic names is governed by the following regulations:

(a) A Greek or Latin word adopted as a generic name retains its classical gender. In cases where the classical gender varies, the author has the right of choice between the alternative genders. In doubtful cases general usage should be followed.

(b) Generic and subgeneric names which are modern compounds formed from two or more Greek or Latin words take the gender of the last. If the ending is altered, the gender is that of the new ending in the language of origin.

## DENTISTRY

Discussions in current dental periodicals indicate that the dental profession is somewhat dissatisfied with the progress made in systematizing and improving the nomenclature of dentistry.[27] A first step in the organization of dental terminology was taken in 1849 when Chapin A. Harris published his *Dictionary of Dental Science*, but even yet there is no officially adopted guide to the formation and usage of dental terms. No official dental dictionary is presently in print which includes the words that have entered the vocabulary

---

27. See, for example, *Proc. Amer. Assn. Dental Schools*, XXIII, 1946, 294-97; *Jour. Dental Education*, XIV, 1949, 38-44 where also is found a useful bibliography on the subject. Near the end of the article appears this paragraph: "*Conclusion:* The preceding observations show that there is a wide difference of opinion about what needs to be done in dental nomenclature, what should be done, how it should be done, and by whom it should be done. The only uniformity of attitude encountered is the opinion that something should be done." *Jour. Amer. Dental Assn.*, XL, 1950, 104-06; and XLII, 1951, 345-50 which contains a brief history of attempts to systematize the nomenclature of dentistry. *Jour. Mich. State Dental Assn.*, XXXIII, 1951, 204-6. *British Dental Jour.*, LXXIII, 1942, 204.

since the latest dictionary was published in 1936. In attempting to improve the situation, the American Dental Association at first assigned the problem to a Committee on Nomenclature. In 1948, however, the task of developing sound and uniform standards of nomenclature in the field of dental science was given to the Bureau of Library and Indexing Service of the American Dental Association.[28] This Bureau is actively engaged in a thorough investigation of the problem by taking into account the historical, linguistic, and practical factors involved. It is giving attention to the terminology already developed in specialized fields of dentistry such as in Orthodontics, Periodontics, and Endodontics[29] and to all efforts by local, national, and international societies and organizations to systemize and improve the terminology in their particular areas. The Bureau's recent publication *The Vocabulary of Dentistry and Oral Science — A Manual of Dental Nomenclature* by George B. Denton (American Dental Association, Chicago, 1958) presents in considerable detail the several aspects of the nomenclatural problem in dentistry. This book will surely have considerable effect toward improving and systemizing terminology in the field of dental science. Appearing prominently on the pages of Dr. Denton's book and included in the agenda of the Bureau are studies of the language sources for the terminology and the principles that apply to the formation of dental terms from those sources. Those language sources and principles are predominantly in the ancient Greek and Latin languages.[30]

## *ZOOLOGY*

In 1914 the firm of Imprimerie Oberthur in Rennes, France, published in French the full *Report of the Proceedings of the Ninth International Congress on Zoology* held at Monaco in March, 1913. Incorporated in this report was the *International Rules of Zoological Nomenclature*

28. Cf., *Jour. of the Mich. Dental Society*, XXXI, 1949, 158-61.
29. Cf., *Amer. Jour. of Orthodontics*, XXXIV, 1948, 178-91; *Jour. of Periodontology*, XIV, 1945, 47-49; 110-12; 140-41; XVII, 1946, 24-27; XIX, 1948, 147-49; XXI, 1950, 40-43; *Jour. of Endoaontia*, III, 1948, 58-59.
30. Recognizing the value of a basic understanding of the classical languages for intelligent formulation and use of dental terms, the Fédération Dentaire Internationale at its meeting in Brussels in 1951 passed a resolution to require of all students of biology an elementary course in the Latin and Greek languages; Cf. *Internat. Dental Jour.*, II, 1952, 427, and III, 1953, 438.

which since that time has served zoology as the official code for the nomenclature of that science. In order to establish a systematic procedure for the many dubious cases which unavoidably and perpetually arise in naming and classifying the vast number of new genera and species of the animal kingdom, or in changing the orthography or classification of names already in use, the profession established the International Commission which periodically publishes *Opinions and Declarations Rendered by the International Commission on Zoological Nomenclature*.[31] This Commission in 1943 established the *Bulletin of Zoological Nomenclature* as the official organ and medium for publication of the comments, suggestions, and proposals received by the Commission regarding the several aspects of zoological nomenclature. Through published notices in the leading scientific periodicals, the Commission solicits comments and suggestions on certain proposals and gives notice of the date on which it will vote on the cases.[32] In spite of this regularized procedure regarding the terminology and the taxonomic system to be used, the *International Rules* and recommended procedures have at times not been observed by the profession, nor have officially published copies of the *Rules* been easily available.[33] Accordingly, the Thirteenth International Congress of Zoology in 1948 took steps to revise the *Rules* and to reaffirm them as the official guide to zoological nomenclature. It was decided that, in advance of the Fourteenth Congress in Copenhagen in 1953, criticisms and suggestions be solicited so that official approval for the *Rules* might be made at the Copenhagen meeting and concrete steps taken to make the *Rules* available in printed form as soon as possible. Awaiting such publication of the revised *Rules*, the Commission (through its Publications Office, 41 Queen's Gate, London) made available the book titled *Copenhagen Decisions on Zoological*

---

31. Begun in 1939, but with the earlier volumes incorporating opinions rendered before that time, the series has been published continuously. Present publications office is 41 Queen's Gate, London S.W. 7, England.

32. For samples of such notices, see *Science*, CXVI, Oct. 17, 1952, 433 and 546; CXVII, (Jan. 2 and 30, 1953), 16-17 and 112.

33. Only recently has official action been taken to publish the *Rules* in English and to make them easily available to zoologists. Privately printed or typwritten copies have appeared, of which one of the most common and recent is that in *Procedure in Taxonomy* by Edward T. Schenck and John H. McMasters (Stanford University Press, 1936; third edition [1956], enlarged and partly rewritten by A. Myra Keen and Siemon W. Muller) which was in turn reprinted from *Proceedings of the Biological Society of Washington*, XXXIX, 1926, 75-104.

*Nomenclature* which was to serve as an interim code and which contained a record of all the actions and decisions at the 1953 meeting.

The latest official complete publication of the *Rules* is given in *Bulletin of Zoological Nomenclature*, XIV, June 1958, i-xxviii; Official Text of the *"Règles Internationales de la Nomenclature Zoölogique"* (English text as it existed up to the opening of the Paris Congress in 1948), Francis Hemming, editor. The immediate reason for this publication was to assure a uniform version and ready availability of the present *Rules* for the Colloquium on Zoological Nomenclature in London in 1958.

Attesting further to the continuing and genuine interest in nomenclatural matters are numerous articles dealing with the subject of terminology in leading biological publications. Some of these articles discuss the subject in general terms, others devote themselves to problems of naming and classification in limited and specialized areas.[34] Problems of appropriate classification, descriptive techniques, transliteration of stems from Greek and Latin, and protests over linguistic offenses in the formation of scientific terms from foreign words are some of the matters treated in the columns of the periodicals. Much discussion also revolves about the Law of Priority (Article 25 of the *Rules*), whether greater or less restriction should be placed on the Commission in the use of its plenary powers to make decisions in matters pertaining to priority of names. The chief objective in all these efforts is to promote stability and universality in zoological nomenclature.

A large part of the contents of the *International Rules of Zoological Nomenclature*, established as they were long ago when knowledge of Latin and Greek was part of the equipment of most students of the science,[35] presents today's students with linguistic and orthographic

---

34. For example: *Science*, XXXII, 1910, 295-301; LXV, 1927, 194-99; LXXI, 1930, 26-28; CXV, 1952, 63-64; *Parasitology*, XXXI, 1939, 255-62; and *Amer. Jour. Human Genetics*, IV, 1952, 347-49, referring to steps taken in 1952 by the American Society of Human Genetics toward the formulation of an international code for nomenclature in the field of human genetics.

35. This quotation from the Stricklandian Code, published in 1842 and the parent of the present *Rules*, expresses a sentiment perhaps too hopeful to be appropriate for inclusion in today's *Rules*: "In the construction of compound Latin words there are certain grammatical rules which have been known and acted on for two thousand years, and which a naturalist is bound to acquaint himself with before he tries his skill in coining zoological terms" (quoted from P. L. Sclater's edition of 1878).

matters which may not be altogether meaningful to them unless they are familiar at least in an elementary way with those classical languages. The following extracts from the *Rules* will serve to illustrate this point and, further, to indicate the relevance of some of the contents of the *International Rules* to the subject of this text:

*Article* 3: The scientific names of animals must be words which are either Latin or Latinized, or considered and treated as such in case they are not of classic origin.

*Article* 8: A generic name must consists of a single word, simple or compound, written with a capital initial letter, and employed as a substantive in the nominative singular. Example: *Canis, Perca, Ceratodus, Hymenolepis.*

*Recommendations.* — The following words may be taken as generic names:

a) Greek substantives, for which the rules of Latin transcription [transliteration (see Appendix F)] should be followed. Examples: *Ancylus, Amphibola, Aplysia, Pompholyx, Physa, Cylichna.*

b) Compound Greek words, in which the attributive should precede the principal word. Examples: *Stenogyra, Pleurobranchus, Tylodina, Cyclostomum, Sarcocystis, Pelodytes, Hydrophilus, Rhizobius.*

This does not, however, exclude words formed on the model of *Hippopotamus*, namely, words in which the attributive follows the principal word. Examples: *Philydrus, Biorhiza.*

c) Latin substantives. Examples: *Ancilla, Auricula, Dolium, Harpa, Oliva.* Adjectives (*Prasina*) and past participles (*Productus*) are not recommended.

d) Compound Latin words. Examples: *Stiliger, Dolabrifer, Semifusus.*

e) Greek or Latin derivatives expressing diminution, comparison, resemblance, or possession. Examples: *Dolium, Doliolum*; *Strongylus, Eustrongylus*; *Limax, Limacella, Limacia, Limacina, Limacites, Limacula*; *Lingula, Lingulella, Lingulepis, Lingulina, Lingulops, Lingulopsis*; *Neomenia, Proneomenia*; *Buteo, Archibuteo*; *Gordius, Paragordius, Polygordius.*

f) Mythological or heroic names. Examples: *Osiris, Venus, Brisinga, Velleda, Crimora.* If not Latin, these should be given a Latin termination (*Aegirus, Göndulia*).

g) Proper names used by the ancients. Examples: *Cleopatra, Belisarius, Melania.*

*Article* 14: — Specific names are:

a) Adjectives, which must agree grammatically with the generic name. Example: *Felis marmorata.*

b) Substantives in the nominative in apposition with the generic name. Example: *Felis leo.*

c) Substantives in the genitive. Examples: *rosae, sturionis, antillarum, galliae, sancti-pauli, sanctae-helenae.*

*Recommendation.* — The best specific name is a Latin adjective short, euphonic, and of easy pronunciation.

Latinized Greek words or barbarous words may, however, be used. Examples: *gymnocephalus, echinococcus, ziczac, aguti, hoactli, urubitinga.*

It should be noted that while the term "specific name" in zoology is the second component of the name of a species, the term "specific name" in botany means the entire name of the species, consisting of two components. The term "specific epithet" in botany is equated with "specific name" in zoloogy.

The 1953 publication, *Copenhagen Decisions on Zoological Nomenclature,* which has been referred to above, contains several specific recommended revisions and additions for inclusion in the forthcoming edition of the *Rules.* Quoted below are four examples of those recommendations (the numbers are used for purposes of reference to the separate items in the publication):

82. "The Colloquium recommends the insertion in Article 8 of a *Recommandation* urging authors, when proposing generic names consisting of compound words, to avoid selecting words of which one term consists of, or is derived from, a Greek word and the other a Latin word." (p. 49)

83. "The Colloquium recommends the insertion in Article 8 of a *Recommandation* urging authors, when proposing generic names based upon Greek or Latin words, (i) to determine, if necessary in consultation with a competent authority, the gender of the words concerned, and (ii) to include in the description of the genus a statement regarding the gender of the name and its etymology." (p. 49)

93. "The Colloquium recommends that a provision should be inserted in Article 14 prescribing that, where a specific name consists of a compound word, the use of any connective (phonetic) vowel is permissible. (p. 55)

102. "The Colloquium recommends that a *Recommandation* as follows should be added to Article 20:

Authors, editors and others concerned with the publication of books and serial publications relating to zoology are strongly urged to avoid the use of false diphthongs, that is, to avoid linking vowels together, because of the risk of errors of transcription by later authors." (p. 58)

## BOTANY

*The International Code of Botanical Nomenclature* (until 1950 called *The International Rules of Botanical Nomenclature*) was formulated by the Third International Botanical Congress at Vienna in 1905. It has been modified at various subsequent international congresses, the last being in Paris in 1954. Since the publication in 1737 of Linnaeus' *Critica Botanica*, in which the binomial system of naming plants (whereby every species is given a name consisting of the name of the genus to which it belongs, followed by the name of the species) was introduced, most efforts to establish a workable system of rules for the nomenclature of plants have not been in the direction of abandoning the Linnaean system but rather of improving it.[36] The number and complexity of the taxonomic problems that challenge the botanist may be partially appreciated when one realizes that between 500,000 and 1,000,000 species of plants have now been named and described.[37] At times some difficulty has been encountered in enforcing the provisions of the *Code*; moreover, there have been periods when a botanist could only with difficulty procure a printed copy of the *Code*. For several years after the 1935 meeting of the International Botanical Congress in Amsterdam, at which time several revisions of the rules were made, no text of the *Code* was readily available to workers in plant taxonomy. An unofficial special edition was published in *Brittonia* (pp. 1-20) in April 1947 and from this a reprint made in 1948.[38] Such a situation would seem to indicate that the official rules did not enjoy the prestige which many scholars thought they deserved. Dissatisfaction with the status quo resulted in active discussions and several symposia on the subject.[39] A widespread desire was expressed

---

36. For an excellent brief summary of the history of the *International Code*, see *Amer. Jour. Botany*, XXXVI, 1949, 5-7. This summary is recommended for all students who have an interest in botanical studies. See also XXVI, 1939, 229-31.

37. Cf., *Amer. Jour. Botany*, XXVII, 1940, 339-47. Contains a summary of the system of botanical terminology and a useful bibliography on the subject. See also XXXVI, 1949, 22.

38. W. H. Camp, H. W. Rickett, and C. A. Weatherby, *International Rules of Botanical Nomenclature* (Chronica Botanica Co., Waltham, Mass., 1948).

39. Cf., *Amer. Jour. Botany*, XXXVI, 1949, 1-32. Reference is made to the requirement laid down by the Vienna Congress in 1905 that after January 1, 1908 all new groups of plants must have a Latin diagnosis, but that the international bodies failed to enforce this requirement and later set the date for the enforcement of such Latin diagnosis forward

that the provisions of the *Code* be re-examined, revised conservatively wherever needed, and reaffirmed through official action at an international congress; and that thereafter revisions by subsequent congresses, though not forbidden, be strongly resisted. Such actions were taken at the Seventh International Botanical Congress in Stockholm in 1950, and in 1952 a preliminary printed version of the *Code* was made available. Special committees contined to work on nomenclatural problems and at the Eighth International Botanical Congress in Paris in 1954 a revised version of the *Code* was adopted. Published in 1956, the *Code* in its present form is printed in English (the official version), French, German, and Spanish.[40] Rearrangements and changes, such as separating the Preamble and Principles from the Rules and Recommendations, have rendered obsolete the Section-Article numbering of the previous versions of the *Code*. In general, the nature of the changes and additions made in the latest version reflects a realistic and determined effort to make this *Code* the one universally acceptable guide to the nomenclature and taxonomy of plants.

Quoted below are a few extracts from the 1956 *Code* which deal with matters closely related to the subject of this text:

*Principle V*: Scientific names of plants are Latin or are treated as Latin.

*Article* 20: The name of a genus is a substantive, or an adjective used as a substantive, in the singular number.

*Recommendation* 20 *A*: Botanists who are forming generic names should comply with the following suggestions:

(a) To use Latin terminations insofar as possible.

(b) To avoid names not readily adaptable to the Latin tongue.

(c) Not to make names very long or difficult to pronounce.

(d) Not to make names by combining words from different languages.

(e) To indicate, if possible, by the formation or ending of the name the affinities or analogies of the genus.

---

to January 1, 1935. The effect of such actions, it was pointed out, was that the international body gave validation to much work published in defiance of the *Code* and at the same time rendered invalid various plant names that had been established in a spirit of cooperative adherence to the rules. Principle V and Articles 34, 36, and 40 of the 1956 *Code* reaffirm the requirement that scientific names of plants be Latin and that diagnoses be written in Latin.

40. J. Lanjouw et al., *International Code of Botanical Nomenclature* (Kemink en Zoon N. V., Utrecht, 1956).

(f)  To avoid adjectives used as nouns.

(h)  Not to dedicate genera to persons quite unconnected with botany or at least with natural science.

(i)  To give a feminine form to all personal generic names, whether they commemorate a man or a woman (see Rec. 73 B).

*Article* 23: The name of a species is a binary combination consisting of the name of the genus followed by a single specific epithet. If an epithet consists of two or more words, these must either be united or hyphened.

The specific epithet, when adjectival in form and not used as a substantive, agrees grammatically with the generic name.

Examples: *Helleborus niger, Brassica nigra, Verbascum nigrum; Rubus amnicola.*

*Recommendation* 23*A*: Names of men and women and also of countries and localities used as specific epithets may be substantives in the genitive (*clusii, saharae*) or adjectives (*clusianus, saharicus*).

*Recommendation* 23*B*: In forming specific epithets, botanists should comply also with the following suggestions:

(a)  To use Latin terminations insofar as possible.

(b)  To avoid those which are very long and difficult to pronounce.

(c)  Not to make epithets by combining words from different languages

*Article* 34: In order to be validly published, a name of a new taxon of recent plants, the bacteria and algae excepted, published on or after 1 Jan. 1935 must be accompanied by a Latin diagnosis or by a reference to a previously and effectively published Latin diagnosis.

In order to be validly published, a name of a new taxon of algae published on or after 1 Jan. 1958 must be accompanied by a Latin diagnosis or by a reference to a previously and effectively published Latin diagnosis.

*Article* 45, *Recommendation* 45*G*: The etymology of new names and epithets should be given when the meaning of these is not obvious.

*Article* 73: The original spelling of a name or epithet must be retained, except that typographic or orthographic errors should be corrected.

The consonants *w* and *y*, foreign to classical Latin, and *k*, rare in that language, are permissible in Latin plant names.

*Note* 2: The use of a wrong connecting vowel or vowels (or the omission of a connecting vowel) in a name or an epithet is treated as an orthographic error (see Rec. 73G).

*Recommendation* 73*A*: When a new name or epithet is to be derived from Greek, the transliteration to Latin should conform to classical usage. The *spiritus asper* should be transcribed in Latin as the letter *h*.

*Recommendation* 73*B*: When a new name for a genus, subgenus, or section is taken from the name of a person, it should be formed in the following manner:

(a)  When the name of the person ends in a vowel, the letter *a* is added (thus *Bouteloua* after Boutelou; *Ottoa* after Otto; *Sloanea* after Sloane), except when the name ends in *a*, when *ea* is added (e.g. *Collaea* after Colla).

(b) When the name of the person ends in a consonant, the letters *ia* are added, except when the name ends in *er*, when *a* is added (e.g. *Kernera* after Kerner). In latinized names ending in *-us*, this termination is dropped before adding the suffix (*Dillenia*).

*Recommendation 73C*: When a new specific or infraspecific epithet is taken from the name of a man, it should be formed in the following manner:

(a) When the name of the person ends in a vowel, the letter *i* is added (thus *glazioui* from Glaziou, *bureaui* from Bureau), except when the name ends in *a*, when *e* is added (thus *balansae* from Balansa).

(b) When the name ends in a consonant, the letters *ii* are added (*ramondii* from Ramond), except when the name ends in *-er*, when *i* is added (thus *kerneri* from Kerner).

(c) The syllables not modified by these endings retain their original spelling, unless they contain letters foreign to Latin plant names or diacritic signs (see Art. 73).

(d) When epithets taken from the name of a man have an adjectival form they are formed in a similar way (e.g. *Geranium robertianum*, *Verbena hasslerana*).

If the personal name is already Latin or Greek, the appropriate Latin genitive should be used, e.g. *alexandri* from Alexander, *francisci* from Franciscus, *augusti* from Augustus, *linnaei* from Linnaeus, *hectoris* from Hector.

The same provisions apply to epithets formed from the names of women. When these have a substantival form, they are given a feminine termination (e.g. *Cypripedium hookerae*, *Rosa beatricis*, *Scabiosa olgae*, *Omphalodes luciliae*).

*Recommendation 73D*: An epithet derived from a geographical name is preferably an adjective and usually takes the termination *-ensis*, *-(a)nus*, *-inus*, *-ianus* or *-icus*.

Examples: *Rubus quebecensis* (from Quebec), *Ostrya virginiana* (from Virginia), *Polygonum pensylvanicum* (from Pennsylvania).

*Recommendation 73E*: A new epithet should be written in conformity with the original spelling of the word or words from which it is derived and in accordance with the accepted usage of Latin and latinization.

Examples: *silvestris* (not *sylvestris*), *sinensis* (not *chinensis*).

*Recommendation 73 G*: A compound name or an epithet combining elements derived from two or more Greek or Latin words should be formed, as far as practicable, in accordance with classical usage (see notes 2 and 3 to Art. 73). This may be stated as follows:

(a) In a true compound (as distinct from pseudocompounds such as *Myos-otis*, *nidus-avis*) a noun or adjective in a non-final position appears as a bare stem without case-ending (*Hydro-phyllum*).

(b) Before a vowel the final vowel of this stem, if any, is normally elided (*Chrys-anthemum, mult-angulus*), with the exception of Greek *y* and *i* (*poly-anthus, Meli-osma*).

(c) Before a consonant the final vowel is normally preserved in Greek (*mono-carpus, Poly-gonum, Coryne-phorus, Meli-lotus*), except that *a* is commonly replaced by *o* (*Hemero-callis* from *hemera*); in Latin the final vowel is reduced to *i* (*multi-color, menthi-folius, salvii-folius*).

(d) If the stem ends in a consonant, a connecting vowel (*o* in Greek, *i* in Latin) is inserted before a following consonant *Odont-o-glossum, cruc-i-formis*).

Some irregular forms, however, have been extensively used through false analogy (*atro-purpureus*, on the analogy of pseudo-compounds such as *fusco-venatus* in which *o* is the ablative case-ending). Others are used as revealing etymological distinctions (*caricae-formis* from *Carica*, as distinct from *carici-formis* from *Carex*). Where such irregularities occur in the original spelling of existing compounds, this spelling should be retained.

*Note.* The hyphens in the above examples are given solely for explanatory reasons. They should all be eliminated in botanical names and epithets except in *nidus-avis, terrae-novae* and similar Latin pseudo-compounds.

*Article 75, Recommendation 75A*: The gender of generic names should be determined as follows:

(1) A Greek or Latin word adopted as a generic name should retain its gender. When the gender varies, the author should choose one of the alternative genders. In doubtful cases, general usage should be followed. The following names, however, whose classical gender is masculine, should be treated as feminine in accordance with botanical custom: *Adonis, Diospyros, Strychnos*; so also should *Orchis* and *Stachys*, which are masculine in Greek and feminine in Latin. The name *Hemerocallis*, derived from the Latin and Greek *hemerocalles* (n.), although masculine in Linnaeus, Species Plantarum, should be treated as feminine in order to bring it into conformity with all other generic names ending in *-is*.

(2) Generic names formed from two or more Greek or Latin words should take the gender of the last. If the ending is altered, however, the gender should follow it.

Examples of names formed from Greek words: The generic name *Andropogon* L. was treated by Linnaeus as neuter, but it, like other modern compounds in which the Greek masculine word *pogon* is the final element (e.g. *Centropogon, Cymbopogon, Bystropogon*), should be treated as masculine. Similarly, all modern compounds ending in *-codon, -myces, -odon, -panax, -stemon* and other masculine words should be masculine. The generic names *Dendromecon* Benth., *Eomecon* Hance, and *Hesperomecon* E. L. Greene should be treated as feminine, because they end in the Greek feminine word *mecon*, poppy; the fact that Bentham and E. L. Greene respectively ascribed the neuter gender to the names *Dendromecon* and *Hesperomecon* is immaterial.

Similarly, all modern compounds ending in *-achne*, *-carpha*, *-cephala*, *-chlamys*, *-daphne*, and other feminine words should be feminine. The generic names *Aceras* R. Br., *Aegiceras* Gaertn., and *Xanthoceras* Bunge should be treated as neuter because they end in the Greek neuter word *ceras*; the fact that Robert Brown and Bunge respectively made *Aceras* and *Xanthoceras* feminine is immaterial.

Similarly, all modern compounds ending in *-dendron*, *-nema,*, *-stigma*, *-stoma*, and other neuter words should be neuter. Names ending in *-osma* should be feminine, since that is the gender of the Greek word *osmé*. Names ending in *-anthos* (or *-anthus*) and those in *-chilos* (*-chilus* or *-cheilos*) ought strictly speaking to be neuter, since that is the gender of the Greek words *anthos* and *cheilos*. These names, however, have generally been treated as masculine: hence botanists are recommended to assign that gender to them. Similarly, it is recommended that those ending in *-gaster*, which strictly speaking should be feminine, should be treated as masculine in accordance with botanical custom.

Examples of compound generic names where the termination of the last word is altered: *Hymenocarpus*, *Dipterocarpus*, and all other modern compounds ending in the Greek masculine *carpos* (or *carpus*) should be masculine. Those in *-carpa* or *-carpaea*, however, should be feminine, e.g. *Callicarpa* and *Polycarpaea*; and those in *-carpon*, *-carpum*, or *-carpium* should be neuter, e.g. *Polycarpon*, *Ormocarpum*, and *Pisocarpium*.

(4) Generic names ending in *-oides* or *-odes* should be treated as feminine irrespective of the gender assigned to them by the original author.

# BIBLIOGRAPHY

## Dictionaries

1. *The Oxford English Dictionary* (Oxford, at the Clarendon Press, 1933).

2. *Webster's New International Dictionary of the English Language*, 2nd Ed., Unabridged (G. and C. Merriam Co., Springfield, Mass., 1957).

3. *Dorland's Illustrated Medical Dictionary*, 23rd Ed., (W. B. Saunders Co., Philadelphia and London, 1957).

4. *The Macmillan Medical Dictionary* (The Macmillan Co., New York, 1954). Published in England under the title *The Faber Medical Dictionary*.

5. *Blakiston's New Gould Medical Dictionary* (The Blakiston Co., Philadelphia, 1949).

6. *Stedman's Medical Dictionary* 19th Revised Ed., (The Williams and Wilkins Co., Baltimore, 1957).

7. I. F. Henderson and W. D. Henderson, *A Dictionary of Scientific Terms* (D. Van Nostrand Co., New York, 1952).

8. Benjamin D. Jackson, *A Glossary of Botanic Terms*, 4th Ed., Reprinted (Gerald Duckworth and Co., Ltd., London, 1953).

9. William B. Dunning and S. Ellsworth Davenport, Jr., *A Dictionary of Dental Science and Art* (P. Blakiston's Son and Co., Inc., Philadelphia, 1936).

10. L. E. Hinsie and J. Shatsky, *Psychiatric Dictionary* (Oxford University Press, New York, 1940).

11. Robert S. Woods, *The Naturalist's Lexicon* (Abbey Garden Press, Pasadena, 1944).

12. Ernest Weekley, *An Etymological Dictionary of Modern English* (John Murray, London, 1921). A Concise and Revised Edition of the Same (E. P. Dutton and Co., New York, 1952).

13. Joseph T. Shipley, *Dictionary of Word Origins*, 2nd Ed., (The Philosophical Library, Inc., New York, 1945).

14. C. T. Lewis and C. Short, *Latin Dictionary* (Oxford University Press, New York, 1957). Formerly, *Harpers Latin Dictionary*.

15. C. T. Lewis, *An Elementary Latin Dictionary* (American Book Co., New York, 1918).

16. H. G. Liddell and Robert Scott, *A Greek-English Lexicon*, Two Volumes, Revised by Henry S. Jones (Oxford University Press, London, 1951).

17. —————— and ——————, *An Intermediate Greek-English Lexicon* (Oxford University Press, London, 1945).

## Books

1. Agard, Walter R. and Howe, Herbert M., *Medical Greek and Latin at a Glance*, Third Ed. (Paul B. Hoeber, Inc., New York, 1955).

2. Andrews, Edmund, *A History of Scientific English* (Richard R. Smith, New York, 1947).

3. Beard, John G., *Latin for Pharmacists* (University of North Carolina Book Exchange, Chapel Hill, 1942).

3a. Breed, Murray and Smith, *Bergey's Manual of Determinative Bacteriology*, Seventh Ed. (The Williams and Wilkins Co., Baltimore, 1957).

4. Brown, Charles B., *The Contribution of Greek to English* (The Vanderbilt University Press, Nashville, 1942).

5. ——————, *The Contribution of Latin to English* (The Vanderbilt University Press, Nashville, 1946).

6. Brown, Roland W., *Composition of Scientific Words* (United States National Museum; published by the Author, Washington, D. C., 1954).

7. Campbell, F. R., *The Language of Medicine* (D. Appleton and Co., New York, 1888).

8. Cooper, J. W. and McLeran, A. C., *Latin for Pharmaceutical Students* (Sir Isaac Pitman and Sons, London, 1930).

9. Currie, George W., *Essentials of General and Scientific Latin* (Chapman and Grimes, Inc., Boston, 1945).

10. Darwin, Francis, *The Life and Letters of Charles Darwin*, Vol. I (D. Appleton and Co., New York, 1887).

11. Denton, George B., *The Vocabulary of Dentistry and Oral Science — A Manual for the Study of Dental Nomenclature* (Bureau of Library and Indexing Service of the American Dental Association, Chicago, 1958).

12. Dobson, Jessie, *Anatomical Eponyms* (Bailliere, Tindall and Cox, London, 1946).

13. Dorfman, J. S., *Pharmaceutical Latin* (Lea and Febiger, Philadelphia, 1938).

14. Effler, Louis R., *The Eponyms of Anatomy* (McManus-Troup Co., Toledo, 1935).

15. Eycleshymer, Albert C. and Schoemaker, Daniel M., *Anatomical Names* (William Wood and Co., New York, 1917).

16. Field, E. J. and Harrison, R. J., *Anatomical Terms: Their Origin and Derivation* (W. Heffer and Sons, Ltd., Cambridge, 1947).

17. Garrison, Fielding H., *An Introduction to the History of Medicine*, Third Ed., (W. B. Saunders Co., Philadelphia, 1924).

18. Gray, Asa, *Manual of Botany*, Eighth Ed., revised by Merritt L. Fernald, (American Book Co., New York, 1950).

19. Hough, John N., *Scientific Terminology* (Rinehart and Co., New York, 1953).

20. Jaeger, Edmund C., *A Dictionary of Greek and Latin Combining Forms Used in Zoological Names* (Charles C Thomas, Springfield, Ill., 1931).

21. —————, *A Source-Book of Biological Names and Terms* (Charles C Thomas, Springfield, 1944).

22. —————, *A Source-Book of Medical Terms* (Charles C Thomas, Springfield, Ill., 1953).

23. Johnson, Edwin L., *Latin Words of Common English* (D. C. Heath Co., Boston, 1931).

24. Judson, Harry P., *The Latin in English* (Henry Holt and Co., New York, 1896).

25. Lewis, Carolyn, *Medical Latin* (Marshall Jones Co., Francestown, N. H., 1948).

26. Melander, Axel L., *Source Book of Biological Terms* (The City College of New York, 1937).

27. Mettler, Cecilia C., *History of Medicine* (The Blakiston Co., Philadelphia, 1947).

28. Pepper, O. H. Perry, *Medical Etymology* (W. B. Saunders Co., Philadelphia, 1949).

29. Roberts, Ffrangcon, *Medical Terms: Their Origin and Construction* (William Heinemann Medical Books, Ltd., London, 1954).

30. Savory, T. H., *Latin and Greek for Biologists* (University of London Press, Ltd., London, 1946).

31. Seifert, M. J., *Synthesis of Medical Terminology* (D. Appleton and Co., New York, 1925).

32. Skinner, Henry A., *The Origin of Medical Terms* (The Williams and Wilkins Co., Baltimore, 1949).

33. Smock, John C., *The Greek Element in English Words* (The Macmillan Co., New York, 1931).

34. Spilman, Mignonette, *Medical Latin and Greek*, Second Ed., (Edwards Bros., Inc., Ann Arbor, 1952).

35. Staples, Clarence L., *Professional Latin in Modern English* (Thesis, University of Pennsylvania, Lancaster, Pa., 1914).

36. Wiken, Erik, *Latin för Botanister och Zoologer* (Gleerups, Malmö, 1951).

## Bulletins and Tracts

1. *Bulletin of Zoological Nomenclature*, XIV, June 1958, i-xxviii.

2. *International Bulletin of Bacteriological Nomenclature and Taxonomy*, Ames, Iowa State College Press, Vol. I (1951), 97-102 and 113-25; Vol. II (1952), 64-68; Vol. III (1953), 63-69; and Vol. IV (1954), 167-87.

3. *Society for Pure English Tracts* (Oxford, at the Clarendon Press):
   a. John Sargeaunt, "The Pronunciation of English Words Derived from Latin," Tract No. 4 (1920), 1-31.
   b. William C. Morton, "The Language of Anatomy," Tract No. 9 (1922), 3-19.
   c. C. G. Darwin, "Terminology in Physics," Tract No. 48 (1937), 280-86.

4. Frederic E. Clements, "Greek and Latin in Biological Nomenclature," *University Studies* III, No. 1 (1902), 1-85; University of Nebraska.

5. Walter Miller, "Scientific Names of Latin and Greek Derivation," *Proceedings California Academy of Sciences*, Third Series, Zoology, Vol. I, No. 3 (1897), 115-43.

6. P. H. Yancey, S. J., *Introduction to Biological Latin and Greek*, Third Ed., (Bios Classroom Series, No. 1, 1946); reprinted from *Bios*, Vol. XV.

7. —————, *Origins from Mythology of Biological Names and Terms* (Bios Classroom Series, No. 5, 1945); reprinted from *Bios*, Vol. XVI. Available from F. G. Brooks, Mount Vernon, Iowa.

8. Report(s) on Second (and Third) Nomenclature Conference(s) (Bureau of Library and Indexing Service of the American Dental Association, Chicago, 1953 and 1954).

## Codes and Rules of Scientific Nomenclature

1. *Nomina Anatomica*, proposed revision of the B. N. A. by the International Anatomical Nomenclature Committee; published and distributed by The Williams and Wilkins Co., Baltimore, 1956. Also in *Nomina Anatomica Parisiensia (1955) et B. N. A. (1895)*, M. W. Woerdeman, Editor (A. Oosthoek Publishing Co., Utrecht, 1957).

2. *Standard Nomenclature of Diseases and Operations*, Fourth Ed., by Richard J. Plunkett (Published for The American Medical Association by The Blakiston Co., New York, 1952).

3. *International Code of Nomenclature of the Bacteria and Viruses* (Bacteriological Code), edited by R. E. Buchanan, Ralph St. John-Brooks, and Robert S. Breed and published in *Journal of Bacteriology*, LV, 1948, 287-306. The 1953 amendments are published in *International Bulletin of Bacteriological Nomenclature and Taxonomy*, IV, 1954, 167-87.

4. Edward E. Schenk and John H. McMasters, *Procedure in Taxonomy*, Third Ed., enlarged and in part rewritten by A. Myra Keen and Siemon W. Muller and including a Reprint in Translation of the *Règles Internationales de la Nomenclature Zoölogique* (Stanford University Press, Stanford, Calif., 1956). Official Zoological Code in English published in *Bulletin of Zoological Nomenclature*, XIV, June 1958, i-xxviii. Interim Code: *Copenhagen Decisions on Zoological* Nomenclature: Additions to, and Modifications of, the *Règles Internationales de la Nomenclature Zoölogique*, edited by Francis Hemming (Office of the International Trust, 41 Queen's Gate, London, S. W. 7, 1953).

5. W. H. Camp, H. W. Rickett, and C. A. Weatherby, *International Rules of Botanical Nomenclature* (The Chronica Botanica Co., Waltham, Mass., 1948).

6. J. Lanjouw *et al.*, *International Code of Botanical Nomenclature* (Kemink en Zoon N. V., Utrecht, 1956; and The Chronica Botanica Co., Waltham, Mass., 1952).

## Periodicals

1. *American Journal of Botany* XXVI, 1939, 229-31; XXVII, 1940, 339-47; XXXVI, 1949, 1-32.

2. *American Journal of Clinical Pathology* XVIII, 1948, 443-50; XIX, 1949, 56-60.

3. *American Journal of Human Genetics* IV, 1952, 347-49.

4. *American Journal of Medical Technology* XIV, 1948, 324-36; XV, 1949, 264-72.

5. *American Journal of Orthodontics* XXXIV, 1948, 178-91.

6. *American Scientist* XXXVI, 1948, 150-51.

7. *Annals of Medical History* X, 1928, 180-98.

8. *British Dental Journal* LXXIII, 1942, 204.

9. *International Dental Journal* II, 1952, 427; III, 1953, 438-39.

10. *Journal of the American Dental Association* XL, 1950, 104-06; XLII, 1951, 345-50.

11. *Journal of the American Medical Association* CXII, 1939, 1843 and 2423.

12. *Journal of the Association of American Medical Colleges* XXII, 1947, 298-301.

13. *Journal of Bacteriology* LV, 1948, 287-306.

14. *Journal of Clinical Investigation* XXXIV, 1955, 899.

15. *Journal of Comparative Neurology* CII, 1955, 348.

16. *Journal of Dental Education* XIV, 1949, 38-44.

17. *Journal of Endodontia* III, 1948, 58-59.

18. *Journal of Investigative Dermatology* IX, 1947, 213-18.

19. *Journal of Iowa State Medical Society* XXXII, 1942, 217-18.

20. *Journal of Michigan Dental Society* XXXI, 1949, 158-61.

21. *Journal of Michigan State Dental Association* XXXIII, 1951, 204-06.

22. *Journal of Michigan State Medical Society* XXXV, 1936, 374-85.

23. *Journal of Periodontology* XVI, 1945, 47-49, 110-12, 140-41; XVII, 1946, 24-27; XIX, 1948, 147-49; XXI, 1950, 40-43.

24. *Journal of Washington Academy of Science* XXXI, 1941, 135-40.

25. *The Medical and Surgical Reporter* LXX, 1894, 339-43.

26. *New York State Journal of Medicine* XL, 1940, 1260-62.

27. *Parasitology* XXXI, 1939, 255-62.

28. *Proceedings of the American Association of Dental Schools* XXIII, 1946, 294-97.

29. *Science* XXXII, 1910, 295-301; LXV, 1927, 194-99; LXXI, 1930, 26-28; XCVI, 1942, 272; CXV, 1952, 63-64; CXVI, 1952, 433 and 546; CXVII, 1953, 16-17, 40-41, 112.

30. *Transactions of the American Philological Association* LXXVI, 1946, 333-57.

31. *Washington University Medical Alumni Quarterly* VI, 1943, 88-97.

# INDEX

Ablative case in Latin, its uses, 33-34

Ablaut, *see* Vowel gradation

Accent: of English words, 247-49; of Greek words, 45-46; of Greek words not transferred in anglicization, 46; of Latin words, 31, 247; and meaning of Greek word, 46

Accusative case in Latin, its uses, 32

Achilles' tendon, 280

Acrostic names, 17-18

Acute accent, 45

Adaptability of words, 21-22

Adjectives: agreement with nouns, 35-39, 300, 304; comparison of, 32, 37; as generic and specific names, 295, 300; Greek, declension of, 50-51; Latin, declension of, 35-39; listing of in word lists, 85-86, 147; as substantives (nouns), 143-45, 234, 295, 300; suffixes (adjectival), 79-81, 143-45

Affective meanings, 12, 26

Affixing characteristic of Greek and Latin, 27-28

Agreement, *see* Adjectives

Alpha-privative, 135

Alphabet: of Greek, 44-46; of Latin, 30-31

American Dental Association, 297

Analogy: false, 268-69, 306; power of, 239-40, 242, 261, 263

Anatomical nomenclature: anatomical equivalents in Greek, Latin, and English, 251-52; *B. N. A. (Basle Nomina Anatomica)*, 249n, 282, 289-91; development of, 289-91; Latin-derived terms in, 252; *see also Nomina Anatomica*

Anatomical Society, 289

Anglicization: of foreign words, 243; of Greek suffixes, 140-45; of Latin suffixes, 75-83; *see also* Transliteration

Anglo-Saxon, as a source of common and scientific English words, 24

Antepenult, 31, 247

Article, the Greek definite, 47

Aspirate, *see* Breathing marks

Assimilation, 67-68, 262

Asterisks, their meaning in the word lists, ix, 86, 148

Bacteriological nomenclature: development and control of, 239 and n., 286, 293-96; *International Code* of, quoted, 294-96

Base: definition of, 4; derived from genitive case, 32, 48-49, 235; of Greek and Latin words, 34-35, 48-49; participial, 40-41; "short" base, 261; variations and errors in 235-37, 267-70; *see also* Stems

Basedow, Karl Adolph von, 283

Binomial system, 18, 55n, 285, 293, 302, 304

Biology, functions of terminology in, 17, 18-19

*B. N. A. (Basle Nomina Anatomica)*, *see Nomina Anatomica*

Botallo, Leonardo, 283

Botanical nomenclature: development and control of, 302-03; *International Code* of, quoted, 303-07

Breathing marks: effect on consonants, 46-47; how noted in transliteration, 59-61, 262, 267, 304; smooth and rough, 46

Bureau of Library and Indexing Service (American Dental Association), 297

Case-endings: corresponding endings in Greek and Latin, 48, 55-57; tendency to drop or change, 44, 55-57; *see also* Declensions, Suffixes

Cases: agreement in, 35-39; names and uses of, 32-33, 47-48

Celsus, 27n

Changes: consonant, 42-43, 53-55, 134; in meaning and form of words, 9-10, 14, 23, 26-27; vowel, 6, 42-43, 52

Chemistry: basis of naming chemical compounds, 17; function of nomenclature in, 16-17; system of suffixes in, 82-83

Cicero, v

Circumflex accent, 45

Classification, a function of nomenclature, 15, 298, 302

Codes of nomenclature: of anatomy, 249n, 282, 286, 289-91; of bacteriology, 239n, 286, 293-96; of botany, 239n, 302-07; of dentistry, 296-97; of diseases and operations, 286, 292; of human genetics, 299n; international recognition of, 287-88; revisions of, 288; of zoology, 281, 297-301

Coined words: definition of, 7; numerous in scientific terms, 231; similarity to native words, 27; *see also* Word coinage

Combining form: definition of, 6; importance of, 64-65

Combining vowels: definition of, 5-6; final vowel of stem as, 237; in Greek words, 237-38; in Latin words, 238-39; in modern word coinage, 237-42, 295, 301, 304, 306; variations in, 239-42, 262, 296, 304

Comparison of adjectives, 32, 37

Compound words: component elements of: arrangement of, 258-61, 270, 300, coordinate and subordinate, 232-34, 258-60, recognition of, ix, 1, 64-65, syntactical relationships between, 231-34; excessive dissection of, 65; formation of, 231-42; gender of, 234-35, 296, 301, 306; more numerous in Greek than in Latin, 231; and the synthetic nature of Greek and Latin, 27-28, 30, 231; *see also* Word-elements, Names, Malformations, Misnomers, Neologisms

Concealment of information, 28-29

Congress, *see* International Congresses

Conjugations: conjugation defined, 30; of Latin, 39-42; of Greek, 51-52

Connecting vowels, *see* Combining vowels

Consonantal *i*, 31, 43

Consonants: changes of: in Greek, 53-55, 134, in Latin, 43, 67-68; double, 244-45; false, 263, 268; of Greek, 45; of Latin, 31; pronunciation of, 244-45

Context, and meaning, 64, 65

Coordinate compounds, 232-33

*Copenhagen Decisions on Zoological Nomenclature*, quoted, 301.

Darwin, Charles, 280-81

Declensions: declension defined, 30; in Greek, 47-51; in Latin, 32-39

Definitions: of frequently used terms, 3-8; tentative, 64; in word lists, 64

Degree of adjectives, 32, 37-38

Dental terminology: function of, 15; present status of, 296-97

Derivatives: definition of, 7; as "laboratory" material, 62-63; from Latin, 85; learning of, x; not defined in word lists, 63-64

Descriptiveness of terms, 13-14, 16-18, 291

Descriptive tracts: in French and English compared, 11-12; in Latin, 28; pseudo Greek-Latin aspect of, 25, 28n

Diagnoses: written in Latin, 28-29, 302n, 303; technical language of, 28-29

Dictionaries: as authorities, 9; use of in word study, xi

Diminutive suffixes, 78-79, 142

Diphthongs: false, 245-46, 301; of Greek, 45; of Latin, 31; pronunciation of, 245-46; transliteration of, 43, 58-59, 263

Diseases, nomenclature of, 286, 292

Diseases and Operations, nomenclature of, 292


Economy in terms, 21

Elision: definition of, 6-7; in Greek, 53; irregularities in, 68, 134, 241-42; of prefixes and stems, 68, 133-34, 306

Emotional meanings, 14, 26

English language: adjectival suffixes in, 144; its debt to Greek, Latin and Anglo-Saxon, 24; "technical" and "vernacular" English compared, 9-12

Endings, see Case-endings

Entry-words: in Greek dictionaries, 47-48, 50-51; in Latin dictionaries, 32, 35-36, 39; in words lists: alphabetical, 62, irregularities in listing, 86, meanings of, 65-66, memorization of, 64-65, number of, 86, 148

Eponyms: attitude toward in Codes, 285-86; Darwin on, 280-81; definition of, 280; Oliver Wendell Holmes on, 281-82; latinization of, 305; number of in medical dictionary, 282; references to in Codes, 291, 295, 300, 304-05, 306; and synonymy, 258, 284; in terminol-

ogy of science, pros and cons of, 280-86

Errors: in naming, 271-74; orthographic, reference to in Codes, 295, 304, 306; in word analysis, 65, 224-30; in word formation, 265-74, 295-96; in transliteration, see Transliteration

Etymology: and meaning of word, 256-57; of new scientific names, 295, 296, 301, 304

Etymology of scientific names, required, 20, 295, 296, 301, 304

Euphony of terms, 20-21, 275

Examinations, suggestions for construction of, x


"Fancy" names, 17

Flajani, Giuseppe, 283

Folk-terms, see Vernacular language

"Foreignness" in terms, 28

Functional facility of terms, 21-22

Galen, 26, 27n, 283

Gamma-nasal, 45, 57

Gender: agreement in 35-39, 300, 304; of compound words, 234-35, 295-96, 301, 306-07; in Greek, 47-48; in Latin, 32, 34, 35, 39; of personal generic names, 295, 296, 304; of specific epithet, 304

Genitive case: used as base, 268; as the source for the base of a word, 32, 48, 235-37; in descriptive phrases, 32; for specific names, 301

Generic names, see Names

Gerundive, 42

Grammar, see Syntax

Grave accent, 45

Graves, Robert J., 283

Greek (classical): alphabet and pronunciation of, 44-47; inflections of, 47-52; as the language of science, 26; as source of English words generally, 24; as a spoken language, 26-27; synthetic nature of, 27-28, 30, 231; in the terminology of science, v, 2, 24-29, 252, 294, 297n, 299-300; transliteration of, 55-61, 294, 295; its value to the scientist, 29-30; word lists of, 132-223

Haplology, 265
Harris, Chapin, A., 296
Harvey, William, 283
Hippocrates, 26, 27n, 262
Holmes, Oliver Wendell, 281-82
Homer, 280
Hooker, J. D., 280
Hybrid Words: in Bacteriological Code, 295, 296; in Botanical Code, 303, 304; meaning of, 8, 274, 278-79; and synonymy, 253-54; in terminology of science, pros and cons, 274-80; in word lists, 63; in Zoological Code, 301
Hyphenation of words and names, 241-42, 306

Imperative mood, 41
Infinitives: in Greek, 51-52; in Latin, 40-41
Inflected Latin forms in English, 85
Inflections: inflection defined, 31; of Greek, 30, 47-52; of Latin, 30, 31-42
Instructional procedures, ix-xi
International character of scientific language, 10-11, 15, 28
International codes of nomenclature, see Codes of nomenclature
International Congresses: of Anatomists, 290; of Botanists, 302-03; of Dentists, 296n; of Microbiologists, 293; of Zoologists, 297-99
Iota-subscript, in transliteration, 58

Lachèse, Sanoaville de, 274
Language: a changing phenomenon, 9, 10 and n.; for communication

and preservation of ideas, 9; general and scientific, 9-12; international aspect of scientific language, 10-11, 28; vernacular, see Vernacular language
Latin: alphabet and pronunciation of, 30-31; as a conversational language, 26; in diagnoses and descriptions, 28-29, 291, 302n, 304; inflections of, 31-42; in medical prescriptions, 28; in the Middle Ages, 26; for the scientist, 29-30; as source of English words generally, 25-26; synthetic nature of, 27-28, 30, 231; in the terminology of science, v-vi, 1, 24-29, 250-52, 289-91, 294-96, 297, 299-301, 303-307; universality of, 28; word lists of, 66-131
Latinization: of Greek, 55-58, 278-279, 294 and n., 295-96; of names in gross anatomy, 289-91; of names in bacteriology, 294; of names in botany, 303-07; of names in zoology, 299-301
Law of Priority, 23, 266, 299
Length of words and names, 16-18, 21, 294, 295, 303, 304
Linguistic correctness of terms, 20
Linguistic purity: sometimes sacrificed, 278; in terms, 20; see also Hybrid words
Linnaeus, 55n, 293, 302
Loan words: definition of, 7; from Greek, 146-47; from Latin, 85
"Long" stem, 235-37

Malformations, 259-60, 262-63, 265-270
Meanings: changes in, 10 and n., 14, 23, 26-27; emotional or affective, 14, 26; established by usage or arbitrary decision, 256, 261; precision of, 14, 16-18, 26-27; primary and secondary, 27n, 65-66, 67, 132; stability in, 9-10, 14,

23, 26-27, 29; uniformity of, 14, 28; of words in word lists, 63-66
"Meaning-units" of compound words, 65
Medical terminology: functions of, 15-17; broad scope of, 1, 288-89; *see also* Anatomical nomenclature, Bacteriological Nomenclature, Diseases and Operations
Metathesis, 258-61
Misnomers, 271-74
Mithradates and mithradatism, 280
Mood of Latin verb, 32, 41-42
Mutes in Greek, 45, 53-54
Mythological names, 280 and n., 300

Names: acrostic, 17-18; choice of, 23, 265-66; "fit", 271; generic, 294-96, 300, 301, 303-07; hybrid, *see* Hybrid words; length of, 16-18, 21, 294, 295, 303, 304; as mnemonic necessity, 9; mythological and heroic, 280 and n., 300; need for new, v; personal, *see* Eponyms; specific, 294-96, 300-01, 304-06; as significant symbols, 2, 15; as tags or meaningful epithets, 15, 295, 303; of taxa above genus, 294; vernacular, *see* Vernacular language; *see also* Nomenclature, Misnomers
Nasal gamma, 45, 57
Neologisms: definition of, 7; constructed to meet specific needs, 85; similarity to native words, 27
Nomenclature: of anatomy, 289-91; of bacteriology, 293-96; of botany, 302-07; of dentistry, 296-97; desiderata in, 16-23, 295, 300, 303-304; of diseases and operations, 292; of human genetics, 299n; and history, 26; meaning and functions of, 15-16, 287-88; 303-304; nomenclatural criteria, 2; of zoology, 297-301; *see also* Terminology of science

*Nomina Anatomica*: development of, 289-90; eponyms in, 282, 286, 291; *Introduction* of, quoted, 290-291; synonymous words in, 249n
Nominative case, 32, 47-48
Nominative stems, 236-37, 261, 269-270
Notebooks, suggestions for use of, x-xi
Nouns: as adjectives, 144; gender of, 32, 34, 39, 47-48; Greek, declension of, 47-50; Latin, declension of, 32-35; noun suffixes, 75-79, 139-42; in word lists, 85-86, 147
Number: agreement in, 35, 38-39, 300, 304; of generic, subgeneric, and other names, 294; singular and plural, 32, 34, 42, 47-49
Numerals: Greek, list of, 145-46; Latin, list of, 83-84

Operations, nomenclature of, 286, 292
Orientation of terms, 18-19
Orthographic variants, in *Codes*, 295-96, 304
Osler, William, Sir, 283

Parry, Caleb, 283
Participles, in Latin, 40-42
Pathology, favors Greek-derived terms, 252
Penult, 31, 247
Person of verb, 32
Pharmacology, terminology of, 16
Plants, naming of, 1, 17; *see also* Botanical nomenclature
Plural, *see* Number
Precision in meaning of terms, 14, 16-18, 26-27
Prefixes: definition of, 5; and elision, *see* Elision; Greek, list of, 132-39; incorrect use of word "prefix", 5, 132; Latin, list of, 66-74; separable and inseparable 66, 132;

several in one word, 67, 133; as starting point in study of word lists, ix; variable force of, 67, 132

Prescriptions, language of, 28-29

Principal parts: of Greek verbs, 51-52; of Latin verbs, 39-42

Priority, Law of, 23, 266, 299

Pronunciation: affected by observing word makeup, 248; "correct" or "standard", 243; of English words, 243; of Greek words, 44-47; of Latin words, 30-31; practice-words in, 249; of technical terms, 243-49

Proprietary names, 16

"Purebred" words, 274-75, 278

Purity, see Linguistic purity

Quantity of syllables, 31, 246

Restrained descriptiveness of terms, 16-18

Roots: definition of, 3; of Greek verbs, 52; number of, 47

Rough breathing, see Breathing marks

Rules of nomenclature, see Codes of nomenclature

Sanction of terms, 23

Scientific language: cohesion and unity of, 29; dual linguistic base of, 250; compared with general language, 9-15; international aspect of, 10-11, 28; see also Descriptive tracts, Prescriptions

Semantic change, 10 and n., 14, 23, 26-27

"Short" stem, 235-37, 261, 268, 269, 270

Shortening of words, 16-18, 263, 264-65

Simple words, 231

Singular, see Number

Specific names, see Names

Specificity of terms, 19-20

Spelling: changes in, 9-10, 14; variations in, 295-96, 304, 306, 307; see also Malformations

Stability of terms, 10, 14, 23, 26-27, 29

*Standard Nomenclature of Diseases and Operations*, 286, 289, 292

Stems: definition of, 4; irregular and incorrect, 267-70; "long" stems, 235-37; nominative or "short" stems, 236-37, 261, 268, 269-70; participial, 40-41; separable and inseparable, 4; similar, 224-30, 268, 269-70; stem and base compared, 4, 35, 49; verbal, 39-41, 51-52, 235; vowel-endings of, 4, 35, 49; see also Base

Strickland, Hugh, 281, 299n

Subjunctive mood, 41

Subordinate compounds, 232-34

Substantives: adjectives used as, 143-45, 300; suffixes (substantival), 75-79, 140-42

Suffixes: adjectival, 79-81, 143-45; adverbial, 82; in chemistry, 82-83; definition and function of, 5, 75, 139; diminutive, 78-79, 142; Greek: list of, 139-45, English versions of, 140-45; Latin: list of, 75-83, English versions of, 75-82; primary and secondary, 75; substantival (noun), 75-79, 139-42; verbal, 82, 140

Syllables: in English, 244; in Latin and Greek, 31, 45, 244; quantity of, 31, 246

Symbols for words, 15

Synonyms: in gross anatomy, 289, 291; causes of, 240-41, 249-63, 284; examples of, 240-42, 249-63; in literary and technical language, 249; by usage although not etymologically, 256-57

Synonymy, see Synonyms

Syntax, 30

Synthetic nature of Greek and Latin words, 27-28, 30, 231

Technical terms: Greek and Latin in, 2, 29; the large number of, 1; mixed with nontechnical, 14; in "technical English", 10-12; semi-technical terms, 13; stability of, 10
Tense, 32
Terminology of science: characteristics of, 1, 9-23; "foreignness" of, 28; international aspect of, 28; *see also* Nomenclature
Transliteration: definition of, 9; faulty, 262-63, 266-67, 295; of Greek, 55-61, 294; of Latin, 43-44
Trousseau, Armand, 283

Ultima, 31, 247
*UNESCO*, 288n, 290n
Universality of Greek and Latin, 28

Varolio, Costanzo, 283
Verbs: Greek, 51-52; Latin, 39-42; stems and bases of, 40-42, 51-52; suffixes (verbal), 82, 140; in word lists, 86, 147-48
Vernacular language: in anatomy, 291; in scientific terminology, pros and cons of, 12-15, 19-20; and technical, compared, 9-12; mixed with technical, 13, 14
Vocabulary: of Greek and Latin, how constructed, 30, 66, 75, 132, 139, 231; newness of, v; as part of language, 30; lists, *see* Word lists; of science, 1; *see also* Language
Voice, of verbs, 32, 42
Vowel gradation: definition of, 6; in Greek, 52; in Latin, 42-43; 86
Vowels: changes in, *see* Vowel gradation; combining, 5-6, 237-42, 262, 295, 301, 304, 306; elision of, 6-7, 68, 133-34, 306; final, pronunciation of, 244; of Greek, 45; of Latin, 31

Word-analysis: errors in, 224-30; faulty, 65; skill in, 1-2
Word coinage, 2, 294; *see also* Coined words
Word-elements: frequently confused, 224-30, 268-69; metathesis of, 258-61; *see also* Compound words
Word lists: Greek: general, 146-223, numerals, 145-46, prefixes, 132-39, suffixes, 139-45; hybrid terms in, 63; Latin: general, 85-131, numerals, 83-84, prefixes, 66-74, suffixes, 75-83; method of listing in, 62-63, 85-86, 147-48; purpose of, ix, 1-2, 62-63; selection of words in, 63-66; how to use, ix-xi, 64-66; of word elements frequently confused, 224-30

Zoological nomenclature: extensiveness of, 1; development and control of, 281, 297-301; *International Code* of, quoted, 300-01